D1241269

FINLAND IN CRISIS
1940–1941

by the same author

*

SIR ARTHUR INGRAM
c. 1565–1642
(*Oxford*)

FINLAND IN CRISIS
1940–1941
A study in small-power politics

by
ANTHONY F. UPTON
Lecturer in Modern History
St. Salvator's College, St. Andrews

CORNELL UNIVERSITY PRESS
Ithaca, New York

First published in the United States of America, 1965
Cornell University Press
Printed in Great Britain
© *1964 by Anthony F. Upton*

TO
THE PEOPLE OF FINLAND

Contents

Illustrations

PLATES

MAPS

Foreword

Two factors principally have led to the writing of this book. Firstly, for personal reasons, I became deeply interested in Finland and acquainted with the Finnish language. Secondly, as a professional historian, I noticed that many questions arising from this crucial period of modern Finnish history seemed to be unanswered. The urge to try to find some of the answers was irresistible. The reader will readily appreciate why Finnish historians have found this a painful and delicate period to write about.

This is not a definitive history of its subject. Such a history cannot be written as long as important sources of evidence are closed to the historian. On the Finnish side, for example, the private papers of Marshal Manner-heim will not be open to research for many years to come. They may contain much vital information. Outside Finland, there is little first-hand material available from the USSR, and Soviet statesmen do not publish memoirs. For this reason, I did not consider that my inadequate knowledge of Russian was too grave a handicap. I should add that where I have used sources in the Swedish language, this has been translated for me by my wife. Considerable archive material is available from Germany, but even here some of the relevant archives were destroyed or lost in the war. Subject to these limitations I have tried to write as full an account as the available sources permitted.

I should like to thank the many people in Finland who helped me with my work. They were invariably courteous and patient with a troublesome foreigner. In particular I should mention Professor Arvi Korhonen. The use I have made of his published work in this field will be apparent to the reader, but in addition he has shown me many personal kindnesses for which I shall always be in his debt. Colonel K. J. Mikola, Director of the Historical Section of the Finnish Armed Forces, went to considerable trouble in order to answer my questions. Hallitusneuvos Olavi Merimaa, of the Ministry of Justice, arranged for me to read the transcript of the War Responsibility Trial. I was greatly assisted by various members of the staff of the Sota-arkisto and the University Library in Helsinki. The

Library was generous in its arrangements for lending microfilm and books from its collection. Finally I should mention Mr and Mrs R. Halonen, whose generosity and hospitality were a major contribution to the work.

I am indebted to the Court of the University of St Andrews for grants from their travel and research funds. Acknowledgments are due to the Imperial War Museum for the use of the copy of the Halder Diary, and to Her Majesty's Stationery Office for the quotations from the published series of German documents. The quotations from V. Tanner, *The Winter War* are by permission of Stanford University Press: from J. K. Paasikivi, *Toimintani Moskovassa ja Suomessa*; E. W. Juva, *Rudolf Walden*; A. Korhonen, *Barbarossa suunitelma ja Suomi*; are by permission of Werner Söderström Osakeyhtiö: from G. Mannerheim, *Muistelmat*; O. Paavolainen, *Synkkä yksinpuhelu*; E. Heinrichs, *Mannerheim*; W. H. Halsti, *Kesäsota*; are by permission of Kustannusosakeyhtiö Otava: from C. O. Frietsch, *Suomen kohtalonvuodet*; V. Tanner, *Itsenäisen Suomen arkea*; by permission of Kustannusosakeyhtiö Tammi: from H. Greiner, *Die oberste Wehrmachtführung*; W. von Blücher, *Gesandter zwischen Diktatur und Demokratie*; by permission of Limes Verlag: and from the Halder Diary by permission of W. Kohlhammer Verlag.

My wife has had an exceptionally important share in the making of the book, indeed, but for her it would never have been written.

September 1964   A. F. UPTON

Introduction
by Michael Futrell

Probably most people over thirty have some recollection of Finland's resistance to Russian invasion during the Winter War of November 1939 to March 1940. This savage clash of Russia and Finland coincided with the strange inactivity in Western Europe during the early months of the Second World War. While we in the West were singing boastfully about the Siegfried line, the Finns, with small population and long frontiers, were bloodily denting the juggernaut of the Soviet army. In the icy darkness and Arctic cold of the frozen forests, whole divisions of Russian troops were cut off and surrounded by the incomparably tough and resourceful Finns.

As the author of this book writes, 'the struggle of this virtually unknown country had caught the imagination of the world ... the Finnish war had in it something for everyone. It was David versus Goliath ...' Britain and France even planned a relief expedition through Norway and Sweden.

Then, in the spring of 1940, only a few weeks after the Winter War had ended with Finland yielding to overwhelming Russian force, the German blitzkrieg was unleashed in the West. The Low Countries and France were overrun. Britain concentrated on survival. The following year, Germany invaded Russia; Japan swept the Far East. In the conflict of giants, Finland attracted little attention.

Now, we all have our own personal clusters of memories and feelings associated with Dunkirk, Pearl Harbor, Alamein, Stalingrad ... But Finland? For most people, Finland during the years immediately following the heroic episode of the Winter War is simply a blank. Yet by 1945 Finland had fought two more wars, very different but both truly tragic: the war (in company with Germany) against Russia during 1941–4—known as the Continuation War—was followed by a grim campaign of several months against a 200,000-strong German army which systematically devastated Northern Finland during its slow retreat towards Norway.

Finland is a country with many war graves. Finnish cemeteries are often movingly beautiful, tree-filled, spacious with air and light, with an occasional sculptured monument of the same imaginative simplicity that

16

distinguishes modern Finnish architecture. I remember particularly the
graveyard of a certain remote village I once visited in the forests of central
Finland. Row upon row of soldiers' graves bore the same date—that of the
battle for the key town of Tornio near the Swedish frontier in 1944. The
battle was between Finns and Germans, with whom the Finns had just
fought side-by-side for three years against Russia . . .

This book is not an account of Finland's tragic wars of 1941–5; it is an
account of the equally tragic events that led up to them, of what happened
in Finland betweeen the end of the Winter War in March 1940 and the
beginning of the Continuation War in June 1941. It is an excellent piece
of historical investigation and reconstruction, solidly based on Finnish
material; but it is more than that. Why, after all, should anyone but a
specialist bother to read a book dealing with merely fifteen months of the
history of Finland, one small country among so many others?

Finland in Crisis will be absorbing reading for many people, besides
specialist historians.

In the first place, anyone who follows the unfolding events will be
gripped by their sheer human drama. By ineluctable geography, Finland
throughout its modern history always has been what it was then and is now:
a small and sometimes humiliated neighbour of a large and sometimes
threatening Russia. In the summer of 1940, as the author emphasizes, many
people in Europe quite naturally believed that Britain had lost the war and
that Germany would dominate continental Europe. The handful of
undoubtedly strong and clever men, Mannerheim and his colleagues, who
formed the core of the Finnish government, were impaled between two
dictators—Hitler and Stalin. It has the remorseless fascination of classical
tragedy to see how these Finns, under ever increasing strain, with ever
decreasing room for manœuvre, step by step approached the fateful days
of June 1941, when Finland joined in the German onslaught on Soviet
Russia.

But this is more than just a good—if terrible—story well told.

Understanding of Finland has been hindered not only by the country's
remoteness and by the difficulty of its principal language, but also by ill-
informed interpretation and uncritical appreciation. Although Finland
resembles the Scandinavian countries in its high material and cultural
standards, its political and social history have been very different. Ruled
by the Russian Tsar for more than a century until attaining independence
in 1917, Finland was at once, during the first half of 1918, rent by bitter
civil war of Reds and Whites, ending in the victory of the latter. This conflict
left a legacy of strife that formed—and still forms—a dark background to
the picture of Finland drawn by sympathetic visitors, who often see Finland as Scandinavian sophistication salted with a dash of Finnish tough-

ness. In fact, the wounds of 1918, and the permanent anxiety—or stimulus!
—of proximity to Russia, have produced not only intense patriotism, but
also deep and long-lasting cracks and sores in Finnish society and politics.

An outstanding merit of this book is that the author combines understanding and sympathy for Finland with unfailingly balanced and dis-
passionate judgment. To put it bluntly, he reveals not only Finnish courage
and determination, but also the conceit and narrowness which sometimes
accompany that courage and determination. With the skilful penetration of
a surgeon he dissects the ambiguous tissues presented by the Finns; but as
a historian who knows intimately Finland and the Finnish people, he
never forgets that he is concerned with living, striving and suffering men.
'If there is a moral to this story,' he concludes, 'it is perhaps that a small
nation can pay too highly for entrusting its affairs to men of boldness and
vision.'

Every friend of Finland will hope that this book will be widely read.
With particularly keen anticipation do we await the reactions of the Finns
themselves . . .

Note

The spelling and pronunciation of Finnish words and names is phonetic and regular. The letters have approximately the same values as in English, except that y is a vowel equivalent to the German ü. Every letter is sounded, double vowels are long, single vowels are short. Each word is stressed on its first syllable.

In 1940, the exchange value of the Finnish Mark was approximately 196 to the pound sterling.

CHAPTER 1

The Peace of Moscow

A t noon on March 13, 1940, the Treaty of Moscow between the Republic of Finland and the USSR came into force and began a new era in Finnish history. The treaty terminated more than three months of bitter and continuous fighting which had been opened by a series of Russian attacks on November 30, 1939. Although the conditions created by the outbreak of the second World War had prevented much effective aid from reaching Finland, and the disparity between the resources of the contestants was so great, the Finns had more than held their own in the early stages. But a Russian offensive, which had continued without pause since the second week of February, was wearing the Finnish army down to the point where sheer lack of trained manpower threatened to cause a breakdown of organized resistance. Unless there were immediate and weighty intervention by a third power in Finland's favour, the war was lost by the beginning of March 1940, and the commander in chief of the Finnish forces, Marshal Mannerheim, had made this clear to his government. After prolonged and agonized sessions, in which the ministers tried to weigh what they knew of the probable Russian peace terms against the possible sources of outside aid, it had been decided to send a delegation to Moscow to make peace.

The immediate origins of the war are to be found in the non-aggression treaty of August 1939, between the USSR and Germany. In the secret protocol to this treaty the boundaries of the spheres of influence of the contracting parties were defined, and Finland fell within the sphere of the USSR. Once Poland had been defeated, and the booty shared out, the Soviet Union had begun a series of moves to secure the Baltic approaches to its territory. It had forced the three Baltic republics of Estonia, Latvia, and Lithuania to accept treaties of mutual assistance and permit the establishment of Russian bases on their territory. When this had been done, Finland was called on to send a delegation to Moscow to discuss 'concrete political questions' which turned out to be a set of similar demands. These comprised some adjustments of the frontier, for which territorial

19

compensations were offered, and the lease of a Finnish port as a naval base. An initial demand for a treaty of mutual assistance was quickly dropped. This in itself showed that Finland was being treated on a slightly different footing from the three Baltic republics. Stalin, who led the negotiations for the USSR, was prepared to make genuine concessions to the Finnish point of view in an effort to reach agreement. But the Finnish government had chosen to stand firmly on its rights as a neutral sovereign state, protected by valid treaties, including one of non-aggression with the USSR. Its own proposals had been rejected by the Soviet government as totally insufficient and the negotiations had been broken off. Shortly after, a frontier incident was made the pretext for denouncing the Russo-Finnish non-aggression treaty, and this was followed by the invasion of Finland. At the same time, the Russians established a puppet government of Finnish communist exiles led by Otto Kuusinen, which they declared was the sole legitimate government of Finland, and with which they solemnly concluded a treaty of mutual assistance. By this action the Soviet Union made negotiations with the real government of Finland impossible, since they no longer recognized it, and declared their intention of incorporating the whole of Finland in the Soviet Union.

It seems obvious now that the Soviet leaders were misled in part by information fed to them by Finnish exiles, in part by their own memories of the Finnish civil war of 1918, and in part perhaps by their own ideological preconceptions, into supposing that the campaign would be a formality. All manner of evidence suggests that it was really expected that the toiling masses of Finland would welcome the Red Army as liberators from their bourgeois oppressors, and that the Finnish conscripts would turn their weapons against their class enemies in the officer corps. The Russians made the terrible mistake of behaving as though their propaganda picture of the outside world were true. It was a fact that the bloody memories of the Finnish civil war and its aftermath had left deep scars in Finnish society, and perpetuated a bitter sense of class division which is still a political force to the present day. But the crude assault by the hereditary enemy,[1] accompanied by the insulting attempt to impose Kuusinen's government upon them, aroused the deep national pride and will to independence of the Finnish people. Instead of precipitating the dissolution of Finnish society, the attack created the famous 'unity'[2] which has been the theme of almost every public pronouncement in Finnish politics from that day to this. There was little significant opposition[3] to the Finnish government's decision to defend national independence. In consequence, the Russians found themselves obliged to fight a full-scale war for which they had not made adequate preparation and in the process suffered some striking and humiliating defeats.

When the Finnish government discovered that the USSR refused to have any further dealings with it, it appealed to world opinion through the League of Nations. The world responded enthusiastically with bitter condemnations of the Russian aggression and unbounded praise for the gallant Finnish resistance. While this unquestionably helped to maintain domestic morale in Finland, it did nothing more to help avert an eventual defeat. Despite all the goodwill so freely expressed very little effective help reached Finland before hostilities had ended, and nearly all of this came from Sweden. The Swedish government was most anxious to preserve an independent Finland as a buffer between herself and the USSR and sent all aid short of war. But this proviso was of crucial importance. Sweden consistently refused to send her army to help Finland, which was one means by which the military outcome might have been altered in Finland's favour, and equally refused to allow Britain and France to send troops to Finland through Swedish territory, which was, in theory, the only other means. From the one great power that could have helped directly, Germany, Finland got nothing,[4] not even sympathy.

Towards the end of January 1940 a major change occurred in the policy of the Soviet government. They let it be known through neutral channels that they were prepared to discuss peace with the Finnish government. This meant that they were ready to renounce the attempt to take over the whole of Finland through the agency of Kuusinen's government and settle for more limited gains. The Swedish government, which was anxious to see the war ended at almost any cost to Finland, acted as mediator in the negotiations which followed the Soviet move. There were various reasons why the Finnish government was slow to close with the Russian offer. One was the severity of the conditions demanded as the price of peace. The government felt that as long as their armies were undefeated it was worth holding out for easier terms. Another was the hope that the military and political situation might be transformed by the intervention of Britain and France. These two powers were thinking of sending an expeditionary force to Finland through neutral Norway and Sweden. But the value of the assistance tendered was reduced by the fact that the rendering of assistance to Finland was not the primary purpose of the scheme. The real objective of the allied governments was to use the expedition as a pretext for occupying the port of Narvik and the Swedish iron ore fields, thus denying the vital ore supplies to Germany. They also expected that as a result of German reactions they could open up a second front in Scandinavia. If circumstances permitted they would also help Finland, but this aspect of the plan, though the pretext for it, was definitely secondary to its main purpose. Because of this the proposals made to Finland tended to be unspecific, except towards the end, when in an effort to prevent Finland making peace, more concrete promises were made. Although the Finnish commander in chief, Mannerheim, could not know the reasons for the unsatisfactory nature of the Anglo-French proposals, it became increasingly clear to him that the assistance offered would be too little and too late, so that in the end he advised his government to reject it and make peace. In the end, the Marshal's views were decisive. Although the Finnish government felt the peace terms offered were outrageously harsh, they did not feel able to reject Mannerheim's assessment of the political and military situation, that to continue the fight was to court total military and political disaster. It was decided that a delegation led by the prime-minister, Risto Ryti, should fly to Moscow and negotiate a peace on the basis of the Russian terms communicated through Sweden. If this effort failed, it would still be open to them to fight on and call in the Anglo-French assistance.

The expectation that the delegation would be able to negotiate a peace treaty proved false. Although there were several hours of talks between the Finnish representatives and Molotov and Zhdanov who acted for the Soviet government, there were no negotiations in the proper sense of that word. These talks were rightly characterized by Paasikivi, one of the Finnish delegates, as 'pretty fruitless'.[5] The Treaty of Moscow was a dictated peace. From the start the Soviet representatives made it clear there could be no concessions and no haggling. They took the line that Finland was fortunate to be let off so lightly, and that if the terms were not accepted at once, any future settlement would be harsher. If the Finnish government tried to fight on, it was made clear that the Soviet government was prepared to proceed with the total conquest of Finland, and the imposition of Kuusinen's government. There was no response to Ryti's suggestion that if Russia were generous in the hour of victory the settlement would be more readily accepted by the Finnish people, and would become the basis of a new and better relationship between the two countries.[6] Molotov consistently maintained that the terms proposed were in fact extremely generous in view of the military and political situation. So in the end the terms accepted by Finland were unchanged in any important respect from those read out by Molotov at the beginning of the talks.

Therefore the Treaty of Moscow may be taken to embody the views of the Russian government, at that time, of the correct relationship between the USSR and Finland. Molotov maintained that its terms were solely based on considerations of the military security of the USSR, and were consistent with the sovereignty and independence of Finland.[7] First, Finland had to cede most of the province of Karelia, the south-east corner of the country. The new frontier, with minor alterations, was that established by Peter the Great in 1721. It gave the USSR a broad belt of land in which the northern defences of Leningrad could be organized and control of two

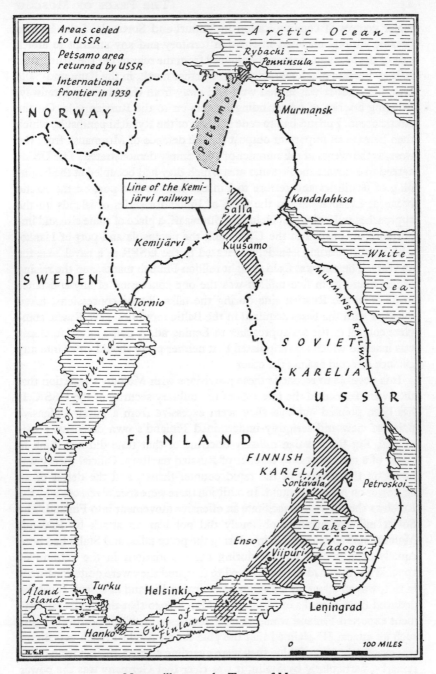

Map to illustrate the Treaty of Moscow

major centres of communication in Viipuri and Sortavala. Lake Ladoga
became entirely enclosed in Russian territory and any attempt to attack
east of the lake and threaten Leningrad from the rear or cut the Murmansk
railway became much more difficult. Further north, in the Kuusamo-Salla
area, the frontier was moved west and away from the Murmansk railway,
bringing a series of commanding heights on to the Russian side. On the
Arctic ocean, Finland had to cede her half of the Rybachi peninsula, which
then became an important outpost for the defence of Murmansk from the
west, as the events of the summer of 1941 amply demonstrated. The USSR
agreed to evacuate the Petsamo area which they had occupied at the beginning of hostilities and restore to Finland her ice-free port on the Arctic
ocean at Liinahamari. In the Gulf of Finland a series of islands on the
approaches to Leningrad, including Suursaari, a place of some size and importance, was ceded to the USSR and the peninsula and port of Hanko,
with its surrounding islands, was leased to the USSR as a naval base for
30 years. The rent was fixed at eight million Finnish marks, and the raising
of this figure from five million was the one concession of any substance
made from the Russian side during the talks. These concessions, taken
together with the bases acquired in the Baltic republics, gave Russia complete control of the sea approaches to Leningrad. A non-aggression clause
was inserted which also stipulated that neither party should enter into any
alliance directed against the other.

It is possible to reconcile these provisions with Molotov's assertion that
they were framed in the interests of the military security of the USSR. It
has been pointed out that they seem excessive from a purely defensive
point of view and seriously undermined Finland's own defensive possibilities. But the Russian military doctrine of that time did not think in
terms of a merely passive defence of Russian territory. Official theory was
based on the concept of the rapid counter-thrust, and the defeat of an
aggressor on his own ground. In addition there were special reasons why the
Russians should wish to facilitate an offensive movement into Finland. The
Soviet military planners obviously did not fear an attack by Finland.
Molotov said so quite explicitly during the peace talks, and Stalin had been
equally definite on the point during the negotiations in the autumn of
1939. What they had both professed to fear, and they were quite consistent
in this, was an attack by a foreign power using Finland as a base. It can be
deduced from remarks of Molotov in March 1940 that the Soviet government expected Finland would at least acquiesce in, if not positively assist
such an attack. He claimed that the plan for an Anglo-French expedition
was exactly the sort of thing they were guarding against, though from other
remarks, particularly by Stalin, it was clear that Germany was the power
they really feared in this respect. Stalin and Molotov stated openly that

they could not take seriously Finnish assurances that Finland would and could defend her neutrality against all attempts to use her territory for an attack on the USSR. For these reasons Soviet military planning wanted to be able to launch a preventive offensive into Finland if a threat of this kind developed. The changes enforced by the Treaty of Moscow all improved the prospects for such an offensive. The new south-eastern frontier was nearer to vital centres of population and communications and was much longer and more open than the old one, which was of great importance for the power which was certain of having a great superiority in numbers. The base at Hanko was big enough to support an offensive task force which could strike directly at the essential communications between Helsinki and the ports of access in western Finland. The salient created by moving the frontier in the Kuusamo-Salla area would facilitate a stroke across the waist of Finland to the Swedish frontier which would cut land-communications with the west. The cessions on the Rybachi peninsula gave Russia complete control over the sea approaches to Liinahamari.

There was one clause of the treaty which was supposed to be based on economic grounds and to be without military significance. This required Finland to provide a railway link between the Murmansk line at Kandalaksa and the Swedish frontier at Tornio. Finland would have to construct a line through wild forest and fells from the existing railhead at Kemijärvi to the new frontier at Salla. The Soviet government always asserted that the sole purpose of this railway was to open up Russian trade with Scandinavia, and Finland was required to allow transit rights over the railway for Russian goods. In fact the railway remained a minor enigma of Soviet policy. Since it had not been completed when war broke out again in June 1941 its economic potentialities were never tested, but it is difficult to see what real economic purpose it could have served. Consequently it seems simpler to assume that in fact it had a military purpose like all the other clauses of the treaty. The railway had obvious value for an attack down to the Gulf of Bothnia across country that was otherwise entirely lacking in communications. Whatever their motives, the Soviet government attached great importance to the Kemijärvi railway. They tried to insist that it should be completed before the end of 1940, but the Finnish representatives gained their only other concession in having this modified to 'as far as possible' by the end of 1940.

Molotov had claimed that the treaty fully respected the sovereignty and independence of Finland. Apart from the prohibition on joining alliances directed against the USSR this was formally true. The original Soviet terms, communicated through Sweden, had revived the demand for a treaty of mutual assistance, but this had been dropped before the talks began. Molotov pointed out, as an example of the unparalleled generosity of his government, that there was no indemnity to be paid to the victor. It is perhaps more surprising that there were no military limitations written into the treaty. Finland was not even required to demobilize, and could maintain any kind of armed forces that could be afforded. In the course of the talks Molotov had said that Finland was free to build as many fortifications as she wanted behind the new frontiers.[8] This was consistent with Molotov's declaration that the USSR was not afraid of anything Finland might do by herself, and his further declaration that his government fully respected the sovereignty of Finland and had no wish or intention of interfering in either the internal or external affairs of Finland. He reinforced this with the statement that the Soviet government regarded the treaty as settling all the questions outstanding between the two countries.

The Treaty of Moscow is the starting point for all that followed. The above analysis of its terms is a deliberate attempt to present it from the Soviet point of view. From that point of view the treaty is a self-consistent document which embodies a clear and comprehensible policy. It assumed that Finland could be used by a great power as an approach route for an attack on the USSR. In the autumn of 1939 Germany was the power they had in mind, but the Anglo-French plan for an expedition to Scandinavia had suggested that a threat from these powers also existed. It was further assumed that the Finnish government would not be able and would not want to prevent such a use of its territory. Its basic hostility to the USSR was taken for granted. If it is accepted that these assumptions represent the basic Soviet view then the Treaty of Moscow makes good sense, especially bearing in mind current Soviet military doctrine. The fact that Finland would be deeply embittered and antagonized was of no importance if her basic hostility was taken for granted. But it must be recognized that there was a further dimension to the Finnish policy of the USSR which developed logically from the previous assumptions. No security arrangements on a purely military level could give complete insurance against the intrigues of a Finnish government whose hostility was assumed. The only final solution of the Finnish problem was to establish a pro-Soviet government in the country. This had been attempted with Otto Kuusinen's government during the war, and represented what may be called the total solution of the Finnish question, in contrast with the partial solution embodied in the Treaty of Moscow. Although the treaty implied the shelving of the total solution, it remains one of the major enigmas of the following 18 months whether the total solution had been shelved indefinitely, or merely postponed. It will be shown that there are grounds for believing that the total solution had not been rejected entirely, but would be revived when circumstances seemed to favour it. It is less easy to determine how seriously such reversion was considered between March 1940 and June 1941. It is certain that the existence of this alternative policy was a major factor poisoning the atmosphere between Finland and the USSR, and cannot be ignored when evaluating the significance of the Treaty of Moscow. With the best will in the world it would not have been easy to exorcize the ghost of Otto Kuusinen's government and it remained to haunt all subsequent Russo-Finnish relations.

It would assist the evaluation of Soviet policy on this point if it were known why, early in 1940, the Soviet leaders, and that meant ultimately Stalin, decided to switch from the total to the partial solution of the Finnish question. It is true that the offer to negotiate with the Finnish government came at a time of military stalemate, so that it is possible that it had been decided that the military cost of the total solution was too high. But this explanation is insufficient. On the one hand, earlier in January, when the military position was the same, the German government had been told that there could be no dealings with the Helsinki government, though the basis of the Kuusinen government could be broadened if that would help to bring about a solution. On the other hand, Soviet policy did not change when the military situation altered in Russia's favour. The situation in January was certainly unpromising, but at any time after February eventual victory was in sight. The answer may be found in Soviet internal politics. There are expert sovietologists who consider that the policy adopted in November 1939 can be identified with Zhdanov and the Leningrad party which he directed. At first the war did appear to be almost a private enterprise of the Leningrad military district rather than an all-Russian effort. It is conceivable that Stalin had always tended to favour a partial solution, as his attitude in the autumn of 1939 suggested, but decided, when that failed, to give Zhdanov a chance to try his solution. When this miscarried, Stalin reasserted his policy. This must remain pure speculation. But Molotov did drop hints about pressures within the USSR opposing any compromise solution, sometimes identifying these with 'the military', and while he might simply have invented this concept as a weapon to use in his talks with the Finnish representatives, it could be that some such pressure group did exist, and if so it would almost certainly have had Zhdanov and the Leningrad party as its core.

But in part at least the decision of January 1940 and its successful execution through the Peace of Moscow in March were related to the general international situation. In this field, the prolongation of Finnish resistance threatened to cause complications because of which even the Russian successes of February and March were insufficient to justify a further reversal of policy. Although the final breakdown of Finnish resistance was in sight by March 1940 it was not near enough to guarantee the USSR against possible embroilments with other powers. It seems to have been Stalin's

settled policy between 1939 and the German invasion of Russia to remain
outside the European war at almost any price and to use the position so
gained to pick up any booty that might be had. Such a policy demanded
the ending of the Finnish war on several counts. There was the intervention threat by the allied powers. However hare-brained this may have been
as a military enterprise its political effect would have been to involve the
USSR in the European war as the ally of Germany. This in itself would
bring Stalin's policy down in ruins. Since the phoney-war was still on and
the outcome quite uncertain, it was no time to get committed to one side
or the other. Further Stalin must have wanted to get his hands quite free
of entanglements in the spring of 1940. The Finnish war, for all its limited
scale, involved considerable parts of the Red Army and seems to have been
causing awkward economic strains, particularly on the transport system.
This was unacceptable at the time when the campaigning season was about
to open. If the allied powers and Germany were serious about their war,
the decisive campaign must begin in April or May. When this happened
it was most important for the USSR to be free to exploit any opportunities
that might arise, or ward off dangers. If these speculations on the motives
of Soviet policy makers are correct, the decision to defer the total solution
of the Finnish question becomes very natural. There were more important
matters which demanded priority. The eventual implementation of a total
solution could be postponed to a more favourable time.

Before considering the Finnish reactions to the Treaty of Moscow it
may be well to describe the attitudes of other interested powers. On the
whole these reflected the healthy national egotism of each. The country
most closely involved was Sweden. Swedish policy had been based on an
intelligent and hard-headed assessment of her national interest. The
Swedish government held in mind two considerations, to keep out of the
European war, and in particular prevent Sweden, and if possible the rest
of Scandinavia, from becoming a theatre of war and to preserve Finland
as an independent state and a buffer between Sweden and the USSR. The
combination of these two aims was not easy, and where they conflicted
there was no doubt about the priority of the first of them. This emerged
in Sweden's refusal to intervene in Finland with her armed forces[9] or to
allow the allied powers to send troops across her territory. The Swedish
problem would have been easier if it had not been bedevilled by sentiment.
Sweden subscribed to the ideals of Scandinavian brotherhood and co-
operation, and there is no doubt that in Sweden many people had a bad
conscience about not helping Finland unreservedly. It was a platitude of
Swedish public oratory that Finland's fight was also Sweden's. If this were
so, the logical conclusion was obvious. The dilemma of the Swedish government, when faced with the demand for transit facilities for the Anglo-

French expedition, was painful. But the Swedes declined to let their hearts rule their heads. Germany had made it quite clear that if Anglo-French troops entered Sweden, whatever the pretext, Germany would strike at them on Swedish territory. Hence the adamantine Swedish refusal to consider the request. It is unfortunate that some Swedish circles then and later gave the impression that Germany also used threats to prevent Sweden sending her own troops to help Finland. There appears to be no good foundation for this view, since, to judge from Hitler's remarks to Sven Hedin, the Swedish writer, he had so poor a view of Sweden's military potential that he did not think Sweden's intervention would make any difference. The one certain way of reconciling the twin aims of Swedish policy was for Finland to make peace as quickly as possible so that the Swedish government was at all times eager to mediate. It had provided the main channel of communication between the contestants. It had done more, since the Swedish government never concealed from Finland its belief that the Russian terms ought to be accepted and its actions were all calculated to induce Finland to do this. On the negative side was the refusal to intervene or allow other powers to do so. On the positive side the Finnish government was assured that if it made peace, Sweden would give all possible economic and financial assistance for reconstruction, and in addition would be ready to consider joining with Finland, and possibly Norway too, in a Scandinavian alliance to preserve the new status quo. These undertakings did much to persuade the Finnish government to accept the Russian conditions. It must be added that some people in Finland thought that in their eagerness to get a settlement the Swedish government had misrepresented the Soviet peace terms, making them appear more favourable than they really were. There seems no good foundation for this belief which stems from misconceptions on the Finnish side, particularly their belief that if they sent a delegation to Moscow the Russians would be prepared to negotiate in the proper sense of the word, so that the terms could be modified. It was true that the frontier changes in the Salla-Kuusamo area were not included in the terms transmitted through Stockholm, but that was the doing of the Soviet government. A more serious complaint from the Finnish side was that Sweden, by making it abundantly clear that she would not intervene herself or allow others to do so, weakened the Finnish bargaining position. The Finnish foreign minister, Väinö Tanner, felt so strongly about this that he openly voiced the complaint in his radio address explaining the treaty. He implied that the conduct of Sweden in this respect had made the terms more onerous. But Tanner, and those who shared his view, were the victims of a delusion. Finland had no bargaining position. The peace treaty was in no sense a bargain, it was a diktat. There is no evidence to suggest that Soviet knowledge of Sweden's position had any influence on the terms offered. There is no doubt that Sweden welcomed the Treaty of Moscow. It gave her what she wanted and Finland paid the price so there was every reason for satisfaction. The Swedish government had done all it could to induce the Finnish government to accept the terms. It was a main aim of Swedish policy after the conclusion of peace to see that Finland observed the treaty. No blame attaches to the Swedes for this. Their government showed an intelligent appreciation of where the national interest lay and acted in accordance with it. This was their duty to their own people. Within the limitations imposed by their policy, the Swedish government did all it could to help Finland materially and to dissuade her from lines of policy which Sweden considered could only end in disaster.

The interests of Germany in the Finnish question were in many ways similar to those of Sweden. German policy was based on a realistic assessment of the national interest, which clashed with a tradition of sentimental friendship and goodwill towards Finland. Consequently Germany too wanted a quick end to the war, hoped that this would preserve Finnish independence, and feared above all that the Finnish war would lead to an Anglo-French intervention in Scandinavia. German policy was inevitably dictated by the exigencies of her war with Britain and France. Hitler had decided to resolve this by a spring offensive in the west. This left him no choice but to pay whatever price was necessary for the passive acquiescence of the USSR in the east. He had agreed in August 1939 that as part of this price the USSR should have a free hand in Finland. He kept his word and paid the price loyally. This involved abandoning traditional German policies. Ever since the German intervention in Finland in 1918, Germany had felt a protective interest in Finland. There had always been friendly contacts between the two countries, particularly between their armed forces. Germany naturally did not want to see the position of the USSR in the Baltic strengthened at Finland's expense. Germans who believed in this traditional policy, and they included the German ambassador in Helsinki and permanent officials of the German Foreign Office, were all deeply disturbed by the development of Hitler's policy, though they swallowed their distaste and obeyed their orders. German policy had been quite consistent. Before the outbreak of hostilities she had urged Finland to accept the Russian terms. During the fighting she had refused to assist Finland, or to allow others to do so, and refused to mediate without the prior approval of the USSR. The German press and diplomatic service were instructed to say nothing that might encourage Finland. The foreign minister, von Ribbentrop, explained Hitler's policy to the ambassador in Helsinki in January 1940. He revealed that Hitler and the Nazi party chiefs harboured some resentment against Finland, whose press had often been critical of their policies before the war, and whose government in the years before 1939 had seemed deliberately to move away from Germany and seek closer ties with the democracies. Even so Ribbentrop was not happy about the Russo-Finnish war, and was aware that his policy was opposed by strong and influential sections of opinion in Germany. He hoped for a quick end to the war, and thought the Kuusinen government had been a mistake which was preventing a reasonable solution of the problem. But Germany had to face political reality, and could do nothing to offend the USSR. 'Wir müssen eiskalt Politik machen,'* the ambassador was told. So Germany, like Sweden, remained formally neutral, but where Sweden was neutral in Finland's favour, Germany was neutral against her. She stopped Italy sending fighters to Finland through Germany. She offered the USSR various facilities. Above all she threatened Norway and Sweden in a way which made it certain they would not voluntarily permit Anglo-French troops to cross their territory. And she rejected every approach for intercession made by Finland, or on Finland's behalf. To all such approaches the German government returned the same answer. Finland must make peace with the USSR on whatever terms she could get. So Germany welcomed the Treaty of Moscow with genuine relief. It freed her from a situation which had been embarrassing and had threatened to become mortally dangerous. The German press praised the moderation of the peace terms and implied that it was hoped that Finland had now learned a lesson and would in future adapt her policies to the existence of a Russo-German hegemony of the Baltic.

The attitudes of Britain and France were very different. They did not conceal their disappointment at the ending of the war which was to have been the pretext for their Scandinavian campaign. Of the two, the French felt most bitter. The British government, with its naval tradition, had been thinking primarily in terms of plugging a hole in the blockade by seizing the Norwegian ports and the ore fields. When the fighting ended, the British intended to go ahead and seize the ports in any case. But the French had desperately wanted to transfer the main seat of war away from French territory by opening a second front in Scandinavia. Both powers had done all they could to dissuade Finland from making peace. The British government had declined to transmit the Soviet terms to Finland on the ground that they were unreasonable. As the Finnish government showed signs of weakening the offers of the allied powers became more concrete and alluring. They gave the impression that Finland had only to say the word and the expedition would set sail. It is an impressive tribute to Finnish strength of character that in the end they rejected these offers. The main credit is Mannerheim's, who perceived that from a military point of view,

*'We must be ice-cold in our politics.'

to say nothing of possible political complications, the proposed expedition was fundamentally unsound. In their desperation to keep the war going the allied powers even tried to frighten Finland into being helped. The French prime minister, Daladier, told the Finnish ambassador that if Finland rejected the allied offer, the two powers would undertake no responsibility for any territorial settlement concerning Finland which might be made at the end of the war. This was a shrewd thrust since, as will be shown, some Finnish politicians only brought themselves to accept the Treaty of Moscow in the belief that it would be revised at a peace conference which they supposed would follow the end of the European war. Consequently Britain and France tended to see the Treaty of Moscow as a defeat for themselves. The measure of their disappointment was the vehemence with which the press in Britain and France abused Norway and Sweden whose behaviour was held responsible for the collapse of the allied plans.[10] So strong were feelings in France that the Treaty of Moscow was a major cause of the downfall of Daladier's government. The British were more philosophical once they had decided to go ahead with the essentials of their plan to cut off the iron ore supplies. But this still left the allied powers, like Sweden, with a bad conscience about Finland, a feeling that they had failed her. This was to have its consequences later when the British government, faced by an increasingly obvious pro-German orientation in Finland, showed itself shame-faced and hesitant in taking any counter-measures. This did not in the end prevent the British government declaring war on Finland in December 1941, when the demands of her Soviet ally made it expedient. But the British government had the grace, like Maria-Theresa partitioning Poland, to do it with a heavy heart.

One interested power alone had policies that rose above the sordid considerations of self-interest that affected all the others. This was the United States of America. In the American mythology of foreign affairs, Finland had a special place. Finland was the country that had paid its debts. Further there was a vocal minority of Finnish Americans who conducted a vigorous propaganda on Finland's behalf, and they found a ready hearing in a country where the USSR had few friends. So that although the United States had no interest of her own at stake, she selflessly took up the Finnish cause. It was unfortunate that for a wide variety of political and constitutional reasons her efforts were virtually useless to Finland, and cost the United States very little in real terms. But the most cynical commentator cannot deny the great good will that underlay American policy. In the field of diplomacy the American government had taken several initiatives in Moscow urging moderation on the USSR. These were backed up after the outbreak of war by the threat of a trade embargo. But the Soviet government remained unmoved, indeed in its public pronouncements it was apt

Finns reading the news of peace, 13 March 1940

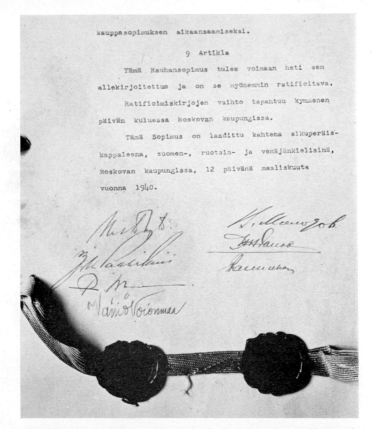

kauppasopimuksen aikaansaamiseksi.

9 Artikla

Tämä Rauhansopimus tulee voimaan heti sen
allekirjoitettua ja on se myönnemmin ratifioitava.

Ratifioimiskirjojen vaihto tapahtuu kymmenen
päivän kuluessa Moskovan kaupungissa.

Tämä Sopimus on laadittu kahtena alkuperäis-
kappaleena, suomen-, ruotsin- ja venäjänkielisinä,
Moskovan kaupungissa, 12 päivänä maaliskuuta
vuonna 1940.

The Treaty of Moscow. The principal signatories are Ryti and
Paasikivi for Finland, Molotov and Zhdanov for U.S.S.R.

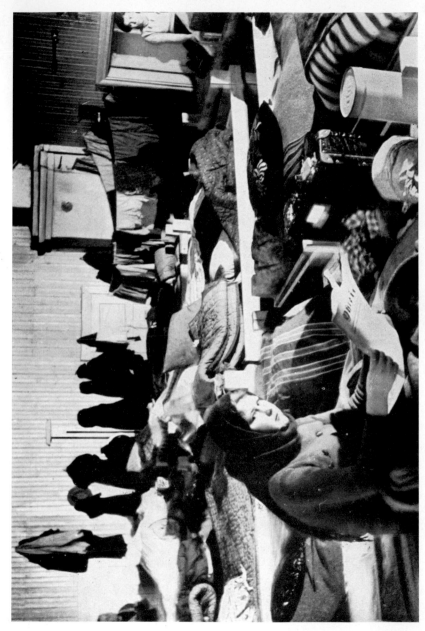

Yugoslav refugees in their billets

to be less than respectful about the course of American policy. Otherwise
the United States had provided credits for Finland and facilitated the sale
of arms to Finland in spite of the neutrality laws, and gave loud and enthusiastic encouragement to Finland in her fight. President Roosevelt expressed the sentiments of the United States in a message sent to both
governments on the conclusion of the Treaty of Moscow:

'. . . the Finnish nation by incomparable courage and strong resistance
against an overwhelming superiority of armaments has won for itself for all
time the moral right to live in peace and independence in the land which it
has so bravely defended.'

The position of the United States after the Treaty of Moscow remained
one of the warmest goodwill towards Finland. It was Finland's misfortune
that such a quantity of goodwill generated so little action of any practical
value to herself.

Indeed there was an almost universal feeling of benevolence towards
Finland in March 1940. It was extraordinary how the struggle of this virtually unknown country had caught the imagination of the world, and
almost displaced in its interest the major war between Germany and the
allied powers which should have held the centre of the stage. In truth, the
Finnish war had in it something for everyone. It was David versus Goliath
and everybody could enjoy the setbacks suffered by the Russian colossus.
For the democratically inclined it was the gallant fight of a small nation,
with a strong tradition of democratic politics and progressive social policies,
against a ruthless dictatorship. For the not so democratically inclined it
was the struggle of an outpost of Christian civilization and decent social
order against the Asiatic barbarism of Stalin's Russia, and for the real enthusiasts a war of the children of light against the dark horrors of an un-
speakable bolshevik menace. So the chorus of praise and encouragement
re-echoed from democratic Denmark and Norway to fascist Italy and
Hungary, from the model democracy of the Netherlands to the nastiest of
Latin American dictatorships, from those whose hope had been the
League of Nations to those who, like Japan, had been among the first to
encompass the ruin of that organization. It must be said that this universal
shout of acclaim did Finland much practical good. Nobody can calculate
how important it was, when the prospect was so grim and the country had
to face the consequences of defeat that the Finnish people could feel that
they had done their duty to civilization and that the world recognized this.
They could believe, for the world told them so, that theirs had been a
righteous war, and that in the end righteousness must prevail. These
feelings kept Finnish morale high in face of a lost war and a peace so un-
expectedly harsh that it might well have broken the national spirit. The
approbation of the world was not confined to verbal encouragement. Many

3

countries had opened funds to help Finland and throughout the period following the Treaty of Moscow gifts of money or materials trickled in, as far as the developing war situation would allow. Only two countries stood out against this wave of good-feeling. They were the USSR and Germany, and even in the latter the sympathy of the general public for Finland could not be entirely prevented from finding expression. But it was the policies of these two countries, more than any other factor, which were to determine Finland's future.

CHAPTER 2

Finland and the Treaty of Moscow

It is unlikely that any Finn who was old enough to have been aware of events around him will ever forget March 13, 1940. Every source available testifies to the sense of shock produced by the news of the peace terms. Flags were spontaneously lowered to half-mast, people wept openly in public places, the nation mourned as a private family might mourn the loss of a favourite child. The shock was the greater because the public was little prepared for what had happened. The socialist newspaper, *Suomen Sosiaalidemokraatti*, in its editorial on the following day, noted how the sense of tragedy was deepened because 'the Finnish people generally have not been able to prepare themselves for such news'.[1] This was partly because the Finnish government had exercised a strict and effective censorship. The linguistic isolation of the Finns tended to cut them off from foreign sources of news. All they could learn for certain was what appeared in their press or was broadcast over the state radio. Both these channels were closely controlled throughout the war years. Outside sources of information were virtually closed to the average Finn. He could neither receive nor understand foreign broadcasts, nor read foreign newspapers. Only a minority had the opportunity and the linguistic equipment for this. Educated people could read the Swedish press, but the government could and did, when necessary, hinder the import of Swedish papers. This same minority could listen to the Swedish radio which provided a source of uncensored news, but they were not numerous. Official propaganda had concealed much in an entirely reasonable effort to keep up the national morale. In particular they had never revealed the full seriousness of the military situation and had naturally striven to paint an optimistic picture of the prospects of outside assistance. Although, at the very end, it had been revealed that peace talks were in progress, the general optimism of the news prepared nobody for the severity of the terms. Further it is fair to say that at the best of times the average Finn had little knowledge or experience which would help him to make a reasoned or realistic assessment of international problems. There was no tradition in Finland of open

35

public debate about foreign policy. The absence of this in the public press
is a striking feature of it. The correspondence columns are not comparable
with their counterparts in the national press of Western countries, being
occupied with letters on strictly personal or local topics. The editorials and
the political commentators failed to provide informed discussion since they
followed the guidance of the censorship and repeated the official line of the
moment, and always in very general terms. Needless to say there were no
discussion programmes on the radio. On the contrary there was a whole
tradition which deplored and discouraged open argument about foreign
affairs.

This is reflected in the provisions of the Finnish constitution. The
president of Finland is wholly responsible in law for the conduct of foreign
policy. But in this field as in all others it is the custom in Finland that the
conduct of the president is not publicly criticized or discussed. This same
tradition was followed in the Eduskunta, the single-chamber parliament.
The Eduskunta had the right to be informed of foreign policy developments
and to express opinion about them through its foreign-affairs committee,
but it had no tradition of public debates on foreign affairs. These were in
fact almost never discussed on the floor of the Eduskunta. Even the foreign
affairs committee was not fully informed of what went on, was required to
treat as confidential much of what it did learn, and its proceedings were
not made public. The Eduskunta only discussed foreign affairs formally
when called on to ratify treaties or decide war and peace, or in the annual
discussion on the report of the Ministry of Foreign Affairs for the pre-
ceding year. Further, there are good grounds for the belief that the Eduskunta was quite incapable of informed discussion of foreign policy. The
Finnish Eduskunta, unlike the British parliament, was literally representative of the Finnish people. Finnish politics are organized on a multi-
party system in which each party represents a given social grouping and
exists for that purpose. The party members in the Eduskunta truly reflect
the opinions of their voters, sharing also their prejudices and their ignorance of foreign affairs. Finland, unlike Britain, is a genuinely democratic
country. There is no social or class division between the members of the
Eduskunta and those who elect them. This does have the effect of thrusting
the direction of foreign policy into the hands of the very limited circle of
men with some experience in and understanding of international affairs.
The Finnish people, and their representatives in the Eduskunta, proved
well content to follow any lead they received from those whom they trusted
in a field where most people felt lost and out of their depth.

The required lead did not come clearly from the speech of Väinö Tanner,
the foreign minister, on March 13. Tanner, the man who had remade the
Social Democratic party after the civil war, and built up one of the most

powerful co-operative movements in Europe, shared his countrymen's awkwardness in dealing with foreign affairs. He had never been happy with them and had undoubtedly made a mistake in leaving the sphere of internal and economic policy in which he could find full scope for his great abilities. Tanner's speech mirrored the bitterness and also the bewilderment of his countrymen in face of the disaster. He told them how well they had fought but gave no idea of how close they had come to military catastrophe. He could not easily reconcile his picture of the war with the harshness of the peace, which he said was out of all proportion to the enemy's military achievement. In this statement alone Tanner revealed his own failure to grasp what had happened. He offered as his one ray of hope the assurance that the USSR would not interfere in the country's internal or external affairs. This was to be proved worthless in a matter of days. Tanner could not conceal his bitterness and sense of bafflement at the unfairness of things. 'Peace has come back to the land, but what a peace. Henceforth our country must endure mutilated . . .' In his bitterness Tanner sought scapegoats. Sweden and Norway were the obvious ones. They had betrayed Finland by refusing transit rights to Britain and France. They had undermined her bargaining position by proclaiming openly their refusal to help. So Tanner reflected the anger and frustration of his countrymen. While he did not perhaps go so far as the group of ladies from Aavasaksa who sent him a telegram stating that it was 'a swinish disgraceful peace we shall never submit to',[2] he could not bring himself to think of it as the final settlement of Russo-Finnish relations. Tanner had told the government on the previous day that in his opinion 'this peace of ours was an interlude and we did not know how the final peace settlement would look'.[3]

It was the following day when the Finnish people got the directive they needed from the one man who could give it and be sure of being heeded. This was Mannerheim. The Marshal was as untypical of an average Finn as anyone could be. There had in fact been little to connect him with Finland except the accident of birth into one of Finland's few noble families. Mannerheim never really learned to use the language of most of his countrymen. His upbringing was entirely alien from theirs. Mannerheim had made his career as an officer in one of the most exclusive Russian cavalry regiments, and his environment had been that of the imperial Russian Court. When he returned to Finland in 1918 to lead the White forces in the civil war, he was a foreigner to his countrymen. He had nothing in common with the politicians whose training had been as leaders of a national resistance movement to attempts at the russification of Finland. His whole mental outlook was different from that of most Finns.

The Finns are intensely self-centred and mentally tend to live in a world of their own of which the centre is Finland. This is probably inevitable among a people isolated by geography and language, and whose difference from others had been accentuated and stressed by the strong nationalist strain in their politics. Small nations like Finland, and there were fewer than four million Finns in 1940, can only keep their identity and hence their independence by a fierce and self-conscious concentration on those things which mark them off from others. This characteristic fennocentric view of the world was a factor which had prepared their failure to cope with the realities of world politics which had led them into war in 1939. This tendency was one reason why Mannerheim was so important. He had lived in the great cosmopolitan society of upper-class Europe. He was accustomed to being on equal terms with leaders and statesmen, and was familiar with the ways of Courts and Chancelleries. He knew the realities of European politics. Mannerheim, with his mental outlook free of the fennocentric bias of most of his countrymen, could see situations more clearly. But this was only of value to his country because his personal prestige gave him a hold over the Finns which made them willing, after November 1939, to do whatever he told them they must do.

It had not always been so. In 1918, Mannerheim was the victorious White general whom the defeated Reds had some cause to label 'the butcher'. The politicians, once he had won the civil war for them, found his authoritarian concepts of government irksome. They had discovered that where Mannerheim ruled no one else could expect any share of real power. When the new republic elected its first president, Mannerheim was rejected and retired into private life. During the inter-war years he succeeded in transforming his public image. He was helped by the official mythology. This had set about changing the civil war into a 'war of liberation', as if it had really been a struggle against the Russians aided by a minority of traitors and honest, but misguided, Finnish workers. The deaths of more than 80,000 Finnish Reds in the fighting and the repression which followed it are sufficient proof that this was a travesty of what had really happened. But the official version of the events of 1918 gained such currency in Finland that even today it is only beginning to lose its place in the orthodoxy of Finnish history. It certainly helped Mannherheim to become established as the liberator, the hero of national independence. The general himself, by his own efforts to promote conciliation, by refusing to lend himself to the schemes of right-wing extremists, and by avoiding any suspicion of personal political ambition, made a characteristically intelligent contribution to his own transformation. Already in the early 1930s there were abundant signs of the widening acceptance of Mannerheim as the country's national hero. He returned to public life as the chairman of the defence planning committee with the understanding that in time of war he would take command. By 1938 even Tanner, as

leader of the Social Democratic party, had met and been reconciled with
Mannerheim and told his supporters, most of whom had been Reds in
1918, that Mannerheim was an honourable man who had done his duty as
he saw it in the civil war. Even so, Mannerheim's position was not quite
established. He could not make the politicians accept his full defence programme. In the autumn of 1939 they would not listen to his urgings that
they must make realistic concessions to the Russians and come to terms.
The politicians even whispered that senility was creeping on and the old
man was losing his nerve. But when war came and proved that Mannerheim had been right over the previous years, and the politicians wrong,
they turned to him as the only possible commander in chief, and he
accepted. His conduct of the war finally gave him unquestioned and un-
questionable authority as the real first citizen of the republic, the one man
whose word, in the last resort, would be accepted by the whole nation.

Mannerheim's proclamation to the Finnish nation was in form an order
of the day to the armed forces, but as he noted himself 'in reality it appealed
to the whole Finnish people and for that reason was read on the radio and
fixed to the wall in every church in the land'.[4] It is a document which shows
great insight and intelligence, reflecting accurately the mind and background of the author. For instance he said, addressing the soldiers, 'I am
proud of you as if you were my children'. That was the voice of the aristocratic Tsarist officer speaking to an army of peasants. The sentence looked
oddly out of place in the middle of the 20th century and the context of
modern Finland. But in general the text was masterly. It had a dual purpose, to raise the national morale while at the same time telling the nation,
gently but firmly, that it had lost the war and must make the best of the
peace. All sections of society got honourable mention from the General
Staff to the factory workers, and each part of the country got its individual
praise. He told them that the war had been lost because of the overwhelming superiority of the enemy in men and materials, made worse by their
own neglect before the war, and the inadequacy of outside assistance
during it. He called on the nation to rebuild and repair what remained to
them, to make a better life for all, and to defend their diminished fatherland with the same determination as they had shown during the war. He
assured the whole nation that it had done its duty and that the world outside had recognized this. He asked the people to be satisfied with this,
accept their fate, and do the best job they could in the new circumstances.[5]

The order of the day has some interesting details. There was no bitterness or reproach expressed towards Sweden for her conduct in refusing
transit rights to the Anglo-French expedition. Mannerheim's biographer
has pointed out that he could not honestly have done this. In public he
was obliged to give this refusal as the reason for not accepting the aid offered,

since otherwise it would seem inexplicable to the people. In fact he had urged the rejection of the offer because he thought it insufficient, and might lead to embroilment with Germany. Thus the Swedish refusal was not decisive in Mannerheim's view. Further he felt, as he had throughout the 1930s, that the only real solution for Finland's international problems lay in alliance with Sweden. Thus he was far from wishing, at a time when this alliance seemed more than ever desirable, to say anything that would make it less acceptable in Sweden or Finland. Mannerheim also expressed in one passage something of what the Finns felt to be so intolerable about the peace. It is not easy for the outsider to appreciate what the loss of Karelia meant to ordinary Finnish people, even if they had never been there and had no personal connection with it. Mannerheim caught the essence of what they felt when he wrote:

'Ours is a hard fate, when we are compelled to give up to a strange race, with a different world outlook and different moral values, land which we have cultivated for centuries with sweat and suffering.'

For the Finns thought of themselves as a frontier people in both the usual senses of that expression. That is, they were a people who had extended the area of civilization by populating and cultivating the natural wastelands of forest and swamp that cover most of Finland. This pioneering tradition went back to the obscure times when the Finnish tribes first moved into their homeland. The process of taming nature had been continuous ever since and continues now. It is the reason why the Finns have made first-rate migrants, whether in exploiting the backwoods of Sweden in the 17th century or in America and Australia in recent times. The pioneering tradition is part of their inheritance. Hence the passionate attachment to the actual geographical area which they and their ancestors had made habitable, and the deep sense of loss at surrendering parts of it to others. This was what Mannerheim alluded to by his talk of sweat and suffering. But when he spoke of a strange race, different world outlook, different moral values, he referred to the other sense in which Finns regarded themselves as a frontier people. They were one of the bastions of western, Christian civilization against the alien culture to the east. This tradition too had deep historical roots. When Finland was attached to Sweden it had reflected a simple political fact. Sweden on one side and Russia on the other had represented two alien and hostile cultures and Finland was one of their main battlegrounds. In the 19th century, when Finland was attached to the Russian empire, and when the cultural gap between Russia and the west was being bridged to some extent, it appeared that the role of Finland as a bastion of the west had lost its importance. The russification campaign in Finland at the beginning of the century, and more dramatically, the Russian revolution, had suddenly recreated the old conditions, and revived old habits of thought. Russia was once more a hostile culture which menaced the very foundations of western civilization, or was thought to do so.

This was what the newspaper *Helsingin Sanomat* had meant when, in its editorial of March 13, it had written that 'the Finnish people has honourably discharged its guard duties . . .'[6] Mannerheim concluded his order of the day by formulating the concept quite concisely:

'We are proudly conscious that we have a historical mission which we are still carrying out: the protection of western civilization which for centuries has been our inheritance.'

By appealing to the two-fold frontier tradition Mannerheim was seeking to raise the national morale. It seems to be essential for any healthy nation to possess some concept of its historic mission. Such concepts play a major role in justifying the national existence, and in fortifying the national identity. A nation in defeat can easily sink into apathy and disintegrate. Finland might well have been expected to do this in 1940. But in the end national self-confidence endured, and it seems foolish to underrate the importance in this process of the consciousness that as a nation they had a duty and a purpose. Indeed the value of an appeal to the pioneering tradition at such a moment was obvious. There could be no better psychological basis for tackling the problems of national reconstruction. The reminder to the nation that it was the advance guard of western Christendom against the East had less happy consequences. The sedulous encouragement of this concept by Mannerheim, by other public figures, by the Lutheran church, through the state schools and their textbooks, in the press and in public propaganda was a major factor in preventing the Finnish people from seeing the world situation, and their own relationship with the USSR, with the cool, calculating perception that was needed. To political groupings of the Right, the concept of the outpost of the West was very dear. It was particularly fostered by the important student society, the Akateeminen Karjalan Seura. There is reason to believe that, as a habit of thought, the concept was deeply entrenched among the educated classes, that is in the civil service, the professions, the officer corps, in short in those elements in society who played the greatest part in formulating public opinion and policy. Even the Social Democrats, who were formally internationalists, and opposed to all such concepts, subscribed to their own version of it. Particularly in the speeches of Tanner one finds the image of their party upholding the true socialist ideal against the insidious bolshevik perversion which was only a cloak for Russian imperialism. It would of course be absurd to pretend that the mass of ordinary Finnish farmers and townsmen consciously thought of themselves as the frontier guard of Western culture. It is not in the nature of ordinary people anywhere to waste time thinking about such things. But it can be said that when, in times of crisis, the ordinary citizen did turn his attention to politics, he would have been so conditioned by his education, and organs of public opinion, that such a concept would seem quite natural to him.

The religiously inclined added a twist of their own to the idea of Finland's frontier mission. They were prone to present it as a God-given duty and to teach their countrymen to regard themselves as a chosen race, whose mission was a divine one. It was not only the clergy who are to be found preaching and writing in this sense, stressing of course the godlessness of the USSR, there were plenty of laymen to echo such ideas. They can be found in the secular press. *Satakunnan Kansa*, a sober provincial paper, told its readers that 'God directs the fate of our nation and he will not forsake us'.[7] In an Easter editorial *Uusi Suomi* made the direct comparison between the sufferings of the Son of God on the cross, and the recent trials endured by the Finnish nation. It would be wrong to lay too much stress on these phenomena. A historian is always in difficulties when seeking to assess anything so intangible and immeasurable as the psychology of a whole people. But it is difficult to make any sense of the events under consideration unless it is recognized that Finns in general did have their own characteristic attitudes and ways of thought, clearly derived from their own history and environment. If these are ignored, the behaviour of the Finnish people will often appear absurd or inexplicable to an outsider. Finns did not of course go about saying to one another that their nation had been specially chosen by God for its historic mission. But when such notions were expressed most Finns did not find them unreasonable.

The cumulative effect of such ideas was a flat rejection of Russia and things Russian, it was a negative rather than a positive effect. The Finnish writer, Olavi Paavolainen, writing of what he called 'the church-village mentality' of some of his countrymen, noted how they regarded themselves as 'the front-rank of Christendom and advance guard of the West against the godless East'. Such people took up an attitude of 'derisory contempt towards everything Russian, as though that were the most natural thing in the world'.[8] Urho Kekkonen remembered that in his student days in the 20s, it was commonly believed that 'love of one's country has two different aspects: love towards our own land and hatred of the Russians'.[9] Except on the extreme Right, this mental climate had not led to any serious advocacy of participating in an attack on the USSR. No responsible political party or politician, much less any government, had entertained such notions since 1920. What the Finns had done was to attempt to live and plan as though the USSR did not exist, or else was not to be taken seriously. Many serious observers have noted how the Finns not only knew nothing about the

USSR before 1939, they clearly did not want to know anything. It was notorious then, and still is today, how difficult it is to persuade any Finn to take up the study of the Russian language. Everything that was published about Russia in Finnish between 1920 and 1939 was propaganda for one side or the other. Very few Finns availed themselves of such facilities existed to travel in the Soviet Union. The level of trade was completely insignificant. In short, despite the long common frontier, there was an absolute minimum of contact between Finland and the USSR. This had the dangerous consequence that Finnish ideas about Russia were built on impressions gained during the last period when there had been contact, the period 1918 to 1920. It had been a period when the USSR was trying to export revolution to its neighbours, and when civil war and intervention had reduced her to a second-rank power. There was almost total ignorance in Finland of the changes wrought by Stalin in the 1930s. Their concept of Russia was based on the Russia of 1920 with which they had made their peace.[10] It is therefore fair to say that when Finland had to deal with the USSR, her ability to shape a policy was hampered by the mental habits of her people. Most Finnish minds contained a series of mental road-blocks which obstructed a rational appraisal of Russian policies, or realistic thinking about their own relations with the USSR. In such a situation, the lead given by Mannerheim and the leading politicians was unusually important. If they wanted to lead the nation along paths which conflicted with the ingrained prejudices of their countrymen, they would have to work hard, and with deep conviction.

It was quickly apparent that the war had failed to stimulate any tendency towards a reappraisal of traditional attitudes to the USSR. On the contrary it had served to strengthen old prejudices. The tone of immediate post-war discussion was backward looking. Frietsch, a member of the Eduskunta, remarked on this aspect of the debate on the peace treaty. This "showed that we still lived in our old mental world, thoughts were running, as before, in their accustomed channels'.[11] It might have been expected that after a war which had ended so badly there would have been room for some discussion of how it had begun, and whether there had been mistakes which might be avoided in the future. Voices were raised in favour of this. *Helsingin Sanomat*, on March 13, had said that now the war was ended it was time that some 'full and convincing explanations' were given about a number of 'open questions'.[12] Some tentative beginnings were made. A letter in *Uusi Suomi*, with the revealing heading, 'an unbeaten army and a dictated peace',[13] blamed the misfortune on politicians. It was the pre-war party system which had produced leaders 'tied up and blinded' by their party obligations, who had failed to assess the dangers. They must be replaced by far-sighted, non-party men with experience of modern diplomacy.

However, the censorship came down on the debate before it had really got started. Thereafter the whole weight of official policy opposed any open inquests into the past. There seem to have been two main reasons for this. The one publicly stated was that such discussions might imperil unity and become offensive to foreign powers. The unstated reason was that official propaganda had to go on stressing that the war had not been in vain.[14] It is obvious why this was felt to be necessary in order to sustain the national morale, but it precluded any discussion of the origins of the war which might suggest that it had been avoidable. The government was loyally supported by almost all the press and in public speeches in pursuing this line. *Uusi Suomi* in an editorial on March 19 recognized that discussion must for the time being be restrained. Tanner, in two major policy speeches admitted that there was much in the recent past that merited discussion, but that unfortunately the times were too delicate to permit it. The Turku paper, *Sosialisti*, came out with a strong attack on those who suggested even in private discussion that a policy of concessions in the autumn of 1939 might have been more profitable. It branded such people as communist agents.[15] It seems probable that even if free discussion had been allowed, few Finns would have been convinced that the war had been a mistake. Even today, when discussion has been free for years, it is very rare to find anyone who holds this view. It is one of the ironies of the situation that such an opinion, branded then as communist subversion, was in fact held by Mannerheim both before and after the war.

General Heinrichs, Mannerheim's chief of staff, and later his biographer, asked the Marshal his opinion a few days after the fighting had ended. Mannerheim said that by buying peace in November 1939 by extensive concessions, they would have gained time to equip the army and make some kind of alliance with Sweden. He went on to remark that the 1939 frontier had been unrealistic 'as a frontier between two independent states, of which one was weak, and the other large and powerful, it could not have been lasting'.[16] Very similar views were held by J. K. Paasikivi, in 1940 an elder statesman, and of all Finns the best informed about Russia. Writing in 1944 in the last phases of a new war, he argued that the war of 1939 had been a mistake for Finland. He concluded, 'the Winter War certainly earned us honour and reputation and the goodwill of the world, but it did not prevent and it was no compensation for the unhappy peace of Moscow.'[17] But the Finnish public knew nothing of this, Mannerheim and Paasikivi deemed it expedient to keep their thoughts to themselves. It was in fact their duty not to do anything which might upset the idea that, as *Suomen Sosiaalidemokraatti* wrote on March 14, 'the sacrifices have been heavy and costly, but it would be fundamentally shortsighted to say that they have been in vain.'

The Finnish people were quick to accept the government's line that all was not lost and even that something had been gained from the war. Many believed, with Tanner, that the peace treaty would not last and the lost territories would be regained. It was said that the eventual defeat of Germany by the Allies 'would also lead to a restoration of the old Finnish boundaries'. A foreign office official suggested to the German ambassador that there might be a revolution in the USSR, and went on, 'kein Finne erkenne die neue Grenzführung für die dauer an.'*[18] But on a less sophisticated level, the belief was an act of faith, a simple popular trust that so iniquitous a treaty could not endure. This was often supported by references to previous fluctuations in the Russo-Finnish frontier. In the early days, before the government realized how dangerous the expression of such feelings could be, many letters appeared in the press about the inevitability of revision. They reveal the total failure of the writers to grasp the realities of the international situation, and among some, a failure to understand that their country had been defeated in the recent war. A letter in *Uusi Suomi* on March 22 said:[19]

'Now, when our nation mourns the loss of Karelia, our faith in the future is "No, No, Never." Can he who has won the war lose it?'

Some writers dwelt on the moral wrong, 'we must believe and we do believe that the wrong which our nation has suffered will be corrected.' Others cited the lessons of history:[20]

'Once before the province of Viipuri was torn away from us by war. Building on wise policies and statesmanship, it was recovered. Finnish history gives many proofs of the fact that peace brings back what war has taken away.'

In some of these letters it was stated quite bluntly that the writers did not regard the Treaty of Moscow as a valid or binding instrument. A correspondent of *Uusi Suomi* declared, 'we have now concluded a peace which is no real peace. Everyone knows that.' One of the most outspoken statements appeared in the newspaper *Ilkka* which said:

'We are not willing to see, we cannot bear to see, we simply are not able to see in the decision that has happened anything final or enduring.'

It seems reasonable to conclude that very few Finns, if they thought about the matter at all, accepted the Treaty of Moscow as a final settlement. This does not mean that they harboured any plans to overthrow it. They felt that such a manifest injustice must be corrected some time. In consequence, if they felt that an opportunity had come to put things right, few of them would have any scruples about taking it. In March 1940, ideas like this were harmless, and useful in upholding morale. It was only

*'no Finn will accept the new frontier for long.'

at a later stage that such habits of thought led to danger. The newspaper *Sosialisti* summed up feeling in an article on March 15:[21]

'History shows that unjust alterations of frontiers, brought about by bloody violence, have never lasted for ever. So let us raise our heads, clench our teeth and build a new Finland.'

Over and over again a famous line from a national poet was quoted in writing and speech—'viel' uusi päivä kaikki muuttaa voi'—come another day and everything can change. These sentiments were natural and even healthy, but they were no help when it came to constructing a new relation with the USSR. Anyone could see that the great change which the Finns were dreaming of could only result from the USSR suffering diplomatic or military defeat at the hands of some other power or powers. It became apparent very quickly that the expression of these feelings had not passed unnoticed in Moscow, and by the time the censorship silenced their public utterance, it was too late, and the damage had been done.

Another consolation that many Finns found in their hour of defeat was the idea that the war had taught the USSR to respect Finland, so that she would be more careful in future before putting pressure on. There was an element of truth in this. The USSR certainly never repeated its error of November 1939 in supposing that Finland could be taken over and put under a puppet government without a hard fight. But this was as far as the respect went. Marshal Timoshenko put the matter bluntly to the Finnish military attaché when he praised the courage and skill of the Finnish army but added, 'for an army to produce results it has got to be a big one'.[22] The USSR knew now that it would have to fight hard to break Finland. But it also knew, as was obvious, that if Finland stood alone it would be an unpleasant job, but well within the capacity of the Red Army. Paasikivi commented bitterly that while he was ambassador in Moscow he experienced very little of this respect which the war was supposed to have created. His countrymen undoubtedly made too much of this factor but it too helped to keep up their spirits. And it was true, as Paasikivi agreed, that the consciousness that the reduction of Finland would demand a full-scale war must have had a moderating influence on the policy of the USSR.[23]

However, when the Finns were casting up the war's balance sheet, they always made the most important item on the credit side the creation of national unity. It has been noted earlier that independent Finland was born out of a civil war and this gave a special element of bitterness to its politics. The communist movement had always been persecuted by the authorities and was finally made altogether illegal in the 1930s. The legitimate political aspirations of the defeated Reds had been forced to find expression through the Social Democratic party. This was the largest single party in the country between independence and the outbreak of war. It had retained a formal allegiance to Marxism and still thought and talked in terms of the class-war. It still professed to see in the bourgeois state and its organs the class enemies of the workers. In spite of this the Social Democrats had taken part in constitutional politics and even co-operated with their class enemies in forming governments. Tanner declared as late as 1938 that 'there is no cause to give up the class struggle. The whole of political life is an unending class war . . .',[24] but by that stage the range of class enemies was being somewhat cut down. Even so, formidable sections of conservative opinion continued to think of Tanner's party as enemies of society who should be treated accordingly as outcasts from normal political life. Between these elements and the socialists, the civil war was still being fought. One formidable enemy was the Lutheran church, which was established, and enjoyed the nominal allegiance of nearly 95% of the population. In 1936 Tanner complained of the use of the church as an instrument of anti-socialist propaganda, and said his party was being 'abused and insulted from almost every pulpit'.[25] A more serious enemy than the church was the Suojeluskunta, the Defence Corps. This body was directly born of the civil war and was a semi-official militia. Its members did military training as volunteers although this did not affect their obligation to do their regular military service as conscripts. Each parish had its own unit and the members including the officers were elected. There was a pyramid of command headed by a general staff and a chief of staff who commanded the Defence Corps. He too was elected subject to the approval of the president of the republic. The relations of the Defence Corps to the state were ambiguous. The salaries of the officers were paid out of state funds and arms were provided at public expense. Other expenses including the provision of uniform were met by private contribution. In time of war the Defence Corps came under the command of the president of the republic, and was integrated into the armed forces. But in peacetime it had a measure of autonomy and could formulate its own policies, acting as a powerful pressure group in Finnish life.

It was by nature conservative in its politics. It opposed the socialists and refused to admit members of the Social Democratic party into its ranks. In fact it was tacitly recognized that the purpose of the Defence Corps was primarily to suppress internal threats to the established order of society. In face of this the Social Democrats had consistently campaigned for its dissolution, particularly since the occasion when the Defence Corps had provided arms and organization for an attempted Rightist *coup d'état* in 1932.[26] They would accept its continued existence only if it became a truly national militia and ceased to exclude socialists.

This state of latent and often active hostility between the country's largest political party, the state church, and the semi-official state militia was the outward sign of deep divisions in society which the civil war had intensified. After 1936, the tensions had eased a little. The Social Democrats had made an alliance with the second largest party, the Agrarian party representing the farmers. This 'Red-Mud' alliance commanded a majority in the Eduskunta which had been maintained in the general election of 1939, and had given the country its most stable and successful of pre-war governments. In 1937 the alliance had elected as president of the republic Kyösti Kallio, an elderly and much respected Agrarian politician, who made an excellent figure-head, seemed to embody the idea of the sturdy Finnish farmer, and could be relied on not to use the extensive presidential powers to interfere with the control of the government by the cabinet and the Eduskunta. On the eve of the war it was clear that the Social Democrats, having won a major share of political power, had once more been integrated into normal political life. The scars of the civil war were healing at last.

This process was completed by the war itself. For the successful Left-inclined coalition government before the war had faced the bitter opposition of the Right-wing parties. They had found themselves virtually excluded from their traditional political influence, and this had intensified the acrimony of their attacks. On the outbreak of war, when Ryti had formed a coalition that included all parties except the fascists, political conflict had ceased and national unity—yksimielisyys—was born. It is easy to understand how very many Finns who remembered the arid bitterness of pre-war party politics thought the new state of affairs highly desirable and wished it to continue. War had brought them this one clear advantage which they were anxious to keep. In this respect a lead was given, and the keynote sounded, by Hakkila, the socialist speaker of the Eduskunta, in a radio address on March 14. He declared:[27]

'Our nation has acquired a lively perception of what the full and integral unity of the whole nation means. It alone has been able to create a durable foundation for our survival during an arduous conflict. We have made many sacred promises during this period to preserve this unity into the future as well. For we have learned to recognize what limitless strength it has concealed within it, and how by its means miracles can be achieved in peace as well as war.'

The outside student of this period is apt to find the endless repetition and embroidery of the unity theme tedious. It is inescapable wherever one turns. But this conscious drive to preserve unity was intensely realistic politics. Even in great powers it is generally held undesirable that the nation's foreign policy should become a subject of party conflict. For a small power such a process can be fatal. Not only must a small power be able to use the whole of its strength to pursue its aims, for there is none to

Refugee property

Marshal of Finland C. G. Mannerheim

spare, but it is particularly vulnerable to great power exploitation of its internal conflicts. Hence E. Hiitonen, writing in *Suomen Sosiaalidemokraatti*, was stating a basic fact of political life when he declared that:[28]

'Above all else, a small nation must be unanimous about its foreign policy. Internal political questions must not get mixed up in foreign policy, but the major national aims must be kept common for all.'

The conscious pursuit of national unity was a correct policy in the circumstances of 1940 but it had its dangers. The government was led to trying to maintain harmony by forcibly preventing the expression of views which called the correctness of current policies into question, on the grounds that this might cause controversy. This was especially true of foreign affairs, where there was the additional incentive of wishing to avoid offence to foreign powers. The socialist press at the time was alive to the dangers, and made certain reservations about the implications of preserving unity. It pointed out that as a fact there were conflicting interests in Finland, which could not be resolved without discussion and even controversy.[29] Even in the field of foreign affairs there should be some room for discussion:[30]

'There is no need to start from the idea that because our difficulties are terrible, and external danger great, as long as the world war continues, we must create a silence of the grave in this country. Constructive discussion and the exposition of opinions which give rise to understanding is, on the contrary, necessary. Great restraint is certainly demanded of us, but not a forced silence.'

Official opinion did not agree with this. In fact the silence of the grave was enforced to prevent any public debate on foreign policy, and the idea was prevalent that any sort of political argument, even over purely domestic policies, was to be deplored and prevented. In these circumstances, criticism of the government was inhibited, and became the monopoly of irresponsible and extremist elements. The absence of responsible and moderate opposition voices was a serious weakness which distorted the proper working of the democratic system. But the Finns had little time to spare for these abstract considerations. They were conscious that they stood in mortal danger, they believed rightly that their achievements in the war would have been impossible if the impulse to national unity had not overwhelmed, for a time at least, the old conflicts and bitterness. They were sufficiently alarmed for the future to feel certain that their united strength was vital to their survival. Such was the mental and emotional background against which the Finns faced the consequences of the Treaty of Moscow.

The formalities of ratifying the peace treaty went through without difficulty. This is in itself remarkable since most members of the Eduskunta, whose level of information was little better than that of the general public,

4

would have rejected it out of hand if left to themselves. The government had prepared the ground, through conferences with the leaders of the party groups, and they knew, among other factors, that the Marshal was unequivocally in favour of the treaty. In any case, the representatives were faced with a *fait accompli*. The treaty had already come into force, and it was no longer practical politics to reject it. So in bitterness and resignation the Eduskunta ratified the treaty with only three votes cast against. These three were all Agrarians, just as in the cabinet the two ministers who resigned in protest were Agrarian. While Niukkanen, the defence minister, had personal reasons for this, since he felt that the admission of defeat was a slur on his own work as minister, there were good reasons why the Agrarians should feel so much more strongly about the treaty than other parties. The ceded areas in Karelia had been predominantly inhabited by small independent farmers, and such people were the backbone of the Agrarian vote. Karelia, and the city of Viipuri, had been citadels of the party's power. The Agrarian party naturally felt the loss of its home base more keenly than other parties. Urho Kekkonen, who had begun his party career in Viipuri, voted against the treaty, and he was no fire-eating chauvinist. This bond between the Agrarian party and the Karelians was to become an important factor in post-war politics. When the treaty had been approved by the Eduskunta, it was ratified by the president of the republic, another Agrarian, who had accepted the treaty with the utmost reluctance because he could not stand out against the advice of Mannerheim and the majority of the cabinet. On March 18, J. K. Paasikivi and Professor Voionmaa set out for Moscow for the formal exchange of ratifications.

Before they arrived at their destination, the first of the post-war difficulties between the two countries had arisen. It was mentioned earlier how the Finnish government, when it was considering the Russian peace terms, had sounded out the Swedish government on the possibility of forming a Scandinavian defence alliance between Sweden, Norway, and Finland, which should guarantee the new *status quo*. The Swedish government, aware that it would be a strong inducement to Finland to make peace, had indicated that it was ready to consider it. Mannerheim attached the greatest importance to the idea and his enthusiasm was shared by the Finnish government. They literally did not lose a day before taking the first steps. President Kallio mentioned it in his speech to the nation on March 14, when he expressed the hope that 'the necessity of a Scandinavian defence alliance has become clear to our neighbours in this time of war.'[31] The Swedish press discussed the idea on March 13 and was mostly in favour of it. On March 14 the Speaker of the Norwegian parliament, Hambro, also gave favourable mention to the scheme in a radio address.

Unfortunately this was not all Hambro said. He openly expressed the belief that Finland's new frontiers could not last, 'no unjust, false peace can last long'.[32] The speech was to become a classic example of the dangers of thinking out loud in an age of mass communications. Hambro's speech was heard in Moscow. In Finland too there was careless talk. Everyone could see what the motivation of the proposed alliance was. *Helsingin Sanomat* was foolish enough to say it explicitly. In an editorial welcoming the idea it said:[33]

'. . . to Moscow, the present peace is nothing but a step on the way, with which on this occasion it has seemed best to be satisfied, in order on some subsequent occasion to continue its march to the west.'

The Swedish government while repeating that it was ready to discuss the idea, struck a cautious note, stressing that there must be guarantees that members of the alliance would not be endangered by one of their number launching into a policy of adventure.[34] This was a polite way of saying that they suspected some leading elements in Finland of harbouring ideas of revenge, and that they did not have complete confidence in the cool-headedness and maturity of some Finnish politicians.

Much depended on the reactions of the USSR. From an objective point of view the USSR should have welcomed the proposed alliance. It would have been their best guarantee that Finland would really accept the Treaty of Moscow. It would relieve Finland of feelings of insecurity, which otherwise would always tend to make her seek support from any available anti-Soviet source. Sweden would certainly be the dominant partner in such an alliance and could be relied on to restrain any attempt on Finland's part to pursue a policy of revisionism. It is just possible that at first the project did present itself to the Soviet government in this light, for on March 14, *Pravda* put out a statement that the USSR would not oppose such an alliance. On March 15, the Finnish government made official approaches to Sweden and Norway, and three days later announced to the ambassadors of all interested powers that negotiations had started. By this time the Swedish government was already aware that something had gone wrong. When Paasikivi passed through Stockholm on his way to Moscow, the Swedish foreign minister told him of a conversation between Molotov and the Swedish ambassador. Molotov had declared that the proposed alliance would be a breach of the peace treaty, and also a breach of neutrality by Sweden and Norway, because it was directed against the USSR.[35] The Soviet government had changed its mind. This was confirmed on March 20 when Tass published an official statement. This said that Hambro's speech in particular had revealed that the so-called defensive alliance was directed against the USSR. In consequence it would be a breach of article three of the Treaty of Moscow in which the contracting parties engaged not to enter any alliance directed against the other. It is impossible to believe that Hambro's speech was really the cause of a change of policy by the USSR. It is easier to believe that the original statement in *Pravda* had been issued without full consideration. On consideration the alliance must have appeared to the Soviet leaders somewhat in this light. It was obviously directed against the USSR. The fact that it would equally operate against a German or any other aggression in Scandinavia could not alter this fact. If the USSR really harboured further designs against Finland then it must oppose the alliance. If the USSR did not harbour any such designs, then the proposal was an unwarranted slur on the honour and integrity of the government of the USSR since Finland needed no protection. Either way it was reasonable to oppose the project.

The whole question was discussed on March 21 at a meeting between Molotov and the Finnish delegates Paasikivi and Voionmaa. Molotov confirmed that it was the view of the government of the USSR that the alliance would be a breach of the peace treaty on Finland's part, and a breach of neutrality by Norway and Sweden. All the Finns could say in reply was that the alliance was 'defensive' and that the neutrality of Norway and Sweden guaranteed it could be nothing else. Molotov alleged that Hambro's speech and press comments in Sweden and Finland proved his assertion that it was directed against the USSR. The Soviet Union 'intends to observe the treaty. We regard all questions with Finland as finally settled. Now we want to improve relations between our countries'.[36] The heart of the argument was in the following exchange:[37]

Paasikivi: You cannot believe that this alliance is directed against you.

Molotov: Hambro and others have revealed its purpose.

The whole discussion illustrated the futility of diplomatic exchanges between two parties of unequal strength when mutual confidence is lacking. Neither speaker could have believed what he was saying. Paasikivi knew that the alliance had no meaning for Finland if it was not directed, defensively of course, against the USSR. Molotov, unless he were certifiable, could not have believed that Sweden, Norway, and Finland harboured aggressive intentions against the USSR. But since in diplomatic discussion no one may call a spade by its right name, this kind of empty meaningless argument seems inevitable. The outcome was clear enough. As Paasikivi noted, 'the Soviet government had laid down its position".[38] If Finland had been stronger, or not directly open to armed intervention by the USSR, she could have told the Soviet government that she disagreed with their interpretation of the treaty and intended to go ahead with the alliance. As it was, the Finnish government had to drop the negotiations. The Swedish government, whose position was much less vulnerable, seemed inclined to defy Molotov's warnings. At least the tone of the Swedish press and speeches by the prime minister and defence minister on March 25 suggested this. Even in Finland there were some who had failed to grasp one of the war's chief lessons. An editorial in *Helsingin Sanomat* on March 22 referred back to Tanner's assurance that the USSR had been given no right to interfere in Finland's internal or external affairs. It went on:[39]

'It is clear that Moscow's attitude to the question of a defensive alliance means precisely an attempt to interfere with foreign policy. For this reason we must from the beginning take a serious stand. We have not made peace in order to give up our freedom and right of self-determination. This must be made clear on all sides.'

These were admirable sentiments but quite divorced from the realities of politics. They are quoted to show that there were responsible men in Finland who, after all their experiences in the past three months, still believed that great powers could be expected to take seriously the rights of small powers, when it did not suit their own ends. The answer to the editor was that he must recognize that Finland, having been defeated by one great power, and enjoying no counter-support from any other, must do as she was told. Fortunately the Finnish government no longer harboured any illusions on this point. To make quite sure that nobody else should, the Soviet government sent notes to Sweden and Norway on March 28 setting out its view that an alliance would be a breach of neutrality, and on March 29, in a major policy speech to the Supreme Soviet, Molotov repeated, in unequivocal terms, his government's view that such an alliance would disrupt the peace treaty. The incident was closed and in Finland it was never officially revived.[40] The Swedish press continued defiant, but it could afford to do so.

The effect of this whole episode inside Finland was disastrous. Paasikivi had pointed out to Molotov how the Russian attitude must hamper the efforts of those in Finland who were working for better relations between the two countries.[41] Mannerheim remarked, in characteristic understatement, that this 'negative attitude towards a Scandinavian defence alliance did not diminish distrust of the intentions of the Soviet government'.[42] Most Finns could draw only one conclusion from what seemed to be an utterly unreasonable Soviet position. The USSR must indeed regard the peace treaty as no more than a step on the way. She had not yet finished with Finland. It would be absurd to argue that the business of the Scandinavian alliance gave rise to this belief. As has been shown, it was widely held in any case. But it certainly helped to promote and strengthen it. One can only speculate on whether Finnish apprehensions were right at that time. Probably the Soviet leaders did not know themselves what they would do. In March 1940 they were still waiting to see what might turn up. But whatever this might be, they wanted Finland kept weak and isolated so that if necessary she could be squeezed further, and in any case would be reminded that she belonged in the sphere of influence of the USSR. The price of this policy does not seem to have worried them. They shared the sentiment of a famous Roman emperor, let them hate as long as they are afraid.

While this first external crisis developed, Finland was also engaged on the reconstruction of her government. The wartime coalition of Risto Ryti had been formed to bring the war to an end. Its task had been fulfilled. In addition two Agrarian ministers had resigned so that some reconstruction was inevitable. It has been mentioned that the immediate pre-war government had been a coalition of Agrarians and Social Democrats with one or two small centre groups included, and the Right in opposition. Since there was no thought of holding elections it would have been possible in theory to resurrect this government. But there were strong reasons against this. It was agreed that wartime unity must be preserved and it followed that the Right must be brought into any government formed. There were some on the political right, particularly in the Kokoomus, or conservative party, who hankered after a new system. The Kokoomus newspaper consistently tended to condemn what it called a return to the party politics of pre-war days, and it got several letters from readers both at this time and later arguing in this sense. What they wanted was a 'strong' government that could protect the national interest because it was not at the mercy of the sectional interests represented by the political parties.[43] The most important figure supporting this line was the great industrialist, virtual founder of the modern Finnish paper industry, Rudolf Walden. In 1932, at the time of the so-called Mäntsälä revolt, an abortive Right-wing *coup d'état*, Walden had been intended for the strong man who should lead the new régime. Despite his equivocations at the time, there is little reason to think he would have refused in case of success. Walden admitted himself that he was a rarity among Finns, 'a real man of the Right ... Such an outlook on life is met with rarely in this country, and this basically brings it about that the necessary balance is lacking in ordinary political life'.[44] Walden, as a business man with wide international contacts, was another of the small circle of Finns who were familiar with the great world beyond their country's borders. Like many of this group, he could not help despising what seemed to him the shallowness, irresponsibility, and ignorance of many party politicians. These seemed too absorbed in the pursuit of their selfish sectional interests to care adequately for the nation's affairs. Because he felt like this, Walden had held proudly aloof from pre-war politics, built up his industries, ruled his model factories as a benevolent despot, done all he could to support the Suojeluskunta, and refused to have any dealings with trade unions. Walden had a further, and almost unique importance. He was a close personal friend of Mannerheim, one of the very few Finns who could be called that. The two men had co-operated closely in 1918 and held many political views in common. They shared contempt for party politics and politicians. They were both realistic about foreign affairs. They both believed in strong government and strong defences. On those occasions when Walden was approached about re-entering politics, he always stipulated that Mannerheim must become commander in chief at the same time. The two men had dominated the pre-war Defence Council, which had been set up as an advisory body to the government to ensure continuity in military planning. During the war, Walden had been in Helsinki as Mannerheim's personal emissary to the government, though not a member of it. In spite of that the government seems to have consulted him on most major questions. Walden would certainly have nothing to do with a government based on the pre-war pattern, and that meant that Mannerheim too would oppose it. This by itself ruled out such a government in the circumstances. Nobody could form a government in March 1940 without the blessing of the Marshal.

In these circumstances, Walden and his friends tried to suggest their favourite scheme for a strong government. They embodied it in an editorial in *Uusi Suomi* on March 17, which was nominally a comment on the Marshal's order of the day. It stressed the value of the confidence which the whole nation felt in Mannerheim and continued:[45]

'Only by the aid of this authority and confidence is it possible to carry out the peace terms. There could be no happier outcome of our misfortunes than that the Marshal's command should continue not only over the armed forces, but over the general direction of the country's fate. We do not need a dictator, but we do need a commander who can hold down all party and other struggles for advantage by his personal authority and prestige and can preserve that national readiness for sacrifice and front-line spirit which emerged during our heavy trials, and which alone can guarantee the successful realization of the gigantic programme which is now before us.'

It was not made clear under what constitutional form this was to be done, or whether president Kallio was to be replaced by Mannerheim. It did not matter, since the proposal was more than the regular politicians could swallow. The socialists in particular did not like the sound of it nor did its origins recommend it to them. It was true that during the war Walden, and the employers' associations generally, had made gestures to the socialists. They had agreed with the socialist Trade Union Federation on a general recognition of the unions. The Suojeluskunta too had made a treaty with the Social Democrats for future co-operation on the basis of the free admission of Social Democrats to the ranks. Even so the politicians knew that under a Mannerheim-Walden régime they would be, for all practical purposes, out of a job. *Suomen Sosiaalidemokraatti* answered *Uusi Suomi* on March 18. There must be a reconstruction of the government, but it must be on a democratic, that is a parliamentary basis.[46] The following day their political commentator repeated this, adding that it would be strange if, after a struggle in which all had freely served, the country found itself in a condition of total, forced unanimity.[47]

The political leaders who alone could command a majority in the Eduskunta were clearly not willing to abdicate power in the Marshal's favour, so a compromise had to be hammered out. Its basis was the continuation of Ryti's wartime coalition of all parties except the fascist IKL. Walden's unofficial position as Mannerheim's spokesman was regularized by making him minister of defence, on the clear understanding that he was to have a free hand in defence policy, and that the necessary money and legislation would be voted without question. It seems that Walden and Mannerheim took a joint stand on this, making it clear that they would only continue in their functions on their own terms. Mannerheim was as closely consulted as the party leaders in forming the new government, almost as though he was himself part of the constitutional machinery. Mannerheim and Walden also stipulated that there must be legislation to free the commander in chief from dependence on the minister of defence, who in normal circumstances would be a party politician like Niukkanen, making his authority almost independent of political control. Walden also insisted that he must be regarded as a non-party minister, although he was at least nominally a supporter of the Kokoomus.

The other posts were allocated among the party leaders with the exception of the foreign ministry. It was clear that Tanner was not happy in this office. He was not temperamentally suited to it. More serious he was known to be obnoxious to the Soviet government and to a lesser extent also to the German government. The Soviet leaders have always pursued a bitter personal vendetta against Tanner, presumably because his Social Democratic party successfully led the bulk of the Finnish workers away from communism. Tanner had never concealed his dislike of all forms of fascism and this had angered the Nazi leaders. So he moved to the control of economic affairs. This left the foreign ministry vacant, and it can be understood that it was not a very attractive post. Few politicians felt themselves qualified for the job, yet with Kallio as president the presidential right to direct foreign policy was practically in abeyance. In the end the choice fell on Professor Rolf Witting. It seemed difficult in retrospect to see how this patently unsatisfactory appointment came to be made. Witting died in 1944 leaving no written evidence of his own. Very few people could be found to say a good word about him after he had gone. When Ryti was asked at his trial why the appointment was made, he said, admitting many defects in Witting, that 'he had good points as well. He was unusually intelligent and he could express himself. And there was no one else even of his standard to put in this delicate position'.[48] Witting was another untypical Finn. Though born in Viipuri his family was German speaking, and he himself spoke German and Swedish more readily than Finnish. He had been in politics before as a member of the Swedish People's party, but he did not regard himself as a party man, nor did his views on foreign affairs agree with those of the party to which he belonged. Witting was never able to establish a good and confidential relationship with the foreign affairs committee of the Eduskunta, perhaps because of language difficulties. It is established that he fed this committee with partial information to an extent which amounted to deception. Witting seems to have shared the contempt for politicians which was so common, and believed with some justification that anything he said before the committee, however confidential, would leak out. His relations with the members of the Eduskunta were further queered by a difficulty of temperament. Witting was of an ironic disposition, and given to a realistic, if not cynical manner of exposition. This, combined with language problems, meant that many of his hearers were uncertain what he meant, or how far he was to be taken literally. Members of the foreign affairs committee often had rather naïve and idealistic views on foreign policy and certainly did not regard them as a fit subject for humour. One member recalled that Witting 'gave the impression that the subject was not being presented with that seriousness which its nature called for'.[49] Witting's brand of ironic humour passed over the heads of many of the representatives and left them baffled and dissatisfied. As government spokesman on foreign affairs to the Eduskunta, Witting was a failure. He was also by background and inclination pro-German, and this gave a bias to his policies. Witting was an intimate of the German ambassador,[50] whose aristocratic person represented the old Germany which Witting admired, as compared with the new Nazi Germany for which it is unlikely that Witting had much sympathy. Ryti was probably correct in saying that Witting was appointed in the end because there was nobody else remotely qualified and willing. Kallio, for reasons not now explicable, was keen to have him, while Mannerheim felt unable to oppose the choice although he told Ryti by telephone that 'I am afraid that the choice of Witting will not prove successful'. The situation was one which commonly arises in small states. They do not have any reserve of men qualified by training and experience to handle foreign affairs. The local politicians are usually unsuited for the work, and the tendency is to turn to intellectuals or professional men, like Professor Witting, to plug the gap. They at least generally know foreign languages and are presumed to understand the world outside.

The prime minister, Risto Ryti, had long been noted as one of Finland's coming men, and a probable future president of the republic. Ryti was thoroughly Finnish in background, but had made his reputation as a financial expert and governor of the Bank of Finland. In this capacity he had been involved in dealings with the world of international finance and commerce, and so belonged to the group of Finns who were familiar with the great world outside their country's borders. In addition, as an orthodox banker, Ryti had become a well-known anglophile. He naturally found a conservative Britain sympathetic, and the unorthodox commercial and financial practices of Nazi Germany distasteful. When the war broke out, Ryti was immediately asked to form a national coalition, and in March 1940 there was no other candidate to head the reformed government. Ryti added one more to the number of ministers who were not regular party politicians. His own party allegiances were purely nominal. The new government was formally installed on March 27. It had the support of the whole of the Eduskunta except the fascist IKL, numerically insignificant, although on some questions there was a group of dissident Agrarians, led by former defence minister Niukkanen, which was inclined to go into opposition. Yet the fact that this government enjoyed the support of such an overwhelming majority tends to obscure the fact that its relations to the Eduskunta were abnormal. Of the four leading figures in it, Ryti, Walden, Witting, and Tanner, only the latter was a professional party and parliamentary politician. Further the crucial fields of defence and foreign policy were wholly in the hands of non-party men, and there is reason to think that Walden and Witting rather despised the politicians of the Eduskunta, and Ryti showed strong tendencies to do the same. So that although the government was nominally based on wide parliamentary support, there were some respects in which a gulf existed between the government and the Eduskunta, and mutual confidence was lacking. Certainly in retrospect, many observers thought that the relations of the country's leaders with its elected representatives in the Eduskunta left much to be desired.

CHAPTER 3

The domestic economy and the refugee problem

The new government was compelled to give its immediate attention to serious economic and social problems which were partly the result of the war with Russia and partly caused by the European war. The latter had wrecked the structure of Finland's foreign trade and raised acute problems of supply and employment. There had been a time, not very remote in 1940, when Finland had had a primitive but almost self-sufficient agrarian economy. The farmer and his immediate neighbours had been able to produce almost everything necessary for life. In the 19th century, the industrial revolution came to Finland, and with it the usual phenomena of urbanization and population increase. The economy ceased to be self-sufficient and foreign trade developed. After independence the process had raced forward and brought hitherto undreamt-of prosperity to the country. But the self-sufficiency of the old economy was gone beyond recall.

The broad pattern of Finland's foreign trade was a simple one. There were three main kinds of import. Foodstuffs, especially grain, to feed the towns and their swelling populations were the first. Then there were textiles and raw materials for the native textile industries. Third were the materials for Finland's newer industries, metals and machinery, coal and oil. Although wood was the main domestic fuel, and was also used in industry to some extent, and helped to keep transport going by firing the railway engines and even producing a kind of gas for internal combustion engines, a certain amount of imported fuel was vital for keeping industry and transport going. There were no domestic sources of coal or oil. Exports too fell into three main groups. First, farm produce, of which butter was the most important single item. Then came the products of the forest industries, raw timber, and timber processed as pulp, cellulose, or paper. Third came raw metals, mainly copper and nickel, of which Finland possessed some of the richest deposits in Europe. The pre-war trading economy had been a healthy one. It had recovered quickly from the Great Depression and usually showed a balance of trade in Finland's favour.

Great Britain had taken most of the exports and supplied most of the imports. Germany had come second, and far below her the United States and Sweden. The most striking feature of the pattern of trade was the insignificant share of the USSR. Before 1914 Russia had been Finland's biggest market. Since independence she ranked with countries like Norway as a very minor trading partner.

The European war had wrecked this trading pattern by closing the North Sea and destroying trade with Britain. It automatically boosted the importance of Germany since supplies of fuel, grain, and engineering products had to come almost entirely from that country, or through her territory. Only Sweden was in a position to supply a certain amount of produce which was not entirely dependent on the good will of Germany. The German seizure of Denmark and Norway in April 1940 reinforced this state of affairs. Finland retained one precarious link with the world beyond continental Europe. This was the port of Liinahamari in the Petsamo area, which was on the Arctic ocean. Unfortunately, Liinahamari, though ice-free all year round, had only a single highway connecting it to the rest of Finland, and this automatically put serious limits on its capacity, especially in view of the shortage of motor transport and fuel in Finland. Further, even trade to Liinahamari was subject to the blockade regulations of the belligerents. Even so a valuable trickle of trade with the United States and the Southern Hemisphere was maintained through it.

The threatened collapse of Finland's foreign trade posed grave problems for the government. The fall in imports threatened shortages of basic food, clothing, and fuel. The fall in exports threatened unemployment and foreign exchange difficulties. In these circumstances the government had two tasks, to stimulate the development of domestic resources and achieve the maximum possible degree of self-sufficiency, and to develop new trading outlets where that was possible. In practice there were only three possible major trading partners left, Germany, Sweden, and the USSR. It was easiest to deal with Sweden, which was pricked by a bad conscience over the war. The Swedish government was ready to do all it could to help Finland. In addition to money and materials for reconstruction, which will be mentioned elsewhere, Sweden did as much as her limited resources permitted to find supplies of food and raw materials. She gave extensive credits and joined with Finland in the exploitation of the port of Liinahamari. But with the best will in the world, Sweden could make only a limited contribution. For major developments the Finnish government had to look to Germany. Fortunately Finland had a major asset in her supplies of copper and nickel which were both important as blockade-free sources of supply for the German arms industry. There were some difficulties in developing Finnish-German trade. The Finnish government did not like the German system of barter and clearing agreements. But necessity had to be recognized, and negotiations for the enlargement of Finnish-German trade were soon begun. In June 1940, a new trade agreement was concluded which got a warm welcome in Finland since it assured the supply of some basic necessities for the following twelve months and looked forward to a permanent large expansion of mutual trade.

At the same time the government set about negotiating a trade agreement with the USSR. This had been anticipated in article 8 of the peace treaty, and on the Russian side there was considerable enthusiasm expressed. Both parties realized that the pre-1939 level of trade had been absurdly low, if judged by purely economic criteria, but of course it never had been. There were economic problems, the chief one being that the USSR did not want any large quantities of Finland's main exports of timber products or minerals. But this had not been the main obstacle to trade. Both sides saw the difficulties as political. Responsible opinion in Finland, even that of Paasikivi, an advocate of better relations, feared to give the USSR any kind of economic hold over Finland.[1] The USSR had also insisted in the period before the war that a satisfactory settlement of political issues was a pre-condition of any trade agreement. Now that they had declared that all outstanding issues were settled, this was no longer any reason for delay. So as early as March 27, Moscow Radio declared that the prospects for Russo-Finnish trade were good. It claimed that Finnish business circles had long been dissatisfied with their excessive dependence on Great Britain. 'Now Russo-Finnish trade will be a corner stone of the Russo-Finnish peace treaty'.[2] The enthusiasm on the Finnish side was notably less. The newspaper *Työn Voima* probably took an extreme line when it declared that 'we ordinary people hope sincerely that fate will spare us, in present circumstances, from touching with our hands any product made by the oppressor'.[3] The government knew that the country needed the trade. It also believed, as so many people still do despite all evidence to the contrary, that the development of international trade automatically improves international relations. A Finnish delegation led by the minister of commerce went to Moscow in May and had no difficulty in agreeing on the broad outlines of a treaty. The basic principles were settled by May 27. The details took a little longer to arrange, but by June 23 the full agreement was ready for signature and was formally concluded on June 28.[4]

It provided for a balanced trade in the first year of operation of seven and a half million United States dollars in each direction. Finland would supply engineering products and ships, the USSR would send grain, petroleum products, and raw materials. The value of the trade proposed was modest, as a proportion of Finland's total trade, but the grain and the oil would be especially valuable. If the agreement had been fulfilled, it would have represented about 9% of Finland's foreign trade in the period June 1940–June 1941. Thus it was not big enough to give the USSR a serious economic hold over Finland. The treaty also provided for a system of payment, for increased Russian consular representation in Finland, and for transit rights for Russian goods. The treaty got a general welcome in Finland as a sign that relations were developing normally. The Tampere newspaper *Aamulehti* pointed out that although the value of the exchange was so much less than that provided for in the treaty with Germany, 'its greatest value is on the political side',[5] as showing that relations between the two countries were correct. Svento, the foreign affairs commentator of *Suomen Sosiaalidemokraatti*, also stressed the political implications and hoped that his countrymen now understood that correct political relations with the USSR were a prerequisite for the development of trade.[6] The Eduskunta considered the USSR and German trade agreements early in July and approved them without dissent. Witting used the occasion to try to raise public confidence in Finland's international position. It will be seen that there was ample cause for this in the circumstances. Witting claimed with some plausibility that the government had made an energetic and successful response to the threatened collapse of the country's foreign trade. He claimed that the agreements provided for a level of trade four times greater than had seemed probable in March. The agreements also showed the fundamental goodwill of the USSR and Germany towards Finland. Germany had shown great understanding, and Witting implied that she was really buying more than she strictly needed in order to help the Finnish economy. The USSR had shown her desire to help by offering, at the moment of signing, a considerable increase in deliveries of petrol. These things were signs of normal healthy relations.[7] In fact Witting was well aware how far this was from the truth. It will be shown that at this point relations with the USSR had taken a particularly disturbing turn. And however welcome the trade was for its own sake, any observer could see the dangers inherent in a situation where Finland's two totalitarian neighbours, then outwardly working together, completely dominated her foreign trade.

By these trade agreements the danger of economic disaster was averted. But a measure of dislocation and hardship could not be prevented. Native ingenuity and enterprise found substitutes for some of the worst shortages, exploiting the abundant supply of native timber. Finns gradually got used to such novelties as paper sheets for their beds, shoes made of wood and paper, and buses and lorries running on gas produced from small wood-burning stoves towed along behind. In spite of all efforts, hardship and austerity crept over the national life. It can be measured by the spread of rationing. There had not been much rationing during the war, except for obvious things like coffee. Bread rationing was announced on May 19, followed shortly by butter. As people came to realize that they might be in for a hard winter,[8] food hoarding became a major problem and no amount of severe sentencing of offenders could prevent it, nor suppress the flourishing black market which developed, and was the subject of endless denunciation and moralizing in the press. The exceptionally cold winter of 1939–40 had killed almost all the fruit trees and bushes, adding a further dietary problem since substitute supplies were not easily obtained. As a result of the war, and the loss of Karelia, there had been heavy cattle losses, perhaps amounting to 10% of the nation's herds. In November, meat was rationed. Clothes rationing preceded it by a month. When Tanner was interviewed in October about the prospects for the coming winter, he was gloomy.[9] The harvest of 1940 had been mediocre, the trade agreements looked more impressive on paper than they were in performance, food was bound to be short in the spring. The minister of commerce, in a speech to businessmen at the same time, tried to be more cheerful, but without much conviction. The economic situation was not hopeless but it would be difficult.[10] In face of general shortages the government would be compelled to introduce price-control for all goods before long. A grim and peculiarly exasperating danger was that there would be a shortage of firewood in the cities. This could have been catastrophic in a climate like that of Finland. The problem was peculiar in that there was of course no absolute shortage of wood in a country covered in forest. The shortage was of labour to cut it, and transport, particularly motor transport, to get it to the cities. The threat was so serious that the government passed a law in June compelling all forest owners to cut a quota of firewood and sell it at controlled prices.[11] They also took power to conscript the unemployed to help get it in. Many could not understand how it was that at a time of high unemployment in cities, and when many Karelians were living on public assistance, there could be such a shortage of labour in the forests. Some estimated that an extra 45,000 men could be found work there. It was Ryti, in a speech to the Eduskunta on June 7, who pointed out some of the difficulties. Forest workers needed suitable clothing and tools, and unemployed city workers and Karelian refugees often did not have them and could not buy them. The raising of money to travel to distant parts of the country was also an obstacle.[12] In this field, as in others, the government's measures averted disaster, but could not prevent hardship. Nor could it prevent the development of patches of unemployment, especially during the summer of 1940, and particularly in Helsinki. In June there were many complaints by demobilized servicemen that they had come home to find their old jobs gone, and could not find others.[13] At first it was mainly the socialist press which agitated for relief, but by August the government was alarmed. The natural discontents of the unemployed were being exploited by what the minister of the interior, in a radio broadcast calling for self-discipline, called anti-social elements.[14] He meant communists, but dared not say so openly for fear of offending the USSR. By this time even the conservative press had recognized that unemployment was a danger to national security, and was calling for vigorous measures to alleviate it. The government did what it felt able. There were jobs available, working on the fortifications in the east, or building roads in Lapland, but it was not so easy to get Helsinki workers to go to them in remote parts of the country, and under primitive conditions. Fortunately unemployment remained a localized phenomenon and did not present a major political or economic danger. In general it is worth remembering that, while Finland was undergoing one of the most testing periods of her history, the ordinary citizen was contending with the steady erosion of his standard of living, and facing the prospect that in the winter and spring of 1941 even the most basic necessities of life might be in short supply. The strain on his nerves and his morale was correspondingly increased.

To any government and people in any country, economic and social problems such as those just discussed would have been a heavy burden. To the Finnish people, they were only the background against which they struggled with the vast problem of the Karelian refugees. The refugee issue was the dominant internal political question of the period under consideration. It arose from the provisions of the peace settlement which allowed the inhabitants of the areas ceded to the USSR to move into Finland if they wished. The Soviet government had been quite willing to agree to this and its behaviour suggests that it preferred the inhabitants to leave. They even allowed those who had not moved before the Soviet troops took over the territories to leave if they wished. This is quite consistent with the view that the main motivation on the Russian side was one of military security. From that point of view it was better not to have a large potentially hostile population in the new frontier zone. It was better to have an empty region which could be colonized by Russians.

The exodus of the inhabitants of the ceded territories was a most remarkable phenomenon. Official Finnish versions of it give the impression that everyone simply rose up and left without the slightest hesitation. The Soviet propaganda version was that the populace was driven out by the terrorist activity of the retreating Finnish army, and forcibly prevented from staying to enjoy the blessings of life under socialism. The Soviet version is sheer fantasy. No doubt instances did occur, in the haste and confusion of evacuation, where pressure was put on those who either wanted to stay, or could not make up their minds. But there is such a lack of evidence of people being forced to go, that there cannot have been any significant number of them. A tiny minority did stay behind, but they were so few that it is fair to say that everyone went. This had not been either planned or anticipated by the Finnish government. Its delegation in Moscow spent some time trying to get Molotov to discuss guarantees for the civil rights and religious liberties of the population of the ceded areas. The Finnish version of events is undoubtedly the correct one. The migration of the Karelians was voluntary and spontaneous. But it needs to be pointed out that a large proportion of them did not really have any choice. Those whose homes had been in or close to the battle areas had been evacuated before the fighting ended. This applied, for instance, to most of the 75,000 inhabitants of Viipuri, the only large town affected. It is unrealistic to suppose that the Finnish authorities would have facilitated the return of these people, even if they had wished to go back. But when all allowance has been made for this factor, and for the fact that many heads of families were serving in the army, so that their women and children decided to go without being able to consult them, and for the fact that a Karelian villager would have needed great strength of character to decide to stay when all his neighbours were leaving, because the social pressures would have been very great in favour of going along with the majority, it remains true that of those who were free to choose, virtually all decided to abandon their homes, their land, and much of their worldly goods, and make a new life in what was left of Finland.

This was a demonstration of public opinion far more impressive than any election or plebiscite could provide. Most of these people were small farmers who had owned their own farm. They were passionately attached to their land. To many, the interior of Finland was like a foreign country which they had never visited. Even the language was not quite the same, for in rural Finland dialects were still strong in 1940. The radio and universal education were steadily spreading the standard version of the language, but a Karelian villager of 1940 who moved into a province speaking a different dialect would have had real difficulties of communication. These people committed an act of faith. They left the only life they or their ancestors had known and took the risk of whatever might come in an unpredictable future. They had no sort of guarantee of what their treatment would be. Yet they did not hesitate. By migrating, by voting with their feet, they declared on the one hand what they thought of Finland, and on the other how they regarded the USSR. To them, being and remaining Finnish meant far more than leaving homes which they and their forefathers had often inhabited for generations. On the other hand, the idea of becoming Soviet citizens aroused no positive response at all. It was simply unthinkable. The migration of the Karelians in 1940, and again in

5

1944, is a striking testimony to the vitality of the idea of Finnish nationalism. There is no reason to think that in this respect the rest of the Finnish people differed from the Karelians, and every reason to think that this intense, living national feeling was typical of the bulk of Finnish people, as was the equally intense rejection of Russia and things Russian. The vitality of this idea is one of the secrets of Finland's extraordinary achievements.

There were about 420,000 refugees, or 11% of the population of pre-war Finland. The largest group were the Karelians. They were made up of some 85,000 town dwellers from Viipuri, Sortavala, and Käkisalmi, the workers from the industrial plants of the Vuoksi valley, and the rural population of the Karelian isthmus and the ceded area north of Lake Ladoga. These people had lived by farming and forestry, mostly on family-owned farms, though a few thousand were fishermen-farmers from the coasts and islands of the Gulf of Finland. The next largest group of refugees were the inhabitants of the Hanko area, some 15,000, of whom half had lived in the port of Hanko, and the rest were fishermen and farmers from the surrounding region. The last group was a few thousand farmers and foresters from the Kuusamo-Salla area. The evacuation of these people, or such as had not already left before the fighting ended, had to be done in a matter of days. Every available train and vehicle was pressed into service. Sweden helped by sending a fleet of lorries and their crews. The job was forwarded by the grim determination of the Finns to leave nothing behind for the Russians if they could help it. They were required by the peace treaty to hand over the ceded areas undamaged, but they could and did strip them of everything moveable where circumstances permitted this. A great mass of property was got away and, after first piling up at the communication centres nearest to the new frontier, it was sorted and put in government stores, often hastily improvised. The farm people generally tried to take their livestock and implements as well as household effects, and the livestock presented a grave problem. In March, with the full rigour of the coldest winter in decades prevailing, the stock needed shelter and fodder and much had to be slaughtered in the end.[15] As far as possible the refugees were kept in their original community groups, and when they too had been dumped over the frontier they were sorted out and distributed round the country either in billets, or camped in public buildings such as schools. The preservation of the refugee communities was deliberately done. In this way communal life could be preserved, and this would be administratively convenient, and it was hoped, would aid the morale of the refugees. They were considered to be a charge on public funds, and a relief organization was set up to see that they were clothed and fed, and pay them a small dole while they were unemployed. Each refugee community got a government administrator who directed its affairs in consultation with representatives of the refugees and their host communities.

There had never been any doubt about how the Karelians should be received. From the beginning it was acknowledged that the country owed a debt of honour to them because in part it had purchased its freedom and independence at their expense. This was the theme of an editorial in *Uusi Suomi* on March 20, and in many other articles and speeches. It was the main theme of a radio address by President Kallio on April 12.[16] In addition it was obvious that in the long run the refugees were an asset and not a burden to the community. There was plenty of room in Finland, which in area is one of the larger countries of Europe, and one of the most thinly populated. The manpower of the refugees, and the wealth they could create once they had been resettled, was of the highest value for the future of the whole nation, and was recognized as such. So the Finnish people seem, almost without reflection, to have accepted that they should make heavy sacrifices in order to absorb the refugees and enable them to rebuild their lives. The former town dwellers presented the easiest problem. Finland's towns and cities had been absorbing a steady flow of migrants since about 1880, and although this large new influx created temporary problems of housing and employment, the urban refugees could virtually resettle themselves given time and some short-term assistance. They were joined by many of their rural brethren, large numbers of whom did not wait to be resettled in country communities, but moved into the towns and settled there. Similarly it was not very difficult to place the refugee schoolteachers, civil servants, and professional men. A young and growing country like Finland could always use their talents and skills. The core of the refugee problem lay in the farmers and fishermen who wished to remain in their old way of life.

Once more there was no hesitation in recognizing what must be done. The refugees must be given land and set up once more as independent farmers, at whatever cost to the rest of the community. This was assumed by editorials in *Uusi Suomi* and *Helsingin Sanomat*, and indeed in most of the press, within a few days of the peace. It was also recognized that they would have to be compensated for their lost property and that this too must be a charge on the fortunate majority whose possessions had been preserved by sacrificing those of the Karelians. Committees were immediately established by the government to report on how this was to be done. In the meantime, the mass of the refugees had to sit around and wait, often finding themselves pushed round the country like flocks of sheep as the authorities grappled with the problem of finding suitable places of settlement.[17] There was much bitter complaint that this process was not carried out with the required efficiency and that in the course of it much unnecessary suffering and hardship was caused. Urho Kekkonen, who was in general charge of refugee affairs, came in for much criticism over this. Considering the size of the problem, and the degree of improvisation involved, this was probably unfair. The lot of the refugees was bound to be an unhappy one. While there were some among them who came to like living in idleness at public expense, even wandering around trading on their hard-luck stories, they were a minority. There were enough of them to lead the government, in June, to make regulations requiring all able-bodied refugees on public assistance to register for work, on pain of losing their dole.[18] But the vast majority of refugees longed to get to work again. Most Finns, and especially the small farmers, are fiercely independent people. They find the very idea of living idly on public assistance profoundly repugnant and personally degrading. In these circumstances discontent developed quickly, and the refugees began to grumble and agitate at what they regarded as the dilatory proceedings of the authorities. It was inevitable too that friction should develop between the Karelians and their hosts. The Finns are a remarkable people, and their patriotic desire to do right by the Karelians overcame many obstacles, but Finns are also human, and the circumstances were particularly difficult. The hosts had to share their houses, their community buildings, and in time their fields and cowsheds. It was obvious from the start that resettlement was going to involve some redistribution of existing farmland, and no farmer in the world would view with equanimity the prospective surrender of part of his holding, even if he acknowledged that there was no choice. The knowledge that these involuntary guests were going to take part of the hosts' fields as well did not help to breed warmth of feeling. There was the additional stress set up by regional differences. The problem of dialect has been mentioned. A letter in *Uusi Suomi* in May revealed that there was a tendency to regard the Karelians as backward and primitive.[19] There were naturally differences of social and agrarian custom. There is no doubt that both sides commented on the funny habits of the other, and such comment was not always kindly taken. The Karelians no doubt talked much of the excellence of the lands they had lost, and this would lose nothing in the telling. They must sometimes have conveyed the impression that they thought their hosts' countryside was decidedly inferior to what they had left, and the hosts must have wished at times that they had never left it. This kind of friction tended to develop as time passed and forced inactivity became more irksome, and the original flush of patriotic enthusiasm wore off.

More serious were the manifestations of open hostility with which some communities had met the refugees from the beginning.[20] Apart from general unfriendliness there were cases of refugees being cheated, particularly when they sought to sell their possessions or stock to raise a little ready money. Sharp practice in such deals was sufficiently widespread for the government to introduce legislation to provide for the subsequent revocation of bargains in which the refugee had been manifestly exploited. Refugees accused their hosts of indifference and unfriendliness. The hosts complained of fecklessness, idleness, even social exclusiveness, alleging that the Karelians refused to mix or intermarry. It would be quite wrong to exaggerate the importance of these phenomena. Only a miracle, or super-human behaviour on both sides could have avoided them. On the whole the marvel is how little trouble there was, and how genuine and permanent good feeling did develop between the refugees and their hosts. The situation was fraught with many of the most awkward kinds of social problem, but on the whole the sense of obligation and a common nationality, the firm determination to do right by the Karelians and repay in kind the obligation created when they had decided to come in with their country-men rather than stay under alien rule, triumphed over formidable diffi-culties. At the beginning of April, Kekkonen made a radio address in which he rebuked those who had not received the refugees in a friendly spirit, and reminded the nation of what it owed them. This address, and much press comment on the same theme, shows that a serious problem existed. But it also reveals the strong public sense of shame that there were Finns who were failing to live up to the high standards of unselfish and patriotic behaviour which were expected of them as a matter of course. What is significant is not that some Finns failed to keep these standards, but that the government could confidently expect that most people would do so, if the question was put to them fairly.

The Karelians did not confine themselves to private grumbling. They began to organize to protect their rights. On April 20 a meeting of refugee delegates in Helsinki formed the Karelian League, and drew up a pro-gramme.[21] They sent a delegation to the president to demand that they be resettled in community groups in the south of Finland, and that they should receive full compensation for their lost property. This remarkably swift organization of refugee opinion was assisted by the Agrarian party as part of its campaign to keep hold of the refugee vote. The Karelian League developed into a powerful pressure group which fought unremittingly for the rights of the refugees. It was a symptom of the vigour of the refugee community.

By the end of April the committees on resettlement and compensation were ready with their reports.[22] The resettlement committee, headed by Professor Kivimäki, had its proposals largely accepted by the government. The principle of resettlement was to be the provision of a farm for each refugee family. As far as was possible refugees should be settled as communities. The necessary land would be obtained by voluntary sale, or compulsory purchase where that failed. The farms would not themselves be compensation for lost property, they were conceived as a means of livelihood for a family unit. They would be of a standard size, in general, 15 hectares of cultivable land and 15 hectares of forest. Buildings were to be provided. Half the holding was to be handed over in cultivable condition, which virtually meant it would have to be made up from existing farms. It was laid down that no existing farm should be reduced below a minimum size, or be made unworkable, so that it was inevitable that existing large farms would have to give up a bigger proportion of land than small ones, and that the areas containing most large farms would have to take a larger proportion of refugees. It followed from this that north Finland, where large holdings were virtually non-existent, was exempted from the obligation to provide land. This also met the refugee demand that they be settled in the south of the country. All parishes would be surveyed and the quota of land which they must contribute assessed. It would then be up to each parish to find the land either by voluntary sale or compulsory purchase. The latter would be at a fair market price to be determined by the state. Any landowner who had to provide land was given a limited time to find and purchase equivalent land elsewhere, instead of surrendering his own. This provision was meant to allow large landowners to prevent the break-up of their estates, which were often, from an economic point of view, the most efficient. The resettled farmers would repay the value of their holdings to the state in annual instalments of 4%.

This scheme was more than a simple resettlement scheme. It was at the same time a major agrarian reform, comparable in scope with the enfranchisement of tenants and sharecroppers after independence. The effect would be to multiply small independent farms at the expense of large estates.[23] It had been the consistent aim of agrarian policy since independence to make a rural society of small family-owned farms the backbone of Finnish social structure. Naturally conservative voices were raised which doubted the wisdom of seeking to put through a major social reform at such a time. This view was expressed in *Uusi Suomi* on May 14. It was generally expected that the number of farms to be created would be about 36,000. It calculated that no less than 30,000 of these would get a bigger area of field in their new farms than they had possessed on their old.[24] It was feared that the break-up of existing farms on the scale required might prove a serious set-back to agricultural production and efficiency. *Uusi Suomi* had already canvassed the alternative idea of clearing new land in the north to relieve the pressure. It was recognized that it would be wrong to force the Karelians to go north against their will, but suggested that their reluctance to consider this was based more on prejudice than fact. The climatic conditions in north Finland were little different from those in the eastern parts of Karelia. In the final version of the resettlement law inducements were offered to refugees to go north, in the form of bigger holdings and easier financial terms, but very few seem to have been tempted by this. It was in fact clear that a speedy resettlement must involve the splitting up of existing farms. There was not time to procure the amounts of land needed by clearing forest and swamp.

The draft law, known as the 'pika-asutus' or speedy settlement law, was introduced into the Eduskunta by Ryti in a speech of April 30.[25] There was no opposition to the principle of the law, only a few conservative representatives who deplored the use of compulsory purchase on such a scale, and were unhappy about the redistributive aspects, but even they did not deny the fundamental rightness and inevitability of the scheme. The bill then went into committee. Here the Right tried to enlarge the right to purchase alternative land, and the Left opposed any concessions as being designed to shelter big property owners at the price of slowing down the process of resettlement. While the Eduskunta dealt with this long and complicated piece of legislation it became increasingly apparent that the actual process of resettlement would be a lengthy one, and that little could be done, except on paper, before the spring of 1941. The Karelian League became increasingly embittered as this was realized and sent a strong protest to the president on May 24.[26] They declared that 'as goodwill weakens and removal from place to place continues, and the weeks pass by, the mood of the Karelians is depressed, even bitter'. It was the knowledge of this bitterness and frustration that made everyone sensitive about doing anything which might slow down the process even further. The law finally passed the Eduskunta by 165 votes to 3 on June 18. The work of receiving and deciding on claims, and surveying and apportioning the quotas for each parish could begin. It was found that estimates of the number of families involved had been on the low side. The number of valid applications for holdings under the terms of this law exceeded 40,000.[27] The government quickly appropriated Fmk.945 million for resettlement within the current year but it did not expect to be able to start preparing more than 9,000 farms in that time. So various emergency relief measures were enacted. The most important was the compulsory provision of allotments on which refugee families could raise a crop for their own consumption in the current year. All farms over 10 hectares had to give up land for this purpose.[28] This would relieve refugee families from rotting away in complete idleness. Various inducements were also offered to those refugees who were able and willing to strike out for themselves. In addition to an estimated 50,000 who moved off into the towns,[29] many of the more fortunate or more enterprising managed to buy or lease land by their own initiative, and the state encouraged this. Even so the bulk of the refugees had to accept the fact that it would be twelve months or more before they could expect to be able to set up on their own.

The disappointment of their dreams of a really speedy resettlement had the effect of making the refugees more sensitive about the associated compensation proposals. These were to provoke much more controversy, partly because the government, dominated as it was by conservative financiers like Ryti and Walden, badly misjudged the mood of the country. Ryti explained the government's compensation proposals to the Eduskunta in his speech on April 30. He started off on the wrong foot by his statement that the refugees had only a moral, and not a legal, right to compensation. Ryti went on to say that compensation in full was unthinkable until such time as the national income recovered to its 1939 level, and this might be a long time. Nor could compensation be in cash, which would only stimulate inflation. As far as possible the compensation should be a clearing operation, a direct transfer of goods and property from the taxpayer to the refugee. The basis of the scheme was to be a capital levy on all property. The government calculated that if property valued at less than Fmk.100,000 was exempted, this might raise Fmk.4,500,000 to form the compensation fund. By dropping the exemption it might be possible to raise 5,000 million marks. Ryti was insistent on the principle that the amount of compensation must be rigidly limited to the amount yielded by the levy. It followed that full compensation was ruled out, and the government proposed graduated compensation to favour the poorer claimants.[30]

Ryti's speech was badly received, since his critics felt that the just rights of the refugees were being sacrificed to the claims of financial orthodoxy. This was nothing to the storm that burst when the government's detailed proposals were brought forward in the beginning of June. They suggested the full compensation would only be paid for the first Fmk.10,000 of any claim and that it would be paid on a diminishing scale above that figure. Moreover no more than 3,000 marks was to be paid in cash, the rest would be in 4% bonds. To finance this the levy on property would be on a sliding scale rising from $2\frac{1}{2}\%$ to 20% on the largest properties. There was a howl of protest from the Karelian League. It was claimed that they were entitled to full compensation, and what the government proposed would pauperize the Karelians. Ryti defended his proposals in the Eduskunta on June 4. He stressed that the Karelians were not the only charge on public funds. National income was sharply reduced, but the claims of the unemployed, or of families that had lost their breadwinner in the war were just as valid as those of the Karelians. They too would need help. He would not sanction the proposal put forward from many sides that state property should be liquidated to pay for it, in particular that the vast state forests be used. Whatever scheme was adopted, it must be paid for out of taxation. The debate which followed was notable for the failure of any group in the Eduskunta to give the government wholehearted support. The Agrarians led the attack, with Niukkanen and his followers in the lead. They at once tabled a counter-proposal for compensation in full up to Fmk.500,000 to be paid for by extensive sales of state property. Ryti had added fuel to the flames by a personal attack on Niukkanen. He had suggested that Niukkanen was the last man entitled to criticize, since it was his failures as defence minister before the war which had helped bring about defeat, and given rise to the whole problem. Niukkanen felt bound to defend himself, and accused the government of having made peace prematurely and in a mood of panic. It was a measure of the passions aroused that this normally unmentionable topic was actually aired on the floor of the Eduskunta.

The press agreed with the politicians that the government's proposals were quite unrealistic. Public opinion, faithfully mirrored in the Eduskunta, would never accept them. Some were unkind enough to point out that there were too many votes at stake. Even the Right felt that the government's proposals flouted the basic rights of property. The proposals had now gone to committee, and it was universally recognized that drastic changes would be made, and that the government would have to accept them.[31] The political storm did not abate in the meantime. It developed into a campaign to bring down the government that was unique in this period. The core of the attack was to be found in the dissident Agrarians organized by Niukkanen and his principal lieutenant Hannula. The latter controlled an important provincial newspaper *Pohjolan Sanomat*, which became the mouthpiece for the campaign. The aim was to form a more popular government, by which they meant one more responsible to the Eduskunta. It was alleged that the Agrarians in particular had almost no voice in the government. It was insinuated that the government was controlled by an extra-parliamentary clique of bankers and businessmen, meaning of course Ryti and Walden. Hannula went further and tried to drag in the language issue. He described the government as dominated by the 'bosses of our big industry, and for the most part Swedish-speaking'. When the Agrarian Party Congress met on June 21 it was clear that Niukkanen had most of the party with him. Speaker after speaker attacked the compensation law, and it was resolved that if this were not drastically changed so as to give something like full compensation the Agrarians must leave the government. To reinforce this Hannula was suggesting that the decisions of the Congress were mandatory on the Agrarian members of the Eduskunta. This in itself provoked some press controversy about the constitutional issue involved.[32]

On June 29, Ryti addressed a Karelian festival in Helsinki, and in a long speech tried to explain how the economic situation made full, or even generous, compensation impossible.[33] He made no impression. A day or two later the Karelian League put out a statement that the government's proposals must be rejected.[34] The only group to show some signs of rallying to the government were the Social Democrats. They had few votes at stake, and on the other hand disliked the various proposals to finance compensation by selling state property, so they were able to take a highly moral line, and condemn all the bourgeois parties for their shameless bid for the refugee vote. In particular it was shameful of them to threaten a government crisis.[35]

Early in July there was another full debate on the floor of the Eduskunta. It became clear that the government was giving way. Pekkala, the finance minister, took the line that if the Eduskunta wanted to pay out more compensation, the government would not object, provided that they were ready to finance it by taxation. Ryti said that the government was not unshakeably attached to its proposals. It had no other wish than that 'the matter should be decided in the best way possible'. Only the Social Democrats showed any inclination to stand by the government, so that it really had little choice but to surrender gracefully.[36] The law now went back into committee and a compromise was hammered out. The final form passed the Eduskunta on August 2. It provided for full compensation up to Fmk.320,000, with a graduated scale thereafter. It was still to be financed out of the capital levy, but in addition the state would contribute 3,000 million marks to the compensation fund out of taxation.[37]

The business of the compensation law was an interesting example of Finnish democracy at work. The original government plan had been a typical product of orthodox financial minds bent on preserving the soundness of the currency. It had asked for an unrealistic amount of restraint and self-sacrifice from the refugees, disappointed as they were at the slowness of resettlement. The refugee reaction had then found its proper channel of expression through the Agrarian party. This party had demonstrated its unique importance in Finnish politics. This lay in its ability to be a party of the Right or of the Left according to what suited it at any given time. On the resettlement law the Agrarians had worked with the Social Democrats to prevent amendments favouring big landowners. On compensation they had joined the parties of the Right in defending the principle of property rights. Further the reality of Finnish democracy had been demonstrated. The Eduskunta had represented the view of the people in rejecting the government's proposal. The government had yielded to the popular will. But the Eduskunta too had been responsible. It had conceded that the compensation proposals should not be wildly inflationary. The two principles of the original scheme, that compensation must be partial only, and that it must be financed out of taxation, had not been entirely ignored. Finally it is worthy of notice that in passing the resettlement and compensation laws the government and the Eduskunta had produced a scheme that was firmly practical in detail, but equally firmly based on principles of social justice. It is a striking tribute to the health of Finnish democracy that schemes of this magnitude could find, in the end, unanimous acceptance.

CHAPTER 4

The military consequences of the peace

The military successes of the Finnish army during the war, and its
ability to fight on unbroken until the end, had not been entirely the
product of the superb courage and fighting qualities of the Finnish
soldier, the unusual rigours of that winter, and the mistakes of the Soviet
military command. All these had played their part. But the Finnish military
machine, with all its deficiencies, had been the product of careful planning
and preparation, particularly after 1930 when the Defence Council, under
Mannerheim's presidency, had been established. The plans of this body
had been frustrated to a considerable extent by the refusal of pre-war
governments to provide the money needed. This had been reflected during
the war in the inadequacy of fortifications and equipment. Even so, the
Finnish armed forces had been able to operate within the framework of a
carefully conceived plan.

In some respects the Finnish military problem had been an easy one.
There was only one potential enemy, the USSR, and all attention could
be concentrated on meeting an attack launched by her. At first sight this
may appear to have posed questions to which there could be no answer.
The disparity of numbers and equipment is too great. On closer examina-
tion it appears that Finland did have the possibility of putting up a successful defence. In the first place, before 1939, it was never supposed that Finland could or would have to fight the USSR alone for any length of time.
War could come in two ways. Either it would develop out of a conflict
between the USSR and some power to the west, in which case, when the
conflict spread to Finland, the USSR would already be committed on other
fronts, and Finland would have allies. Alternatively the USSR might
launch a war of aggression against Finland, in which case Finland could
expect assistance under the charter of the League of Nations. In either case
the military task of the Finnish army was only to hold an initial Russian
assault until outside events brought about a decision, and this was a much
more practicable proposition. An important helping factor was the un-
developed nature of the Russo-Finnish borderlands and the meagreness

76

of communications. These put severe limits on the amount of force which the USSR could bring to bear. If Finland could mobilize her full potential and get it into the field in time, the power relationships in the actual battle front would not be hopelessly unequal, although in the long run the fact that the USSR could provide unlimited replacements, and Finland could not, would be decisive. But Finland did not contemplate a long run against the undivided power of the USSR. Geography too favoured Finland before 1939. In practice the main Russian assault must come up the Karelian isthmus, between Lake Ladoga and the Gulf of Finland. This formed a narrow front, plentifully strewn with water obstacles and difficult terrain, so that by a judicious fortification of the weak points, a strong defensive line could be formed, which could not be outflanked, but would be difficult to assault in sufficient force. The possibility of major outflanking movements north of Lake Ladoga, or in the wilderness of northern Karelia and Lapland, was thought to be ruled out by difficulties of communications and supply. In this respect the Russians had sprung some unpleasant surprises during the war, showing great boldness and enterprise. But the Finns had stopped and contained all such attempts, and won some of their most spectacular successes in the process. Further, the 1939 frontier was distant from any vital centres of population, industry, and communications. This meant that the Finns could fight a delaying action, buying time with space, until their field army had mobilized and manned the main line of defence.

Finland had possessed no regular army in the sense in which powers like Great Britain or the United States did. There was a frontier guard, which in war became part of the army, but otherwise, professional soldiers formed a mere skeleton for which the flesh was provided by an annual intake of conscripts. These served for 350 days with the colours and then passed into the reserve, where they were liable for recall for refresher courses from time to time. Thus at any given time the standing army consisted of the professionals together with one year's intake of conscripts, and this body had to provide the covering force until the reservists had been mobilized. For the mobilization Finland had adopted an excellent scheme, well adapted to the scattered population and poor communications. The whole country had been divided into nine military districts each of which would provide one division for the field army. Generally, each unit was locally based, and officers and men were peace-time neighbours. On receiving the order for mobilization, the men went to local mobilization points and picked up their equipment. The local centres were usually the base of a battalion of infantry. When the battalion had formed, it moved off to the agreed place of concentration and formed part of its division. The specialist arms moved up in the same way. The units thus formed had been the basis of the peace-time training schemes, their tasks had been worked out long before and frequently practised, the officers and men knew one another, the equipment was gathered beforehand at appropriate points, and the whole concentration could be carried through with a minimum of administrative difficulty. When it was tried out in 1939, this area system had worked very well. The defects had been those imposed by lack of money. Heavy equipment had been outdated or altogether lacking. There was virtually no armour, or anti-tank weapons, and many of the troops had never seen a tank. The air force was too small even to cover the most essential places, and there was a severe lack of anti-aircraft guns. But the most tragic shortage of all had been the lack of ammunition for the guns that did exist. The Finnish artillery seems to have been excellent, in spite of the age of much of its equipment. Yet, in the decisive battles on the Isthmus it was often nearly silent for lack of shells. This, in outline, had been the military situation before the war.

The peace had created a crop of new military problems. The geographical situation had been seriously altered by the new frontier. It had given the Russians a continuous land front, undivided by Lake Ladoga, and provided with fair lateral communications. This was entirely to their advantage in enabling them to deploy larger forces. The new frontier was not devoid of natural obstacles. There was the complex of lakes in the Saimaa region, penetrated by narrow isthmuses, which gave good defensive possibilities. This left a broad coastal plain between the lake district and the Gulf of Finland. But the most serious change in the geographical position was that the new frontier ran close to vital centres of population and industry, in particular the valley of the Kymi river, the Lahti region, and Joensuu. Finland could no longer afford to buy time with space. The Finns were compelled to stand and fight on or near to the frontier. The problem was complicated by the way in which the Russians set about developing roads and railways, and building airfields both in the ceded areas and further north. These threatened new and dangerous flanking movements. There were other difficulties caused by the way in which the new frontier cut across roads and railways, and severed communications on the Finnish side. Then the area scheme of mobilization had been wrecked by the cession of the Karelian region. It would have to be rebuilt from the beginning. The old fortifications had all been lost. Equipment had to be replaced, the pre-war deficiencies made good, the chaos created by panic wartime purchases of arms sorted out. Finally, the whole basis of pre-war strategic planning had vanished. There was now every likelihood that Finland would have to meet the undivided strength of the USSR alone, and that no effective outside help would reach her. This was particularly true after the German occupation of Denmark and Norway in April 1940. The long-term military problem appeared to be insoluble. Yet the Finns did not give up. Their military leaders began methodically to make the best of the existing situation. They were determined to fight again if attacked, even if there seemed no chance of prolonging a successful resistance. Finns believed deeply that God helps those who help themselves. They would do their part and trust in providence to help them out when the time came.

The transformation in the atmosphere of military planning after the war, as compared with pre-war days, was striking. Then, the Defence Council had prodded and begged a sceptical government to implement its schemes, often in vain. Now, in effect, Mannerheim spoke the word, and the thing was done. It is fair to say that the military authorities got a blank cheque to do what was needed, which is the same as to say that Mannerheim got a blank cheque. There was no move to revert to pre-war conditions. The president of the republic continued to delegate his authority as commander in chief to the Marshal. When Walden became minister of defence, Mannerheim also controlled that ministry, the only potential centre of authority in military matters apart from his own. Whereas Walden ought to have been a bridge between the commander in chief on the one side, and the cabinet and the Eduskunta on the other, he was in fact merely the embodiment of Mannerheim's will in the machine of civil government. The eminent Finnish authority, Professor Puntila, has commented on this state of affairs:[1]

'In military matters Walden felt himself weak and during the war, in this respect, he really only represented the viewpoint of Head Quarters in the government, neglecting to act in the opposite direction, that is, he was unwilling to represent the government's problems to the commander in chief. Walden had perceived that in Finland there was need for one great man armed with authority.'

It has been mentioned above that Mannerheim and Walden did not intend that this happy situation should depend on the accident of their personal relationship. They had demanded that the ministry of defence be stripped of its most important pre-war power, the purchase of military equipment, and that this should be given to the commander in chief. This was a condition of Walden entering the government, and Mannerheim retaining command.[2] It was embodied in legislation in August 1940 and made the legal control of the commander in chief over the whole field of defence policy absolute. The minister of defence was reduced to the constitutionally absurd position of representing before the Eduskunta and in the cabinet, and demanding the money and legislation for, policies in the making of which he had no legal voice at all. The reasons for the change were no secret, it was a precaution against the danger that 'the defence minister might be someone other than Walden',[3] or, as Mannerheim's biographer put it, to ensure that the difficulties which could arise when such matters as the purchase of equipment 'were the responsibility of a member of the government responsible to parliament'[4] would not arise in future. Since Walden continued to be defence minister until 1944 the system was never put to the test. Because Walden was trusted by Mannerheim he did in fact remain in charge of the military procurement programme, although he always went through the formality of consulting Mannerheim's headquarters for all important decisions in this field.[5] It is probable that this development of Mannerheim's power was necessary in the circumstances. But although formally his authority was limited to matters which were purely military, his actions were bound, on occasion, to have important political repercussions. The situation was most peculiar from a constitutional point of view. Neither the civil government nor the Eduskunta had any real voice in the making of military policy. They merely passed the necessary legislation and voted the funds which it required. Only the president of the republic had any legal power to call his commander in chief to account. Neither Kallio nor Ryti showed any inclination to exercise their power, or even to keep themselves very closely informed of what Mannerheim was doing. If anything was considered to be a military matter, and this covered a very wide field indeed, then it was the Marshal's affair, and it was not for anyone else to raise doubts or ask questions. Exceptions to this rule are extremely rare. The situation amounted to an abdication of lawful, constitutional authority by the president, the government, and the Eduskunta which was quite at variance with the basic principles of parliamentary democracy. But it would be hard to pretend that any alternative existed. The nation needed Mannerheim and had to take him on his own terms.

The working of the system was illustrated at an early stage by the way in which the budget for the post-war procurement programme was put through. Mannerheim told Walden what was needed. Walden's first reaction was that it could not be done but he was called to conference at Mannerheim's headquarters and quickly persuaded that he was mistaken. Walden then put the plan to Ryti as prime minister. Ryti, the banker and orthodox financier, was horrified, 'Who can have drawn this up and yet maintain that such sums can be raised?'[6] But Ryti's resistance collapsed before the Marshal's authority. Mannerheim had decided the money could be found and it was. Military credits were rarely discussed, much less opposed, in either the cabinet or the Eduskunta. It is fair to say that Mannerheim got everything that he asked for.[7] The decisions were made by him personally. The Marshal was a man to whom open debate and argument were anathema. His method of working was to surround himself with competent specialists, listen to what they had to say, and then make the decision by himself, after which the subject was closed. He remarked once, 'synthesis is my job'.[8] When General Heinrichs became chief of staff in June 1940, Mannerheim was quite open about his methods. He told Heinrichs, 'I do not want to be one man's prisoner . . . I must be able to discuss things with absolutely anyone, whether he belongs to the staff or not, and make the decisions myself.'[9] Thus, although the details of military policy were worked out by a circle of experts, General Hanell on fortifications, General Heinrichs on strategic planning, Walden and the chief of military economics, Colonel Bäckström, on the procurement programme, all the ultimate major decisions were Mannerheim's alone.

The question of fortifications policy illustrated this fact. Mannerheim remarked in his memoirs on the importance of fortifications in the new conditions. 'In the long frontier zone it was necessary to build fortifications which would to some extent compensate the lack of manpower'.[10] He had had the troops digging field works as soon as they had retired behind the new frontier. The younger generation of staff officers would have advocated a system of fortification in depth to meet the demands of modern mechanized war. Mannerheim insisted on what many of them thought to be an outmoded scheme of strong linear defence works. His biographer remarks, Mannerheim 'seems in these matters to have followed only his own views'.[11] After all he was 72 years old and it would have been unreasonable to expect of him a 'new and revolutionary attitude'. The age of the Marshal did not prevent a speedy and vigorous execution of his plans. On March 22, Mannerheim called in his advisers, and crawling on his hands and knees over a large-scale map spread on the floor decided the line for the vital sector across the coastal plain from Klamila to Luumäki.[12] The order went out the next day for the troops on the spot to return detailed plans by April 5. On March 30, Major-General Edward Hanell was put in charge of fortifications, and on April 11, promoted and made chief of staff so as to overcome any obstruction by lower commanders who did not agree with the programme. The plans went to the ministry of defence on May 9, backed by a letter from Mannerheim saying how much money would be needed. On May 29, Hanell's position was further reinforced when he was made personally and directly responsible to the Marshal alone for the execution of his work. A great amount of money and manpower went into the fortification of the new frontiers. The first stage in the coastal sector, the so-called 'Swedish line', was constructed with labour and funds provided by Sweden.[13] But the Finns did most of the work themselves, and the fortifications played a useful part in keeping unemployment down. Many of the Karelians found their way to the work camps. From this point of view the scheme probably paid a social dividend at least. Whether the fortifications would have fulfilled their military purpose,

or whether Mannerheim's critics were right, and they were based on outdated concepts, will never be known. They never underwent the test of
an attack.

The next task was to demobilize the army and at the same time reconstruct the shattered system of mobilization. Mannerheim had laid down
from the start that the new frontier demanded a larger standing force than
the old, because it was no longer possible to buy time for mobilization by
yielding ground. When the government was being formed in March, he and
Walden had stipulated that there must be a change to two-year military
service, thus doubling the size of the covering force. The law enforcing
two-year conscription passed the Eduskunta without opposition in December 1940.[14] Until it became effective, the numbers were maintained by
keeping reservists with the colours, and by calling in men who had been
liable for service before 1939, but had been exempted for various reasons.
The standing army was by these means maintained at three times the level
prevailing before 1939. A consequence was that the demobilization of the
men who had fought in the war was slow and partial. Many reservists became embittered about this, unable to understand why the regular rule of
demobilizing by age groups, the oldest first, was not adhered to. There was
a flood of letters to the papers from servicemen on this subject, and although
the socialist press took the lead in championing the cause of speedier demobilization, most papers carried articles sympathizing with the reservists.[15] They would hardly have done this if they had realized that there
were good reasons for the policy being followed, but the military authorities
seem to have ignored the need to explain themselves to either the reservists
or the press. Apart from the wish to keep a larger force on foot, there were
important economic and social considerations. One set concerned the
Karelians. It seemed unwise to release them when they had no homes to go
to, and no fixed address from which they could be recalled. Secondly on
general economic grounds it was unwise to release too many men who had
no jobs to go to. So a policy was adopted of releasing key workers first,
and retaining those with nowhere to go.[16] Associated with this problem
was the question of what to do with the reservists' equipment now that the
area system had broken down. As a temporary measure it had to be dumped
near the frontier, often in hastily improvised stores.[17]

The creation and realization of a new area scheme was one of the army's
most urgent problems. It was decided to use the opportunity for a major
reform, and increase the number of military districts from 9 to 16. This
would provide a field army of 16 infantry divisions. It had been known
before 1939 that the country's manpower ought to be sufficient for a 16-
division army. Various considerations had led to the choice of a 9-division
force. Lack of money had been one, it would have been impossible to equip

16 divisions on the pre-war military budgets. Another was a failure to realize the improvement in the physical condition of the rising generations. The planners had over-estimated the proportion of conscripts who would have to be rejected on medical grounds. With all the money that they needed, and a more realistic appreciation of the manpower potential, the planners decided on the 16-division basis for the new scheme in May 1940. It remained to map out the new districts, register the men, organize the new formations, their staffs, depots, and mobilization plans, and send out mobilization instructions to every reservist. The equipment had to be sorted and distributed, some of it from the dumps established after demobilization, some of it newly purchased. In spite of the complexity of the task, the bulk of the work had been completed early in 1941, and by March–April of that year the new scheme was in full working order. It functioned extremely well when the time came, and Mannerheim has recorded the relief he felt when it was once more possible to carry through a complete and speedy mobilization. Until this had been achieved, mobilization, based on hasty provisional plans, would have been difficult, and this was a major factor influencing the outlook and policy of the military command.

The new area scheme was organically linked with the new defence plans. These in turn were influenced by the new frontier and the existence of a larger standing force produced by two-year military service. This was organized in sixteen peace-time brigades, each of which would be joined after mobilization by two regiments of reservists. These would come from their mobilization centres in fighting order and form a division. Thirteen of these brigades were camped in or near the positions in which they would have to fight, and their job was to hold these until the two reserve regiments joined them. Nine of the brigades were grouped as the nucleus of four wartime army corps along the south-eastern frontier zone. One faced the Russian base at Hanko, three others covered the long northern frontier. The last three were based in the interior and were to form the strategic reserve. In addition the army had its *élite* troops, two light, or Jäger brigades, picked units with augmented transport facilities, and the cavalry brigade which was in process of being motorized. They too belonged to the reserve. When fully mobilized, Finland could, under this plan, put over 400,000 men in the field.

It is worth stressing the way in which the revised area scheme was tied in with the new plan for the defence of the frontier. The Finnish army did not mobilize and then take the field as an army. It concentrated in the field in its actual battle positions. The mobilization plan was adapted for a single purpose, to repel a Russian invasion. Its dispositions for this end could not be changed without wrecking the elaborate mobilization machinery. Thus, whatever the Finnish command might ultimately intend to do, its troops would first have to form up in defensive order. Only when mobilization was complete could any major changes be made in the dispositions of the troops. Finnish commentators had tended to put great stress on the defensive formation of their army in June 1941, as if this necessarily proved the lack of any offensive intent by their military command. In fact it proves nothing about their intentions one way or the other. The Finnish military planners had their hands tied by their own mobilization scheme. The revised area scheme is a reflection of the formidable military talents of the Finns and their commander in chief. It is perfectly adapted to the available resources and to the most probable situation that could arise, and takes full account of the special limitations imposed by Finnish conditions. The speed with which it was conceived and executed, and the efficiency with which it worked, prove a very high level of competence in military administration.

The other major military development in this period was the re-equipment of the armed forces to modern standards. The basic equipment of the Finnish army had been inherited from the Imperial Russian army, both the small arms and the artillery, some of which dated back to 1877. Plans had existed before 1939 to remedy the worst deficiencies but some had been unrealized for lack of money, and others had been slowed down because the government preferred where possible to manufacture equipment under licence in Finland rather than purchase it ready-made from abroad. Thus permission had been obtained for the construction of Bofors anti-aircraft and anti-tank guns, and for a 120 mm. mortar, but few had reached the army when war began. One major item of equipment the Finns had invented themselves, and that was the Suomi machine pistol, a light automatic weapon especially suited for forest fighting. Even so there were only 8,000 machine pistols and automatic rifles in 1939.[18] Equipment generally was for nine divisions, and by no means complete even for them. Then, during the war, all kinds of material had been ordered or given from many different sources. For instance, by the end of the war the army had 108 different types of gun, and the field artillery needed seven different calibres of ammunition.[19] There was no modern radio equipment and very scanty amounts of motor transport and modern aircraft.

As soon as the fighting was over Mannerheim and his staff had begun to plan the re-equipment of the forces, and it has been noted how the government agreed to find the money. Home production was greatly developed. In addition to proceeding with the anti-aircraft, anti-tank guns and mortars, the government set up the production of 105 mm. howitzers. Probably the greatest achievement of domestic industry was in the improved supply of artillery ammunition. By December 1940 the position in this respect was regarded as satisfactory and the worst single shortage experienced during the war had been overcome.[20] Events in the world outside raised new difficulties. After the invasion of Norway quite a lot of equipment destined for Finland was seized by the Germans in Norwegian ports. Some stuff continued to come in from the United States through Petsamo, including 200 75 mm. guns and 32 heavy field guns, but there were severe limitations on the capacity of this channel of supply. The truth had to be faced that war material could only be obtained on a large scale from Germany, or with German permission, and Germany as a faithful ally of the USSR refused to let anything through. This situation lasted until late August 1940, when a secret emissary from Field Marshal Göring, Colonel Veltjens, came to Mannerheim with an offer to sell military equipment. The full story of Veltjens' mission belongs to another chapter, but as a result of it Finland was able to purchase large quantities of war material from Germany. In addition the German government released the supplies belonging to Finland which had been detained in Norwegian harbours, and where the Germans themselves had used them up, compensation was given. The basic purchases from Germany were of artillery, 23 light and 40 heavy batteries of field artillery, with 28 batteries of anti-aircraft artillery and 150,000 mines. There was also an order for modern fighter aircraft.[21]

The result of fifteen months' vigorous replanning and retraining and re-equipment was seen in June 1941, when the Finnish army went into battle once more. Its 16 divisions were reasonably equipped with modern weapons, above all with adequate artillery and anti-tank guns. Transport and communications had been enormously improved. There was the nucleus of an armoured division. The capacity of the country's air defences had been increased many times by the acquisition of modern aircraft and anti-aircraft guns. Finally the numbers of trained men available, and the level of their training, were both much higher than they had been in March 1940. The Finns could be satisfied that they had done all that was in their power to overcome the military handicaps imposed by the peace treaty. In very difficult circumstances they had met and overcome its challenge. The outside observer can only admire the intelligent determination and vigour of the whole military reconstruction programme. The comparative smoothness and efficiency with which it was executed reflected the driving intelligence behind it. Mannerheim's memoirs reflect his quiet satisfaction with what he had achieved.[22] In this field he had fully justified the blind confidence which the Finnish people and their government had placed in him.

CHAPTER 5

An ominous pause

The end of the excitement over the proposed Scandinavian alliance marked the beginning of a period of superficial calm, during which Finland appeared to have been by-passed by stirring developments elsewhere. Although the calm was deceptive, the period between the end of March 1940 and the beginning of June did represent a kind of breathing space, during which national attention was mainly focused on internal problems, which were absorbing enough. The beginning of the pause is marked by the speech delivered to the Supreme Soviet by Molotov on March 29. This contained a review and a vindication of the Finnish war. There were passages in the speech which might have reassured Finland. Molotov stressed that the peace terms were dictated solely by considerations of military security and that the USSR fully respected the sovereignty and independence of Finland. The benevolent intentions of the USSR towards Finland were proved by her magnanimous self-denial in not proceeding to conquer the whole country when that had been militarily possible, and by her waiving any demand for an indemnity.[1] Any favourable impressions these assurances might have given were nullified partly by the obviously unfriendly tone of all the references to the Finnish government, and by the fantasies with which the speech was embellished. Paasikivi remarked of it sadly, 'the information and the allegations contained in Molotov's speech did not correspond with the truth'.[2] The war was justified by Molotov on the grounds that it had really been an attempt by Britain and France to attack the USSR. The Finnish government had been the willing tool of their designs. The scale of western military aid to Finland had been such that in reality the Red Army had defeated not Finland alone, but the united strength of several powers. The bitter hatred of the Finnish government for the USSR was proved by the atrocities committed by the Finnish troops. Finland had paid for her folly with 300,000 dead and wounded. This poisonous rubbish could perhaps be written off as intended for domestic consumption or as a typical attempt by a government to veil its errors and stupidities in a fog of justifications. But it did not make an encouraging starting point for an attempt to build up a new and better relationship between Finland and the USSR. Paasikivi commented:[3]

'I asked myself, what is going to come of this, when both sides have completely opposite ideas about the facts, to say nothing of the suspicions which they have of the other's intentions.'

The speech was followed within two days by a move which seemed most sinister in Finnish eyes. It was announced that the former Karelian Autonomous Socialist Soviet republic was to be promoted. The areas ceded to the USSR under the Treaty of Moscow, with the exception of those in the immediate vicinity of Leningrad, were to be joined to this republic. It would then become the twelfth constituent member of the Union of Soviet Socialist Republics under the title of the Karelian-Finnish Soviet Socialist republic. Zhdanov, who moved the change in the Supreme Soviet, said that the new republic 'will promote the future cultural and economic development of these neighbouring peoples and strengthen their brotherly comradeship'.[4] The government of the new republic was headed by Otto Kuusinen, whose puppet government, according to the official Soviet version, had gone into voluntary liquidation at the end of the war to save further bloodshed. Many Finns suspected that the new republic was intended to form a nucleus to which in time the rest of Finland was to be added.

Their suspicions were almost certainly correct. They only erred in supposing that there was any immediate intention by the USSR of consummating the union. The new republic was for the moment simply an element in a plan that might one day be realized. It provided a decent base for Kuusinen and his colleagues to operate from, and it could be used to help build for the future. Its immediate importance lay in the field of propaganda. A powerful radio station at Petroskoi, the capital, became the chief channel for beaming Soviet propaganda to Finland. It was a constant theme of this propaganda that the happy, prosperous life of the Finnish inhabitants of the republic contrasted sharply with the miseries of their brethren who languished under oppression in capitalist Finland. During the quiet months however, this comparison was implied but not stated. There were plenty of glowing descriptions of the vigorous reconstruction of the ceded areas, but odious comparisons were avoided. An official Finnish study of Soviet propaganda, published during the war, and not strictly impartial, recognized that in this phase, Soviet propaganda about Finland was 'explanatory and defensive. In so far as there were attacks, they were cautious and veiled'.[5] Thus the policy of the USSR remained consistent with the line suggested by Molotov's speech. For the moment they had no further designs on Finland, but would await the outcome of the European war before deciding on any further moves.

In a perverse way, this view is confirmed by the many small unpleasant-
nesses which developed out of the execution of the peace treaty. While
they amply demonstrated the basic hostility of the government of the
USSR towards the government of Finland they equally showed that the
USSR was taking the treaty seriously and meant to screw the utmost advantage out of it. There was good reason for the USSR to be careful in her
handling of Finland. The continued desire of Britain and France to intervene in Scandinavia was very obvious, as was the wish of the USSR to
avoid being dragged into conflict with them.[6] This went so far that there
appeared a distinct coolness in Soviet attitudes to Germany at this point,
evidenced by mysterious hold-ups in promised deliveries from the USSR.
Her government wished to appear genuinely neutral in the European war.
The allied powers declared their intentions in notes delivered to Norway
and Sweden on April 5. Besides announcing their intention of stopping
the supply of raw materials to Germany through Scandinavia, they said
that in the event of an attack on Finland, whether by the USSR or Germany, they would come to Finland's assistance. Any attempt by Norway
or Sweden to hinder such assistance would be treated as a hostile act.[7]
Thus for a brief period Finland enjoyed a unilateral guarantee of her integrity. While the Finnish government, which had not been consulted
about the move, made no attempt to profit by it, it remained true that
there was little likelihood of the USSR taking any serious steps until the
outcome of the struggle for the control of Scandinavia was known.

The business of implementing the Treaty of Moscow proved long and
tiresome. Paasikivi, the ambassador in Moscow, has recorded how he had
to visit the Kremlin almost daily to sort out with Molotov, or his deputy
Dekanozov, the many points of difficulty which arose.[8] The first task was
to demarcate the new frontier, and with one exception this led to no serious
difficulty. A mixed Soviet-Finnish commission was set up in April and the
job was done scientifically on the basis of the maps annexed to the treaty.
The Russians had tried at first to take the demarcation line between the two
armies as the basis but the Finns argued successfully that the maps provided the only valid foundation for the work, and in this way regained for
Finland some 400 square kilometres of territory.[9] On one point the commission was deadlocked. This was at Enso, where there was a valuable
industrial plant and power station. According to Finnish measurements
the new frontier just left this inside Finland. The Russians insisted it was
on their territory. On the instructions of their government the Finnish
representatives conceded the point, although they were almost certainly
right, and Enso was lost. On April 9 the new frontier was unanimously
confirmed by the commission. In spite of this Paasikivi tried to save Enso
by an appeal to Molotov, pointing out that the Russian map was faulty,

and that while Enso was of great economic value to Finland, it was of no
military value to the USSR, but he made no impression.[10] The same sort
of thing happened over the Hanko leased area. Finland maintained that her
shipping was still entitled to use the waters of the area, and that the USSR
should pay for any private property in the area which she used, but both
requests were rejected. The USSR having agreed to pay the stipulated
rent, proposed to treat the area as though it was Soviet territory.

Before the new frontier could be marked out on the ground there was a
succession of incidents caused by Finnish nationals straying over the line.
Such people were at once arrested and disappeared into the Soviet prison
system. No efforts by the Finnish government could secure their release.
On the contrary Molotov treated the incidents as deliberate provocations.
On April 17, in conversation with Paasikivi, Molotov became thoroughly
unpleasant about this subject. He threatened that if the border crossings
did not cease, there would be 'unfortunate consequences'.[11] Typical of the
pathological suspicions of the Russians was the fuss made by Molotov
because one unfortunate transgressor had a Russian name. Molotov alleged
he was a Russian White Guard. Paasikivi had to make special inquiries of
his government in order to assure Molotov that the man had been born in
Finland and lived there all his life. Faced by these absurd and sinister
phenomena Paasikivi told his foreign minister, 'it is probable that they feel
great distrust towards us, which it will not be an easy matter to remove,
or even diminish'.[12] By the middle of May the two sides had agreed on the
process of marking the new frontier on the ground, usually by cutting
away a strip of forest, and even that the Finns could do the job and carry off
the timber.[13] Once this had been done, accidental crossings ceased.

The other major question which arose out of the peace treaty concerned
property removed by the Finns from the ceded territories, particularly
machinery. The whole issue arose from article 6 of the treaty which stipulated that in the process of withdrawing the troops behind the new frontiers
care was to be taken that no damage was done to plant or installations. The
Finnish government took the view that this clause could only cover areas
occupied by their troops on March 13, which seems to be the reasonable
interpretation, and that it did not preclude the removal of such private
property as small machines or other movable plant. On this point they
were probably wrong. The clause does seem to mean that all industrial
plant was to be left in the state it was in on March 13.[14] In a long conversation with Paasikivi, on April 17, Molotov accused the Finns of having
removed installations, contrary to the treaty provisions, and handed over
long lists of the items concerned. He demanded their return.[15] As the
exchange of views developed it became clear that the Russians were really
claiming that the ceded areas be restored to the condition they had been in

at the outbreak of hostilities, war damage excepted, and that installations evacuated during the war must also be sent back. Molotov claimed that when the USSR troops evacuated the Petsamo area they had even replaced the glass in the windows of the houses. Even if this had been true there was no comparison to be made between restoring the sparse buildings in the desolate Petsamo area, and a complete rehabilitation of the developed areas of Karelia.

The Finnish government gave its considered reply on April 25, holding to its view that it had no liability for property removed before March 13 or in areas not then in Finnish possession, and commenting systematically on the Russian lists, which contained some items that had never existed.[16] The reply was not well received. On May 7, *Pravda* published a prominent article accusing Finland of breaches of the peace treaty, and including the very points which the Finnish government had just refuted. Paasikivi wrote to *Pravda* pointing out various mistakes, and revealing that the Finnish government had agreed to restore any property that had been improperly removed. The embassy staff and diplomatic colleagues were surprised when *Pravda* published the reply.[17] The two governments agreed to set up a mixed commission to settle the claims and its work dragged on for months, since as soon as one batch of claims had been settled, the USSR produced a fresh lot. After much tedious haggling the USSR did concede that Finland's liability was limited to property removed or damaged after March 13 in areas under Finnish control. Finland agreed to return certain other property, legitimately removed before that date, against compensation from the USSR. Thus in spite of Russian unreasonableness at the beginning, it proved possible to work out a sensible solution in the end. In June the Soviet government extended the principle to the Hanko area, which the Finnish government tried to reject altogether, on the grounds that this region was in an entirely different position from the ceded territories. But it did not feel strong enough to maintain its position, and in the end a compromise was worked out so that public property in Hanko was returned, but private property was not. It took until November 1940 to dispose of all the claims to physical assets. The seemingly interminable argument then passed on to the question of compensation for property which could not be returned or had been deliberately damaged or destroyed after March 13. The USSR said that the damages amounted to 145 million rubles, but as a generous concession they would settle for 90 million. It was clear from these figures that they were trying to go back on the principles already agreed, and to extend their claims to property removed before the end of hostilities. The gap between the two sides can be measured by the Finnish reply, presented in January 1941, which offered 8 million rubles for damage occurring after March 13. Further, since the

USSR owed Finland compensation for property removed before March 13, and voluntarily returned, there was in fact a balance in Finland's favour of 38 million rubles. War broke out again before this argument was settled.[18]

Many Finns at the time and since have alleged that the business of the return of property in the ceded areas was a disguised war indemnity. They were both alarmed and indignant at what seemed an unjustified exaction. Yet it would be unfair to the government of the USSR to accept this Finnish view. However obtuse and unpleasant the Russian methods were, they were generally prepared to accept a literal interpretation of the treaty, though they certainly sought to strain this interpretation as far as they could in their own favour. There were probably two factors which made the Russians especially difficult to deal with in a question of this kind. First their concepts of property were quite different from those of the Finns. What they were demanding would all have been state property in the USSR. With the best will in the world it was not easy for Soviet officialdom to understand and respect Finnish arguments based on the sanctity of private property. Secondly, as the article in *Pravda* showed clearly, they suspected the Finns of having stripped the ceded areas out of spite. This did the Finns an injustice. The Finnish cabinet had discussed the possibility of devastating the ceded territory on March 12, but had rejected the idea.[19] A further reason which made many Finns ascribe the attitude of the Soviet government to simple malice was that the fuss was made over assets whose value to a small country like Finland was considerable, but to a huge country like the USSR should have been trifling. Even Paasikivi held this view, showing a lapse of his usual understanding of Soviet motivations.[20] It overlooked the fact that the USSR was still economically backward in 1940 by comparison with advanced European countries. Further the drive to develop the economy was so intense that these assets may have possessed a value in Soviet eyes quite different from their valuation by one of the advanced powers of the West. The attitude of the USSR to this question, and also its attitude to the border dispute over the Enso area, suggests a fanatical interest in every machine and installation they could possibly lay claim to. This must be why they demanded such things as cinema equipment, hotel furnishings, even small privately-owned circular saws, and that proportion of the locomotives and rolling stock of the Finnish State Railways which could be regarded as belonging to the Hanko area.

The difficulties encountered in the implementation of the Treaty of Moscow all contributed to poisoning even further Russo-Finnish relations. The Finns could only feel that such obtuse and baffling attitudes sprang from implacable and malicious hostility. These endless and tedious arguments were to be completely overshadowed by much more serious and threatening disputes, but they produced a formidable quantity of bad feeling. It was Paasikivi who remarked of the Russian conduct in them that 'they were either bad psychologists, or they did not care about the mood of the Finnish people'.[21] Both things were true. They were bad psychologists, as they repeatedly demonstrated in this period, and they did not care what the Finnish bourgeoisie and its government thought about them. They believed that it hated them and would only respond to the crudest kind of pressure. So, largely by its own conduct, the government of the USSR made sure that what it believed would be true. This same Russian attitude was apparent in dealing with the modest requests which the Finnish government made for concessions or facilities which should have caused little trouble between two civilized states supposed to enjoy friendly relations. Finland sought such small concessions as the maintenance of fishing rights in what had suddenly become Soviet territorial waters, or the right, if only for twelve months, to continue using the Saimaa canal, severed by the new frontier, or even the return of the archives in the ceded areas. In all these cases the Soviet government either refused outright, or agreed to consider the matter and then did nothing further about it.

The Finnish public knew nothing certain about these disputes. Instead there were persistent rumours of new Russian demands and threats. The rigid censorship, then exercised by the military authorities, was in large part to blame for this. The press had not given up its call for greater freedom of public discussion and information which had appeared as soon as the war ended. It grumbled continuously at the restrictions which bound it. In April *Satakunnan Kansa* referred to the demoralizing effects of finding that 'foreigners knew more about Finland's affairs than the Finns themselves'.[22] *Pohjolan Sanomat* urged that in internal affairs at least the censorship could be lifted.[23] These modest requests were not made irresponsibly. All the papers realized that the delicate international situation would not permit the free discussion of foreign affairs. The socialist commentator Svento warned his readers that small powers needed to be careful not to offend powerful states. 'The harsh conditions of war will not tolerate irresponsible talkers'.[24] But the authorities were very slow to heed the call for even a partial restoration of freedom of expression.

Their caution was reinforced by the misfortunes of Denmark and Norway. Feeling in Finland was almost entirely sympathetic towards these Scandinavian neighbours. This was especially so among those members of the public who could not forgive Germany for her pro-Russian attitude in the war.[25] There was some little malicious satisfaction that Norway, which had blocked the sending of aid to Finland, was now experiencing aggression herself, especially when her resistance was so feeble compared with Finland's. But in the main sentiment and cold reason both fostered sym-

pathy for Norway. It was easy to see that if Germany succeeded in occupying Norway, Finland would be further cut off from the outside world, and
more exposed to the pressures of the totalitarian states. But at the same
time recent precedents and bitter experience suggested that small states
should keep quiet. The permitted public reaction to events in Scandinavia
was cool. The editorials in the Finnish press on April 11 were all sympathetic to Norway, but took up no stand against Germany's action. Rather
they tended to stress that the western allies too had broken Norway's
neutrality. Witting took the same unemotional line when discussing the
invasion of Norway with the German ambassador, he adopted 'im Gegen-
satz zu manchem seiner Landsleute einen realpolitischen Standpunkt zur
Besetzung.*[26] The ambassador sensed correctly that many liberal-minded-
Finns would have liked to express their condemnation of Germany's
aggression, but the censorship was adamant. It is true that on May 11,
after Germany had also attacked Holland, Belgium, and Luxembourg,
Helsingin Sanomat ventured to point out in an editorial that although Germany was constantly accusing the western allies of seeking to spread the
war, each new extension so far had come through a German initiative.[27]
But such cautious comment as this went far beyond the usual limits observed.

At the same time it is true that the Finns, who had become thoroughly
disillusioned at the return by the great powers to naked power politics, did
not make much distinction between the various powers. They certainly did
not see the European war which had begun in 1939 as a crusade against
fascism. It was the socialist commentator, Svento, who reiterated the
theme that all the great powers were the same, except that what he labelled
the satisfied powers, meaning Britain and France, did not need to commit
aggression against small neighbours. But morally they were all alike, and
the current war was just one more in the series of imperialist wars.[28]
The conservative Paasikivi held the same views. He noted in his memoirs
on several occasions that all the great powers are the same underneath, 'all
great powers are imperialistic'.[29] But Paasikivi added something which few
other Finns paused to consider, 'perhaps it is only weakness which pre-
vents the small ones from travelling the same road'.

The Finnish government watched events in Scandinavia with keen
attention. They were quickly convinced by the German successes in Norway that Germany was a power they could not afford to offend. This
appeared in the steps which they took to defend the Åland islands from a
possible attack by Germany. These islands, which block the entrance to
the Gulf of Bothnia, lay across the shipping route by which Swedish iron

*'a realistic political standpoint on the question of the occupation, in contrast to
many of his fellow countrymen.'

ore passed to Germany. They were demilitarized under an international convention drawn up in 1921. Early in April warnings came to the Finnish government from Paris that Germany might try to seize the islands, although in fact Germany had no such intention.[30] The government and the commander in chief took the danger seriously and transferred a regiment from the frontier to man the defences of the islands.[31] Sweden was asked whether she would like to share in the defence, since the islands also commanded the approaches to Stockholm. The Swedish government was interested but wanted to inform Germany and the USSR of any move that was made. At this the Finnish government dropped the idea, it had no wish to draw the attention of Germany to a step that was obviously directed against her. The foreign affairs committee of the Eduskunta was told of the episode in May, and approved the government's action. It was significant that several speakers expressed the view that it would be best not to defend the islands against Germany.[32] They represented the strong current of Finnish opinion that saw in Germany the natural counterpoise to the USSR, and was desperate to do nothing that might offend her. Even at this early stage all rumours of friction between Germany and the USSR were eagerly received in Finland.[33] The government knew that there was no evidence of any Russo-German split, so for the moment they must take care not to offend either dictatorship.

This policy of remaining neutral between both the dictatorships seemed to be the only one possible. Despite the concern which all the leading men in government felt because of the behaviour of the USSR they recognized that this must not stop them doing everything possible to soothe the suspicions of the Soviet government and try to build up a tolerable relationship between the two countries.[34] Their ambassador in Moscow never stopped urging them to adhere to this policy. The reduction of Russian mistrust must be 'the main object of our policy'. The theme was expanded in Paasikivi's first official report to Witting on May 14, 1940. The opening of the report was bleak:[35]

'Although I do not believe that the Soviet Union has any new intentions regarding us, if the contentions which are occurring cannot be cleared up by agreement, she would not scruple to renew violent measures against us.'

It was his opinion that Finland could only continue to be conciliatory and hope for the best. The government had already assured Paasikivi that it accepted his views completely. Walden had written to him on April 27 to assure him that the whole government and the Marshal shared his opinion. 'The beginning and end of our foreign policy must be the preservation of good relations with our eastern neighbour.' Walden went on to make a further significant remark. 'Public opinion also will certainly have to recognize, little by little, that there is no longer any room for fanaticism'.[36]

In other words the general public must be got to revise its traditional attitudes to the USSR. It is a major indictment of the Finnish governments of this period that they did so little to bring about a change whose necessity they recognized. They controlled all the means of communication so the responsibility was their own. They needed to get the public used to the idea that the Treaty of Moscow was a long-term, and not an interim settlement, and that the USSR, as a great power and a neighbour, had interests which must be respected by Finnish policy, however distasteful that might be. Only on this basis could a realistic solution of Finnish-Russian relations have been sought. It was true that the government did take certain negative measures to this end. It suppressed any open expression of hostility to the USSR. But on the positive side it neglected measures which might have shaken the popular image of Russia as the eternal hereditary enemy with whom no lasting peace was possible. It is very clear that most members of the Finnish government, even the more radical socialists, were afraid that if they promoted friendliness towards the USSR, they might weaken the national resistance to communism, and so to the next Russian aggression when it came. From this psychological impasse only a few exceptional minds, like Paasikivi's, could break free. In the end, the government became to some extent the prisoner of a public opinion it had done little to enlighten.

The whole weight and direction of public propaganda was directed to fostering the cult of national unity and reconciliation. Mannerheim took the lead. Until 1939, there had been a national holiday on May 16 to commemorate the entry of the White forces into Helsinki in 1918. Consequently the festival was not highly regarded by the defeated Reds and their heirs. On May 9, 1940, Mannerheim ordered that in future May 16 would not be observed. Instead May 19 would be dedicated to the dead of the recent war, and also to the dead of both sides in the civil war who, to use the official phrase, 'had died for their convictions'. This demonstrative act of conciliation was welcomed wholeheartedly by the Social Democrats. They recognized that it represented a considerable concession. The victors of the civil war would now admit publicly that the Reds of 1918 had not been a gang of traitors, criminals, and bolshevik hirelings, but were men who, however mistakenly, had fought honestly for a high ideal. When Mannerheim had given the signal, all the organs of public opinion set to work to ensure that May 19 should be a memorable festival of national unity. As far as can be judged they were very successful. Ryti broadcast an address on reconciliation. He declared 'the era of distrust is—or so we hope—ended, and with it the period of our people's spiritual wandering in the wilderness.'[37] The day did produce one tragi-comic incident. It happened that the new Soviet ambassador, Ivan Zotov, arrived in Helsinki on May 19. Zotov was a thoroughly unpleasant man, whose tenure of the embassy did immense harm to Soviet-Finnish relations. On this first day Zotov set the tone which he followed consistently thereafter. He observed that all the flags in Helsinki were at half-mast. Zotov at once demanded to know the meaning of this open provocation to the ambassador of the USSR. The foreign office officials who were receiving him explained the significance of May 19. Zotov listened, thought, and then declared that it was nevertheless a crude demonstration of hostility and a provocation that would damage friendly relations. It was to be Zotov's most unpleasant characteristic that he would never accept even the most obvious explanations. May 19, 1940, did not entirely extinguish feelings of distrust between White and Red. This was evident on the day itself. Generally it was marked by ceremonies in which Reds and Whites joined to commemorate all the dead at war memorials throughout the country. But there were isolated instances, particularly among members of the Suojeluskunta, of refusal to join with their former enemies. These incidents helped to feed the continuing distrust of the socialists for the Suojeluskunta. In spite of the agreement between this body and the Social Democratic party, which now officially encouraged its members to join, there were complaints that the Suojeluskunta was not keeping its side of the bargain, particularly it had not retired certain especially offensive members, as was proved by the incidents on May 19. The socialists also pointed out that it would be fitting if certain legislation offensive to the losers of 1918 were repealed.[38]

For the government, the cult of national unity yielded a major political dividend. It disarmed nearly the whole of the potential opposition. Only small extremist groups on the Right or the Left refused to be silenced in the sacred name of yksimielisyys. Early in April 1940 certain radical socialists began an agitation for the ending of the state of emergency and the restoration of normal civil liberties. The leader of this group of socialists, which included some members of the Eduskunta, was Wiik, who had quarrelled with Tanner and his policies before the war. The Wiik group was very typical of the kind of radical splinter movement which plagues all Social Democratic parties and seeks to overthrow the established, moderate leadership. The politics of the Wiik group were always confused by their duality of purpose. They could never decide whether it was the government, or Tanner's leadership of the Social Democratic party, which was enemy number one, and they tended to attack both together. Wiik had opened his civil liberties campaign by putting down an interpellation in the Eduskunta on April 11, asking when the censorship would be lifted. Walden, who had replied for the government, had said that they could not take the responsibility of lifting it while the state of international relations was so delicate.[39] On May 15, the Eduskunta had to debate the emergency regulations, since they were due to expire. The minister of the interior argued for their continuance, although he said that the government hoped to be able to relax them 'in the near future'. Only Wiik and his followers spoke against renewal.[40] The press generally poured scorn on his protests and accepted the government's assurances that they would be liberally administered. Only in the one field of censorship did a general agitation continue. The League of Journalists, meeting in the middle of May, issued a very strong protest, and on May 30, the constitutional committee of the Eduskunta recommended that censorship should be transferred from the army to the ministry of the interior.[41] The army at once put out a statement defending its régime from the criticisms which were the basis of the recommendation, but it was obvious that the Eduskunta was determined to end military control. So was the press. *Suomen Sosiaalidemokraatti* declared that dissatisfaction was nearly universal. The officers who ran the censorship were politically illiterate and quite unqualified for such a function in peacetime. When the committee's recommendation was debated in the Eduskunta on June 7, the government was prepared to give way. It announced that it would transfer the censorship to civilians within the ministry of the interior. Further it laid down the general principles they would follow. The censorship would not be applied to the discussion of internal affairs. It would only be used to restrain publication on questions concerning foreign affairs, internal conditions in foreign countries, and defence questions.[42]

The debate on June 7 was unusually vigorous, for the more radical members of the Eduskunta were not quite satisfied with the government statement. Frietsch, a member of the Swedish Peoples' party, complained of the 'colourlessness' of the press resulting from enforced uniformity. In particular he resented the suppression of articles expressing sympathy with Norway and Denmark. Svento declared that the government ought to be more ready to restore civil liberties and trust the maturity and intelligence of ordinary people. Unity and reconstruction would be better served by free discussion than forced unanimity of sentiment. The most radical attacks naturally came from the Wiik group. Wiik himself accused the government of abusing the censorship to prevent the expression of legitimate opposition against its own policies. The censorship was exercised 'purely to protect those in power'. Räisänen, another member of the group, pointed out how the bourgeois press always supported the government, and since Tanner controlled the socialist press, it tended to do the same. There must at least be enough relaxation of the law to let the opposition find expression through a paper of its own. 'This especially is a time to be able to criticize how public affairs are being run'. The strength of feeling can be measured by the vote on an opposition amendment rejecting

the government plan. It was carried by 106 votes to 16. Only on very rare
occasions could a Left opposition raise as many as sixteen votes in the
Eduskunta.[43] There was certainly some justification for opposition complaints about the effects of censorship. It probably did hinder the ordinary
citizen from obtaining a realistic picture of the contemporary world. In
particular it prevented him forming a balanced views of either Germany or
the USSR. Nothing could be published to reveal what the Nazi régime was
really like, or what methods it habitually used. The only aspect of Nazi
oppression that was fairly fully reported was the behaviour of the occupation authorities in Norway. This was described, though no critical
comment was allowed. Even here the impression was given that Quisling
and his followers, rather than the German authorities, were responsible for
what was happening. There were occasional brief items reporting measures
taken against the Jews in occupied Europe, but again no comment or discussion. The Finnish newspaper reader could have formed no adequate
picture of what was happening to European Jewry as a result of the deliberate policies of the German government. In short, nothing that might
be offensive to Germany could appear. The same rule applied to the USSR
with this vital difference. That while articles and news items conveying a
favourable, even enthusiastic impression of Nazi Germany and her policies
appeared freely, nothing was published favourable to the USSR. Indeed
the great eastern neighbour was usually not mentioned at all. It would of
course have been nearly impossible to give a balanced picture of the USSR
which would not have been offensive to the Soviet government. That being
so it may have been that there was no alternative to silence on this subject.
The total effect of all this was undoubtedly to deny the ordinary Finnish
citizen any chance of forming a realistic picture of the two great powers
whose policies controlled his own fate.

The fuss over the censorship was only one sign of the stirring of radical
opinion in the summer of 1940. By the beginning of June there had been
founded the Suomen-Neuvostoliiton rauhan ja ystävyyden Seura—the
Finnish-Soviet peace and friendship society—usually referred to by the
initials SNS. The founder of this organization was a young doctor, son of
a prominent Social Democrat, who had been an active radical before the
war, Mauri Ryömä. He had been joint editor of a Left-wing paper Soihtu,
and his activities had finally earned him expulsion from the Social Democratic party in 1937. For this, Ryömä naturally blamed Tanner, and hatred
of Tanner was one of the driving forces of his career. Ryömä had been
called up in 1939 and served in a military hospital. In December 1939 he
published a long letter attacking Tanner's foreign policy and blaming him
for the war. For this Ryömä was taken into protective custody from which
he was released on April 30.[44] Ryömä was a socialist intellectual of a type

that has been common in western Europe since the Russian revolution. Although he was never a communist himself, his radical convictions blinded him to the realities of communist practice, made him advocate the formation of a common front with them, and made him an easy tool for communist manipulation.

On May 22, 1940, Ryömä presided over a meeting of some 20 people, some of them radicals like himself, some members of the proscribed Finnish communist party, and it was decided to form the SNS. At first Ryömä had made what was probably an honest effort to get the co-operation of the authorities. There had been discussion with the minister of the interior, von Born, a man of liberal inclinations, and he had approved in principle of the idea of a Finnish-Soviet Society.[45] The newspaper *Soihtu* was to be refounded as the mouthpiece of the new organization. Its avowed methods were to be 'the publication of literature, and the organization of meetings, festivities, and lectures'. From the very beginnings there were signs of trouble to come. On May 23 an article in *Soihtu* on conditions in the USSR was forbidden by the military censors, though it did subsequently appear in July under the civilian régime. More sinister was the composition of the organizing committee. The vice-chairman was one Lauri Vilenius, a lorry driver with a long police record for criminal and political offences, and a communist. There were other members of the illegal communist party on the committee. It seems apparent that in spite of the influence of Ryömä himself, and others of like views, the SNS was from the first run by its communist members, and intended to be the cloak for a revival in Finland of the proscribed communist party. This was revealed by the policy of *Soihtu*, which continually reviled Tanner and his policies, and the Social Democratic leadership of the Finnish Trade Union Congress. Tanner was quick to strike back. He told a socialist party conference on June 9 that SNS was 'clearly a communist organization' and 'a fifth column which seeks to live in the shelter of Russia's broad back'. Tanner demanded that it be dissolved forthwith, and the Social Democratic party proscribed it, refused to allow its premises to be used by the SNS, or its press to accept SNS advertisements. These efforts were backed by the government. The censorship harried *Soihtu*, and prevented the press in general from accepting SNS notices or reporting its activities. But the government did not dare to take Tanner's advice and dissolve the SNS, for it enjoyed the ostentatious patronage of the USSR. On June 1, at the Soviet embassy in Helsinki, the leaders of SNS gave an interview to the Tass representative, and after that the whole Soviet propaganda machine made a great feature not only of the activities of SNS, but even more of the hostility which it was meeting with from the Finnish government. The Soviet embassy and its officials did everything they could to demonstrate that SNS had the full official backing of the Soviet government and in face of this, the Finnish government hardly dare take so provocative a step as dissolving the Society however much it disliked its activity. In these circumstances the SNS enjoyed a rather spectacular popular success. Within two months of its foundation it had some 115 local branches and over 35,000 paid-up members. A proportion of these must have been secret members of the communist party, and other fellow travellers who regarded SNS membership as an insurance against possible future developments, but even so it is apparent that the SNS did have some genuine popular appeal, though so far as can be judged, this was predominantly among the urban working class.

As May moved to its close, the quiet period too was coming to its end. The invisible forces that had preserved a precarious stability for Finland weakened and collapsed. The outcome of the European war was becoming apparent. Ever since the invasion of Norway a German success had seemed increasingly likely. By the beginning of June it was almost certain.While there had been the possibility that the western allies would win the war Finland had been indirectly sheltered from further interference by the USSR. Now that shelter had gone. Both the people and government of Finland began to draw the obvious conclusions from a changing situation. In future the attitude of Germany would be of crucial importance, for Finland, as for every other country in continental Europe. The new facts were reflected in a reshuffle of embassies that took place in May. Professor Kivimäki was appointed ambassador in Berlin from June 1. Kivimäki was a leading national and political figure, who had held high political office, and was known to be of pro-German leanings. His appointment was recognition that Berlin had become one of the key embassies. The newspaper *Ilta Sanomat* commented on this:[46]

'Professor Kivimäki's appointment to Berlin takes effect on June 1. Berlin is and will remain a post of the first importance in our overseas representation, for which reason it can be understood that there should be sent to it a politician who has a long career in public life and long-term experience as a member of a government, and who has a name outside his own country's borders. It is clear however that Minister Vuorimaa's transfer and Provessor Kivimäki's coming in his place gives no ground for making baseless political speculations one way or another.'

The final sentence was a reproof to those Finns who were indulging in dangerous political speculations. Many were wondering whether, now that Germany had won the war in the west, she would turn her interest to the east. If this happened then Germany might resume her role as a protector of the border states from Russian expansion. If this were to happen then Finland should lose no time in getting on close and friendly terms with Germany. Any bitterness felt over her conduct during the war would have to be forgotten. The prevalence of this line of thought in Finland, and the dangerous implications it involved, were enough to cause Svento to issue two warnings against it in his column within three days, one on May 31 and another on June 2.[47] Svento singled out those who advocated gambling on a breakdown of Nazi-Soviet relations by openly throwing in Finland's lot with Germany:

'I should like once more to warn those circles in Finland, who have the power to decide the fate of the Finnish people, against such mistakes . . . we do not want to experience a second time the sort of thing in which we were recently involved.'

In the second of the articles, Svento specifically mentioned those bourgeois circles who did not acknowledge that Germany had changed since 1918. Svento was alluding directly to the manifest fact that pro-German tendencies were strong in the upper levels of Finnish society. It was broadly true that among those who had been to university, and in the officer corps of the army, a majority shared this sentiment. It would be mistaken to make too much of this essentially psychological phenomenon, which cannot be measured, or even defined with any precision. But it is a fact that Finland has both culturally and politically strong traditional ties with Germany. Among the many factors involved can be cited the common bond of Lutheranism, the choice of German as the first foreign language for study in schools, which in turn meant that university students relied heavily on German language textbooks, and if they studied abroad, tended to make Germany their first choice of country. Then there was political sentiment. It was a corollary of Finland's negative attitude to Russia that she should adopt a positive attitude towards Germany. The events of 1918, when Germany had intervened in the civil war, and helped to speed up and clinch the victory of the Whites, had strongly reinforced this attitude. There were special factors which reinforced pro-Germanism among the officers. The majority of the men who had moulded Finland's army, and filled the top posts in 1940, were drawn from the Jägers of 1917. These were volunteers who had left Finland illegally in the first World War, and enlisted in a special battalion of the Imperial German army. The influence of these men had ensured that friendly sentiments towards Germany should predominate in the officer corps whose traditions they themselves had founded. Throughout the inter-war years there had been cordial professional relations between the German and Finnish armies. Such feeling was also strong in the Suojeluskunta.

Pro-German feeling was widespread and had survived Germany's behaviour during the war with Russia, though many observers think that it then suffered a blow from which it never really recovered in full. Letters in such papers as *Uusi Suomi* in the period just after the peace sometimes expressed the bewilderment of the writers at Germany's current unfriendliness, some blaming it on the behaviour of the pre-war, Left-inclined governments.[48] But such sentiment did not amount to an organized political force. The most that can be said with confidence is that in the upper ranks of Finnish society in 1940, the idea of drawing closer to Germany would evoke a positive response, would be felt to be a natural line of policy. Svento hinted that this sentiment took no account of the nature of Nazi Germany. It was based on an image of the old imperial Germany of 1918. To get a true perspective on Finnish pro-Germanism it is necessary to remember the existence of counter-influences. The largest party in Finland, the socialists, had long been actively anti-fascist, and had a record of opposition to Hitler and his régime. The events of the war had only served to reinforce their dislike. Nor was pro-Germanism strong in the inmost circle of the government. Mannerheim had never been infected by it. He had been brought up in the Russian army, and done much of his campaigning against Germany. He had been bitterly opposed to inviting the Germans to intervene in the civil war and anxious to get rid of them when it had ended. The Marshal always seems to have preserved a cool scepticism towards the Germans, even when he was working with them. It has been noted that Ryti was a notorious anglophile, and Tanner had been so outspoken about Germany before 1939 that the Nazi government for a long time declined to have any dealings with him. The position of Walden is less certain, but he was known for his admiration of English culture and civilization, and gave no positive sign of pro-German tendency. In the inmost circles of power only Witting can be safely called Germanophile.

There was in any case no need for the Finns to have any special tradition of pro-German feeling in order to conclude, in the summer of 1940, that their best interests might be served by rapprochement with Germany. It was dictated to them by the logic of events. It has always been very difficult for the British in particular to remember that they had lost the war in the summer of 1940. But it was quite clear to most other observers at the time. The fact that eventually, Hitler's insane policies rescued the British from the consequences of their defeat does not alter the fact that by any rational calculation they were beaten in June 1940. This was obvious in Finland as elsewhere and the correct conclusions were drawn. Germany was going to dominate the fate of continental Europe in the foreseeable future, so that even if the Finns had loathed Germany and the Germans, political realism would still have impelled them to seek the best relations they could with her. Since in fact so many of them felt as they did about Germany, they had little difficulty in reconciling themselves to the idea of a new European order in which Germany would be the dominant power.

Even Svento accepted this as a fact of life. What he was warning against was betting on a Soviet-German quarrel. Svento continued to believe to the end that Germany stood to lose so much by abandoning her co-operation with the USSR that no German leader could be insane enough to do it. He under-estimated Hitler. So now he reminded his countrymen of what too many wanted to forget. That Germany had sold Finland out to the USSR in August 1939, and would not scruple to do so again if it suited her.

In early June 1940, ordinary Finnish citizens, preoccupied with the increasing material difficulties of life, and the implications of the resettlement and compensation questions, still had energy enough to be fascinated by the drama being enacted in western Europe. They followed it as best they could, perhaps grumbling that the censorship obscured their view, and not unhopeful that something good for Finland might emerge from the changing situation. Only the men at the top knew that so far Germany's victories had been Finland's defeats. They left Finland even more helpless between the two dictatorships whose co-operation showed no sign of weakening. But these gloomy thoughts they kept to themselves. The nation's attention was directed to unity and reconstruction, while the lonely men who ran its government waited to see how the USSR would react to the new European balance of power, and wondered whence their own salvation might come. They were on the brink of three of the worst months of their lives.

CHAPTER 6

Cold War

The next stage in the story was opened by a new phase of Soviet policy which was marked by the annexation of the Baltic republics. The reasons for this new phase, though necessarily unverifiable, can be assumed with some degree of plausibility. It has to be supposed that Stalin, like everyone else including the Germans themselves, got a shock when France and Britain collapsed so suddenly under the German onslaught. He concluded, in early June 1940, like all sensible politicians, that the continental war was over, and that Britain would face this fact and make peace. Hitler would then be free to reorganize Europe according to his taste. Since Hitler's predilections for expansion in the east were no secret, there was the serious chance that he would turn in that direction. Even if he did honour his pact with the USSR, the position of the two partners had been changed in Germany's favour. In August 1939, Germany had been a suppliant needing favours from the USSR. But if Germany was free of embarrassments in the west, and had the whole continent of Europe at her disposal, she would be the stronger partner, and would dictate the terms of the relationship. Thus whether Hitler intended to revert to his ideas about destroying bolshevism and winning living space in the east, or whether he was ready to continue working with Stalin as a partner, it was still an obvious move for the USSR to secure the maximum advantage out of the pact of August 1939 before Germany had mopped up the western allies.

In the mutual assistance treaties between the USSR and the Baltic republics of Estonia, Latvia, and Lithuania, the full sovereignty of these countries had been solemnly guaranteed, even though they were all fascist dictatorships whose basic hostility to the USSR was not in doubt. The USSR had been scrupulous in observing the treaties, making good propaganda about how they demonstrated the possibility of peaceful co-existence between Russia and her small neighbours, despite differing social systems, and how they showed that the security needs of the USSR could be met without in any way infringing the rights of neighbouring countries.[1] There had been one or two incidents in Lithuania, which being nearest to Germany probably seemed least secure to the USSR. Incidents involving soldiers of the Soviet garrisons had caused protests in March, and more ominously in May. But the Lithuanian answers had seemed to satisfy the USSR.

On June 14, when the decision in the west was beyond doubt, Russia struck. The Lithuanian government was given an ultimatum. It was accused of hostile acts against the Soviet garrisons, and of conspiring with Estonia and Latvia against the USSR. It must install a new government which could honestly perform the obligations of the mutual assistance pact, and permit Soviet troops to occupy the whole country. Lithuania complied and was occupied on June 15. After that it was a mere formality to present similar ultimatums to Estonia and Latvia and occupy them in the days which followed.

In Finland the developments were followed with an interest that was heightened and alarmed by the news on June 15 that a Finnish airliner, on a flight from Tallinn, the capital of Estonia, to Helsinki, had crashed in flames. A commission of inquiry reported that it had been destroyed by an explosion of unknown origin, but probably due to external causes.[2] In fact the government knew, and the public seems to have learned, that it had been deliberately shot down by Russian fighters. From later evidence it seemed possible that this was done in order to secure the diplomatic bags being carried on board by a French diplomatic courier. The incident caused a wave of anger among ordinary Finnish people, fed by the obvious impotence of their government in face of a brutal and criminal act.[3] It was decided that in such a delicate international situation no protest could be made. Across the water, in the Baltic republics, Soviet commissars had appeared in each capital, Left-wing political demonstrations were organized, the old régimes were dismantled, and new radical governments installed. There was a flood of rumours that Finland's turn was coming. These became so persistent that on June 21 the government issued an official statement that there had been no Soviet demands on Finland.[4] A few days earlier, Witting had told the foreign affairs committee of the Eduskunta that 'relations with Russia are normal'.[5] There was indeed nothing as yet to cause serious alarm. Only the attention being given in Soviet propaganda to the activity of SNS was a little disturbing. Its first big public meeting in Helsinki, addressed by Dr. Helo, one of the more radical socialists, had struck a reasonable tone, or so it seemed to Paasikivi watching from Moscow.[6] The same could not be said of the first SNS circular to its members, issued on June 14, which bitterly condemned the late war as caused needlessly by the policy of the Finnish government, drew comparisons with the more sensible behaviour of the Baltic republics, and declared that the Soviet base at Hanko 'protects Finland's independence'. On June 19, the whole executive committee of SNS was ceremonially and ostentatiously received by Zotov in the Soviet embassy.[7] Then, on June 23, Paasikivi was suddenly summoned to the Kremlin. He shared the feeling of gloom and fear which this summons caused among his embassy staff, 'I feared that now it was Finland's turn, and that Molotov would present us with demands.'[8]

Paasikivi was right about this, but it was not the kind of demand that he and his colleagues had dreaded. He found Molotov in a good humour. Molotov remarked that he had not seen Paasikivi for some time, and then said that the USSR was interested in the nickel deposits in the Petsamo region. He asked whether Finland would give a concession to exploit them to the USSR, or alternatively set up a joint Russo-Finnish company for the purpose. Paasikivi was taken by surprise, and supposed that Russia wanted the produce for herself. So he pointed out that the concession was already let to the Canadian-British Mond Nickel Company, but he was sure that they would sell the USSR all the nickel she wanted. Paasikivi sent the request back to Helsinki and recommended an answer on these lines.[9] The motivation of this demand, whose consequences were to bedevil Russo-Finnish relations until the outbreak of a new war, is not easy to determine. It does not make much sense as a question of economics. The USSR, as fas as is known, produced all the nickel she needed at that time. She might have wanted to build up a semi-monopoly position in nickel production which would have been a valuable bargaining counter with Germany, who desperately needed this metal for her armaments industry, but there is little evidence to suggest that this was a primary motive. It must be concluded that the reasons were probably political, and that the main objective was to expel British influence from the Petsamo region and replace it with Russian. Molotov said as much to the German ambassador in Moscow when they discussed the Soviet position in July.[10] The fact that the possession of the concession had not given the British any political influence in the area seems to have been ignored by the Soviet government. It was felt that the concession was some kind of link between Finland and Britain and they wanted it broken, in order to make Finland's isolation more complete. But there could be a further reason why the demand was presented at this time. On June 14, the German occupation authorities in Norway had announced that they would extend German occupation into the northern tip of that country, Finmark. On June 15, the German flag was raised in its only important town, Kirkenes. It was so difficult to move troops into this remote country that the concentration proceeded very slowly, but from that time there were German armed forces in an area which bordered on northern Finland, and was divided from Soviet territory by the narrow sleeve of the Petsamo area. The vital ice-free port of Murmansk, with its vulnerable railway connection to the south, was not far from the frontier. This helps to explain the keen curiosity which the Russians always displayed about what was happening in the Petsamo area. If they could establish control of the nickel mines, they would have an excellent observation post from which the whole area could be kept under surveillance.

The demand put the Finnish government in a genuine difficulty. It could not afford to offend the British government by confiscating its concession. Britain was certainly weakened, but she had the power to cut off the sea traffic to Liinahamari if she was provoked. It was also repugnant to Finnish concepts of law to cancel a valid concession without legal cause. Further Germany had to be considered. During the recent trade talks, Germany had asked for the concession herself and been refused. She had then offered to take up to 75% of the output of the mines. Germany would surely be displeased if the concession that had been refused to her was given to the USSR. Yet all the signs were that it would be dangerous to refuse the Soviet demand. On June 25, the day set for signing the Russo-Finnish trade agreement in Moscow, the Finnish delegation was suddenly informed that the signing must be postponed. The following day, in Helsinki, the SNS held a meeting at which the terms of a letter to the Speaker of the Eduskunta were approved. Ostensibly the letter was occasioned by a debate on the censorship, of whose operations the SNS strongly disapproved. But its implications went much further than this. The letter declared:[11]

'Instead of the government having worked to bring about confidential and friendly relations between Finland and the Soviet Union, it has tried to put a stop to developments here which would promote our national interests . . . the writing of the press, controlled by the state, is still hostile to the Soviet Union, but at the same time they try to prevent that broad current of national opinion, which favours friendly relations between these countries from getting publicity . . . For these reasons the Society considers that the present government is unwilling and unable to organize the relations of the Soviet Union and Finland in the manner demanded by the interests of the Finnish nation, and awaits the formation of such a government as will honestly endeavour to develop economic, political, and cultural relations between Finland and the Soviet Union . . . and thus will safeguard our people's livelihood and our country's peaceful and happy development.'

The most significant feature of this manifesto was the way in which it echoed the demands being made by organized left-wing demonstrations in the Baltic republics at this point. The SNS pointedly sent telegrams of congratulation to the new governments organized there under Soviet supervision. It enjoyed the same kind of encouragement from the Soviet government. Naturally the comparison was not missed by the Finnish government. In these circumstances they returned what was intended to be a soft answer on the nickel question. Paasikivi saw Molotov on June 27 and stated that his government was willing to divide the output of the mines equally between the USSR and Germany.[12] Molotov pointed out that this was not what the USSR had asked for. She wanted the concession itself, and she wanted British influence expelled from the Petsamo region. When Paasikivi pointed out that the legal rights of the Canadian-Mond Nickel Company were an obstacle to complying with the Soviet request Molotov merely said that he was sure the Finnish government could find some way to get round this. Paasikivi then mentioned the unsigned trade agreement, but Molotov said he had another matter to raise first. The government of the USSR noted that Finland was keeping a garrison and fortifications on the Åland islands. These must be removed unless Finland would like to fortify them jointly with the USSR. Otherwise they must be completely demilitarized, and the USSR given facilities to supervise the process.

Paasikivi was once more taken by surprise. The Åland convention of 1921 did indeed require that the islands be demilitarized. When Finland and the USSR had been negotiating in the autumn of 1939, the Soviet government had been prepared to let Finland fortify them. They had in fact been occupied by Finnish forces since the beginning of the war, and as Paasikivi pointed out, it was a little late to protest about this. Molotov replied that the government of the USSR had changed its mind since the autumn. He continued with a phrase that has since become proverbial in Finland as proof of the cynicism and perfidy of the Soviet government, that 'he had not wanted to raise the matter in the peace conference, lest it should create new difficulties'.[13] In other words, the solemn assurance that the peace treaty had settled all political issues between the two countries had been meaningless even when it was being given. Paasikivi undertook to consult his government, and then pointed out that this was no reason for not signing the trade agreement. Molotov agreed and said they could sign next day, the USSR wanted to help Finland, 'which was in a difficult position',[14] but they expected that Finland in her turn would meet the wishes of the USSR over the Åland and the nickel questions. Paasikivi retired to ponder the significance of his conversation, and on the following day advised his government to agree to evacuate Åland, and try to meet the Russian demand for the nickel concession.

This outburst of activity by the USSR had naturally stimulated Finland to look around for possible support which might enable her to resist. This support could only come from Germany, and in the circumstances there was a natural upsurge of pro-German feeling. This found expression in a memorandum, sent to the president by an eminent group of Right-wing politicians. It urged the government to show open sympathy for the German cause, and to take up any advances that might come from Germany. The government was very willing to try. As a gesture, on June 22, it granted formal recognition to Germany's satellite state, Slovakia. In doing this it was in effect condoning the liquidation of Czechoslovakia by Germany. *Helsingin Sanomat* felt uneasy over this, but comforted its readers by pointing out that several other neutral countries had done the same.[15] But there was no response. Kivimäki, the ambassador in Berlin, had been taking soundings and had reported that 'at the moment Finland has nothing but difficulties here. Hitler has among other things twice refused permission to buy arms.'[16] On June 17, Kivimäki went to the German Foreign Office and asked outright what Germany would advise Finland to do if she was presented with demands similar to those made on the Baltic states, adding that he was sure she would not capitulate as they had done. Woerman, who received the ambassador, had no advice or comment to give.[17] On June 29, while the government pondered its reply to the USSR, Kivimäki sent a further despatch. There was nothing to be got from Germany. 'As things are now, Finland cannot evade the fact that she must by all means seek friendly relations with Russia.'[18] He added that it was a pity that Ryömä had been allowed to get in first with SNS. It would have been much better if the government had promoted such a society. Kivimäki's reports were correct. Hitler had no interest in Finland at that time, nor any thought of a war on the USSR which might stimulate an interest. On June 24, he had ordered the partial demobilization of the army and given a directive to concentrate on developing naval and air forces in case Britain proved stubborn. But he believed that Britain would now give in, and he could digest his gains in peace.

Thus the Finnish government had received identical advice from its ambassadors in Moscow and Berlin to give in to the demands of the USSR. This was done, and on July 3, Paasikivi brought his government's answer to Molotov. The evacuation of the Åland islands would begin immediately. Molotov expressed satisfaction, but added that the USSR wished to establish a consul there with power to inspect what was done. He hoped there would be no delay in arranging this.[19] Then Paasikivi announced that his government would open discussions with the concessionaires of the nickel mines with a view to meeting the Soviet requirements. Again Molotov remarked that he hoped there would be no delay. Paasikivi replied that that depended on the other side. Molotov then pointed out that the Finnish government had already compelled the British company to sell its nickel to Germany, obviously against its will, so that it could do what it wanted.[20] Still, Molotov appeared to be satisfied for the moment, and the Finnish government could hope that its conciliatory attitude had won it a breathing space.

No word of these developments reached the public ear. Even the foreign affairs committee of the Eduskunta was left in ignorance. One of its members remarked afterwards that 'we, the representatives of the nation, knew very little of what was happening in the state in the summer and autumn of 1940'.[21] The government did not feel able to thrust the burden of these new worries on a people that had troubles enough, particularly as any discussion that might arise could offend foreign powers and imperil unity. This attitude was demonstrated when the unruly Agrarians, Niukkanen and Hannula, pursuing their campaign against the government, broke the sacred silence in which foreign affairs were usually wrapped. Their paper, *Pohjolan Sanomat*, revealed that during the war the news of Russian peace moves had been concealed even from such key members of the government as the minister of defence. This had been done by the same clique as dominated the present government. The socialist press at once sprang forward to condemn this public washing of dirty linen, since Tanner was one of those aimed at. The revelation caused such a stir that Ryti was obliged to issue an official statement. In this he implied that Niukkanen was misleading the public but refused to be drawn into an argument with him. It was still premature to discuss so tender a topic as the late war, and such public controversy was utterly deplorable.[22] The government was under a lot of fire at this point. Wiik and his friends were busy trying to organize an anti-Tanner group inside the Social Democratic party, and steadily agitating against government policies. They had at last succeeded in launching a newspaper of their own, *Vapaa Sana*—Free Speech—in spite of all that the censors and obstructive printers could do to stop them, although they did not get its first number on sale until July 24.[23] These persistent disturbers of unity were a nuisance but no danger. The same could not be said of SNS. It continued to harp on the way in which events in the Baltic republics pointed the way for Finland. A speech by Ryömä was circulated to the members on July 7 which dwelt at length on the example given in Estonia where 'representatives of the workers have secured the direction of their country's affairs'. They were a model for Finland to follow. Meetings of workers were told that 'events in the Baltic states could be taken as a promise of a brighter future'.[24] In view of what was happening in the Baltic states, all this was very disturbing.

The anxieties of the government were betrayed by a visit which Witting paid to the German ambassador on July 4. He told von Blücher:[25]

'. . . die deutschfreundliche Stimmung im Lande wachse "lawinenartig", es bestanden Bestrebungen, eine Regierung zu bilden, die sich ausschliesslich nach Berlin orientieren solle. Die öffentliche Meinung würde stark beeinflusst von der Vorstellung dass Finnland sich in wenigen Monaten mit deutscher Wafenhilfe die an Russland verlorene Gebiete wiederholen könne.'*

Witting probably exaggerated the extent of pro-German sentiment somewhat in order to test Blücher's reaction, although there were plenty of Finns who did think exactly as he described it. Blücher, who genuinely liked the Finns, was tempted to try his hand at policy making. He told Witting to restrain his countrymen's enthusiasm but suggested that the Finnish government might well co-operate secretly with Germany while remaining officially aloof. Witting indicated that they would be glad to do this. In truth, Blücher was a very broken reed for the Finns to grasp at. He had no influence in Germany, where the Nazi leaders regarded him as a typically useless and unreliable example of the old school of diplomacy. When Blücher reported what he must have thought was his very skilful handling of Witting, he got an immediate reproof. He was told not to make such statements in future as they could only raise false hopes in Finland.[26] One more Finnish feeler towards Germany had been fruitless. Germany had no present use for Finland, and even in circles where there was sympathy, there was no anxiety at that moment. General Halder, chief of the army general staff, who occasionally discussed developments in the east with colleagues and foreign office officials, and who was friendly to Finland, noted in his diary on July 9 that 'Finland's position appears to be reassuring'.[27] Germany and the USSR had just been discussing the share-out of the production of the Petsamo nickel mines, and the USSR was willing that for the current year Germany would take 60%.[28] No doubt the impression that nothing drastic would happen had grown out of these talks.

On July 8, the Finnish government received another shock. It had been waiting for some time for Russian proposals to reopen railway communications between the two countries. When this arrived it was discovered that there was a clause permitting the USSR to run trains over the Finnish railway system to their base at Hanko. No limits were proposed either on the number of such trains or their contents. They would be Russian stock, headed by Russian locomotives, with only a Finnish guide on the footplate.[29] Reference to a railway map of Finland shows what was involved. The trains would pass through vital centres of industry and communications over a long stretch of southern Finland. Kouvola, Lahti, and

*. . . pro-German feeling in the country snowballed; there were attempts to create a government whose policies would be based exclusively on those of Berlin. Public opinion was much influenced by the idea that Finland could, with German military aid, retrieve the territory lost to Russia in a few months.

Riihimäki, were places of the first importance. The Finnish government was quite unprepared for this demand. They had assumed that the base at Hanko would be supplied from the sea, though they might have reflected that this would become difficult when the sea froze in winter. As usual, Paasikivi felt that they dared not refuse. He advised his government to agree provided 'this does not create military dangers for Finland'.[30] The government saw both legal and military objections. Legally it was doubtful if a neutral country ought to give transit rights to the armed forces of another power. But since Sweden had just conceded similar rights to Germany for supplying the garrisons in Norway, this argument had little force at such a time. The military danger was the one that mattered. The trains could in theory have been used to seize key communications centres either in connection with a sudden invasion, or in co-operation with internal subversive forces. The route was such that the whole Finnish communication system could be paralysed at a blow by trains properly spaced and timed. It is true that what looks like a brilliant opportunity on paper would have met with all sorts of practical difficulties in execution, but there clearly was a danger, and simply taking the necessary security precautions against it would be burdensome. Further, the Finnish reaction to the demand took into account the whole complex of recent events, and these made it seem much more alarming than it might if considered in isolation. Paasikivi wrote about this:[31]

'We always had the fate of the Baltic states on our mind, which in Moscow diplomatic circles and the world's press was supposed to be awaiting us. The attempt made during the Winter War with the aid of Kuusinen was also never absent from Finnish thinking. The consequence of all these was that, in the summer and autumn of 1940, in our lonely position, feelings of insecurity and fear, and uncertainty of the future increasingly ruled us Finns. I had the continuous feeling that we were on the brink of a volcano.'

That Finnish policy grew out of insecurity and fear is very obvious, and it is no help in understanding it simply to assert that the fears were exaggerated. Only reassuring behaviour by the USSR could have alleviated them, and everything which the Soviet government did worked in the opposite direction. To see the situation as the Finnish government saw it, one has to recall that they had been assured on several occasions that the Treaty of Moscow settled all political questions. Now, against the background of what had happened in the Baltic states, the USSR had presented three demands in ten days, all unpalatable, one, on the nickel concession highly embarrassing internationally, and one, the transit demand, militarily prejudicial. But it was probably not the substance of the demands which terrified. They were not in themselves abnormal, coming from a great power to a small neighbour in a time of international upheaval. It was the impossibility of knowing what the next one might be, and the one after that, the never knowing where it would stop, or what the end would be. Too many factors seemed to suggest to Finnish minds that the fate of Estonia and the resurrection and final triumph of Kuusinen were what the USSR intended for Finland. In these circumstances it is surprising, not that the Finnish government was afraid, but that in spite of its fears it never panicked or lost control of the situation.

This is apparent in their handling of the transit demands. First they tried to limit the traffic to non-military stores, eliminating the transport of troops altogether. The USSR refused to consider this. Mannerheim was then consulted on what were the minimum requirements for basic security and replied that the troops must travel unarmed, their weapons being conveyed separately.[32] Since it became clear that the Russians wanted to send whole trainloads of troops, the weapons must go in different trains, and the number of trains on Finnish territory at any one time must be limited. It is probable that the USSR was primarily concerned with the supply of Hanko only, and had no serious ulterior motives. But as always their behaviour bred fear and uncertainty. It is easy to see that it would have been convenient to have the troops take their personal weapons with them. But when the Russians did concede in the face of Finnish objections that they should travel unarmed, why then did they refuse to have this put in writing?[33] Was it considerations of face, the unwillingness of a strong party to go on record as having made a concession, or did they feel that once the agreement was signed, it would be easy, if it proved desirable, blandly to deny that any verbal agreement existed? These were the kind of questions the Finnish government was bound to ask itself.

All three new Russian moves were carefully concealed from the Finnish people. Witting spoke to the foreign affairs committee of the Eduskunta on July 9, but told them no more than that negotiations were in progress over matters arising out of the peace treaty. A few days later the public was informed that current talks concerned the return of property in the ceded areas, which was true, but the least important part of the truth.[34] Further, the report was embroidered with inspired press comment that was misleading. The public was told that relations with the USSR were normal and improving. *Suomen Sosiaalidemokraatti* assured its readers that 'the direction is right . . . goodwill has been shown on both sides'.[35] The people should not listen to disturbing rumours to the contrary. It is unlikely that people were much reassured by government statements. Instead they increasingly scanned the news for some signs of comfort from Germany. At this time the Nazi leaders were fond of making speeches about the New Order which was to be introduced in Europe. Finns were keen to know if there was a place in it for them. On July 10 the Finnish press reported a press conference given by Alfred Rosenberg, a leading Nazi, on the New Order and Scandinavia. He said that the Germanic races of Scandinavia undoubtedly had a place, and they must make up their minds to take it, and throw off their outdated democratic ideas. It was impossible to tell from what he said whether Finland was included in Scandinavia, but easy to see from much Finnish press comment that they fervently hoped that she was. Later in the month *Uusi Suomi* published a major editorial on the new Europe that was taking shape:[36]

'The new Europe is not any longer just a projected programme added to earlier plans. In spite of the fact that the war is still continuing in the European area, the new Europe is now being realized to a great extent. It is already a reality which every European nation and every European person must take note of.'

The paper stressed that Germany would dictate both the politics and the economy of the new Europe, and clearly found nothing repugnant in this. A little later, in a mood of wishful thinking, the paper published a meditation by the poet Koskenniemi on Rosenberg's statements. Scandinavia belonged to the Germanic world, Finland belonged to Scandinavia, she too belonged to the Germanic world. He stressed the many aspects of German influence in Finland. This, he asserted:[37]

'. . . creates an undeniable connection, which cannot be broken without doing violence to the facts of history, and which is also not at variance with the feeling of comradeship in fate, of which Alfred Rosenberg speaks.'

Koskenniemi and the paper *Uusi Suomi* were typical of the rising pro-Germanism in conservative and intellectual circles. The socialists lacked the enthusiasm of such people, but a sense of realities pushed them along the same political road. *Suomen Sosiaalidemokraatti*, like *Uusi Suomi*, told its readers that Finland must conform to the fact of Germany's predominance in Europe.[38] Small countries had to recognize that for the moment they must submit to the decrees of the great powers. Tanner stressed this point in a speech at Oulu on July 15. Small nations, he declared, 'have no possibility of deciding their own fate during these tumults'.[39] Svento was one of the few socialists who, while recognizing German dominance in Europe, reminded his countrymen that the war had not ended and Britain should not be written off. He thought Britain might yet prove to have unexpected staying-power, and produce some surprises. Svento resorted to the technique of quoting an article written in 1918 to draw a comparison between the over-confident Germany of the spring of 1918 and the Germany of 1940. He also warned his readers not to under-estimate the political skill of the British, 'Albion is cold, calculating, self-regarding, and cynical when it is a question of Britain's own advantages. That we saw from here during our own peace negotiations.'[40]

It is apparent from a reading of the Finnish press in July and August of 1940 that the strain of uncertainty over the international position, and the many difficulties on the domestic front, was telling on the morale of the nation. The economy was unsettled and unemployment was particularly bad just at this time. There was an outbreak of minor strikes and labour troubles. Tanner and the socialist press blamed these on the employers and the bourgeoisie who wanted to put the clock back, or were trying to exploit the workers under cover of the cult of unity. *Hämeen Kansa* reminded the bourgeoisie that the workers would not cease to defend their class interests because of a lot of fine words about unity. The social stresses thus revealed showed up in a row over the formation of an ex-servicemen's organization. The pre-war organization had been the Vapaussodan Rintamamiestenliitto—the League of Servicemen of the War of Liberation— which represented the victorious Whites. At the annual congress of the organization in June it announced that it would in future change its name to League of Servicemen and enlist men who had fought in the recent war. The socialists bitterly attacked the League and its pretensions, describing it as a tool of reaction, and contesting its claim to be a truly national organization. The public debate on the issue was in full cry in July.[41] In a lighter vein, the prevailing tension is illustrated by a letter in *Uusi Suomi* which complained that the authorities did not prohibit the holding of dances at such a grave moment in the nation's history. Such levity invited a descent of the wrath of God on the nation, and it should remember the fate of Belshazzar.[42]

In such an atmosphere of petty discontent and recrimination the SNS flourished. Its significance became more apparent in the light of the fate which had finally overtaken the Baltic republics. Their new radical governments had dissolved the old parliaments and ordered new elections on the Soviet system with a single list of candidates. It became clear that when the new parliaments met they would proclaim a soviet socialist republic, and seek admission to the USSR. Nobody in Finland was in any doubt about what was really happening. *Helsingin Sanomat* remarked with unusual frankness on July 14 that the elections were rigged and in no sense represented the will of the people.[43] Events across the Gulf of Finland were fairly fully reported, and a steady trickle of refugees contributed their own story of events. But the official publications of the SNS loudly celebrated the 'liberation' of the Baltic states. The tone of SNS meetings was both jubilant and threatening. There were shouts of 'Long live soviet-Finland', and 'another two weeks and we shall see where we are going', and 'the police will not dare lay a hand on us because the Soviet Union is

behind us'.[44] The significance of such remarks was not in doubt. The SNS
was in fact being backed by the whole strength of the Soviet propaganda
machine, which had entered on a new phase. It now openly compared
the miseries of the Finnish workers with the happiness of their brethren
over the frontier or in the Baltic states, it praised the work of SNS, and
vilified the government, and Tanner above all, for opposing its work.[45]
Paasikivi had noted this disturbing turn in Soviet propaganda, and observed how it exploited reports in the Finnish press of hardships and
dissensions. He wondered if the government could not use the censorship
to deprive the Russians of such ammunition.[46] The ambassador was by
now thoroughly alarmed at the turn of events, his diplomatic colleagues in
Moscow were full of rumours that Finland's turn was coming, and
'although I am not myself so pessimistic, I cannot conceal my anxiety'.
Paasikivi wrote this on July 15, and like so many others he wondered if
something might not be got from Germany. He urged the government to
take soundings. It has been noted that Witting had already done this, as
had Kivimäki in Berlin, but without response. However on July 16, Witting again called on Blücher, and admitted to him officially that the Finnish
government was alarmed about the intentions of the USSR, no doubt
fishing for a reaction. But Blücher could have offered no comfort at this
stage.[47]

   Hitler had discussed with his service chiefs on July 13, the question of
why Britain was so slow to make peace. They agreed that it only made sense
if she was hoping to get help from the USSR.[48] But Hitler was of the
opinion that if necessary Britain could be beaten down by military
means, and the USSR induced to acquiesce in this, or even to co-operate
in the process. Following this the order was issued on July 16 to prepare
an invasion of Britain,[49] and on July 19, Hitler made a peace offer in a
speech to the Reichstag.[50] Hitler said that he knew Britain was counting
on a breach between Germany and the USSR but this was vain. The
co-operation of the two countries was unshakeable. They had finally de-
limited their spheres of influence, and Finland was specifically mentioned
as an area in which Germany had no interests. So Britain should come to
her senses and make peace.[51] Hitler's speech on July 19 marked the nadir
of Finland's hopes and fortunes. As Paasikivi wrote to Witting, his question was now answered. Germany had sold Finland out to the USSR.[52]
Never had Finland been so isolated or so helpless in face of an incalculable
danger. Yet salvation was at hand, though nobody in Finland knew it. For
within the next 14 days Hitler changed his mind about the USSR. When
he had talked to his service chiefs on July 21, Hitler had stuck to the views
he had outlined on July 13.[53] Even so, the army chiefs, Brauchitsch and
Halder, felt it was worth their while to make some preliminary studies for

a possible Russian campaign. In these studies, Halder assumed from the beginning that Finland would be involved. But as it was apparent that no campaign could be mounted in 1940, and as the army chiefs feared that Britain might have made a considerable recovery by the spring of 1941, they concluded that it would be too dangerous to attack the USSR then. With this conclusion the army leaders flew on July 31 to a conference with Hitler. There, no doubt to their dismay, they learned that Hitler doubted whether an invasion of Britain would be successful. This being so the only alternative was to eliminate the USSR and thus deprive Britain of her only hope. Then she must give in. Hitler outlined his conception of a campaign to be launched in the spring of 1941. Finland might be brought in, and in any case in the resulting carve-up of western Russia, Finland could be enlarged perhaps as far as the White Sea.[54] Nobody knows now what changed Hitler's mind between July 21 and July 31. Whatever it was it also decided the fate of Finland.

But nearly three weeks passed before this decision by Hitler had any practical repercussions in Finland. In ignorance of the salvation that was being hatched, the Finnish government underwent its sternest trial. Their dejection was mirrored in a despatch from Paasikivi on July 22. He feared that growing domestic discontent and hardship would eventually undermine the people's will to preserve their independence. 'The next winter especially frightens me'.[55] SNS was obviously a menace, but he urged the government not to suppress it, for fear of the offence this would cause while the USSR so ostentatiously patronized it. 'The danger is that after the Baltic states attentions here will be turned on us, and then everything depends on our people's internal strength'. Two days later Paasikivi thought that Finland's hour had come. A rumour swept through northern Europe that the USSR would present an ultimatum to Finland demanding immediate demobilization. Its centre of origin was Stockholm, whence the German ambassador passed it to Berlin. Simultaneously the German ambassador to Lithuania reported that Soviet troops were being withdrawn from the Baltic states and concentrated for an attack on Finland in mid-August. Blücher was instructed to find out what the Finnish government knew of this, but Witting told him there was nothing in it, and he suspected the reports were spread deliberately to cause alarm and despondency in Finland.[56] But in Moscow, Paasikivi had a call from Assarsson, the Swedish ambassador, who asked if there were any truth in the rumours. Paasikivi was telling him that he had received no ultimatum, nor any hint of one the last time he saw Molotov, when a message came summoning Paasikivi to the Kremlin. He recalls that, 'I thought that Molotov would talk about what Assarsson had just mentioned, and I prepared what I should reply. I was really nervous'.[57]

Paasikivi went to the Kremlin in fear and trembling, by his own account, and to his relief found Molotov in a good mood. The call was over nothing worse than a Soviet draft of an agreement on the Åland islands. This provided first that the islands be demilitarized, and second that the USSR could establish a consulate there, with the right to supervise the demilitarization.[58] There was nothing in it unacceptable to Finland, which had already conceded both points. But Molotov went on to say that he had another matter to raise. It was clear that the Finnish government, and Tanner especially, were doing all they could to oppose the SNS. Molotov said he could not understand this, and added that Tanner had always been opposed to friendly relations with the USSR. He went on:[59]

'Of course the Soviet Union cannot decide who is in the Finnish government. That must be your own affair. But the Soviet Union can decide with whom it prefers to work and have contact. So long as Tanner is in the Finnish government, especially in so important a post as minister for economic affairs, I cannot imagine how the relations of Finland and the Soviet Union can ever improve or be good ... can you not manage without Tanner?'

Molotov had the grace to concede that 'it is disagreeable for you to discuss this matter', but persisted in this question. Paasikivi pointed out that he had no first-hand information about SNS since he had not been in Helsinki. The following exchange then took place:

'M.: Go now to Helsinki since these things can only be dealt with personally.

'P.: I certainly meant to go to Helsinki ... (jokingly). My dentist has said that if I do not come soon, my teeth will fall out of my head.'

'M.: If your dentist has given such an order, then you must go at the first opportunity.'

The discussion ended on this humorous note, the two men being quite alone. Despite Molotov's friendly personal approach, his meaning was clear. The government of the USSR was presenting its fourth and fifth demands of the current series, that the SNS must be given a free hand, and that Tanner must leave the government, and since these were not the kind of demands that could be put in writing, Paasikivi had better go to Helsinki and arrange it informally.

Molotov was very nearly too late to save the SNS. On July 19, Ryömä and Vilenius had been charged with issuing a seditious publication, namely the letter to the Speaker of the Eduskunta.[60] The case should have come into court on July 26, but Molotov's intervention caused the government to pause. It had already decided that it would suppress SNS if necessary, but Ryti now had a personal interview with Ryömä, and offered to let the Society continue if Ryömä would moderate its tone, and purge it of communists.[61] At the same time the press was let loose in attacks on SNS in thinly veiled form, as a subversive and foreign-directed organization, which *Helsingin Sanomat* for instance lumped in with the black marketeers and the criminals behind a current crime wave, as enemies of national unity which could not be tolerated.[62] But to avoid offence to the USSR the SNS was never mentioned by name. It certainly had no intention of abating its campaign, in fact its activity now rose to its peak. On July 26, Zotov, the Soviet ambassador, went on a tour of SNS branches in the principal urban centres. On his way back he visited the Russian garrison in Hanko. Action quickly followed. The branches were circulated with draft resolutions which declared that the charges against Ryömä and Vilenius were a crude provocation against the USSR and called for the overthrow of the government which had authorized them. It was obviously intended to hold a series of public meetings at which these would be passed.

On July 29, the SNS tried to hold a meeting in Helsinki, but the police ordered it to disperse on the grounds that it failed to comply with the regulations, there were non-members present, and even foreigners, meaning two Soviet embassy officials. Vilenius, who was presiding, urged the members not to submit to police oppression and tried to organize a procession to march to the Soviet embassy. The police prevented this and a riot followed. In the following days the SNS caused almost daily street disorders in the capital by trying to hold illegal meetings.[63] The government issued a decree on August 1, forbidding meetings of more than 30 people without special permission. The press discreetly referred to the disturbances as caused by 'Hooligans', and fully supported the government's determination not to be intimidated by them. Ryömä and Vilenius were at once taken into preventive custody. The worst riot in Helsinki was on August 6, when the fire brigade turned hoses on the demonstration, and fires were lit. The biggest of all the disturbances was in Turku, where on August 7, the police had to open fire in order to disperse a riot which even fire-hoses could not control.[64] Thus the SNS, in an obviously concerted drive, openly challenged the authority of the government in the streets, and sought to undermine its authority. The attempt continued, though with diminishing success, until the middle of August. The general tone of the speeches at these occasions was openly threatening, with such remarks as 'things will be different in Finland in the autumn', and 'revenge will be bloody', and 'bombs will fall on Helsinki in a week or two'. There was talk in SNS circles of a coup. It was said that when the USSR had arranged the transits to Hanko, they would be used to seize communications centres at the same time as parachute troops were dropped. 'Many will wake up to the throbbing of aircraft engines: that will be the voice of freedom.'[65] It would be wrong to exaggerate the strength and organization of the SNS. The success of the riots depended to some extent on the participation of idlers and delinquents who had no aim beyond mischief making.[66] It is unlikely that there was in fact any plan for a coup concerted with the Russian forces, rather they seem to have been an attempt by the communists to shake public morale and test the strength of the government. There may have been hopes that the disorders would grow and turn into something more serious, but if that was the case, the communists miscalculated. The government showed no hesitation in face of the challenge. It is clear that the police were given a free hand to use all the force necessary, and certain military precautions were taken. Some reservists were recalled, and the garrison of Helsinki strengthened against the danger of parachute landings.[67]

The SNS must have placed their chief hope of success in the efficacy of Soviet intervention to protect them. The Soviet press and radio gave the whole business great prominence. Lurid descriptions were given of how brutally peaceful demonstrators were beaten and mishandled by the police.[68] The disorders were represented as an attempt by the oppressed and peace-loving Finnish workers to express their rejection of the anti-Soviet policies of a reactionary government. The Soviet embassy in Helsinki did all it could to encourage the SNS and protect it. Above all the Soviet government, on the diplomatic level, treated the business of the SNS as a trial of strength with the Finnish government, and sought to break its will to resist. The first private approaches to Paasikivi by Molotov were followed on August 1 by a public challenge. On that day Molotov addressed the Supreme Soviet.[69] When he came to the subject of Finland, Molotov conceded that the peace treaty had been carried out 'for the most part satisfactorily'. He then continued:[70]

'Considering the development of mutual relations between the USSR and Finland in a direction favourable to both countries, it must be affirmed that this depends chiefly on Finland. It must be understood that unless certain elements in Finnish governing circles cease their oppressive measures against those elements in society who are seeking to strengthen good neighbourly relations with the USSR, this could cause damage to the relations between Finland and the USSR.'

Thus Molotov announced in effect that the treatment of SNS would be used as a test of how far the Finnish government was prepared to conform to the will of the USSR. The government at once showed that on this point it would not yield. It meant to be master in its own capital. The proof of this came in the Finnish press, which was allowed to answer Molotov back, and declare firmly that he was obviously misinformed about the SNS.[71] The press consistently supported the government in its efforts to keep order. The day after Molotov's speech to the Supreme Soviet, he had an interview with Paasikivi. After they had discussed the current state of the Åland islands question and the Hanko transits, Molotov raised the matter of the SNS. The policy of the Finnish government proved its unfriendliness to the USSR. Further proof could be found in the fortifications which the Finns were building opposite Hanko. Paasikivi defended his government. Soviet press reports of SNS activities did not correspond with the facts. Paasikivi cited the threats being shouted at meetings, and suggested that no government could tolerate such conduct. 'Molotov appeared surprised and answered that such things could only have been shouted by provocateurs.'[72] The discussion was futile when neither side acknowledged the facts alleged by the other. At the close Molotov reverted to the subject of Tanner:

'. . . as long as Tanner is in the government nothing will come of constructing good relations between our countries. He opposes it . . . This matter is of course your own internal affair.'

Paasikivi answered, rather brusquely for him, 'it certainly is our own affair'. But Molotov insisted that he was speaking personally in this, 'as we are old acquaintances'. The ambassador was sufficiently moved by the interview to telegraph his government urging it to avoid open repression of SNS, and rely on 'spiritual means'. Fortunately the Finnish government had no illusions about the possibility of fighting a communist directed subversive movement by 'spiritual means'. They continued to rely on the strong arms of their police force. They also attempted to get some diplomatic support from Germany. On August 2, Witting called on Blücher, in a private capacity as he said. Alluding to the recent German intervention in the affairs of Romania and Hungary, he suggested that the Finnish and Swedish foreign ministers might be called to Berlin, presumably to get German blessing for a joint stand against any further Soviet move against Finland.[73] Alternatively, Witting and Ryti might come alone. Blücher reported to his government that he had heard from another source that the Finnish leaders would be prepared to agree to 'a considerable curtailment to the sovereignty of their country in favour of Germany.' In other words they would be prepared to accept some kind of German protectorate. Blücher thought that this was a great opportunity for Germany and urged his government to take it up.

The Swedish government was in fact highly alarmed at the plight of Finland, but had decided that it could only offer to help Finland with the approval of Germany. The Swedish ambassador in Berlin had been taking soundings on this at the foreign office but got no encouragement. Kivimäki too had been at the foreign office and got the same response. When the answer came to Witting's 'private' approach, on August 6, it too was negative. The time was not opportune for a visit to Berlin by the Swedish and

Finnish foreign ministers.[74] But Blücher was told, for his own information, that it 'is recognized here that the Finnish question is beginning to become somewhat more important than it seemed this summer.' These soundings of German policy showed that officially it remained as stated in Hitler's speech of July 19, but even the German Foreign Office now knew that changes might be coming. It could not yet, however, reveal anything of this to the Finnish government.

In holding firm to its decision to fight SNS and defy the Soviet pressures, the Finnish government got no encouragement from Berlin, and no comfort from Moscow. Paasikivi continued to urge that open suppression should be avoided. On August 6, he reported that he was sure the Soviet propaganda barrage concealed 'bad intentions against us', and on August 9, that if the SNS disturbances went on, 'we must reckon with the possibility of intervention from the Soviet side'.[75] But the government went on methodically with its work. Arrests continued until 50 of the leading organizers of SNS were in preventive detention. Tanner launched a new campaign in the Social Democratic party against adherents of the Wiik group and the SNS. On August 9, the government published an official account of what was happening. For the first time the public was told unambiguously that the SNS had deliberately provoked riots for political purposes, and how these had been dealt with by the police. They had also decided that in face of the situation there could be no question of making any concessions on the Hanko transit question. Paasikivi was told on August 9 that if the Russians would not make the necessary concessions to the Finnish point of view, 'we cannot do anything about it if the negotiations for an agreement lapse'.[76] They also worked energetically to keep up national morale. Mannerheim intervened to settle the argument about an ex-servicemen's organization. He had set up a committee to look into the question, and on August 4 it was announced that an entirely new body, the Suomen Aseveljien Liitto—the Finnish League of Comrades—would be established under the Marshal's patronage for all ex-soldiers.[77] The press hailed this as a positive victory for the cause of national unity. The government was also fighting alarmist rumours by a campaign intended to suggest that fundamentally Russo-Finnish relations were developing normally. It was the theme of this campaign that the SNS far from being a body which sought to improve relations, was only harming them. An editorial in *Suomen Sosiaalidemokraatti* on August 1 had developed this thesis, though at that stage without actually naming SNS. The answers to the Molotov speech carried the idea further, trying to write off what Molotov had said of SNS as the product of a misunderstanding which could be easily cleared up. On August 6, the government announced that it had set up a committee to report on how cultural and other relations with the USSR could be genuinely developed and improved.[78] On August 13, when the trade agreement with the USSR was formally ratified, all the press carried articles declaring that this showed how the relations of the two countries were really normal despite the flood of rumours. The tendency was to play down the crisis, rather than take the public into the government's confidence. Some people clearly objected to being treated in this way. *Uusi Suomi* felt it necessary on August 10 to defend the government's way of informing the public about events. It denied that there was any serious lack of relevant information in the papers. It went on:[79]

'Has any one of us really suffered harm because some affairs are related a little generally in our newspapers, even perhaps a little tardily? There is not the slightest need for our ordinary citizens to be continually worrying over all the general affairs of state.'

The paper urged its readers to stop talking politics and get on with their ordinary lives. In fact the government was more open with foreigners than it was with its own countrymen. Social security minister Fagerholm made a speech in Stockholm to assure the Swedish people that Finland was not going to collapse in face of the 'trojan horse' tactics of the communists. 'This plot against the nation's independence is not going to succeed'.[80] There were grounds for belief that the Swedish government and people stood in more need of assurance than the ordinary citizens of Finland. When Paasikivi passed through Stockholm on August 10, he found opinion there was worried, 'even despairing' about Finland.[81]

The wave of disquieting rumours about the intentions of the USSR was reaching its peak at this time.[82] The rumours were so persistent that the Germans too began to fear that some Russian stroke was imminent, a prospect they viewed with some dismay. The naval attaché in Helsinki sent in a gloomy report on August 4 that Finnish morale was wavering under pressure. A few days later reports from Lithuania spoke of 23 divisions with tanks facing Finland, and said that an ultimatum would be sent in the second half of the month. The ambassador in Helsinki was asked to follow up this report, and said that it might be true, but that whatever happened Finland would fight.[83] The military authorities were particularly concerned since they were among the few who knew that Finland might be of value in the next phase of the war. Halder noted three times in his diary that Finland seemed in danger, and even that August 15 would be the date of the ultimatum.[84] Eventually the military authorities asked the foreign office if it would not be possible to ask for restraint in Moscow. The reason given was that a new war might cut off nickel supplies, which would be a serious inconvenience. The foreign office, which was conscious that Finland had been assigned to the USSR sphere of influence, felt that the most they could do was to ask for information, thus showing concern. Finally on

August 12 the Swedish colonel Adlercreutz told the German military attaché in Stockholm, as a matter of urgency, that he had information of an imminent Soviet attack on Finland. It will be shown that the cumulative effect of these reports in Germany now began to produce action.

It can be assumed that the Finnish government in Helsinki got the same reports, or most of them. The lines of communication with Stockholm were many. They must have had the same difficulty as the historian does now in trying to interpret them. There seems no positive evidence to substantiate them, and much circumstantial evidence that suggests that this reading of Soviet intentions in August 1940 was mistaken. In fact the strength of the Soviet forces in line facing Finland varied very little in our period, being usually about 15 divisions. But this was only part of the military picture. The great imponderable was the huge Leningrad garrison, parts of which could have been turned against Finland at very short notice. Throughout the summer and early autumn of 1940 there were very extensive military exercises in the Leningrad military district. These were reported in the Soviet press and even on occasion in the Finnish press. It is possible that the troop movements arising out of these manœuvres fed the speculations about an attack on Finland. While the reports were at their most alarming, Paasikivi returned to Helsinki, and his presence was the occasion of a lengthy review of policy by the Finnish government. He had a series of conferences with Ryti, President Kallio, Witting, Mannerheim, and Tanner, as well as the foreign affairs committee of the cabinet. Out of these, and the subsequent debates, some important policy decisions emerged. Paasikivi recalled that he found the Finnish leaders 'very worried about the political situation, Mannerheim by no means the least worried'.[85]

Paasikivi's view was that there was no immediate danger of armed attack. He thought that events in the Balkans, and particularly German activity in Romania, were regarded as much more important than Finland in the eyes of the Soviet government. In consequence it was unlikely that they would wish to get involved in a full-scale war in Finland at such a time. Paasikivi believed that the open patronage of SNS by the USSR was so ostentatious that something would have to be done to appease them over this. He thought that by a policy of well-chosen concessions it might still be possible to work out a mutually acceptable relationship with the USSR, at least for a time. On the whole the government seems to have accepted Paasikivi's view, except that they were not ready to go so far in concession over SNS as he would have wished. Paasikivi had a long talk with his old friend Tanner. He revealed the implacable personal animosity of Molotov, and persuaded him to resign as a preliminary to a new effort at conciliation. Tanner's resignation was announced on August 15. The grounds given for it were his long period in office, and the need for him to attend to his duties as the chairman of Elanto, the great consumer co-operative organization. It was blandly asserted that the resignation had no political significance.[86] One or two socialist newspapers were so puzzled by the obvious falsity of these explanations that they alleged the reactionaries and enemies of the working class had driven Tanner out of the government, which was nearly the opposite of the truth.[87] Thus a major initial concession had been made to the Russian point of view. It is almost certain that the Soviet government lost rather than gained by this change. While Tanner had been in the government, his had been the most powerful voice against any tendencies to throw in Finland's lot with Germany unconditionally. Now that he was out of it, he threw all his formidable energies into rooting out communist subversion from the Social Democratic party and the co-operative and trade union movements, ensuring the defeat of all their efforts in this field. Characteristically, Tanner had told Paasikivi that although it would be fine to fight the SNS by 'spiritual' weapons, he fully believed in using the police where necessary.[88] Tanner had been fighting the communists for too long to harbour any illusions about how they could be defeated.

The next step was to send Paasikivi to sound out Zotov, and in particular to see if some compromise over SNS might be possible. The interview was a futile one. Zotov readily agreed that the peace treaty had settled most outstanding questions, and affirmed that the USSR had no wish to interfere in the internal affairs of Finland, a somewhat brazen assurance in view of what was just happening. Zotov agreed that on this basis it should be possible to construct good relations. The ambassador then went on to show how devoid of meaning all this was by taking up the question of SNS. He said that the government's new committee on developing cultural relations with the USSR was a welcome step, but it would have to work in co-operation with SNS. The USSR was particularly resentful of suggestions that SNS was a 'trojan horse', a fifth column.[89] Here the interview bogged down in failure, since the two sides could not agree about the sort of organization the SNS really was, and had no basis for constructive negotiation.

Parallel with this, the Finnish government continued its probes of German intentions. Kivimäki called at the foreign office in Berlin on August 14 to ask what attitude Germany would take up if the USSR did attack Finland. He was told that Germany's attitude would be the same as during the late war. Kivimäki then gave a warning that even so Finland would fight to the end.[90] It was desperately hoped that this threat of conflict, which would among other things cut the nickel supplies, might influence Germany. Witting had tried Blücher on the same topic on August 12, without response, and on August 16, Ryti sent for the German

ambassador, to tell him how pro-German sentiment was rising in all levels
of Finnish society, and probing for some encouraging reaction, but Blücher
could say nothing in reply.[91] The same day Witting had a call from Zotov,
which showed how difficult it was going to be to conciliate the USSR.
Zotov complained bitterly of the repression of SNS. What was worse, he
revealed that Tanner's resignation, far from pacifying him, had merely
whetted his appetite.[92] He complained that von Born, the minister of the
interior, and Fagerholm, minister for social security, were also obstacles to
good relations with the USSR. In particular Fagerholm's Stockholm
speech had been noted and was bitterly resented. It is almost uncanny
how the hostility of the USSR pitched on the more liberal members of the
government, the very men who were most likely to promote a moderate
foreign policy. However, since Germany would give no encouragement at
all, the government decided to persevere in a policy of concessions. But
they would not allow the SNS to continue subversive activity, nor allow
any more members of the government to be bullied into resignation, nor
yield any ground on the question of Hanko transits. On the positive side,
Paasikivi was sent back to Moscow armed with massive proof of the subversive nature of SNS, negotiations would be pursued to reach a compromise with its leaders, and Ryti would make a radio address to the nation
declaring that it was the policy of the government and the people of Finland to seek good neighbourly relations with the USSR, not just as a temporary expedient, but as the long-term foundation of Finnish policy.

By mid-August the government had plainly won its battle with SNS for
control of the streets. Some fifty of its leaders were under arrest and the
disorders had ceased. There is some evidence that the Soviet authorities
realized that they had been beaten and called off their men. The vigorous
propaganda campaign about SNS quite suddenly ceased towards the end
of the month. The Finnish government, having asserted its authority, was
now ready to come to terms. A negotiation was carried on with the imprisoned Ryömä, with the radical professor Ruutu acting as intermediary.
The government offered to grant legal registration to SNS if it would
accept two limitations on membership, that members be over 18 years of
age, and without a criminal record. The executive was allowed to meet
Ryömä and Vilenius in prison to discuss the offer, but it was rejected. The
government's intention was to keep out raw youths who would be easily
susceptible to indoctrination, and all members of the communist party,
since all who had been active communists in pre-war Finland were either
in exile, or had convictions for their activities. On this point the negotiation broke down, as had the similar effort a month earlier. The SNS explained publicly that it could not agree to the exclusion of youthful enthusiasts and everyone who had been in some kind of political trouble in

the past. But the government, and most commentators since, concluded that this refusal of the government's moderate terms was the proof of the Society's subversive intent. If the communist leaders could not be sure of keeping the SNS firmly under the party's control, and using it as a cover for their own activity, they preferred that it should not function legally at all. Hence the government went ahead with repression. The trial of Ryömä and Vilenius was allowed to proceed. The efforts of SNS to fight back became increasingly feeble. Those leaders who remained at liberty held a meeting at the end of August to organize a campaign of protest at the arrests. They went to call on Zotov, but it seems probable that Zotov made it clear that his government was disappointed with the performance of SNS, and was no longer prepared to support it on the old scale. At the same time the socialist campaign against SNS was stepped up. In particular, Hakkila, Speaker of the Eduskunta, made a major speech at Tampere on August 24, attacking SNS and its attempts to delude the workers. The socialist press joined in, and now said bluntly that the aim of SNS was to carry Finland along the same road as the Baltic states. It was true that SNS propaganda had scarcely made a secret of this, but it had not previously been publicly acknowledged. The verdict and sentence on Ryömä and Vilenius were announced on September 7. Both got nine months' imprisonment for publishing the letter to the Eduskunta, seeking to bring the government into contempt. The SNS now put in a formal request to be registered as a legal society, and on September 29 the request was finally rejected by the High Court. Its attempt in this same month to publish a new newspaper, *Kansan Sanomat*, failed. Two sample copies were produced, but after the second had been confiscated by the police, they had to give up. However, although refused registration as a lawful organization, SNS had not yet been declared an unlawful organization and there will be cause to note some of its subsequent activities.

On August 18, Ryti delivered a radio address to the nation which was mainly concerned with relations with the USSR. It was intended to be a public affirmation of the basic goodwill of the Finnish government towards the USSR, and to be the final and authoritative refutation of the wave of rumours that had so disturbed the public. The speech made two principal points. The first was that Finland accepted the Treaty of Moscow as final. This was addressed both to the USSR and the Finnish people. Ryti declared:[93]

'. . . we Finns are realists, we recognize facts and we start from the basis of existing conditions. So even the peace, hard as it was for Finland, has been, once it was concluded, accepted without reservation, and on the basis of it we have proceeded to create and develop good neighbourly relations.'

The second theme was how Finland had illustrated in deeds, that is by the various concessions she had made, that she wished to live in peace and friendship with the USSR. Ryti claimed that 'Finland has shown in action her honest desire, without prejudice, to seek to create the best possible relations'. Ryti cited the way in which Finland had met Soviet requirements over property in the ceded areas, over the Åland islands, and on the question of transits to Hanko as proofs of his assertion. He concluded by declaring that the whole Finnish people shared his government's desire for peace and friendship with the USSR. 'We are also convinced that the aim of the Soviet Union is the same'. This speech is riddled with dishonesty, and it is no surprise that it fooled nobody. First it represented as a positive desire something that was in fact a negative acceptance. It was quite true that Finland was prepared to observe the peace treaty, and make reasonable concessions to the USSR, and to seek closer cultural and economic ties. But she did this not because it was her 'honest desire', but because she could see no alternative to giving way before Soviet pressures. For instance, the Finnish government's readiness to concede some transit rights to Hanko did not prove Finnish goodwill. It proved the government's fears of the consequences if it refused, as balanced against its fears of the consequences if it accepted, had led to the conclusion that acceptance was the safer policy. The last sentence contained the second major dishonesty. The Finnish government did not believe that the USSR honestly sought good relations with it. On the contrary, and with every justification, it believed the opposite. The government of the USSR barely concealed the fact that it tolerated an independent Finland under its existing form of government with difficulty, and would gladly put an end to it if it could conveniently do so. It may be said with some confidence that the speech was a complete waste of effort. In so far as it was believed by the Finnish people it tended to mislead them. While in Moscow it got no credence at all.

This was what Paasikivi discovered when he saw Molotov on August 22. The two men then had what was probably their most significant conversation. Paasikivi was reporting on the results of his visit to Helsinki. He had with him a draft for a treaty on the Åland islands, which was put aside for later consideration. Then the ambassador launched into a long justification of his government's treatment of SNS. He explained the conditions which the Society would have to meet in order to be registered, and showed how large was the criminal element in the existing direction of the SNS. He produced detailed evidence of the provocative activity of SNS, and the slogans which had been shouted, and said that these were of a kind which no government could tolerate. Paasikivi could have saved his breath, since Molotov listened with obvious annoyance, he 'apparently did

not want to believe it'. Indeed it was probably a tactical mistake to have
mentioned the matter at all, for the signs are that the Soviet government
had already written off the SNS as of no immediate use, and would have
been ready to forget about it. Instead, Paasikivi's explanation led Molotov
into an attack on the theme that although the Finnish people naturally
wanted to live in peace with the USSR, Finland's 'ruling circles' did not.
Molotov declared:

'You are the only one who wants good relations between Finland and the
Soviet Union, but you are only a single person and you cannot achieve
your aim. The government is following a double policy, it proclaims its
acceptance of the peace treaty, but in the same governing circles it is said:
"There is not a Finn who accepts the Moscow peace".'

Paasikivi now referred to Ryti's speech, and asked who were these
'ruling circles'. Molotov refused to specify, but insisted that unfortunately
'my allegations are true'. He went on to complain of the way in which the
frontier was being fortified, and said that in the armed forces there was
deliberate inculcation of hatred of the USSR. There was not much
Paasikivi could say to this. It is difficult to deny that the building of fortifications does show an unfriendly spirit. As for the army, there is no
doubt that the officer corps was deeply imbued with feelings of hostility to
the USSR. It would have been surprising if they had not passed some of
this on to their men, particularly since fighting the USSR was the
army's sole purpose. However, Paasikivi urged that Mannerheim was certainly for 'good relations and peace', as he had been the previous autumn.
Molotov replied that he knew of the Marshal's attitude the previous
autumn, 'but how things are now I do not know'. But Molotov was not
finished. He said that the Finnish government was calculating that the
European war might take a turn favourable to themselves. Again he refused
to specify what he meant by this. Paasikivi replied that this was the first
time he had heard such an idea. If his answer was honest, he was quite un-
characteristically ill informed. The Finnish press was witness to the extent
of such speculation, if only by its repeated appeals to the public not to
indulge in them. It has been seen how the government was making repeated soundings of Germany's attitude in the hope of just such a change.
Molotov then got on to the subject of Tanner. His resignation was a blind,
he had only withdrawn 'into the shadows', and continued to work against
the improvement of relations. In addition von Born and Fagerholm had
made unfriendly speeches, attacking the USSR. Paasikivi referred to
Ryti's speech. Molotov acknowledged that he had heard of it, but 'Ryti
evaded the heart of the matter'. Again Molotov did not specify what he
meant by this. In taking his leave, Paasikivi fished for some crumb of
reassurance from Molotov. He stated that the government's policy was

9

based on Molotov's own assurances that the Treaty of Moscow had
settled all outstanding issues between the two governments. Paasikivi
expected Molotov to confirm that this was so, but 'Molotov did not answer
anything to this'.[94] It is worth noting that Molotov had said many of the
same things to the Swedish ambassador in Moscow a few days earlier. In
particular he had accused the Finnish government of playing a double
game, and mentioned the fortifications as proof of this, though he had
added that the USSR would be 'very patient towards Finland'.[95]

Paasikivi was most upset by his reception. He had returned to Moscow
hoping to make a fresh start towards better relations, and had been virtually told that better relations were impossible with the existing Finnish
government. Paasikivi concluded that the USSR was so upset about the
SNS because it had really hoped to use it to produce in Finland the same
results as in the Baltic states. In spite of this he urged his government to
continue along the path of conciliation. They must try to legalize the
SNS, they must watch their own tongues, they must find out if anyone in
the army was guilty of careless talk, they must educate the nation to accept
the Moscow peace. But Paasikivi was no longer very confident that even
this would save his country, it would merely give her a clear conscience if
she were attacked. In desperation he urged the government to try Sweden
once more. If it were known in Moscow that in a new war, Sweden would
intervene on the Finnish side, 'I think the Soviet Union would leave us in
peace'.[96]

The unusual bluntness with which Molotov spoke on August 22 gives
grounds for an attempt to assess the policy of the Soviet Union towards
Finland in July and August 1940, and in particular the significance of the
SNS episode. The Soviet government was certainly highly angered by the
repression of the Society, and attached the greatest significance to this.
But it is difficult to accept the superficially attractive thesis that the activities of SNS were part of a careful and deliberate plan by the USSR to
create such a state of weakness and disorder in Finland that a virtually
bloodless takeover by the Red Army would become possible during
August. Most Finns including in the end Paasikivi himself inclined to take
this view. But it seems inconsistent with the other actions of the Soviet
government. There is the apparent lack of any suitable military preparations
during the critical period during the first 10 days of August. More solid
objections are the seriousness with which Molotov pursued his demands
on the Åland islands question, the request for the Petsamo nickel concession, the Hanko transit agreement, and the resignation of Tanner. These
demands would have been superfluous if there had been any serious intention or expectation of taking Finland over within a few weeks of their
being presented. It is more probable that the Soviet leadership had the

more realistic objective of building up in Finland, under cover of SNS, a firm organizational framework for the Finnish communist party, with a view to the future. It would then have been analogous to the setting up of the Karelian-Finnish republic under Kuusinen. A strong SNS under communist direction would come in useful when, and if, it were decided to proceed to the total solution of the Finnish question. But when it became apparent that the Finnish government would resist the development of SNS, an attempt was made to force it to desist from such opposition. It is possible that the local leaders of SNS, and ambassador Zotov, who had personally taken up their cause with such zeal, led the Soviet government to believe that some much bigger success could be achieved, perhaps even a 'Baltic' solution in Finland, or at least the downfall of the existing government, if only they were granted diplomatic and propaganda backing. If this were so, the Soviet government had become completely disillusioned by the second half of August.

The remarks of Molotov on August 22, and of ambassador Zotov to Paasikivi earlier, indicate that by that stage the main significance of the SNS episode was that it had become the yardstick by which the USSR measured the 'goodwill' of the Finnish government. By 'goodwill' they understood the readiness of the Finnish government to meet without qualification all the requests made to it by the government of the USSR, in short to acknowledge that it belonged completely to the sphere of influence of the USSR. By this yardstick the Finnish government stood clearly revealed as lacking in goodwill. Consequently its public professions of peaceful intent and a desire for better relations with the USSR meant only that it was playing a double game. It was further apparent that Molotov could not conceive that they would do this unless they had some promise, or strong expectation, of support from an outside power, which in the circumstances could only be Germany. It was probably inconceivable to Molotov that the Finnish government would dare to defy him without such support. It has been shown that he was wrong on this point. The Finnish government had indeed done everything it could to induce Germany to make some gesture in its favour, but without success. Yet it still chose to defy the USSR. It was true that the Finnish government was well aware that to fight the USSR in isolation would lead to the country's destruction. But despite what Ryti said about the Finns being realists, they also had a strong idealist-romantic strain in their make up. They genuinely thought death preferable to dishonour, preferred to risk having to go down fighting rather than submit to live in bondage. There was always the hope that something would turn up. Later on, a phrase was coined to describe this attitude, sankarillinen itsemurhe—heroic suicide—and this irrational element in Finnish policy-making deceived Molotov. Apart from this

irrational factor, Molotov's reasoning was correct. The willingness of the
Finnish government to meet the requirements of the USSR did generally
depend on its hopes of getting some outside support.

It is highly likely that the episode of the SNS brought about a major
reappraisal of the Soviet policy on Finland. It appears that up to the end
of July 1940, the government of the USSR had assumed that the Finnish
government, though fundamentally hostile, was sufficiently afraid and
isolated to be amenable to Soviet pressures. Now by the end of August
1940, they knew that it was not only hostile, but felt able to translate hostility into open defiance. This being so, it would have to be disciplined
or destroyed as soon as possible. It could obviously not be undermined
from within the country. Control would have to be reasserted as a result
of direct pressure from outside, and this could not be done until it was
known how extensive was the foreign support which the Finnish government enjoyed, and steps had been taken to cut it off. This was the next
phase of Russian policy. For as usual, the Soviet government had succeeded in driving Finland into doing precisely what they accused her of
having done already. If the tone and content of Molotov's conversation on
August 22 had convinced Paasikivi that in the end the USSR intended to
terminate Finland's independence, it may be imagined that the government in Helsinki was reinforced in a conviction which most of its members
had held since the war, and some long before that. They would certainly
redouble their efforts to find outside support as Paasikivi recommended,
and Sweden was not their only hope.

CHAPTER 7

Germany intervenes

The series of events which is now to be described turned out to be the most important occurrence in the period with which this book is concerned. There is a fairly clear account of them from the German side, but a much less satisfactory one from the Finnish. Two of the major Finnish participants, Walden and Witting, died without leaving any record of their side of the story. For this reason alone the whole truth may never be known. Mannerheim gave his version of events both in 1945, and later in his memoirs, and both are manifestly unsatisfactory. Ryti gave an explanation at his trial, in 1945, which cannot be reconciled at all points with Mannerheim's, nor with the German evidence. Further, nearly all Finnish attempts to describe the way in which Finland came to give to Germany the right to transport men and materials for her garrison in northern Norway through the north of Finland are vitiated by a contradiction in their thinking. The pattern was established by Mannerheim in his memoirs. At one point he sought to argue that the agreements made with Germany in September 1940 were so limited in scope and importance that they were not inconsistent with a continued policy of neutrality between Germany and the USSR. At another point he gives the impression that once Finland had concluded these agreements, and he asserts that she had no choice in the matter, her government lost control of events, so that what followed was manifest destiny. There is, therefore, no entirely satisfactory Finnish version of what happened. One can only claim for the account which follows that it seeks to take into consideration all the evidence that has so far come to light.

It has been shown that Hitler's decision of July 31, 1940, that preparations should begin for a spring campaign against the USSR, in case the invasion of Britain proved impractical, had no immediate effects for Finland. The German leaders assumed that Finland would be involved in such a campaign, but her role was always a subsidiary one. On the other hand, any attempt to intervene in Finland would be a flagrant violation of the pact with the USSR, and would necessarily involve serious consequences for Germany. All that Germany had done, in reaction to the renewed Soviet pressure on Finland, was to insist that her share of the nickel output from the Petsamo mines must be safeguarded. This had been laid down on June 26, and several diplomatic contacts with the USSR had followed. It had been determined that Germany's minimum requirement was an assurance that she would receive 60% of the output for an indefinite period. The Soviet government had proved evasive, giving no more than a vague assurance of willingness to share the output.[1] But throughout these exchanges there had been no suggestion that Germany was seeking to intervene between Finland and the USSR or in any way to trespass on the exclusive rights of the latter over Finland.

   A decision to intervene in Finland, and violate the German-Soviet treaty, was of such importance that it could only be taken by Hitler himself. It cannot now be known exactly when or why Hitler became convinced that it was necessary to prop up Finland against Russian pressure. Presumably the flood of reports about a Russian ultimatum and invasion of Finland were important factors. Information was being collected at the beginning of August about the possibility of selling arms to Finland. A Finnish businessman, W. Hilbert, who was known to be interested in buying arms, was urged to go to Berlin, and was questioned about the sort of equipment most urgently needed by Finland. The decision to intervene had certainly been made by August 10. Part of it was communicated by Keitel to Weizsäcker, permanent head of the foreign office, on August 12. Finland was to be encouraged to hold out against Soviet pressure by permitting her to buy arms from Germany. It was hoped that this could be kept entirely secret by using Sweden as the channel through which the arms would be despatched. The same day Halder learned that Hitler had sent for a report on the Finnish armed forces, and the German intelligence service submitted a political report on Finland.[2] This gave the impression of a Finland eager to enter the German camp. Ryti, who had been a noted anglophile, was described as entirely changed since July. Witting was enthusiastically pro-German. Finnish morale was good, public feelings strongly pro-German, while anti-democratic sentiments were fast gaining ground. The report claimed that any Finn, if asked, would agree that he would prefer his country to be a German protectorate rather than go on living at the mercy of the USSR.[3] It will be shown later that this report was of as much, or as little value as are most intelligence reports on the political feelings of foreign countries. It tells less about the country itself than about what its compilers thought their employers wanted to hear. But it would have encouraged Hitler in his new policy.

   On August 13, Hitler returned to Berlin and active measures were taken to execute his decision over the following days. Conferences were held

GERMANY INTERVENES 135

with the military chiefs, including von Falkenhorst, the commander in Norway, on the first aspect of the policy which was military. The far north of Norway was to be garrisoned much more strongly by the German mountain brigade, and some airforce units. In the event of a new Russian attack on Finland, this garrison would move into the Petsamo area and secure the nickel mines. Hitler explained that he wanted a speedy supply of arms to Finland, 'as he did not wish to deliver Finland into the arms of the Russians.'[4] The execution of this aspect of the new policy was largely put into the hands of Göring. On August 14, Hitler, Göring, and Colonel Joseph Veltjens had a meeting at which Veltjens was told that he had been chosen as the ambassador who would explain the new policy to the Finnish leaders. Veltjens was a retired airforce colonel, an old personal friend of Göring, who then held a high position in the administration of Göring's Four Year Plan for the German economy. Veltjens had also been active in the arms trade for many years and had a keen interest in Finland, where he had many friends. He had tried to supply arms to Finland during and after the war, but the German government had forbidden it, in accordance with its treaty with the USSR. Thus Veltjens was an obvious choice for this mission.[5]

He was told that the new policy was intended to strengthen the German position in north Norway and to safeguard the nickel supply from Petsamo. Absolute secrecy was essential, and Veltjens was authorized to speak only with Mannerheim, while what he had to say must not be communicated to anybody outside the inner circle of the Finnish government. The maintenance of secrecy was a condition, without which the business could not proceed. Veltjens was authorized to offer to sell arms to Finland, and to release or replace those stores belonging to Finland, which had been held up in Norwegian ports after the German invasion. In return, and as a condition of the sale of arms, Germany wanted to send a limited number of airforce men, and some equipment to Norway through Finnish territory. Later on, Germany might also wish to send leave-men to and from northern Norway by the same route. By these measures, Hitler expected to give Finland enough encouragement to enable her to resist Soviet pressure.

There were several advantages in supplying the far north of Norway through Finland. There was neither road nor railway up the whole length of Norway, although the construction of a road was about to begin. Sea communications were made difficult by lack of shipping, at a time when everything was earmarked for the invasion of Britain, and by possible British interference. It was both safer and quicker to send men and materials to Finnish ports on the Gulf of Bothnia, whence they could go by rail to Rovaniemi, and on by road to Ivalo. From there it would be easy to improve the existing rudimentary tracks to Kirkenes. The route was so attractive that by August 22 Halder was wondering whether a whole army division could be sent that way.[6] Unfortunately there were two limitations on the route. One was the limited capacity of Finnish railways. Single tracking, low-powered, wood-burning locomotives, lack of rolling stock, and the necessity of not interrupting Finnish civil traffic, imposed severe limits on the amount of men and materials that could be sent. The other limiting factor was political. It might be possible to conceal small transits from the USSR for a time, or at least to represent them as of no significance. But to send a whole division would be an altogether different thing, and a most blatant infringement of the Russo-German pact. As it was, the concentration of German forces at Kirkenes was bound to be interpreted by the USSR as a hostile act, as Halder noted in his diary.[7] Since Hitler was most anxious to prevent any premature breach with the USSR, this factor alone dictated that only small transits could be sent.

On August 15, Veltjens called at the Finnish embassy in Berlin. He outlined the nature of his mission to the ambassador, Kivimäki, stressed the need for secrecy, and asked for a letter of introduction to Mannerheim.[8] Kivimäki willingly complied and a letter was sent by the hand of Baron Wrede, a Swedish diplomat, who was to deliver it personally. It was followed by a copy to Witting. The exact contents are not known, but it certainly announced the purpose of Veltjens' mission, and stressed that it must be kept secret from all but the inmost circles in Finland. On August 17, Veltjens flew to Finland, and Kivimäki sent telegrams to Mannerheim and Witting asking them to meet Wrede at Helsinki airport on the following morning.

Veltjens was taken to Hilbert's summer villa, and there he had a series of conversations with Hilbert and with M. V. Terä, a retired staff officer who was Hilbert's associate. Veltjens told them that the German leaders were convinced that the USSR planned to absorb Finland, and that Hitler had decided that if the attempt was made Finland should not be left to face the attack alone. He spent considerable time stressing the need for secrecy, and insisted that on no account must the Eduskunta or even the whole of the government get to know about his mission. Veltjens outlined his instructions and asked for advice on how best to approach Mannerheim. He was apprehensive that Mannerheim, as an officer and a gentleman, might not like discussing so vulgar a topic as the sale of arms. He was assured that Mannerheim would have no such prejudices, but warned that the Marshal would probably decline to give a decision on the transit question, since this was clearly political, and a matter for the government. Veltjens was advised not to make the transit question a condition of the sale of arms, as this might create difficulties with Mannerheim. In the course of these discussions Veltjens said that Germany's primary interest was to safeguard her nickel supply, and various ways of countering the current Russian demand for the concession were canvassed. Veltjens also maintained that the request for transit rights was mainly a political gesture to encourage Finland, but he added that the Germans would be glad of the opportunity it would offer to get acquainted with the area and assess the military possibilities there.[9]

Kivimäki's proposal that Mannerheim should meet Wrede at the airport on August 18 suited the Marshal very well, since he was due to fly to Jyväskylä that morning. He had invited Walden and Heinrichs to accompany him and they were joined by Witting. Wrede duly arrived and handed over the letter, which the Marshal suggested Heinrichs might read out, but noting that it was not to be shown to anyone other than himself, Walden, and Witting, he asked Heinrichs and Wrede to take a little walk while the letter was read. These two had to stroll up and down for some time before Mannerheim called Heinrichs over. He remarked that the letter had been 'truly interesting—even significant', but he was not at liberty to reveal its contents. He would return from Jyväskylä that evening, and a meeting with Veltjens was arranged.[10] Veltjens unfolded his propositions to Mannerheim, and when the latter was satisfied that the proffered arms would be suitable for Finland's needs, he willingly accepted the offer to sell. This he had every right to do, since arms purchase was now the legal responsibility of the commander in chief. But on the question of transit rights Mannerheim said he could not give an answer, since it was a political question which the government must decide. He suggested that Veltjens might approach Witting, but Veltjens insisted that he was only authorized to speak with Mannerheim, and further that he must be able to send a simple 'yes' or 'no' to Göring by August 20 at the latest. The Marshal then agreed to contact Ryti and give Veltjens his answer in the morning.

Mannerheim says that he did telephone Ryti that evening, and that Ryti authorized him, by telephone, to agree to the grant of transit facilities. Ryti always denied this, even said that he was in the country that evening and not on the telephone. Since this was the evening when he made his radio address to the nation, his story seems unlikely. Ryti was certainly in Helsinki the next day, and had a meeting with Veltjens, which later seems to have escaped his memory altogether. It seems most probable that Mannerheim did have a conversation with Ryti on the evening of August 18, that Mannerheim indicated that he thought the German request should be granted, and that Ryti agreed with him. Ryti never denied that he thoroughly approved of the decision, even though he could not remember taking part in the making of it. The next morning Veltjens was told that the answer was 'yes'. In this way the fatal decision was taken. It seems that the responsibility must rest with Mannerheim. For form's sake he had felt bound to consult Ryti, for Mannerheim liked to preserve the fiction that he was only a soldier, and did not interfere in politics. But everything that is known about him and his relations with the government suggests that his recommendation, however phrased, would decide an issue like this. There could be no question of Ryti making a decision of such importance if he did not know that Mannerheim was in agreement with it. In all the discussion that has gone on over who made the decision, it tends to be overlooked that neither Mannerheim, nor Ryti, had any legal right to say yes or no to the German request. The only man in Finland who had such a right was president Kallio and it is most probable that he was never consulted. There could not be a more striking demonstration of the nominal character of Kallio's presidency in the period after Mannerheim, Ryti, and Walden had taken up positions of authority. Whatever the wisdom of the decision of August 18, it was flagrantly unconstitutional. There is no reason to think that Kallio would have objected. It was simply that nobody thought to ask him.

On August 19, after receiving his answer from Mannerheim, Veltjens went on to see Ryti, Witting, and Walden. Ryti impressed on him, as had Mannerheim earlier, that if Finland was attacked she would fight to the end. Veltjens thought that they were angling for some official response to this, but he declined to be drawn. Instead he urged the importance of playing for time with the USSR. The more time that could be won, the better it would be for Finland.[11] The problem of the nickel concession was discussed, and Ryti offered to give Germany any guarantees she wanted, and suggested that Germany might ask for a right of pre-emption over any mineral concessions in Finland to block the Soviet claim. When Veltjens saw Witting, he stressed that Finland must not use the fact of his mission for diplomatic support against the USSR. Witting expressed alarm about the nickel question, and suggested hopefully that Germany might 'force' Finland to transfer the concession to her. Veltjens discouraged all such notions. Finally Witting said he would send a telegram to Göring, through Kivimäki, stating simply that Finland's answer to the German propositions was 'yes'. The meeting with Walden was a business meeting, and the practical details of the arms purchase scheme were worked out.[12] At the same time, in Berlin, Kivimäki discovered that the German foreign office had caught up with a part of the new development. The ambassador and the head of a Finnish economic delegation were received by Ribbentrop. The foreign minister solemnly announced that Germany had now decided to sell arms to Finland. The German report of the meeting notes that 'the discussion made a deep impression on the Finnish gentlemen.'[13] Kivimäki at least must have been an actor, since he had known about this, and something more, since the time of Veltjens' call at his embassy. Probably he felt it would have been undiplomatic to spoil Ribbentrop's enjoyment by revealing that his news was already stale.

The Germans spent the rest of August in the vigorous implementation of the new policy. On August 26, the plan for the seizure of the Petsamo region in the event of a new Russo-Finnish war was discussed with the army chiefs. Halder noted in exasperation that this was yet another call on his overstretched resources, but the plan was pushed ahead under the code name 'Renntier'.[14] By the beginning of September it was ready. The question of arms deliveries to Finland was given high priority. Göring told Thomas on August 29 that orders had gone out to give especially favourable consideration to Finland's requirements, particularly because at the moment 'Finland is ready to make any concessions'.[15] Hitler took an active interest, discussing the matter with Göring on August 30, and with Halder the following day. Hitler said that he had decided not to allow any further advance to the west by the USSR, and that was why the arms deliveries were so urgent. He told Halder that they would include a lot of first-class material. Hitler had also decided that he would inform the USSR of what he was doing in order to warn her off making any move against Finland. However the information would be carefully veiled, the arms deliveries would be represented as confined to the release of material held in the Norwegian ports, and the transits as dictated by the British threat to north Norway.[16]

The Finns were equally active. On August 22, Colonel Raatikainen left for Berlin with a list of the arms that Finland wished to buy. Mannerheim appointed a committee of three officers, General Talvela, Lt.-Colonel Stewen, and Commodore Sundman, who were to be directly responsible to himself, and were to work out the transit arrangements with the Germans. In the middle of this activity, president Kallio was eliminated from any active participation in events. On August 20, the president had a mild stroke. This did not prevent him attending a cabinet meeting in Helsinki on August 23. It has been assumed that since Ryti and Walden were present, they must have told him about Veltjens' mission and the decision that had followed, though there is no proof of this. Kallio returned to his summer residence, and on August 28 he was due to receive Mannerheim, Ryti, and Walden for lunch. It has been widely assumed that this high-powered triumvirate did not intend to pay a simple social call, but must have had some more serious purpose. The most plausible guess is that the visit was in some way connected with the German transit agreements, though some have gone so far as to allege that the three intended to call for Kallio's resignation so that formal power could be transferred to those who already held it in fact. Whatever the purpose of the visit it was

frustrated. On August 27, Kallio had a severe stroke, which left him par-
tially paralysed, and from which he never recovered fully. Kallio was able to
appear with his guests to be photographed, but that was all. Two days
later it was announced that because of Kallio's incapacity, the presidential
powers would be exercised by Ryti. In this way, the supreme power of the
Mannerheim-Ryti-Walden-Witting group became complete in law as well
as fact.

On August 29, General Talvela and Colonel Stewen were sent to Berlin
to draw up the actual transit agreement. It took some days, since at one
point Talvela and a German officer had to fly to Lapland to survey part of
the route, and the agreement was signed on September 12. Although the
agreement, usually referred to as the 'military' transit agreement, carried
far-reaching political implications for Finland it was in form a simple
working arrangement between the Finnish General Staff and the German
Air Staff, and was signed by Stewen and a German major.[17] It is not clear
whence Talvela and Stewen derived their authority to agree to the passage
and stationing of German troops on Finnish territory, an authority which
only the cabinet, acting through the president, could confer. They had
their military orders from Mannerheim, and seem also to have had verbal
instructions from Walden as minister of defence, but that was all. It must
be assumed that ultimately their right to conclude this agreement was held
to derive from the assent which Mannerheim and Ryti had given to Veltjens, an assent which they had had no legal right to give. Certainly the
making of such an agreement in such a way seems subversive of the basic
rights of the constitutional authorities. The agreement of September 12
does not touch at all on political or legal questions, it was entirely concerned with the technical arrangements for the transits. There were to be
three of these, and the first would travel in Finnish shipping from German
harbours on September 18, and arrive in Finland on September 22. The
others would follow at intervals, concluding in mid-October. The arrangements for the journey were set out in great detail, what rolling stock Finland would provide, where hot tea would be served, what billets would be
provided, and how they would be equipped. The Germans were to be conveyed in sealed trains to Rovaniemi, and would then march to Ivalo, and
after a rest there, move on into Norway. From the point of view of the
future the most important provisions were those which permitted the
Germans to set up camps and depots on the route. The most important
would be at Vaasa and at Rovaniemi. At the latter place, proper barrack
accommodation was to be built, in addition to the tented camp for the men
passing through. At Ivalo there would be a large supply dump. The number of Germans manning these posts would be about 1,100.

This base apparatus seemed disproportionate for its stated purpose.

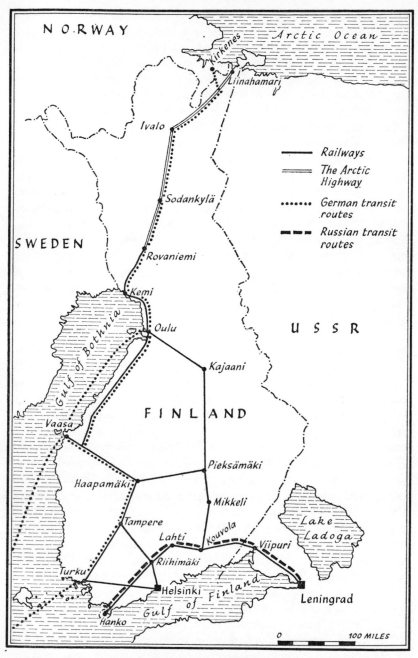

Map to illustrate the transit agreements between Finland and Germany and
Finland and the USSR

The three transits provided for in the agreement involved about 5,000 men altogether. To facilitate this a line of bases was set up manned by over 1,000 men. This suggests that from the beginning the Germans had in mind the possibility of much larger movements. This is more likely since the number of men who eventually established themselves on Finnish soil was 2,200, nearly double what was provided for in the agreement.[18] The significance of these facts would have been obvious to the Finnish military experts who dealt with the matter. From the German point of view this was a very satisfactory way of arranging things. It gave them all they needed for the present, it opened the way for future developments, but it committed them to nothing. In theory the whole arrangement could be wound up in October after the third group had passed through. It was possible to represent the agreement as temporary and of minor significance.

It is interesting to compare the easy informality which marked the conclusion of the German transit agreement with the parallel proceedings over the other transit agreement, the one permitting the USSR to send troops to Hanko. When Paasikivi had raised the matter after his return to Moscow, Molotov had at once agreed that the troops and their weapons could travel in separate wagons. Paasikivi had to say that this was not enough, but that they must go in separate trains. He explained that the agreement would have to be passed by the Eduskunta, and would hardly get through unless this provision was included. Paasikivi then offered a draft of an agreement to this effect. Molotov's reaction was mild, he agreed to consider the draft. Within a few days, Molotov informed Paasikivi that his government accepted the Finnish proposals and the agreement was signed on September 6.[19] In addition to the provision about separating troops and weapons, it provided that the timetable should be so arranged that no more than three Russian trains should be on Finnish territory at the same time. In spite of these safeguards, the Finnish government had held earnest debates on whether the agreement could be made to comply with both Finnish and international law. Because of possible doubts about this, it was decided not to send it for formal ratification by the Eduskunta, but only to communicate the terms to its foreign affairs committee. The agreement would be confirmed under the presidential powers by an exchange of notes.[20] The foreign affairs committee was presented with the agreement by Witting on September 13. Most members thought that the agreement should have gone to the Eduskunta, and they only agreed to accept the government's action by a majority of one vote.[21]

The tough bargaining, and the anxiety over legal and constitutional aspects, which marked the passage of the Hanko transit agreement are entirely absent from the negotiations over German transit rights. Yet the

German transits involved much more serious infringements of Finnish law and of Finland's neutral status. Germany was a belligerent power, while the USSR was a neutral. The Russian troops would pass through in their sealed trains, and never set foot on Finnish territory, and they would be unarmed the whole time they were crossing it. The German troops, once they had detrained at Rovaniemi, would march with their weapons through Finnish territory, while in addition there would be the German camps along the route, manned by armed soldiers. No attempt had been made to clothe the German agreement in constitutional covering, much less was there any thought of submitting it to the Eduskunta for approval. Indeed, the Finnish government never even saw the text of the agreement. Only five copies were made, and all of the three retained by Finland remained in the hands of the military authorities. Ryti declared at his trial that he had never set eyes on the military transit agreement, and this was almost certainly true.

The contrasts in the making of these two agreements are certainly striking, but in the circumstances they are entirely natural. The Finns, from Mannerheim downwards, believed that the USSR intended their destruction in the near future. Their belief was correct as will be seen. No other explanation of their behaviour is needed. In such circumstances they had to accept any assistance that was going, and as the Germans had observed were in a mood to grant any concessions. So that if it suited the Germans, as it undoubtedly did, to proceed in a secret and informal manner, then Finland would oblige them. The obvious disproportion of the German base apparatus did not worry them in the slightest. On the contrary, the more Germans who could be persuaded to settle on Finnish territory the better. Each German soldier was an additional hazard in the way of a Russian attack. The Finnish government wanted the German stake in Finland to be the biggest possible. They were not fools, they knew that Germany was using them for her own ends, and that there would be a price to be paid, but the situation was such that they could not stop to consider the cost. The noted historian, Professor Korhonen, has remarked of this episode that if the angel Gabriel comes down from heaven offering gifts, you do not hold meetings to consider the offer, you accept.[22] Colonel Halsti, a senior Finnish officer, expressed this feeling in his diary:[23]

'The one miracle which could carry us through this autumn and winter without a fresh aggression has happened. It remains to be seen what the price is going to be but it cannot be greater than total destruction.'

The feelings of ordinary people were expressed, in words which could perhaps have been better chosen, by a Finnish lady to the British ambassador. The ambassador had reproached Finland for letting in German troops. She replied:[24]

'Die Finnen nehmen jeden Deutschen mit offenen Armen auf. Das tue ich auch. Je mehr deutsche Soldaten ins Land kommen, desto ruhiger lege ich mich abends zu Bett.'*

There is no cause for surprise that two rather similar requests from Germany and the USSR had been met in Finland with such different responses, nor that all the constitutional proprieties had not been observed. When a nation feels that its very existence is at stake, niceties of international law and constitutional practice tend to be pushed aside. But it was quickly realized in both Finland and Germany that the contrast, and the irregularities, were too striking to be ignored. On the German side, the only worry was how to present their action in such a way that it might seem consistent with the Russo-German pact, or at least that the breaches involved might be explained away as of slight significance. Hitler was already convinced that his actions had produced the results he desired. He told a conference of military chiefs on September 14 that the USSR was afraid of Germany's military might, and that 'this realization has already had a restraining effect on Russian actions against Finland'.[25] Again on September 26, Hitler declared that there was no probability of any developments between Finland and the USSR during the rest of the year for the same reason.[26] In fact, Hitler was deluding himself, there had been no sign of a relaxation of Russian pressure. On the contrary, at this very time the Soviet government had re-opened the Petsamo nickel question in a more forceful way, as the German government had been informed. But Hitler was not a man to let awkward facts disturb his outlook. As far as he was concerned, all that needed to be done over the Finnish question was to devise a plausible account of Germany's action. This was left to the German foreign office and Ribbentrop. When the date of the landing of the first German troops in Finland was known to be September 22, Ribbentrop sent instructions to his ambassador in Moscow.[27]

The ambassador was to find an excuse for calling on Molotov on the evening of September 21, and 'verbally and casually, preferably while engaged on another errand', tell him that in order to meet English threats, some anti-aircraft units were being sent through Finland into northern Norway. Both the extent of the transits and their route were wildly misrepresented. The ambassador was to conclude by saying that 'we are anxious to inform the Soviet government of this step in advance'. He was to urge the USSR to keep the matter a secret. Korhonen has remarked that 'in this announcement the truth was used so sparingly, that it almost amounted to a contempt.'[28] Molotov was bound to realize almost immediately that not only was the exclusive interest of the USSR in Finland

*'The Finns receive all Germans with open arms. I do too. The more German troops enter the country, the calmer I am when I go to bed in the evening.'

Mannerheim taking leave of President Kallio on Helsinki railway station a few minutes before the latter's death

President Ryti (*left*) and Prime Minister Rangell opening the subscriptions for the reconstruction loan

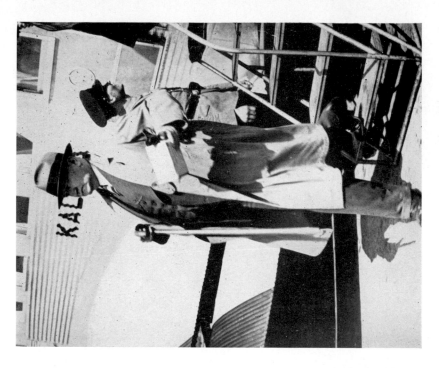

R. Walden

Mannerheim talking to a blinded ex-serviceman

being flagrantly disregarded, but that the Germans attached such small importance to this that they were satisfied to inform him of it through a blatant and unconcealed string of falsehoods. Further the notice that he was given was so short that he was really being faced with an accomplished fact. The whole proceeding reflected Hitler's conviction that the USSR was too frightened of Germany to make any protest. At the same time, Blücher was instructed to tell the Finnish government, on September 21, the terms of the announcement to Molotov. This was done so that whatever lies the Finnish government was proposing to tell would not clash too obviously with Ribbentrop's own. This concluded the formalities over the transit agreement as far as Germany was concerned.

But on the Finnish side there was a sudden consciousness that perhaps the military transit agreement was an excessively informal way of arranging so important a matter. Kivimäki may have been the first to draw his government's attention to the fact that very shortly German troops would be landing in Finland, that this was bound to be noticed, and that it would be thought very strange if such a development was not covered by some kind of agreement between the two governments.[29] The Finnish government, or rather the circle of ministers who knew about the affair, saw the point and took the necessary steps. The military authorities were consulted about what sort of terms should be proposed, since they alone knew what was in the military agreement already concluded. One point of advice which they gave is known. On a copy of the military transit agreement there is a note by Heinrichs which runs, 'referring to the Hanko transit agreement and its corresponding provisions we must demand that soldiers and weapons be transported in different trains'. This was reflected in the first instructions to Kivimäki that an agreement should be based on the terms of the Hanko transit agreement. The following day the instructions were amplified, and he was told that the agreement should specify what ports were involved, the number and dates of sailings, the base organization to be set up in Finland, and the notice to be given of the arrival of transits at Finnish ports.[30]

It was not until September 20 that Kivimäki managed to raise the matter with the German foreign office.[31] According to his own account, he was received by Grundherr, one of the senior officials, who professed that he was 'struck with amazement' to hear that German troops would land in Finland on September 22, and expressed disbelief. State secretary Weizsäcker was reached by telephone, and professed equal ignorance. It is just possible that Ribbentrop, who did know the date, had neglected to inform his subordinates, since he did not expect any diplomatic action would be called for, other than his instructions to Moscow and Helsinki. Kivimäki made it clear that his government was mainly concerned with keeping up appearances, and appearing to treat Germany and the USSR on an equal footing. Kivimäki then outlined what he thought the agreement should contain, as he had been instructed. The suggestion was not welcome to the Germans. Weizsäcker did draft a form of note to be exchanged between the two governments, but when Kivimäki returned to the foreign office on September 21, he was told that the matter was really too insignificant to merit such treatment, and he telegraphed to Witting that Germany appeared to be unwilling to make such an agreement. However, there must have been a misunderstanding somewhere, for later the same day Kivimäki was shown Weizsäcker's draft note. He pointed out that the draft spoke of 'northern Baltic ports' as the places of arrival for the transits, when it should have said ports in the Gulf of Bothnia. Grundherr agreed that this was a mistake, but declined to correct it. Korhonen is inclined to think that this curious incident showed a German desire to keep open the possibility of landing in southern Finland. Finally, on September 22, when Kivimäki and his wife were having tea with Weizsäcker the ambassador was taken into a corner and offered the note to sign, which he did. In this manner, and somewhat late in the day, the landing of German troops was covered by a political agreement, usually referred to as the 'political transit agreement'.[32]

This agreement is entirely different from that concluded on September 12. That had been concerned with the precise details of transporting three defined batches of men and materials. The political agreement was vague and unlimited in its application. It shows every sign of its hasty drafting by Weizsäcker, on the basis of Kivimäki's suggestions, but in view of its authorship it naturally has no inconvenient restrictions on Germany's freedom of action. The agreement had four clauses, the first of which declares that the Finnish government will permit the transit of material and accompanying personnel from its northern Baltic ports, through Rovaniemi, into northern Norway. It is notable here that the emphasis is on materials, the men are supposed to be 'Begleitpersonnel' only, which made the whole thing sound more innocuous. The second clause gives an undertaking that Germany will inform the Finnish government 'in good time' about the transits and their proposed journeys, but oddly there is no obligation to state the quantity of material or the numbers of men, only the number of ships involved. The third clause provides that the notice of times of arrival in Finnish ports will be no less than 24 hours. The fourth clause provides that on the railways, the men and their weapons will travel separately. The number of men who may accompany the weapons is to be the subject of a separate agreement. No such agreement was ever made.[33] In effect, the Germans were permitted for an indefinite period to send any quantity of men and materials they pleased through Finland into northern

Norway. There was no condition attached except that they give 24 hours' notice of the number of ships and their port of arrival.

The agreement has in fact been commonly misunderstood. Kivimäki, at his trial after the war, went to some pains to explain why the political agreement failed to embody effective controls over the German transits. He argued ingeniously that the lack of a time limit was a positive advantage, since the agreement could have been cancelled at any time, and demonstrated that his instructions never required him to set limits to the numbers involved.[34] Such arguments are divorced from the real significance of this document. All the practical aspects of German transits were adequately covered in the military agreement. Indeed, the transits had already started before the political agreement had even been drafted, so little did they depend on its existence. Transit arrangements between Finland and Germany continued to be the exclusive business of the military authorities. In making them, no notice was taken of the terms of the agreement between the governments. These were frequently violated. The military authorities behaved as though the agreement of September 22 had no bearing on the question. In this they were right. The political agreement was for outside consumption only. Weizsäcker told Blücher this in his telegram explaining the agreement. He said that the Finnish government had wanted to be 'covered as respects Russia by a regular agreement between the two governments'. This accounted for all the clauses of the agreement except the first, and was particularly true of point four about the separation of the men and their weapons. Weizsäcker said 'this formulation had been chosen in consideration of the Russian-Finnish agreements on Hango, but that in practice, in the opinion of OKW, the Finns would leave us a free hand'.[35] Experience proved that OKW was correct in this assessment. Thus the German Foreign Office had no illusions about the exchange of notes. They were to be shown to foreign powers in order to create the impression that the transit agreements between Finland and Germany were analogous with those between Finland and the USSR, or those between Sweden and Germany. The instruction to Blücher confirms beyond doubt that both parties regarded the notes exchanged on September 22 as political camouflage only. The practical effects of the arrangements embodied in them were inconsequential.

The execution of the transits was left entirely in the hands of the military authorities. When Ryti was asked what the government did to supervise the carrying out of these agreements, his answer was that the civil authorities did nothing. No instructions were ever given for reports to be sent in on the numbers and activities of the Germans. It is fairly apparent that the government never knew how many Germans there were in the country, or whether they were behaving in accordance with their agreements or not.

Rangell, the prime minister after January 1941, said that at most he got an occasional verbal report from local officials on Germans in their area. A small department of the General Staff handled all transit matters, and Walden was the only minister to whom proper reports were given. Walden occasionally passed on items of information to other ministers or the whole cabinet, but never on any systematic basis. Ultimately, responsibility led back to Mannerheim. This explains the system. The political leaders knew that the Marshal was in charge, and were quite willing to leave him to deal with the Germans as he saw fit. If Mannerheim was in charge, it was not for them to interfere, matters were in safe hands. Only in this way can it be explained how the Finnish government came to abdicate its responsibilities into the hands of a tiny group of soldiers, and left them to take decisions which were bound to have profound political repercussions affecting the whole nation, without even bothering to keep itself informed on what exactly they were doing.

The arrival of the first ships at Vaasa and Oulu on September 22 demonstrated how well secrecy had been preserved. The chief of police at Vaasa, a sorely puzzled man, rang up the ministry of the interior and announced that he had shiploads of Germans standing off the port. He asked for instructions. The minister of the interior, von Born, could tell him nothing, and turned to Ryti for advice. Ryti assured him that 'everything was in order'.[36] Walden had told Ryti three days previously that the first group of Germans was on its way. On the following day, when the text of the political agreement had arrived in Helsinki, Witting communicated it to the ambassadors of Great Britain, Sweden, and the USSR. Zotov displayed keen interest, and asked if Germany had presented an ultimatum. He was solemnly assured that the Finnish government had not allowed matters to reach that stage[37]. On September 24, the Finnish cabinet was informed. Outside observers may think it strange that so important a decision had been made and executed without a word being said to the cabinet, but so it was. Only Ryti, Walden, and Witting had been in the secret. The ministers took the news very well in the circumstances. Two Social Democrats, Fagerholm and Salovaara, said that they thought they should have been consulted before the event rather than after, but when Ryti asked them whether they objected to the actual agreement, they said they did not. One of the Agrarian ministers, Kalliokoski, was also dubious about the way it had been handled, but the other two Agrarians fully endorsed what had been done. The minister of the interior, still feeling a little foolish over the telephone call from Vaasa, agreed with the policy, but wished it had been possible to let his department have some advance warning of the Germans' arrival.[38]

The last to be informed were the Finnish people. Something had to be said, since rumours of the arrival of German troops had been spreading in the wildest forms. Hence a tiny paragraph appeared on the front pages of all the Finnish newspapers on September 25. It gave no details of the agreement, simply said that transits of German troops were currently taking place in accordance with agreed conditions. It described the transits as 'leave men'. The agreement was never communicated to the Eduskunta, although it seems that the leaders of the party groups were told informally of what was happening. Witting addressed the foreign affairs committee on September 29, and tried to convey the impression that the whole thing was of slight importance, 'it in no way altered the existing situation'. He described the Germans as 'leave men', which he knew to be untrue, and according to the chairman of the committee he said that the Germans had 'demanded' the right of transit, and that their ships had already sailed when the demand was presented, so, 'what could we do about it?'[39] In fairness to Witting's memory it should be said that these accounts of what he said were given some five years after the event, and may not be entirely accurate. Even so, it looks as though Witting deliberately deceived the foreign affairs committee about the nature of the agreements. His defence would have been that the Germans insisted on strict secrecy, and that anything he told the committee would leak out. The Finnish leadership has another defence against the charge of misleading the Eduskunta and the general public. They were themselves ignorant of the significance of this shift in German policy. Kivimäki sent a despatch to Witting on September 25 to warn the government against jumping to any premature conclusions on the strength of the transit agreement.[40] The foreign office was still very reserved in its attitude to Finland. In these circumstances it was wise of the government to play down the significance of the whole matter both to its own public and to foreign powers. The fact remains that in the process, the government prevented the Eduskunta and the Finnish public from appreciating what was happening in their own country, or how what was happening was affecting their country's international position.

CHAPTER 8

Finland's fate in the balance

I t is possible to treat of the making of the German transit agreements in isolation because that is how they were made. It is probable that until September 22, fewer than 50 people knew anything about them. After that date, and because of the evasive tactics pursued by both Finland and Germany, it was some time before their significance was grasped and they became an accepted factor in the situation. For a time, Finland's international position remained as precarious as ever, in some ways it was deteriorating. It will be recalled that Paasikivi, in his gloomy reaction to his reception by Molotov on August 22, had urged his government to try Sweden for support. Paasikivi then knew nothing of the German approaches, which Walden had described as 'a very small ray of light flashing out of the dark'. But he probably had heard some talk of a plan then being devised in Sweden to rescue Finland. In mid-August the Swedish government had been alarmed and despondent about the future of Finland, whose position was held to be hopeless. It had decided that if the expected Soviet attack came, Sweden could do nothing to help, unless Germany would give her consent. But Finland had many powerful friends in Sweden who were not prepared to stand idly by. They had a spokesman inside the government in Gösta Bagge, the minister for church affairs, and an organizer of wealth and influence in the industrialist S. Påhlson. These people had devised a scheme for a union between Sweden and Finland.[1] The king of Sweden would be the head of the union, which would have a common foreign policy and common armed forces. It was thought that Mannerheim might command the union forces. A plan on these lines was sent to Walden, a friend of Påhlson, on August 19. The authors of the plan supposed, optimistically, that it would be acceptable both to Germany and the USSR. It was thought that the former would be happy to see Finland saved from the clutches of the latter. On the other hand the plan was based on the acceptance by Finland of its present frontiers, and the foreign policy of the union would obviously be controlled in effect by Sweden. This should assure the USSR that Finland could not embark on policies of revenge, and at the same time save her from the danger of being driven into the arms of Germany. It was a scheme that ought to have satisfied all parties. Walden and the Finnish government showed immediate interest in it, and discussions about it began.

The enthusiasm of the Finnish government was quickened by the growing unpleasantness of the USSR. It was true that the Hanko transit problem had been disposed of but the Åland island question had not. Paasikivi took a draft treaty back with him which was totally rejected by Molotov at the end of August. The USSR would not agree to the Finnish proposals to leave certain installations on the islands standing, such as gun positions, at least as long as the European war continued, nor did he wish to include any mention of the Åland convention of 1921. Molotov claimed that this convention, to which the USSR was not a party, had lost all significance. Only the USSR, Finland, and Sweden had any valid interest in the islands.[2] Paasikivi insisted that the Finnish government did regard the 1921 convention as still binding. A few days later, Molotov produced a new draft clause designed to meet the Finnish position. It did recognize the convention, provided that the USSR was put on an equal footing with the signatories, and in particular should be consulted in advance before Finland took any measures relating to the islands under the terms of the convention. In the discussion which followed it emerged that Molotov had introduced his draft clause only to humour the Finnish government. His attitude was that if they really attached importance to such rubbish as international law and outdated treaties, he would not stand in their way. Paasikivi remarked that Finland could not by herself admit the USSR to all the rights belonging to the signatories of the 1921 convention. They would all have to be consulted first. This was true in law, but absurd in fact. Molotov quickly replied by asking whether Poland's consent would have to be sought. Thus the Åland issue threatened to bog down in a morass of mutual incomprehension. Finland had not raised the matter of the 1921 convention purely out of respect for international law. The Finnish government was sure that there was some ulterior motive behind the demand of the USSR for the demilitarization of the islands, and hoped desperately that they could somehow involve other powers in helping them to resist Soviet pressure. Above all they hoped to stir German interest and Kivimäki lost no time in communicating the text of the Soviet draft treaty to the foreign office, asking what was the German reaction to it. But Germany was not to be drawn and Kivimäki was told that the German government favoured complete demilitarization. Blücher was instructed to follow the course of events carefully, but to 'maintain reserve with regard to the German position.'[3] The hopes of the Finnish government were vain, but understandable. Molotov quickly perceived this aspect of their policy, and refused to take seriously the legalistic scruples of the Finnish government. The new Soviet draft clause was transmitted to Helsinki.

It was probably during this same meeting between Paasikivi and Molotov that the latter demanded to know when he was going to have the Finnish government's answer on the nickel question.[4] This was a shock for the Finns, since they had assumed that the negotiations between Germany and the USSR over the sharing out of output had settled the future of the nickel mines. There was now indeed a fresh complication, since Ryti had promised Veltjens that if the concession were transferred, Germany should have the first refusal of it. It is unlikely that Ryti did this innocently. He must have hoped from the first that such a promise might be used as a bar to any further Soviet claims. Paasikivi however had no instructions on the nickel question, and said so. Molotov assured him that the Soviet government was 'as interested as ever in the concession', and that only Finland and the USSR must be involved in running the mines.[5] Thus the government in Helsinki got one more problem to worry over. What they had hoped was a sleeping dog had suddenly come to life.

It had been part of Hitler's new Finnish policy to boost Finnish morale. If it was not convenient to do much by way of open political or diplomatic support, it was open to Germany to exploit and develop the existing pro-German sentiments in Finland. It has been pointed out earlier that these rested on a dual foundation of Finland's traditional pro-Germanism, and the sense of political realities, the acceptance of the fact that Germany was the dominant European power, and above all the only possible counterpoise to the USSR. The darker aspects of nazism proved no obstacle for most Finns. In part they did not know about them, and the government tried to ensure that they remained in ignorance. In part, the Finns simply turned the blind eye to such things. They could not, in general, see much to choose in the standards of behaviour of the belligerent powers. Everyone knew that unpleasant things happened in wartime, and probably Germany was no worse than anyone else in this respect. The idea was so deeply held that it is common in Finland to this day. So the Finns reconciled themselves to Germany's nazism. They would argue that in any case, as between Germany and the USSR 'we have no room for choice', or 'if we can choose then we will a thousand times rather choose the German, even if he is a nazi'.[6] During the autumn of 1940, however, there were signs of a further movement of opinion, from the mere acceptance of nazism as Germany's private affair to the view that totalitarianism was the creed of the future, and that Germany was setting a pattern which Europe should follow. This sprang from Germany's striking military triumphs. Totalitarian Germany was new and successful, the defeated Western democracies, and their ideas, were old and worn out. A contemporary wrote:[7]

'. . . no observer can fail to notice that admiration of the national socialist ideology—which is again spreading among us, especially in our educated classes and among propertied people—is connected closely with German military power and its military victories.'

A sober expression of this new attitude to the totalitarian idea can be found in an address given to the Finnish-German Society in Helsinki, on October 10, by the distinguished mathematician, Professor Nevanlinna. After developing the theme that Germany and Finland were both young nations, with much in common, the professor continued:[8]

'Is there any country outside Germany, where such warm and widespread feelings of sympathy for Germany have existed and do still exist, as in Finland, as well in the time of distress after Versailles, as in the following period of powerful recovery . . . everyone who tries to examine the present world situation without prejudice can see those signs of greatness which modern Germany presents to the gaze of the world. . . . There is a society completely submitted to the guidance of a great political ideal, where the idea of the individual's responsibility . . . is fused into the living whole . . . a conception according to which the individual has significance only through becoming an inseparable part of that great whole—this of course involves a revolution, and it is no wonder if now and then some things of value are pushed aside to give way to higher values.'

The first important initiative by Germany was the announcement that she would participate in an athletics contest with Sweden and Finland in Helsinki in September. The head of the German state sports organization attended in person, and told von Blücher, and probably many Finns as well, that he had been told to come by Hitler in person, and that this could be taken as a hint of a new turn in Finnish-German relations. Hitler had chosen his ground well. No other gesture could have made a deeper popular impression in Finland. Athletics was almost a second religion to the Finns. It was a truly national sport practised by all those who were young enough, and keenly watched and followed by the whole nation. The Finns were proud of their fame as athletes, and counted their remarkable performances in international competitions before the war as one of their greatest achievements since national independence. The Finnish press leaped to the opportunity. For three days in succession the papers were completely dominated by features connected with the athletics meeting. *Uusi Suomi* proclaimed that 'the three leading sporting nations of Europe, to whom the values of sport are so sacred . . . are meeting one another in brotherly and chivalrous contest'. The public responded with enthusiasm, great crowds filled the Helsinki stadium, while the visitors were showered with hospitality.[9] The public demonstrated its belief that at last the long period of isolation in the face of the menaces of the USSR was coming to an end. From that time on German-Finnish contacts, on the cultural and economic level, were frequent. Delegations of businessmen, soldiers, churchmen, sportsmen, and pressmen passed to and fro between the two countries. Lecturers were exchanged, complimentary public speeches made. The surest sign of the new turn in policy was probably the change in the tone of German press comment on Finland. This was now invariably friendly and encouraging, as Finnish readers could discover from the many translated quotations that appeared in their own press. There were still liberal-minded Finns who were worried where this association might end, but even they would have agreed that dependence on Germany was a happier fate than absorption by the USSR, if that was indeed the only choice.

The Finnish government, which was delighted by all manifestations of German benevolence, was wondering whether this might be stretched so far as to help them with the nickel problem. They knew how important the nickel ore was for Germany, and they were sure that Germany did not want to see the USSR in control of the mines. On September 13, Kivimäki went to the foreign office to explore the ground. He was told that Germany could not intervene at all. The ambassador then said that in that case it was very probable that Finland would have to concede the Russian demand, and in consequence, Ryti's promise of pre-emption given to Veltjens would be void. This stung Weizsäcker into saying that although Germany could not intervene, she would not abandon her claim either. On September 20, Weizsäcker was alarmed to learn through von Blücher that Witting had expressed his satisfaction at what Weizsäcker had said. He hastily telegraphed to say that the Finnish government must not misinterpret what he had said.[10] He was afraid that Witting was going to plead Germany's prior rights as a bar to the claims of the Soviet government. This was of course just what the Finnish government wanted to do.

In the meantime, Finland had tried out the effects of a virtual rejection of Molotov's demand. Paasikivi had presented his government's answer on September 14. In substance it regretted that Finland could not legally dispossess the existing concession holders without their consent, which was not forthcoming. The USSR would have to content itself with sharing the output with Germany.[11] As a consolation it repeated that Germany herself had earlier asked for the concession and been refused. Molotov was not pleased. He made it clear at once that he regarded the Finnish answer as a pretext. If Finland wanted to she could easily circumvent mere legal obstacles. Molotov stressed that it was not just the nickel that interested the USSR. She was as anxious that the British be got out of the Petsamo area. Molotov pointed out that the USSR had freely given back the Petsamo area after the war. There was a clear implication that if necessary she

could take it back. This at least was how Paasikivi interpreted it. He reported to the government that mention of Germany had obviously angered
Molotov and concluded that 'measures of force against Petsamo are not
beyond the bounds of possibility'[12]. In his diary, Paasikivi recorded that
Molotov had looked really angry.[13] He suggested to his government that as
a next step they should propose that the USSR itself ask Britain to give
up the concession, promising if this were done to transfer it to a joint
Finnish-Soviet company.[14] But the government could not do this very
well in face of Ryti's promise to Veltjens, and decided to dig in behind its
legal barricade. In fact, Molotov's anger may have stemmed from another
source. Halder noted in his diary, on September 16, that there was tension
between Germany and the USSR over the division of output of the nickel,
since Russia would not let Germany have more than 60%.[15] This was a
slight oversimplification of the position. Molotov had suggested that
Germany's right to 60% of the output would last only to the end of 1940,
but the German ambassador in Moscow had made it plain that Germany
did not accept such a limitation, and Molotov had indicated that he would
consider the German point of view further.[16]

The Petsamo nickel problem was only one element in the crisis that was
developing in Russo-Finnish relations. The USSR was also casting a jaundiced eye on internal developments. Tanner's resignation from the government had led to a new vigour in the leadership of the Social Democratic
party. Early in September he launched a campaign against Wiik and his
followers. They were vigorously attacking Tanner, as such groups do in
every socialist party, for betraying socialism and selling out to the class
enemy. They called for a renewal of the class war and a more vigorous
defence of the rights of the workers. The official leadership, committed to
the cult of unity, had been obliged to drop the class war. It talked about a
modernized socialism, though suspicious conservatives grumbled that in
its aims, which were still a socialized economy, 'it does not differ from
marxism'. Wiik's paper, *Vapaa Sana*, had been systematically obstructed
by the government and the trade unions. It was at that point being
printed in Sweden because of this. Now the demand was being worked up
for the expulsion of the Wiik group from the party. At the same time, the
Soviet propaganda machine, having largely dropped SNS, took up the
Wiik group as the real voice of the Finnish workers in opposition to the
Tanner clique.[17] Once more Tanner and the Soviet Union were in head-on
conflict.

On September 9, the socialist press attacked Wiik and his followers as
upper-class converts, intellectuals, unscrupulous power seekers who
abused 'genuine proletarian manners of speech' to delude honest workers
and lead them astray.[18] This was the signal for a campaign against them

designed to lead to their expulsion from the party. The press increasingly
urged on the local party organs to demand this. When enough feeling had
been worked up, the party executive did expel Wiik and five other members of the party's Eduskunta group. The bourgeois press applauded
loudly.[19] Soviet propaganda made loud noises of dissent. The Soviet
Union, it said, would take note of how those who worked for friendship
and good relations were treated in Finland. Tanner justified his actions
in a speech to a youth group of the party on October 3. The speech was
quite unapologetic. Tanner attacked the Wiik group for its agitation
against the restrictions on civil liberties. It was absurd to expect the full
exercise of democratic rights when the nation was really in a state of war.
'Democracy had generally been too tolerant. Its weakness has been an
excess of trust'. The Wiik group was playing into the hands of the fascists.
The present era, when reaction was everywhere on top, was no time to be
shouting revolutionary slogans. Also the Wiik group were in effect fellow
travellers with the communists. Tanner alleged that they wanted Finland
to go the way of the Baltic states. This was almost certainly unfair to Wiik
and most of his followers. They were people who genuinely believed in the
possibility of improving relations with the USSR, and they represented
that tiny minority of Finns who thought that if a choice had to be made,
the USSR was preferable to Hitler's Germany. But Tanner was in that
dangerous state of mind which sees everyone who calls for better relations
with the USSR as a hidden communist or a potential traitor.

When they had been got out of the party, Tanner, with the help of the
government, set about shutting off their outlets for propagating their point
of view. In particular, *Vapaa Sana* was virtually suppressed, and reduced
to a duplicated sheet which appeared sporadically. The struggle was also
spread into other fields. The radicals made a bid for control of the trade
union organization, SAK, which was to hold its congress at the end of
October. The opposition attacked such things as the wartime agreements
with the employers and the Suojeluskunta, and called for a return to the
class war, and a vigorous defence of the workers' interests, which were
being neglected in the current preoccupation with unity. It is obvious
that the radicals did have a genuine popular appeal among some sections
of the workers, for it was estimated that they had succeeded in capturing
nearly one-third of the delegations to the congress. The conservative press
found this an alarming state of affairs, but the fact remained that Tanner
and his followers had kept control of the trade unions and beaten off a
determined attempt to infiltrate them.[20] A similar contest occurred for the
control of Elanto, the great co-operative of which Tanner was the chairman. This was an organization of great economic power, so that the
struggle was an important one. Elanto elections were held at the beginning

of November, and it was feared that the radicals might profit by the traditional apathy of Elanto members and gain control. Both the socialist and the bourgeois press ran a campaign to get people to vote. The result was an unusually high poll of nearly 30%, and a loss of ground by the opposition to Tanner.[21] The result of Tanner's campaign was that the opposition on the Left could only find expression through the activities of Wiik and his five colleagues in the Eduskunta, who soon became known as 'the Six'. This tiny group, isolated in the midst of a bitterly hostile Eduskunta, scorned, derided, or ignored by the whole of the national press, harassed by the implacable hostility of the authorities, remained the only effective channel through which the ideas of left-wing dissenters could find expression.

While Tanner and his colleagues were seeking to strengthen the domestic front, Finland's international position remained full of obscurities. In face of the mounting pressures from Moscow, and the unwillingness of Berlin to make any open intervention, the idea of union with Sweden was extremely attractive. Negotiations had got far enough for the sending of a delegation to Stockholm to indicate that Finland accepted the idea in principle and to sound out the leaders of the Swedish political parties. It was composed of Hakkila, Speaker of the Eduskunta, representing the socialists, and Ramsay, a member of the Progressive party, representing the bourgeois parties. The mission left for Stockholm on September 21 and its purpose was supposed to be highly secret. But the USSR, which was usually extremely well informed about events in Stockholm, quickly got wind of it. Two days later the news of the German transit agreement was released to the ambassadors of Sweden, Great Britain, and the USSR. As soon as the Swedish government got to see the text of the political agreement, they perceived that it was very different from their own transit agreements with Germany. The latter embodied very precise controls on the extent and nature of the traffic, while the Finnish agreement contained virtually no controls at all. The existence of the military agreement was of course unknown to them. While there was no inclination in Sweden to blame Finland for her conduct, there was some tendency among exponents of the union plan to have second thoughts. But when it appeared that the traffic was in fact on a very small scale, and there was no sign of a German takeover in Finland, the hesitations mostly vanished. The British government was bound to protest at the granting of facilities to its enemy. It duly did so on September 26. It was pointed out that the Finnish attempt to equate the German transit agreement with the Hanko transit agreement, or those made with Sweden, was unacceptable. The British government was referring to the absence of controls and limitations. This difference was real enough, but there was another and much more fundamental difference, which could not be expressed in diplomatic notes, and which most Finns still persist in ignoring when they try to uphold the equivalence of these agreements. The Hanko agreement, and the agreements between Sweden and Germany, had been forced out of reluctant governments by great power pressure. But the Finnish-German agreement had been voluntarily conceded by Finland. Finland had wanted to make the agreement, and would have granted almost any terms to get it concluded. This is not to say that Finland would have found it easy to refuse the German request if it had been pressed on them. But the attitude of the Finnish leaders had been such that no pressure was called for. The British government seems to have realized this, but it was prepared to wait and see what the practical consequences of the agreement would be, and confined itself to a formal protest at this stage.

The reactions of the USSR would no doubt have been much stronger if her government had not been unready to give open offence to Germany by making any public protest. But the Finnish government was left in no doubt of the concern and displeasure of the Soviet government. Zotov reacted with vigour. He announced on September 26 that he wanted to take a fishing holiday in the Petsamo region, with the very obvious intention of finding out for himself what was going on in the far north. In spite of all the ingenuity of Finnish officials, Zotov succeeded in finding one of the German columns on the march. Further his request was only the prelude to a stream of urgent demands that Soviet embassy officials be allowed to travel anywhere in Finland, even in forbidden zones, obviously to keep watch on what the Germans were doing. When the Finnish authorities refused, a sharp note was sent on October 7,[22] and it was followed up by a series of peremptory demands in notes, or in interviews between Zotov and the Finnish foreign office. But on this point Finland was not to be intimidated. Zotov was told that Soviet embassy officials must obey the same rules as all other foreigners, though no reasonable request would be refused. The Finnish government did in fact make some exceptions where there seemed to be a valid pretext. Inevitably, Soviet officials began making unauthorized journeys, which in turn led to diplomatic incidents and protests. It was extremely difficult for a Soviet official to travel unnoticed in Finland, particularly in the remote regions which interested them. Whatever they did they could hardly fail to be conspicuous, as any foreigner would, in Finnish surroundings.

The main Soviet reaction came from Molotov in Moscow. He was quite dissatisfied with the statement conveyed to him on September 21. The German chargé d'affaires, von Tippelskirch, called on Molotov on September 25. He had to announce the pact just concluded between Germany, Italy, and Japan, for their future common action, and to intimate that

Ribbentrop would shortly invite Molotov to come to Berlin to discuss their mutual relations. Tippelskirch found it hard to interest Molotov in what he had to say, which should have been interesting enough, because Molotov kept on asking questions about the Finnish-German agreement. He pointed out that the failure to give him advance notice of it was a breach of the Soviet-German pact, and demanded complete information, 'against whom it was directed and the purposes that were being served thereby. The agreement was being discussed in public while the Soviet government knew nothing about it'.[23] Tippelskirch, like a good diplomat, regretted that he had no information and said he would inquire. Since the Germans were most reluctant to satisfy Molotov's curiosity, and took their time replying, the full force of his frustration and anger fell on the unlucky Paasikivi, who of all the participants was the least to blame for what had happened.

Molotov had decided that if Germany would not say anything, the necessary information must be bullied out of Finland. On September 27, Paasikivi had a most unpleasant session with Molotov. Molotov demanded full information about the transit agreement. Paasikivi knew nothing about it. He was told to waste no time in finding out. Discussion then turned on the Åland question. Molotov again raised the question of the interpretation of the 1921 convention. Why did the Finnish government hesitate to grant the USSR equal rights with the signatories of this convention? Paasikivi put up his government's legal defences, they could not do so without the consent of the signatories. Molotov said that he could not accept this position. He went on to spring a surprise. He said that the Soviet government had information that Finland and Sweden were making a secret agreement directed against the USSR. The news of the visit of Hakkila and Ramsay had leaked out. Paasikivi truthfully said that he knew nothing and did not believe it could be true. Molotov insisted that it was and added:[24]

'Now we are talking verbally, but if written proofs are produced, the matter will be serious.'

Paasikivi interpreted this as a threat, which it obviously was, and retired hurt to report to his government. But this was only the prelude for a much rougher interview on September 30.

Paasikivi had been summoned to the Kremlin and was asked what he had to say about the transit agreement. He had instructions to say that the number of German troops involved was about 2,000. This figure, which was a lie, had been worked out in consultation with the German foreign office, on the basis that the column spotted by Zotov would suggest something of this order. Molotov was dissatisfied and wanted full information of how many Germans had passed through, and how many more were to come.[25] He passed on to the subject of the alleged agreement between Sweden and Finland and used language even sharper than on the 27th.[26] Paasikivi still had no information. Then it was the turn of the Åland question. Here Molotov became very angry, and said that the Soviet government would never consent to writing round Europe to the signatories of the 1921 convention. He added sarcastically, 'perhaps France for example would not consent'. He proposed that they omit all reference to the convention from their treaty. If the Finnish government liked to go on thinking that the 1921 convention was still valid they could, the USSR could not care less. Finally he said that Finland must stop haggling over the Åland question. The matter had dragged on far too long. An agreement must be signed within a week. Molotov added:[27]

'We cannot negotiate with you: this matter has dragged on for months. With the Germans, the biggest questions can be cleared up in a few days.'

Molotov's ultimatum made its impression. Paasikivi recommended his government to accept the Soviet draft of the Åland treaty. He added, 'I beg you to avoid excessive legalism, because the Kremlin is not a magistrate's court.'

The Finnish government accepted its ambassador's advice. The Soviet draft was adopted as the basis of the new treaty. In doing this, the Finnish government was victim of a curious delusion. They thought that because the Soviet government had, by deleting all reference to the 1921 convention, also dropped its demand for prior consultation before any action taken under that convention, they had won a victory. In fact, by deleting this clause, the USSR returned to its original draft, since the clause had only been introduced in an attempt to satisfy Finland's requirements. But the illusion of having won a point was comforting. The Eduskunta readily agreed to accept the new treaty. Witting represented it as of slight importance, and carefully stressed his government's view that the 1921 convention was unaffected by it. Thus, on October 11, Paasikivi was able to sign the new treaty in Moscow. It simply provided that the islands be completely demilitarized, and that the Soviet consul there had the right to see that it was enforced. On this occasion Molotov was in a good mood. He remarked that the treaty was a step forward in Finnish-Soviet relations.[28] Paasikivi doubted this, though he did not say so to Molotov. Instead he lectured his own government on the unwisdom of their proceedings in the matter. He pointed out that after haggling with the Soviet government for months, 'we have agreed to their original proposal as soon as Molotov struck his fist on the table and issued an ultimatum'.

The story of the treaty for the demilitarization of the Åland islands is a good illustration of the lamentable state of Russo-Finnish relations. The Finnish government had assumed from the start that the Soviet govern-

Foreign Minister R. Witting (*left*) signing the Aland Island agreement,
October 1940

J. K. Paasikivi (*left*) and V. Tanner

The air-raids 25 June 1941. Bomb damage at (*a*) Helsinki and (*b*) Lapeenranta

ment had some sinister motive for its demand. In consequence it had made difficulties and tried to drag in other powers by resort to the 1921 Convention. When this had failed, Mannerheim and Ryti, in conversation with Veltjens, threw out the despairing suggestion that Germany should occupy the islands, and told him that 'Finland would agree entirely to such an occupation.'[29] Veltjens was in no position to respond to so startling a suggestion, and the Finnish leaders had been left no choice but to give in to the ultimatum, deluding themselves into thinking that firmness had paid dividends. From the Russian side, the whole business must have seemed further proof of the unreasoning malice of the Finnish government. The original Soviet draft had been in accord with the acknowledged international status of the islands. They had almost certainly had no ulterior motive in putting it forward. The USSR had no immediate use for the islands herself, and wanted to make sure that nobody else could use them with Finnish connivance. It was true that if the time did come for the final settlement of the Finnish question, it would be as well if the islands were defenceless, but that was a hypothetical situation. The Soviet government would naturally give no credit to the legalistic scruples of the Finnish government, since they reckoned with some justice that they were not absolutely sincere, and in any case legalistic concepts meant nothing to them. To Molotov it must have seemed that Finland had opposed an entirely reasonable proposal out of sheer malevolence towards the USSR and had been forced into surrender at last by a blunt threat. This would accord with the basic image which he appears to have had of the Finnish government and its policies. So that far from having improved Russo-Finnish relations, the Åland settlement had implanted one more seed of hostility and suspicion in the minds of both parties. But it was already quite overshadowed by more serious issues. It was a hangover from the days of June, when the situation had been very different.

The question of the German transits now had priority in all discussions between the USSR and Finland, and also between the USSR and Germany. Berlin and Helsinki kept in close contact to ensure that they presented a united front on the question. On October 2, Ribbentrop authorized Tippelskirch to give a little additional explanation of events. The transits were of no political significance. They were purely military, occasioned by British threats against northern Norway. They were strictly comparable with the transit agreements with Sweden. 'Naturally' there had been no occasion to give advance information about such an unimportant matter. If the USSR wanted to see the text of the agreement of September 22, Germany would supply a copy of the text.[30] It must be said that there is scarcely a true word in the whole statement, which was given to Molotov on October 4. Paasikivi was also given the text of the answer, so that he

could parry any questions that might come to him.[31] Molotov remained
suspicious. He wanted some hard facts, how many troops were involved,
and how many were remaining on Finnish soil. He complained that the
Finnish government was telling him nothing. Tippelskirch promised to
make further inquiries in Berlin, but added that 'as far as I know it was not
our intention to retain German troops in Finland and that moreover the
agreement was conditional upon the threat to Kirkenes by England'.[32]

Molotov was to be frustrated again, since the Germans had no intention
of telling him anything more. Tippelskirch was with Molotov twice more,
on October 10, when he had nothing to add, and on October 14, when he
said that any further Soviet queries should be made directly in Berlin. So
Molotov was driven back to Paasikivi. The latter was anxious to know
what he could say in face of repeated questions. The Finnish government
at first thought of amplifying its original answer by saying that not more
than 2,000 men would be passing through at one time, which was more or
less true. The German foreign office seemed nervous about this, while
Paasikivi advised raising the bid to 5,000. Finally Witting decided to say
that 2,000 had gone through and less than 2,000 were manning the base
system.[33] This was probably what Paasikivi told Molotov on October 9,
when they had a further important encounter. This time Paasikivi was
looking forward to a somewhat easier interview. In addition to his amplified information about the German transits, he could report his government's readiness to sign the Åland agreement, and he had an official government statement which denied that there was any agreement in existence
between Finland and Sweden.[34] This latter was perfectly true as far as it
went, but concealed the fact that talks about such an agreement were still
in progress. Molotov was unimpressed by Paasikivi's offerings. He still
wanted more precise figures about the transits, and merely 'took note' of
the statement about the agreement with Sweden. Molotov did not say
whether he believed it or not. But if the Soviet intelligence from Stockholm was as efficient as it usually was, it is conceivable that Molotov knew
more about these negotiations than Paasikivi did. On top of this unpromising beginning, Molotov raised the nickel question. He demanded to
know when the Soviet government would get an answer to its request for
the concession. The position of the Finnish government had not changed
since September. It still regarded the validity of the existing concession as
an absolute bar to transferring it to the USSR. When Paasikivi said that
the position was unchanged, Molotov got angry. He claimed that the Finnish stand was a pretext only. The British ambassador in Moscow, Sir
Stafford Cripps, had told him in July that the British government would
be quite happy to see the concession transferred to a Finnish-Russian
company. Paasikivi retorted that his government's inquiries in London had

been met with a firm refusal to agree to the transfer. Molotov said he was astonished.[35]

This exchange gives rise to a minor mystery. Had Cripps ever said that, or did Molotov invent the whole thing? If Cripps had said it, was he authorized to do so by the British government? The truth was probably that the British government had authorized Sir Stafford Cripps to say that they would willingly see the concession transferred to a mixed Finnish-Russian company for the duration of the war, provided the company undertook not to supply any nickel to Germany. What Molotov was doing was to ignore the conditions attached to the Cripps offer. Whether Cripps himself had given Molotov any grounds for doing this is unknown. Whatever the truth, Molotov made it clear on October 9 that his government rejected the Finnish position on the nickel question, and would not let the matter drop. What Molotov did not know was that there was now a further complication. On October 1, Veltjens had been back in Helsinki, in order to sign the formal agreements covering Finland's purchases of arms from Germany. The promise of pre-emption over any future mineral concessions in Finland had been added as a clause to the agreements. The Finnish government did not conceal its motive in doing this, for Witting wrote to Veltjens in these terms:[36]

'In connection with point 7 of the explanations . . . I would like to assure you that the Finnish government has assumed the obligation there mentioned gladly. At the same time I would like to express the wish that the Government of the Greater German Reich, in case of possible difficulties which might arise for the Finnish State from the Soviet Union as a result of fulfilling the terms of the contract, would lend its support in eliminating such difficulties.'

Veltjens told the German Foreign Office that he had made it quite clear that the expectations of the Finnish government must be disappointed. Germany was determined not to allow the Finnish government to manœuvre her into giving any open support over the nickel question. Germany did intend to seize the mines if there should be a new attack on Finland by the USSR, but that was not something which could be told to the Finnish government. The constant hints from the Finnish government that if Germany did not intervene, they would concede the Russian demand did not have the desired effect. The whole question was discussed at a conference in the German foreign office. The military authorities and Göring were indeed most anxious that the USSR should not get control of the mines, but Hitler's policy would not allow of open intervention. Therefore the German policy must be to encourage Finland to procrastinate as long as they could.[37] Fortunately for Germany, the Finnish government was very willing to follow their advice.

Molotov must have realized by this stage that the sturdy Finnish resistance to his pressures was inspired by Germany. He could get no further forward on either the transit question or the nickel question. On the former, Witting, encouraged by advice from the German ambassador, had decided that Finland would give no more information. Molotov was to be told that since Finland did not tell Germany how many Russian troops were conveyed to Hanko, she must observe equal discretion over the number of Germans conveyed to Kirkenes. If Molotov insisted on information, he must apply in Berlin. On October 21, Ribbentrop himself told Blücher to encourage the Finnish government to persist in this stand. But by this stage all the urgency had disappeared from Molotov's questions, and in fact he let the matter drop. This was because of a major development in Russo-German relations. On October 17, the German ambassador, von Schulenburg, returned to his post in Moscow, and went to see Molotov. He had a letter from Ribbentrop which invited Molotov to come to Berlin to discuss the whole future of Russo-German relations. The letter did mention the German transits through Finland but added nothing to previous official explanations. However, in view of the invitation which the Soviet government had no hesitation in accepting, it would obviously have been a waste of effort to continue probing for scraps of information from Paasikivi. Molotov would now be able to put his questions to Hitler in person.

The other unpleasant repercussions of the transit agreement were also smoothed over at this stage. The British government had begun to take a more serious view of the matter when it noticed that German troops were not just passing through Finland, but were setting up bases there. It began to hint to the Finnish government that its traffic to Liinahamari was in danger, on the grounds that Finland had become a satellite of Germany, and the goods imported might fall into German hands. On October 23, the British government laid down its conditions for permitting the traffic to continue. The Finnish government must inform them of the numbers of German troops involved, and in addition allow twelve British inspectors to move round the Petsamo region to check that goods imported with British permission did not get into German hands. No doubt the real job of the inspectors was to count the German troops for themselves. On October 29, the Finnish government agreed to the inspectors, but declined to give information about the numbers of German troops. The British government accepted this, the inspectors were appointed, and the traffic to Liinahamari continued.[38]

The plan for union with Sweden was also being driven forward. The main features were agreed by both sides in the middle of October. These would be a joint foreign and defence policy, recognition of the permanence of Finland's 1940 frontiers, and the securing of the prior consent of Germany and the USSR. Witting had already sounded Blücher, who was due to go back to Berlin for a visit. Blücher had the impression that Witting felt that only Germany could give effective protection to Finland against the USSR, but that he was hoping that Germany would provide a special place for Sweden and Finland in her New Order.[39] At the same time, in Stockholm, members of the Swedish government were sounding out the Soviet ambassador, Madame Kollontai. The Finnish government had formally agreed to the basic features of the union plan by October 25, and sent over to Stockholm the required assurance that it renounced all thought of revising its frontiers.[40] A committee of the Swedish cabinet then discussed it and on November 1 agreed to proceed. There was opposition within the cabinet, which was strong enough to insist that any contacts with the Finnish government must be 'discussions' and not 'negotiations' at this stage. These people were aware that the preliminary soundings of Germany and the USSR had not been promising, and were determined that Sweden should not compromise herself in vain.

It is probable that at this stage, the Finnish leaders were still uncommitted for the future. They were convinced that they needed protection from the USSR. In hope of getting this they had drawn closer to Germany as soon as an opening was given to them. They would gladly have widened and deepened their co-operation with Germany if Germany had been willing. But because Germany remained so reserved, and because the Finnish leaders, remembering recent events, could not trust Germany altogether, the alternative policy of union with Sweden, based on neutrality, seemed a more attractive policy, if it was practicable. Some leading figures however, and Witting is probably the most senior, were sceptical of the value of union with Sweden, and preferred to draw closer to Germany, whatever happened. Kivimäki was certainly another of this group. On October 29 he had a discussion with Weizsäcker about the union plan, emphasizing that 'he was not speaking on the instructions of his government'. Kivimäki said that he had no faith in the plan, and in addition thought that the price was too high. 'For such a union would involve Finland in burdensome ties, the most important of which would be renunciation of a revision of the Finnish frontier with Russia.' Kivimäki said he would rather see his country depend on Germany than on Sweden. Weizsäcker remained 'buttoned up', an attitude that was endorsed by Ribbentrop a few days later as the official German policy on the union plan.[41] The same day, Kivimäki wrote to his government outlining his view of the situation.

He assumed, correctly as it turned out, that the new German attitude to Finland meant that she would not permit a renewed Soviet aggression. Kivimäki believed that his country should try to capitalize on this situation while it lasted. Finland should make gestures to indicate that she recognized Germany's New Order in Europe and sympathized with her aspirations and even her ideology. 'Of course, Finland should not on this account set out, nor need she set out, on the road to nazism, far from it.' That would not be necessary. But Finland could to some extent make her social policies accord with German ideas, and she could, for instance, resign from the League of Nations. Kivimäki recognized that what he called 'the Stockholm road', was a valid alternative, but it was only worth considering if Finland wanted to insure against the altogether improbable event of the U.S.A., Britain, and the USSR combining to defeat Germany. Kivimäki thought such excessive caution would be wasted. 'The road to Berlin is straight and therefore to be followed in spite of the highly improbable danger attached to it of the defeat of Germany.'[42] The ambassador felt that whichever choice was made, the time of decision was at hand. In October, this was still the minority opinion in Finland's ruling circle. They preferred to play safe if they could. So apparently did most of the general public. At least German intelligence reports on the reception of the German troops in Finland said that the feelings of relief which greeted their arrival were mixed with feelings of uncertainty. People could not forget Germany had betrayed them during the war, and feared she might do so again. Even the Finnish liaison officers, while polite, showed little over-enthusiasm for their work.[43]

On the other hand there were elements of the Finnish public whose thinking was moving along the same line as Kivimäki, some of whom were willing to go much further than either he or Witting would have considered proper. This was attested by the emergence of a number of Right-wing political movements, all of which advocated that Finland should throw in her lot with Germany, and some of which wanted to establish totalitarianism in Finland. These latter were probably the least significant. The Finnish National Socialist organization began a big publicity campaign in October, with large press notices saying, 'the march of national socialism is beginning'. It naturally claimed to be the movement of the future, as in its notices announcing the founding of its own journal, *The National Socialist*, which declared 'it will rule our nation yet'.[44] The movement made regular appeals for recruits and organized public meetings. The national socialists openly took Hitler's movement as their inspiration. Other similar groups tried to draw their ideas from native sources. Such were the Vapaa Suomi—Free Finland—movement organized by Teo Snellman, and the Gustav Vaasa group of Erkki Räikkänen which claimed to get its ideas from the work of the great Swedish sovereigns of the seventeenth century. Several of these groups, together with the main fascist party, the IKL, held a congress at Lapua in October.[45] There they discussed the formation of a joint programme for all the totalitarian parties, and the place which Finland ought to take in the New Order in Europe. They managed to put together a joint manifesto, calling the Finnish people to take their places in the struggle now raging alongside a 're-born Europe', and to join the common effort to protect 'everything that is holy and precious to our nation'. These phenomena were reported with strong disapproval in both the socialist and the liberal press. The socialists in particular poured scorn on the pretensions of such insignificant splinter groups to speak for the Finnish people. The kind of unity which they advocated would be 'the peace of the graveyard'.[46] The government was called on to keep its eye on these organizations, which could do the nation no good. On the whole, most Finns rejected their ideas precisely because they advocated the importation of foreign, non-Finnish, social and political systems. Attempts to make such rulers as Gustav Vaasa or Gustav Adolf into prototype Hitlers, and thus give a Scandinavian flavour to fascist ideas had little success. The responsible press was united in its attacks on those who wanted to remodel Finland on a foreign pattern. The socialist press also noted bitterly that the authorities often seemed to extend a greater tolerance to these organizations than it did even to the Social Democratic party.[47] It is certain that although these movements really represented only a lunatic fringe, and although their activities did undoubted damage to the international position of Finland, the authorities treated them with a tolerance which was never extended to radicals on the Left.

A much more significant movement which was founded at this point was Nouseva Suomi—Rising Finland—which began with a public meeting on September 25. This was a propagandist movement dedicated to nationalist ideals, but rejecting foreign totalitarianism. Its opening manifesto was clear on this:[48]

'The democratic political system is the most natural for the Finnish people. So the future must be constructed firmly on this basis. But . . . the quantity of consciousness and feelings of personal responsibility must be greatly strengthened in our political life.'

The programme stressed above all national unity, national consciousness, and the Christian basis of Finnish policy. It placed emphasis on the duties rather than the rights of citizens, and strongly supported the armed forces. Nouseva Suomi was respectable and rather academic in origin, and many of its founding fathers came from the Progressive party, a centre party of intellectuals and professional people. Its initial reception showed that people were not at first sure in what direction Nouseva Suomi was going to move. The socialists at once hinted that it was a crypto-fascist movement, but the IKL strongly repudiated it as nothing more than the Progressive party under another disguise. It seems fair to acquit the

movement of the charge of fascism. Its thought, if the platitudes which
constituted its propaganda deserve that name, derived from an older type
of pre-1914 nationalism. The solemn intellectuals who were its founders,
Vilho Helanen, Eero Mantere, Reino Castren, L. A. Puntila, were nationalists not fascists, though Helanen was characterized in the socialist press as a
man of 'known fascist inclinations'.[49] The real common background of these
men can be found in the AKS, the student nationalist society whose considerable influence has been mentioned earlier. Perhaps they were best
summed up by the paper *Kansan Lehti* as 'perpetual undergraduates'. The
press of the Left never ceased to attack the movement, the moderate press
wondered if it was really necessary, while the responsible Right welcomed
it for embodying all that was best in the conservative-nationalist tradition.
Helanen explained that its mission was to unite the nation round its basic
beliefs and to build for the future. It was in this second part of the programme that a more sinister note was heard. Construction must be based
on 'the consciousness that there can be no return to former days',[50] a
phrase which meant no return to the pre-1939 system of party politics.
The wartime yksimielisyys, with its virtual suspension of party politics,
was to be permanent. Nouseva Suomi is significant because there is every
reason to believe that its ideology was shared by most of the non-socialist
members of the government, the administrations, and the professions.
Puntila, for instance, was the head of the government information service.
It represented a system of ideas in which co-operation with Hitler's Germany was a perfectly acceptable concept, but anything less than the total
rejection of the USSR and all things Russian was near to treason.

In a more healthy state of political society, the emergence of the fascist
groups or of a movement like Nouseva Suomi would have produced
counter-movements on the Left. But this could not happen. The socialist
press certainly grumbled vigorously, but public protest went no further
than that. The Social Democratic party had tied its hands by its sub-
scription to the doctrine of unity. It would have been very difficult to
mount a vigorous attack on Nouseva Suomi without appearing to be
attacking the government and its policies, at least by implication. Thus the
natural mouthpiece for radical opinions was gagged by the current party
line. This left Wiik and his friends to wage a lone struggle against the
whole weight of established policies and ideas. Their fight was a hopeless
one. It was typical that when Wiik tried to put down an interpellation in
the Eduskunta asking when the state of war would be terminated, nobody
outside his own group would support it, so that it lacked the necessary 20
signatures that would have forced the government to answer.[51] When the
Eduskunta debated the regulations on the holding of public meetings on
October 25, the Wiik group were joined by one solitary socialist, the

foreign affairs commentator Svento. Tanner made a vigorous speech defending the restrictions. The speeches of Wiik and his group were generally not reported in the press coverage of the debates, but this did not stop the press mocking and abusing them. The political commentator of *Uusi Suomi* rejoiced that the 'chinwagging' of the 'so-called class warriors' was prevented by the emergency regulations.[52] Svento drew a storm of vilification on his head for daring to back their complaints. His speech, which was much interrupted in the Eduskunta, was described in the press as theatrical and irresponsible, unintelligible and illiterate. In describing this as an unhealthy state of affairs, one would not wish to imply that the programme of Wiik and his friends was right. But it was unfortunate that at this point in Finnish history, it was conservative and nationalist groups that took the lead and set the tone of political life, tolerated and encouraged by the government, while no radical answer was made, and those who tried to present one were systematically harassed and obstructed. This may have been inevitable in the circumstances, but it was the negation of a proper system of democratic politics. In effect, as the socialist press had feared, a 'peace of the graveyard' did hang over the political scene, and in so far as it was disturbed, the noises came from the political Right.

In order to see the political scene in full perspective it is necessary to remember the communist threat, which could not be discussed publicly for fear of offending the USSR, but which hung over everything. The SNS, though crippled by the loss of its leaders, was struggling on. It was natural that it should establish links with the Wiik group in face of their common misfortunes. Thus in September, the Wiik group had put down the interpellation in the Eduskunta, criticizing the suppression of SNS activities, while members of the Wiik group were found addressing meetings which the SNS occasionally succeeded in organizing in spite of the authorities. SNS had also tried to launch its own ex-servicemen's organization in opposition to the official body, and actually managed to get one or two branches started, though with a very small membership. But the main SNS effort lay in keeping its own branch organization alive, and using it to rally the hard core of dedicated supporters, and to spread the written propaganda material, of which it got an abundant supply, probably through the Soviet embassy. This was most important when it was extremely difficult to hold any kind of public activity, since even lectures and film shows were usually stopped by the authorities, and the Society's publication, *Soihtu*, had been closed down in October. SNS was still sufficiently alive to hold a congress in Helsinki on October 25, which re-elected the imprisoned Ryömä as chairman, and drew up a most ambitious programme for future activities which were to be concentrated on enlightenment. The farmers must be cured of incorrect ideas about the collectivization of agriculture in the USSR, and a determined effort made to win over the intellectuals by stressing the high position which their kind of people and their activities held in Soviet society. The government's oppressive measures were vigorously attacked, and resolutions sent to Stalin and Molotov congratulating the USSR on the anniversary of the Russian revolution. By itself, the SNS was no danger. Its popular following had dropped off, and it was reduced to a hard core of communists and crypto-communists, with whom the authorities were quite capable of dealing. What gave it menace was the whole tone of the propaganda poured out from the USSR and aimed directly at the Finnish people.

The vicious tone which had come into Soviet propaganda during the summer had not diminished when its patronage increasingly switched from the SNS to the Wiik group. Its purpose remained the incitement of unrest among the Finnish workers and small farmers. It sought to make the most of their undoubted material hardships, and to make out that these were imposed on them by the criminal policies of the Finnish government. If it had pursued policies of friendship towards the USSR it would not be pouring out the country's wealth on armaments and unnecessary fortifications, and by trading with the USSR it could easily relieve all the material wants of the Finnish people. The chief villain was usually Tanner, who was not only responsible for the last war, but was busy conspiring to start the next one. But this state of affairs would not continue long. The day was not far off when 'the workers and peasants rise against the bourgeoisie and put an end to the policies of the Tanner-Mannerheim group'. The workers should join with the communists to fight the class war. They would not fight alone, 'the Soviet Union has strength which can be relied on, it is the force which will carry the workers into a glittering future'.[53] This propaganda, and the evidence from Molotov's Berlin visit, which will be considered below, leads to the conclusion that the Soviet leadership had decided that the total solution of the Finnish question ought to be implemented in the near future. The obvious intrigues of the Finnish government with Germany had perhaps been the last straw. But in face of this situation one can understand why the Finnish government felt unable to tolerate the activities of SNS, and found the tendency of the Wiik group to talk in terms of class war a sinister phenomenon.

The intentions of the USSR were reflected in the much uglier tone of its diplomacy, particularly since the Finnish government continued its delaying action on the nickel question. By the end of October the Finnish government knew from Britain that Cripps had never been authorized to say that Britain would consent to the transfer of the concession, except on condition that nothing was sold to Germany. It had also decided that it would do as Germany desired, and spin out the nickel negotiations as long as possible, even though Germany could not intervene.[54] Kivimäki had informed Weizsäcker of this on October 29, at the same time as he sought Germany's views on a union with Sweden. On the latter point Kivimäki expressed his personal opinion that Finland would not in the end be prepared to give up her claim to the lost territories as the price of such a union.[55] After an interview between Paasikivi and Vishinski, who now became Molotov's deputy for Finnish affairs, it became apparent how difficult this course would be to follow.

Vishinski had opened the interview with a complaint that Finland was trying to hide something in the Åland islands, because she was obstructing the verification work of the Soviet officials there. This allegation seems to have been quite untrue. It arose from the heated imaginations of the enormous Russian consular staff, who had nothing else to do in the islands but ferret around for non-existent fortifications. Then Vishinski raised a second new matter. He complained about the flood of war books that had appeared in Finland. He said that they fomented hatred against the Soviet Union, and the Finnish government must put a stop to their publication.[56] It was apparent that Paasikivi did not make the reading of war books one of his hobbies. Conscientiously he sent to Helsinki for copies. Then came the nickel question. Vishinski declared bluntly that the excuses given by the Finnish government for refusing the request of the USSR were spurious. He said, 'the Finnish government could arrange the matter if it wanted to, but it does not want, and puts up pretexts.'[57] He repeated his version of what Cripps had said, and added that in any case Finland could override British objections. 'Is Finland an English colony? The Soviet Union has treated Finland as an independent state and wishes to honour its independence.' The insolent mendacity of this last remark was striking, even for Vishinski. Finally came the threat, if Finland did not arrange matters, the USSR would take the necessary steps. This conversation was at once reported to the German government. Kivimäki asked for German permission to plead the agreement with Veltjens in bar of the Soviet claim for the concession, but Germany would not permit this.[58]

Two days later, on November 1, Molotov followed up this offensive. He was in an unusually bad temper and flourished a copy of a Finnish book whose cover showed a Finnish soldier running his bayonet into a Russian. 'Is this the way you intend to improve relations between Finland and the Soviet Union?' Molotov demanded. He raged on about the nickel question and other minor items, alleging that 'Finland has not been willing to discuss economic matters realistically with the Soviet Union', and coming back to the war books repeated that 'in Finland, hatred is being fomented against the Soviet Union'. He concluded by repeating Vishinski's threat. Paasikivi supposed that this meant either the seizure of Petsamo, or some

172   FINLAND'S FATE IN THE BALANCE

economic sanctions.[59] In face of this pressure, the Finnish government had decided to retreat to its next barricade. It now prepared to offer, with the air of making a most painful concession, to set up a mixed Finnish-Russian company to run the nickel concession provided that the USSR would arrange matters with the British and German governments.[60] Paasikivi had suggested this to them about a month earlier. Witting, who had just received a further German memorandum regretting her inability to intervene, at once informed Blücher of the new move, which had rich potentialities for delay. But on war books it was decided to make concessions. Within a few days the press began to carry editorials preparing the public for some restrictions on them, certain especially offensive books were at once confiscated, and it was announced that others would be reviewed. On November 14, the government announced an absolute ban on the publication of books relating to the war.[61] This was done on the grounds that they might be offensive to foreign powers, and, a little improbably, that they might reveal military secrets.

It must be conceded that the USSR did have some objective grounds for complaint against the tone of some of the flood of books about the war which had been pouring off the Finnish presses in the summer and autumn of 1940. The main criticism to be made against them is that they presented the war in an unrealistic and highly emotional way. This is apparent from a lively correspondence in *Uusi Suomi* about a book, *Lunastettu Maa*, which had won a literary prize. Some of the criticism was literary, and some technical, but the core of the attack centred on the picture given in the book of the Finnish fighting soldier. Instead of being presented as a knight in shining armour, carried to superhuman levels of courage by his faith in a sacred cause, he was shown as a human being in a real war situation, who grumbled and complained, and even made cynical political remarks. Such realism was obviously highly offensive to many readers. The political commentator of *Uusi Suomi* tried to point out, gently but firmly, that fighting soldiers do not spend much time talking about patriotism or the fatherland, and that most of their energy goes into the effort to survive. Paasikivi was so depressed by the books which he read, and that was all he could get hold of, that he sent a stern despatch to Witting on the subject. The books were full of prejudice, they displayed abysmal ignorance of the opposing side, they consistently represented Finland as the defender of Christian civilization against asiatic barbarism, they repeatedly asserted that in March 1940 the Finnish army was 'unbeaten' or even 'unbeatable'. If his countrymen persisted in their refusal to face the facts about Russia, if they would not accept the Russians as human beings like themselves, and if they went on indulging emotional rather than rational ways of thought about the USSR, they would scarcely avoid ultimate disaster. Paasikivi asked 'do they really want a new war, after which there will be no need of war writers or of war literature?'[62]

At the beginning of November 1940, the whole world focused its attention on Molotov's visit to Berlin, but few watched with keener attention than the Finns, for they surmised correctly that their own fate would be decided there. Indeed, as early as October 14, the Berlin correspondent of *Uusi Suomi* had sent back a very accurate account of the background to the meeting. He said that German-Soviet relations needed readjustment following the German interventions in Romania and Finland, that the USSR was interested in Bulgaria and the future of the Dardanelles, and that Germany would try to interest the USSR in expansion to the south, into central Asia.[63] The Finnish government was well aware that Finland would figure on the agenda, and naturally apprehensive what the outcome might be. This was reflected in the memorandum which they sent to the German government on the subject. The statement handed over by Kivimäki to the German foreign office declared:[64]

'In the event that these discussions also touch upon Finland, Finland would be grateful if, from the German side, Finland's position were strengthened. At the same time the Finnish embassy affirms, that Finland on the one hand seeks to strengthen and deepen its relations with Germany and on the other hand, with regard to Russia, it desires nothing but to live and work in peace, within the area belonging to it under the last peace settlement.'

They clearly feared that Germany might buy the co-operation of the USSR at their expense as she had done in 1939. But this time their fear was groundless. Hitler had decided that he would not permit a fresh Soviet attack on Finland. This was not negotiable. Some commentators have concluded that Hitler did not really want a new political agreement at all, and that the whole initiative of calling Molotov to Berlin was bogus.[65] It seems difficult to accept this view. For instance, Hitler had certainly recalled his ambassador from Turkey in order to find out whether he could offer concessions over the Dardanelles. Further, the German military chiefs had the impression that the negotiations were genuine. Men like Admiral Raeder and Halder believed that if the USSR would agree to join the Tripartite pact, between Germany, Italy, and Japan, and would accept that her zone of expansion should be towards the Persian Gulf, Hitler intended to make a bargain with her. It is true that Hitler's price for such an agreement was so high that there was little chance that the USSR would accept it. In effect Russia was asked to renounce all interest in western Europe including her traditional interests in the Balkans, and the exclusive rights in Finland which had been guaranteed her in 1939, while in return she was offered problematical gains in the south, which would embroil her in complications with Britain, and involvement in the European war as Hitler's ally. It was an unattractive proposition and it may well be that Hitler did not seriously expect Stalin to accept it, or much regret it when he did not. Certainly he ordered the planning for the Russian campaign to go on while the talks were in progress. Still the offer, such as it was, was probably genuine.

As it turned out, the Finnish question was one of the main points on which the negotiation broke down. In a preliminary talk with Ribbentrop on November 12, Molotov indicated that Finland was one of the most important topics which he wished to discuss. He raised it with Hitler during the first of their conversations on the same day. Molotov began by observing:[66]

'. . . the Finnish question was still unsolved, and he asked the Führer to tell him whether the German-Russian agreement, as far as it concerned Finland, was still in force. In the opinion of the Soviet government no changes had occurred here.'

Thus Molotov uncovered his position. He wanted a free hand in Finland, for that was what the 1939 agreement promised him, and he intended to use it for a final solution of the Finnish question, that is he did not regard the situation established by the Treaty of Moscow as adequate to meet Russian requirements. Hitler gave his answer on the following day and in essentials it was contained in the following passage:[67]

'Germany recognized that, politically, Finland was of primary interest to Russia and was in her zone of influence. However, Germany had to consider the following two points:

'1. For the duration of the war she was very greatly interested in the deliveries of nickel and lumber from Finland and,

'2. She did not desire any new conflict in the Baltic sea, which would further curtail her freedom of movement in one of the few merchant shipping regions which still remained to her.'

The rest of Hitler's remarks on Finland were merely the repetition and elaboration of this original statement. In the course of them he would offer only one concession to the Soviet point of view. He promised that when the present programme of transits through Finland was concluded, no more troops would be sent, and he gave the impression that the transits were virtually completed already. Otherwise, Hitler threw out a series of ingenious explanations of why Germany could not allow a new war in the Baltic. There was 'a purely psychological factor that was extremely onerous', namely German popular sympathy for Finland. Germany was engaged in a life and death struggle, and if a new war started in Finland, her Anglo-American enemies might exploit the opportunity by establishing air bases in Scandinavia. But although Hitler's reasons were obviously false, his meaning was in no doubt, a new Russo-Finnish war 'would mean a strain on German-Russian relations with unforeseeable consequences'. In short, Germany would not tolerate any new attack on Finland, and the parts of the 1939 agreement which covered Finland were cancelled or suspended. For Hitler did hint that Russia might be allowed to proceed at some future time. The suspension of her rights over Finland 'would perhaps be only a matter of six months or a year's delay', and 'Russia would, after all, on the basis of the peace, receive everything that in her opinion was due to her'.[68] Hitler was ready, in theory, to surrender Finland at some indefinite point in the future, but Molotov rightly treated this as worthless.

Molotov's contributions to the discussion are most interesting for the light they throw on the Finnish policy of his government. At first he took a stiff line, that all Germany had to do was acknowledge the unfettered right of the USSR to do what she wanted. He stated that 'the Soviet government considered it as its duty to settle and clarify the Finnish question. No new agreement was needed for that'.[69] Germany herself had caused many of the current difficulties with Finland by her behaviour. The presence of her troops in the country encouraged anti-Soviet demonstrations, under which heading Molotov included 'the despatch of Finnish delegations to Germany or reception of prominent Finns in Germany'. When Hitler asked bluntly whether Russia intended to make war on Finland, the German account of the conversations says that Molotov answered evasively:

'. . . everything would be all right if the Finnish government would give up its ambiguous attitude towards the USSR and if the agitation against Russia among the population . . . would cease.'

Molotov was in fact now trying the genuineness of Hitler's objections by the argument that if Russia and Germany acted in concert towards Finland, the danger of war could not arise, and the USSR could solve the Finnish question without war. Asked what the solution would be, Molotov replied that 'he imagined the settlement on the same scale as in Bessarabia and in the adjacent countries'.[70] But Hitler remained quite impervious to any argument about Finland. In consequence, as Molotov told Ribbentrop in their final talk, 'as to the Finnish question, it was sufficiently clarified'.[71] Germany's position was certainly no longer in doubt. She would not permit the USSR to use armed force for the coercion of Finland. Molotov's position remained rather ambiguous. Thus Ribbentrop could declare with truth at his trial that he had no clear impression what measures Molotov had wanted to take against Finland.[72]

However, if one considers what Molotov said in Berlin in connection with previous Russian policy towards Finland, the Russian position can be reconstructed with some plausibility. When Molotov went to Berlin, his government had decided that if Germany could be persuaded to stand by the 1939 agreements on Finland, the final solution of the Finnish question should be implemented in the near future. Molotov's remark about a solution on the lines of Bessarabia or the adjacent countries can only mean this. When Molotov perceived that Germany would not permit the use of force, and Molotov had no illusions that the final solution was possible without this, he was prepared to settle for something less. If the German troops would leave the country, and the Finnish government understood that Germany and the USSR were in agreement, then the USSR would be able to get far-reaching concessions out of the Finnish government without the use of force. It could compel Finland to drop what he called her two-faced attitude, and cease what seemed to Molotov to be the incitement of hostility against the USSR. On this basis Molotov had been able, as his parting shot, to say that 'he did not see any indication of the outbreak of war in the Baltic'.[73]

This modified attitude became the basis of the final Russian position. Molotov carried back from Berlin a draft agreement for the USSR to join the Tripartite pact as a fourth partner, with a sphere of expansion towards the Indian ocean, but at the price of renouncing all interest in Europe west of her existing boundary. It has been pointed out that this offer was so disadvantageous to the USSR that it can be assumed to have been genuine. When Hitler outlined its terms to the Hungarian, Count Teleki, on November 20, he certainly gave the impression that they were sincerely meant.[74] But the government of the USSR would have had to be very feeble to have accepted such humiliating terms, and it felt under no necessity to do so. This became clear in Molotov's answer which was given to the German ambassador on November 25.[75] The USSR was ready to join the Tripartite pact on a number of conditions all of which were quite unacceptable to Hitler. The first concerned Finland. Germany must withdraw her troops and recognize the validity of the 1939 agreement. In return, 'the Soviet Union undertakes to ensure peaceful relations with Finland and to protect German economic interests in Finland'. Thus the USSR called Hitler's bluff by agreeing to his basic requirements over Finland, which were to be embodied in a new secret treaty. The other Russian conditions concerned Bulgaria, the Dardanelles, and the Persian Gulf. This answer sealed Russia's fate. It is almost certain that Hitler's state of mind was such that nothing but the complete and unconditional acceptance of his terms would have induced him to renounce the liquidation of the USSR. She would, in effect, have to agree to become a client state under Germany's patronage. The answer made it so clear that Stalin was not prepared to accept such a status, that Hitler never even bothered to reply to it. Hitler simply went on with his preparations for a military solution and no further political negotiations took place between the two countries. Consequently, Finland was saved, though her government did not know this. As Weizsäcker told Blücher, 'Der Führer hat seinen Regenschirm über Finnland gehalten',*[76] or as Halder noted in his diary, more bluntly, 'Finland: any further Russian action *casus belli*'.[77]

*'The Führer has held his umbrella over Finland.'

CHAPTER 9

The frustration of the union plan

The decision of the committee of the Swedish cabinet to proceed with the union plan was confirmed by the full cabinet on November 5. The following day the chief promoter of the plan, Bagge, flew to Helsinki to deliver a public lecture, and to discuss the plan further with political circles in Finland. The theme of the lecture, which got a warm welcome in the Finnish press, was that Finland and Sweden had profited from close association in the past and could do so again at the present juncture of their affairs. Bagge declared:[1]

'As I understand it, in every field, but especially in foreign policy, unity of aim and effort is as natural as it is necessary . . . We do not in any way want to deny our responsibility in the rebuilding of Europe, but we must put in the first place the independent future of Sweden and Finland. My dearest wish is . . . that both . . . can not only maintain but also widen and deepen their association.'

Bagge saw all the leading figures, and representatives of the main political parties, and all assured him that they welcomed the union plan. Walden was assumed to be speaking for Mannerheim when he said that Sweden and Finland needed each other, because neither could find any other reliable partner. Only Witting seemed less enthusiastic, suggesting that in face of the probable objections by the USSR it might be best to let the idea rest for the present. Both the Swedish and Finnish governments had been taking soundings, though in very cautious and general terms. In Stockholm, the Swedish foreign minister, Günther, and the Finnish ambassador Wasastjerna, made contact with the Russian ambassador, Madame Kollontai. Her attitude was not encouraging, certainly on November 5 she had informed the Swedes that it was unlikely that her government would agree to the plan.[2] The German government was approached by both Sweden and Finland. It was in a difficult position, since Germany obviously did not wish to see the plan succeed, and yet had no plausible reason to offer for opposing it. So Ribbentrop ordered his officials 'to keep entirely aloof for the time being.'[3] But as it became clear that the USSR was opposed to the plan, Germany was presented with a cast-iron reason for advising against it, which Hitler used in conversation with the Swedish writer Sven Hedin on December 6. Hitler said that the union 'would unnecessarily arouse the Russians. This question had better be allowed to rest until the end of the war.'[4] Hitler had seen that on this issue, the USSR and Germany had a genuine common interest, since neither wished to see Finland placed in a position where she would be less amenable to pressure from either. But the German leaders had also seen, by early December, that they could leave the USSR to do their work for them and need not soil their own hands with it.

But by that time there had been a number of parallel developments which profoundly affected the issue. The earliest of these concerned the German transit traffic in Finland. All the transits provided for in the military agreement had passed through by the middle of October, leaving some 1,200 Germans settled in the base camps along the route. The fact that these made no effort to leave showed that the Germans meant the traffic to continue, and in fact negotiations over this were in progress before Molotov arrived in Berlin on November 12. A cable from the embassy in Helsinki to the foreign office in Berlin indicated that on both the political and the military sides, arrangements for a new agreement were well advanced.[5] As in September there was to be a piece of political camouflage in the form of an exchange of notes between the two governments. The form, which had already been drafted, was to be:

'Referring to the discussions and the exchange of notes in Berlin on 22.9.40 (space for name) has the honour to declare that transits of leave-men on the route Kirkenes–Rovaniemi–Turku and in the opposite direction are now to begin.'

This illustrates very neatly how the political agreements had no practical significance, and indeed how carelessly they were drafted because of this. The reference to the exchange of notes of September 22 was meaningless because it had made no provision for the transits of leave-men, mentioning only war materials and their accompanying personnel, and in any case it had applied to north-bound traffic only, whereas the new exchange of notes concerned traffic in both directions. The real agreement was, as before, a secret one drawn up between the soldiers on both sides. A committee of Finnish and German officers met in Helsinki between November 19 and November 22 and drafted the agreement. The pre-arranged exchange of notes took place on November 21.[6] The new military agreement differed from its predecessor mainly in providing for a continuous traffic in both directions in place of three defined transits in one direction only. The port of entry had to be altered to Turku as the only harbour that would be open in the winter. The agreement said that the number of leave-men would not exceed 400 in any one week, a number that was probably related either to the maximum number who could be expected to proceed on leave at one time, or perhaps to the carrying capacity of Finnish railways. There was no mention of the number of Germans who might man the base system, but this was to be enlarged for the new traffic. The Germans would build accommodation for 500 men at Rovaniemi, Sodankylä, and Ivalo. The omission cannot be an accident. The Germans wanted to keep the size of the base system flexible, since they did not know what their future requirements might be, while the Finns still took the line that the more Germans who settled in, the better for themselves. So the agreement suited both parties. Germany had a convenient route for leave-men from northern Norway, who were a genuine problem, and a cover for developing their base system in any direction needed. Finland was now assured that the German presence in Finland would continue indefinitely. The transits continued steadily through the winter and spring at about the level provided for in the agreement. It is worth noting that the preliminary discussion about this matter had been in progress at the very time that Hitler was giving Molotov to understand that the German transits would soon come to an end. It shows how hopeless was Molotov's effort to get the Germans out of Finland. Far from being penitent about his incursion into Russia's sphere of influence, Hitler was actually arranging that it should go on for an unspecified period.

The conclusion of this agreement was in itself some assurance to the Finnish government that it had not been sold out once more during the talks in Berlin. But in addition the German leaders had decided that certain other steps should be taken to assure the Finnish government that it was now in no immediate danger from the USSR. This was made urgent by the development of the Petsamo nickel dispute. While Molotov had been away in Berlin, Paasikivi had had two further conversations with Vishinski, and presented his government's new proposal, that the USSR should itself secure the consent of Britain and Germany.[7] This was rejected by Vishinski on the grounds that no such consent was necessary. Germany had already agreed on the division of output with the USSR. Britain had in effect agreed in the Cripps offer. When Paasikivi insisted that his government had been told this was not so, Vishinski replied that in any case Finland could simply legislate to put an end to the British concession. He declared:

'You will find a means if you want. Legislation is a human activity. Laws can be changed as the need arises. If the necessary law does not exist you can make one, it only requires the will.'

Vishinski continued to hint that if the USSR did not get satisfaction she would simply take the area by force. When Molotov returned from Berlin he called Paasikivi to the Kremlin and made it quite clear that the USSR would no longer tolerate the attempt of the Finnish government to shelter behind the refusal of Great Britain. He repeated that Cripps had given her consent. Paasikivi pointed out that this consent was conditional on not selling nickel to Germany. Molotov countered, 'sell it all to the Soviet Union, we will take care of the matter',[8] in other words pass on Germany's share. After this typical and brutal cynicism, Molotov said that his patience was exhausted, and the nickel affair must be settled without further delay. Paasikivi was convinced that if his government did not give in now, the USSR would certainly act. He reommended that they agree to transfer the concession and expropriate the British, 'if one of the three great powers must be eliminated, then it must unfortunately be England in my opinion, which is distant and least important to us politically.'[9]

In face of this, the Finnish government turned to Germany for advice. Kivimäki went to the German foreign office on November 18, in part because of disturbing reports about what had happened between Molotov and the Germans. The communiqué issued after the talks said that they had agreed on all important issues, and Finland was flooded with alarming rumours and prophecies. So much can be deduced from the press in spite of the censorship. Svento commented on how rumour was fed by ignorance and how this was creating a dangerous mood in the country.[10] Kivimäki did not get much satisfaction. He was told that Germany could not oppose the transfer of the concession to a mixed company, but would insist on a written guarantee of her right to 60% of the output. Finland could certainly make this a condition of any agreement. The Finnish government reluctantly accepted this position. Witting told Blücher on November 22 that he had hoped for German intervention, but would direct his policy as the German government had suggested.[11]

Shortly after this, Germany decided to give Finland enough encouragement to prevent her making embarrassing concessions to the USSR. Göring was the chief mover, Veltjens again the agent. On November 21, Göring wrote to his brother-in-law Eric Rosen. He asked Rosen to convey to Mannerheim that he could be confident of the future. 'Germany neither can, nor ever will desert a friendly Finland.'[12] Veltjens would come to Finland soon to explain things. Veltjens arrived on November 25 with a threefold mission, to clear up certain points about the arms deliveries, to give a version of what had passed during the Molotov visit, and to give advice about the nickel question. It seems likely that Veltjens confined his talks to the military leaders, chiefly Mannerheim. He revealed that Molotov had been told that Germany would not allow any fresh conflict in the Baltic so that Finland could 'remain calm and firm in negotiation' although 'defiance was to be avoided'.[13] There was no need for Finland to make 'improper concessions' over the nickel question, but no mention was to be made of Germany's right of pre-emption. Germany would not oppose the transfer of the concession to a mixed company, but would insist on her share of the output. If Finland could avoid having to transfer the concession so much the better. Veltjens reported that the Finns had been 'grateful and wonderfully cheered up',[14] as well they might be after all the fearful uncertainty surrounding Molotov's visit. Veltjens was told that Kallio would shortly resign the presidency, and asked for his views on possible candidates for the post. He was also given reports of the effects of German air attacks on London, supplied by the Finnish embassy there. This somewhat un-neutral act was a small token of appreciation. The German foreign office followed up the Veltjens mission with measures of its own, to make sure that the message of hope and good cheer had got over to the Finnish government. Blücher was empowered to talk to Witting on the same lines as Veltjens, while on November 30, Weizsäcker told Kivimäki that he believed that the USSR had taken note of Germany's desire that there should be no new conflict in the Baltic.[15] On the practical side, Halder noted on November 18 that Hitler had listed Finland, with Romania and Bulgaria, as one of the neutral countries that was to receive 'accommodating treatment'.

Thus fortified, the Finnish government decided to take the Petsamo nickel question a stage further, on the lines suggested by Veltjens. They now proposed that although Britain still withheld her consent, they would open discussions with the USSR about the formation of a joint Finnish-Soviet company, which should receive the concession if Britain eventually agreed. Paasikivi pointed out that this was useless as it stood. They must make up their minds that if Britain did not agree, she would be expropriated. He wrote to the government:[16]

'We cannot propose negotiations about a mixed company and the transfer of the concession, before we are clear that in principle, we will fix the matter by legislation if England does not consent.'

Reluctantly, the government in Helsinki accepted the ambassador's logic, and agreed that the proposal should be put forward on that basis. Paasikivi then went to present this offering to Molotov. He stressed how the Finnish government was risking having the traffic to Liinahamari cut off by the step it was taking, and that the new proposal was a great sacrifice on its part. He also said that a condition of any final arrangement would be that Germany was guaranteed 60% of the output, as was provided for in existing agreements. Molotov had a quick ear for an inconsistency, and he at once seized on this last point. Had Britain consented to the making of this agreement to sell the nickel to Germany? He had the impression from Cripps that Britain was opposed to any such sales. How had the Finnish government managed to overcome the objections which the British government must have made? Paasikivi reported that he felt caught out, 'I explained the matter as best I could, but with poor success'. He could hardly explain away the fact that Finland had ignored British objections to the sale of nickel to Germany, and at the same time used British objections as a pretext for not giving the concession to the USSR. Molotov rubbed in his debating triumph, 'you have made agreements with Germany, but with me you have procrastinated five months under various pretexts and tried our patience.' Molotov then demanded, did the Finnish government agree to transfer the concession? Paasikivi tried to dodge a direct answer and said that they still hoped that Britain would be got to consent. At once Molotov leaped in to score his point, 'now we were appealing to England, but we had not done that over our agreement with Germany'. Finally Molotov brought out the now familiar threats, the Finnish government must make up its mind to arrange things with the British, there were many in the USSR who regretted that Petsamo had been returned to Finland, 'our relations will not become good in this fashion.' However, he agreed that discussions could be started about the formation of a mixed company, 'although it did not seem to please him. Probably he suspected a trick to drag the matter out.' For once Molotov was quite correct in his suspicion.[17]

This became apparent when in December, a Finnish delegation arrived in Moscow to discuss the setting up of a mixed company. As Paasikivi described it, the Finnish representatives 'were in the grip of optimistic fancies'.[18] They proposed a form of mixed company in which Finland held three-quarters of the shares, and appointed the chairman and two of the four directors. The USSR was to be allowed to appoint an inspector to watch over the actual mining operations. Even so, this company would not itself run the mines. These would be left in the charge of the existing concession holders, who would merely sell the whole output to the new mixed company. On top of that the whole proposal still required that the British should give their consent, and that the negotiations for this should be undertaken by the mixed company itself. As Paasikivi points out, this scheme completely ignored all the basic requirements which the USSR had repeatedly made clear. These were that the mixed company should have complete control of the mines, that the British should be entirely removed from the Petsamo area, and that the USSR would not be involved in any way in negotiations with the British government on the issue. The Russian proposals were simple. The company would be one in which the USSR owned 51% of the capital, the directorate would be equally divided, but the managing director and the manager of the mines were to be

Russians. The Finnish government would be entirely responsible for getting the British out. The Finnish delegation said that their instructions would not allow them even to discuss such a proposal, and the negotiations were broken off. In consequence, six months after the matter had first been raised, Molotov was no nearer his objective than he had been at the start. He must have felt that the Finnish proposals were so unrealistic, in view of what the Finnish government knew of the requirements of the USSR, that they were simply a device for spinning matters out still further. It is clear from Paasikivi's comments that he too was puzzled by his government's behaviour. They took no notice of his repeated warnings that the USSR would almost certainly use force if she were denied her way in this matter. And as he remarked to the leader of the Finnish delegation in Moscow, 'we cannot afford to be carried into the danger of a conflict over such a relatively small matter as the nickel'.[19] He acknowledged that as soon as the USSR had established its control over the mines, it would begin to make trouble and difficulties in the area, just as it had done in the Åland islands by using its rights of inspection there, but Paasikivi did not see how his government could continue to refuse. From this it is apparent that Paasikivi did not know about the assurances from Germany on which the policy of his government rested. As he must have been kept in ignorance deliberately, this is one of the first signs that the government suspected their ambassador was too soft towards the Russians. He no longer had their entire confidence. The breach was destined to widen because the ambassador really wanted to settle the nickel question, and his government did not, yet it did not trust him enough to tell him so.

The support which Germany was giving to Finland's resistance was by this stage based on much weightier considerations than the maintenance of the nickel supply or the facilities for transits into northern Norway. Hitler's interest in Finland had always rested mainly on his desire to use Finland for his eastern campaign, and by early December, this desire had been translated into concrete plans. From the very earliest discussions of such a campaign, German planners had assumed that Finland would be involved, but the serious planning had only started in September, when General Paulus was given the job of producing a plan of campaign under the supervision of Halder and the OKH. Paulus worked out his plans, through a series of theoretical exercises, and in consultation with Halder and the army commander Brauchitsch. At this stage, Hitler merely urged on the work, as when he insisted that the Molotov visit would make no difference to the planning of an eastern campaign, nor to the parallel work being done on possible campaigns in Gibraltar and Greece.

On December 5, all three plans, which had up to then been the work of OKH, were discussed at a conference between the army leaders, Hitler,

and the chiefs of OKW, Keitel and Jodl. In his general remarks, Hitler
said that 'Romania and Finland will go along with Germany in an eastern
campaign, of that there is no doubt'.[20] But during this conference, there
seems to have been no further mention of what part, if any, the Finnish
armed forces might play. The plan produced by Paulus was essentially for
two powerful thrusts at Leningrad and Moscow, flanked by a southern
force which would aim at Kiev. Moscow was the focal target of the plan.
Hitler insisted on certain major alterations being made. He declared that
concepts based on the capture of ground or even cities were outdated. The
object must be to surround and destroy the Russian armies before they
had a chance to retreat into the interior. Therefore the force thrusting at
Moscow was to be diverted. After breaking through the forces in front of it,
it would wheel right and left in order to encircle the Russians in the Baltic
states and in the Ukraine. Only after this had been achieved would the
march on Moscow be resumed. Hitler added a further refinement. The
troops in northern Norway, after securing the Petsamo area and the nickel
mines, would thrust towards the White Sea. Another German division
would be brought in from Narvik, over the Swedish railways, and operate
on their southern flank.[21] Thus, although no specific role was assigned to
the Finnish army, Hitler did assume the use of Finnish territory for
launching his northern attacks. The Finnish government no more knew of
this than did the Swedish government that Hitler meant to use their railways. Hitler added that Finland would be rewarded by enlargement at
Russian expense when the victory had been won.[22]

   In the following two weeks, the plan was developed and put into final
shape in OKW. In the course of these preparations, German intentions to
use Finnish territory were elaborated. The staff of the German forces in
Norway had a plan for bringing three divisions over the Swedish railways,
and even supposed that Sweden might be induced to lend three divisions
of her own troops to cover their assembly.[23] The plans were completed
and approved by Hitler, and issued on December 18 as 'General Order
No. 21' for an operation to eliminate the USSR under the code name
'Barbarossa'.[24] The plan followed Hitler's ideas. The central thrust was to
be interrupted in order to make vast encircling movements, and further
priority was to be given to the capture of Leningrad and the elimination of
the Russian Baltic fleet before the attack on Moscow. The general effect
of the new plan was to make the task before the German armies both bigger
and more complex than envisaged in the Paulus plan. This 'limitlessness',
as Halder called it, made it more than ever desirable to enlist all the available auxiliary forces for the campaign. Further the emphasis on Leningrad
naturally focused attention on Finland's role.

   This was now fairly outlined. First Barbarossa assumed the participation of Finland and Romania. It laid down that in due course talks would be opened for subordinating their armies to German command. Finnish troops would now cover the flank of the German thrust from northern Norway. The more southerly thrust would be based on Rovaniemi, but was dependent on whether Sweden made her railways available, which could not be assumed. The Finnish forces would have to eliminate the Russian base at Hanko, but their main body would be used for an attack to the south-east, as the German advance approached Leningrad, designed to tie down the maximum number of Russian troops. The order made it clear that for the moment the prospective allies were to be told nothing of the roles allotted to them. Even when the time did come, they were to be led to believe 'dass es sich um Vorsichtsmassnahmen handelt für den Fall, dass Russland seine bisherige Haltung gegen uns ändern sollte'.[*25] The wording of the order makes it quite clear that Finland had not been consulted in advance, nor was she told anything about it at this time. The Germans simply assumed that Finland would be willing to play her allotted part, though with much more confidence than they assumed that Sweden would lend her railways. It is obvious that the Barbarossa plan affected German policy towards Finland in three ways. First Germany had to ensure that she developed the confidence and friendship of Finland to the point where she would be willing to take part in the campaign. Second, since surprise was essential, Germany had to avoid an open breach with the USSR before the time set for the attack, and must also restrain Finland from doing anything which might precipitate a conflict with the USSR, or which might provoke a preventive strike at Finland by the USSR. Thirdly, Germany would not allow Finland to escape into independent neutrality, which might remove her incentive to participate. These three themes are the basis of German policy towards Finland from this time forward.

The third of these lines of policy was being severely tested while the plans for Barbarossa were still being worked out, for the scheme of union between Sweden and Finland suddenly came to its critical point. The immediate cause of the crisis seems to lie in two interviews in Stockholm with Madame Kollontai. Günther talked to her on November 27, and Wasastjerna on December 3.[26] As a result she seems to have reported to Moscow that Sweden and Finland were about to sign a treaty of union. Both men claimed afterwards that they had been misunderstood. All they had said was that their two countries hoped to promote 'the closest possible common effort between Sweden and Finland, on the basis that their defence and foreign policies were the same.'[27] The basis of their common policy would be the maintenance of their position as neutrals. Molotov assumed, on the basis of

*'it was all a matter of taking precautions in case Russia changed her present attitude towards us,'

Kollontai's reports, that the old alliance plan was being revived behind his back, and that he was to be presented with the accomplished fact. At least it is difficult to account for the vigour of his reaction on any other basis. He had known for a long time that discussions were in progress. Paasikivi was got out of bed at 11.30 on the night of December 6, and called to Molotov's presence. Molotov then read him a formal note. It declared that Sweden and Finland were preparing an agreement to unify their foreign policies, so that these would be determined from Stockholm. Such an action would dissolve the Treaty of Moscow, which had been concluded with an independent Finland. It went on:[28]

'The Soviet government urges the Finnish government to weigh all that has been said above, and consider the consequences which such an agreement with any foreign power whatever, Sweden included, will entail for Finland.'

Paasikivi, as so often, had not been told by his government what was happening. He had to send to Helsinki to find out. Over the next few days there were urgent consultations between the two governments and their ambassadors in Moscow, in order to frame a common story for presentation to the Soviet government. Finally, on December 9, Assarsson, the Swedish ambassador, went to Molotov to explain that he had been the victim of a misunderstanding. Nothing had yet been concluded. It was the basis of the negotiations that both countries would maintain their obligations to foreign powers unaltered, and further that they would take no decision without the approval of Germany and the USSR. They had believed that the scheme was consistent with the avowed policy of the USSR.[29] The result of this was that on December 12, Paasikivi was summoned to the Kremlin.[30] Molotov opened in a mood of heavy irony by inquiring whether Assarsson's visit meant that Finland had already subordinated her foreign policy to Sweden. Paasikivi replied by telling the same tale as his Swedish colleague and says that 'out of this arose a wide discussion'. Molotov insisted that the new scheme was simply another version of the alliance plan to which the USSR had stated its objections in March. 'Now you want to reach the same result by a side road with another name'. Paasikivi urged that all they wanted to do was to guarantee the existing situation. Molotov replied that on the contrary, Finland and Sweden were trying to upset the existing situation, it was the Soviet Union which 'wanted to keep things as they are'. He complained that they had obviously consulted Germany before asking the assent of the USSR, and asked what the USA and Britain would think of this. It may have been in Molotov's mind that Germany was behind the whole idea. Molotov remained unmoved by Paasikivi's arguments. He declared in conclusion that the government of the USSR stood by its note of December 6. 'It contains the view of the Soviet Union and is a warning to the Finnish government'. The USSR also took counter measures in Berlin. The Soviet ambassador there had a conversation with Ribbentrop on the subject, also on December 12. He explained the stand which the USSR was taking, and said that one reason why she opposed the plan so resolutely was that Madame Kollontai had said that the scheme was intended to free Finland from German influence.[31] As a friendly power, the USSR was bound to resist this. It is hard to imagine a more implausible reason, but it suited Ribbentrop very well to pretend to believe it. In fact the attitude of the USSR to the union plan played right into Germany's hands, and delivered the German government from what might have been a rather embarrassing situation.

The issues involved in the union plan had been earnestly considered in the top circles of Finnish government. The issue, as it appeared to Mannerheim and Ryti and Walden, was whether Finland should seek refuge from the hostility of the USSR with Sweden or with Germany. From the course of events it seems that Mannerheim and Ryti would have preferred to adopt the union plan to the alternative of direct dependence on Germany. But because the assurances that they had recently received from Berlin were the only existing security that they had, they could not risk forfeiting Germany's goodwill by entering the union without her consent. On the other hand there was the minority opinion, almost certainly upheld by Witting, and inspired by Kivimäki, which was sceptical of the value of any arrangement with Sweden, and wanted Finland to associate openly with Germany. Kivimäki had been talking with his German friends about the idea of Finland joining the Tripartite pact, as other small neutrals were doing. He had received some encouragement in foreign office circles in Germany and had been writing to Ryti, who had also discussed the matter in Helsinki. Ryti claimed at his trial that he had always been resolutely opposed to this idea, but this was not the impression that Kivimäki had formed. Kivimäki sent a private letter to Ryti on November 27, in which he argued strongly for Finland's adherence to the Tripartite pact without further delay, and revealed that Ryti had expressed a readiness to consider the idea.[32]

It can be deduced, from the leading part which Mannerheim played in the next phase, that he had thrown his full weight behind the union plan, so much so that he did not let the attitude of the USSR deflect him from his purpose. It seems that he was prepared to defy the USSR and proceed with the union, if Germany would give her consent. On December 16, Mannerheim's personal emissary, General Talvela, accompanied by the Finnish military attaché, called on General Halder.[33] He revealed that he had already been to see Göring to whom he had presumably talked on the same lines as he followed in talking to Halder. Talvela reviewed the situation in Finland, and put great stress on the danger of communist subversion. This was a theme which Mannerheim himself had stressed to the German military attaché in Helsinki about a month earlier. Mannerheim had then claimed that if the USSR got a foothold in the nickel mines, she would make them a centre for subversive activity. One wonders whether Mannerheim was as alarmed as he said, or whether he judged this the most promising way of raising German anxieties. It certainly impressed Halder who made the note, 'Finland threatened by communist propaganda' Talvela went on to describe the military situation, again in terms most likely to rouse German alarm, and Halder made a note, 'Åland–Petsamo–Salla'. Talvela had said that Finland could not defend these with her present resources. But they were all areas vital to Germany if she wished to realize her plans, or even maintain her nickel supplies. Mannerheim was probably fishing for some hint that Germany herself would help to defend these areas if an attack came. Talvela went on to mention that Finland still needed heavy artillery and aircraft, and then came to the core of his mission. If the union with Sweden were realized, Sweden would send five divisions to help Finland, and this would meet the dangers of which Talvela had been talking. Would Germany be prepared to help bring this union about?

It is not known what Halder's reply was, probably that this was a matter for the foreign office to deal with, but it is known what Göring and the German foreign office said. They told both Finland and Sweden to drop the idea. Göring's attitude, as reported to the German foreign office, was that 'Germany was interested in Finland only as an independent nation, not as a Swedish province'.[34] Happily, the USSR had relieved the Germans of the necessity of thinking up plausible reasons for their stand. Both Sweden and Finland were told that the hostility of the USSR was so strong that it would be unwise to proceed. Hitler told this to the Swedish government on December 16, 'it was not suitable just now to realize the idea, taking into account Finland's delicate relations with the Soviet Union'. In other words, Germany was not prepared to quarrel with the USSR in order to enable the union scheme to go through. But she was able to make this clear without revealing that her own hostility to the plan was as great as that of the USSR.

This was what Talvela learned from his mission to Germany, and the knowledge had a decisive effect in shaping Finnish policy. Even Mannerheim seems to have recognized that association with Sweden was impossible, and that there was no alternative to reliance on Germany. It was suggested at the Nuremberg trials that Talvela's visit to Germany in December marked the beginning of joint Finnish-German planning

for an attack on the USSR.[35] This rests largely on the final entry in Halder's diary after his notes on the visit. 'I want to know how much time
would be needed to make quiet preparations for an offensive to the south-
east'.[36] This has been assumed to prove that he discussed the matter with
Talvela. But the use of the present tense suggests that Halder was noting
this as something he must set about discovering, and that Talvela's visit
had reminded him of it. It is most improbable that at this early stage in
planning, Halder would have risked revealing what Germany had in mind
by putting such a question to Talvela.

In addition to the problems of the nickel concession and the union plan,
the Finnish leaders were also grappling with the delicate question of elect-
ing a new president of the republic. The decision to replace Kallio had
been taken some time in November. It was by then clear that he would not
be able to resume his duties, and in so critical a time it was an obvious
drawback not to have the presidential powers exercised by an active and
able personality. It had been recognized from the start that because the
president of Finland was constitutionally the director of foreign policy,
the choice was bound to be of interest to foreign powers. So that as early
as November 23, Veltjens had been questioned about the German attitude
to the possible candidates.[37] This is worth recalling because when the
USSR later expressed opinions on this question the Finns made a great
show of indignation at her intervention in Finland's internal affairs. Since
the choice of a new president was such an important and delicate matter,
it was fortunate that there could be no question of holding a proper election. The mere existence of the refugees, who were still not resettled, and
would have been unable to vote, ruled this out. So it was announced on
November 28 that Kallio had asked to resign, and that the government
would propose a special law to the Eduskunta whereby the election would
be entrusted to the electoral college chosen in 1937 for the last presidential
election.[38]

The editorials in the press, and the political commentators praised the
decision of the government. The new president must be the unanimous
choice of the nation, there could be no question of letting party politics
affect the issue. Officially there were never any declared candidates. In the
very early stages *Uusi Suomi* quoted a Swedish press report that Mannerheim was said to be unwilling to stand and that Ryti was the next most
obvious choice.[39] *Helsingin Sanomat*, on December 4, actually printed a
list of 12 names said to be possibilities, though at least half of these were
obvious non-starters.[40] Blücher too had collected quite a long list of possible candidates by December 2, and reported that there was 'a marked
splintering' in political circles. But some of his names were so unlikely that
the soundness of his information must be suspect.[41] It was of course true

that everyone in Finland knew who were the five serious possibilities. Excluding Mannerheim, who was in a class by himself, the first and obvious choice was Ryti. He had been acting president since the end of August, his election would present no difficulty to the politicians, and would be safe from the point of view of foreign powers, since it would preserve the existing situation and give nobody fresh cause of offence. Then there was Kallio's predecessor, Svinhufvud. His great drawback was that he was unacceptable to the Social Democrats. When they had said that the new president must be acceptable to the workers and represent democratic values, they meant that Svinhufvud was ruled out. His hostility to the socialists was notorious. From a foreign point of view, the election of Svinhufvud would have been a demonstration, for he was notoriously pro-German and fanatically anti-communist. He once expressed his views to Blücher on the Russian question. The Russians had no place in the north, they should be pushed back into the south, and an enlarged Finland, under German protection, set up to keep an eye on them.[42] Another pro-German candidate was Kivimäki. His election was actively canvassed by some of his German friends and their Finnish connections, though not by the German foreign office. Kivimäki maintained afterwards, in a letter to Ryti, that he had never consented to this campaign on his behalf. Moving in the opposite political direction there was Tanner. He was ruled out internally as a socialist. Unity was the order of the day, and old feuds were supposed to be healed, but the parties of the Right would not accept a Social Democrat as president, however sound his views had become. Tanner was also ruled out by foreign opposition. His election would be an affront to the USSR, and would not be viewed with enthusiasm in Germany. Tanner was not a serious starter. That left Paasikivi, whose name was being canvassed. He was the one candidate whose election would have been a gesture of conciliation towards the USSR, and would have implied a real change of policy. This virtually ruled him out, and in any case, Paasikivi declined to stand. His strongest supporter was the USSR. Molotov told him on December 18 that 'we are very glad to keep you here, but we should be glad also to welcome you as president of Finland'.[43] For once there was no doubt that Molotov was telling the truth.

It was an extraordinary way to run a presidential election in a democratic country. *Suomen Sosiaalidemokraatti* assured its readers on December 17 that the foreign press was amazed at the self-discipline shown in Finland in mentioning no names.[44] It is strange to read long editorials on the election, like that in *Uusi Suomi* on December 17, which contain no hint of who is standing, or who might be elected, and call on the people to be confident that the electoral college will choose a man worthy of their unanimous support.[45] It could be argued that in the end, the election was decided by

Germany, the USSR, and Great Britain. German influence seems to have been decisive in one way, in ruling out Mannerheim, who could have had the presidency for the asking. He was in any case the ultimate authority in the state, and it would have been convenient to regularize this situation. General Talvela did make inquiries in Germany on the Marshal's behalf early in December.[46] The Germans did all they could to discourage the idea. Blücher had reported that Mannerheim's chances were slight, because the Finns suspected that the USSR was bitterly hostile to his candidature. The ambassador thought that this was just as well, since in the past 'his attitude toward Germany has wavered'.[47] Ribbentrop was of the same opinion and told Blücher to suggest to the Finns that if Mannerheim were elected he would 'be a liability in their relations with Soviet Russia'. Further, he might be of 'greater value as a military leader than as president'.[48] Blücher himself, and Veltjens before him, had been hinting to their Finnish contacts that both Svinhufvud and Kivimäki 'enjoy great prestige in Germany.'[49] But Blücher had recognized at an early stage that Ryti was the strongest candidate. Since it would have needed all Germany's strength to block his election, if that seemed desirable, Blücher asked for instructions. He noted that Ryti's sympathies for England and his freemasonry were drawbacks in German eyes.

Ribbentrop replied that Kivimäki would be the best choice for Germany, and that Ryti's election was 'less desirable'. But officially Germany would not support any candidate, and Blücher was not empowered to go beyond making his preferences known 'in confidential conversation'. However, on the eve of the election, after Blücher had sent in a more favourable assessment of Ryti, he was told to throw German influence behind Ryti, who 'has recently shown much understanding for German interests' and was to be preferred to 'some weak compromise candidate or Paasikivi.'[50] Blücher claimed subsequently that his announcement of Germany's preference had been decisive in securing Ryti's election. Certainly it would have rallied many supporters of Svinhufvud and Kivimäki behind Ryti. Ironically, the intervention of the British government tended to produce the same effect. It let it be known that it would take a serious view of the election of either Svinhufvud or Kivimäki, but would be quite happy with either Mannerheim or Ryti.

But the most spectacular foreign intervention was from Moscow. When Paasikivi was summoned to Molotov on December 6, to receive the Soviet note on the union plan, he was also read a second communication which ran as follows:[51]

'We do not wish to interfere in the matter nor make any suggestions about the candidates for a new president of Finland, but we are following the election preparations carefully. We shall judge whether Finland wants peace with the Soviet Union according to who is chosen president. It is clear that if someone such as Tanner, Kivimäki, Mannerheim, or Svinhufvud is elected president, we shall conclude that Finland does not wish to fulfil the peace treaty it has made with the Soviet Union.'

It has been noted that this intervention does not justify all the outraged comment which it has drawn from the Finnish side. The Finns had themselves taken the initiative in asking Germany's opinions, and the USSR had as good a right as Germany to voice a preference. What stung them to fury was not so much the fact of the intervention, as the contemptuous cynicism of Molotov's behaviour, reflected in the opening sentence of the note. Molotov repeated this when Paasikivi remonstrated with him, saying 'of course you can elect who you want, but we have the right to draw our conclusions.'[52] At first Paasikivi was inclined to play down the seriousness of the intervention, presumably to prevent burst blood-vessels in Helsinki. He commented that Molotov's message was 'of course improper', but nowadays 'small countries have to endure anything'. But on reflection, Paasikivi feared that his government might jump to the wrong conclusion as a result of his advice, and wrote to Witting to say that Molotov's threat must be taken seriously. The incident added disproportionately to the bitterness which was poisoning Russo-Finnish relations. As Paasikivi remarked, 'the threatening form and tone of the announcement was as offensive as its contents.'[53] Witting was angry because Paasikivi had consented to accept Molotov's communication at all, and Ryti called it 'a great impertinence', and thought that Paasikivi should have returned the note to Molotov, while some of the electors were stirred to talk wildly of defying the USSR. But on reflection calmer counsels prevailed.[54]

In effect, the three great powers unanimously elected Ryti, the only serious candidate to whom none of them voiced any objection. It only remained to go through the formalities and secure him a unanimous election. The vital decision was probably made on December 18, when there was vigorous activity among the various party groups, and some trouble with stubborn minorities on the Right,[55] but at the formal election the following day, Ryti received 288 votes out of a possible 300. There were six blanks, four members of the Wiik group voted for Helo, one of their number, and Svinhufvud and Kivimäki got one vote each.[56] Thus Ryti was elected to a chorus of universal acclamation in the press. It now revealed that there had for some time been no doubt of his election, but there had been fears of a substantial minority vote for other candidates. The result was a triumph for yksimielisyys, and the electors were assured that they had rightly interpreted the will of the people. The socialists seemed especially pleased, Ryti fulfilled all their conditions, and the collapse of the support for Svinhufvud must have gratified them. Mannerheim too expressed his

13

pleasure at the result. He remarked 'a significant outcome—and a remarkable people this Finnish nation of ours'.[57] It must have been the size of Ryti's vote which occasioned this remark, for the result was otherwise no cause for astonishment to anyone so well informed as the Marshal was. On this interpretation it is a fair comment. The politicians had kept their heads and made the best of the circumstances. Germany had been satisfied without Britain or the USSR being outraged.[58] Unity had been demonstrated in spite of all the tradition of bitter personal and party rivalries associated with presidential elections. To Mannerheim, who had always rather despised party politicians, and deplored the pre-war political habits of his countrymen, the outcome must indeed have seemed remarkable.

The election was followed by a drama which deeply moved the Finnish people. Kallio intended to return to his farm on the 19th, and a great popular send-off was arranged at Helsinki railway station, in addition to an official guard of honour. As Kallio passed down the line of soldiers, accompanied by Mannerheim and Ryti, and watched by the great crowd, he collapsed almost into the Marshal's arms, and died within a few minutes. Kallio had not been of major political importance, certainly not since the war began. But he had been the perfect image of the true Finnish farmer, the ideal national type, just as his wife seemed to typify the Finnish farmer's wife. Their simplicity and lack of pretensions had won the hearts of a people that is inclined to take a very hard and cynical view of those in authority, and Kallio's sudden death made an abnormally deep impression.

December 1940 was a month which found many Finns, both high and low, wondering what their future would be. It seems to have been generally understood that the country's relations with the USSR were in a deplorable state. Official statements, like Ryti's inauguration address on December 21, or his New Year message, spoke of the government's will and expectation that relations with the USSR could be developed on a friendly and confident basis. It is difficult to believe that these carried any credence. The ordinary citizen could get little about the Soviet Union out of his newspaper. But he could listen to the Soviet radio from Petroskoi or Tallinn, and judge from the tone of its broadcasts how matters stood. The Soviet propagandists did not conceal what they hoped the future would bring. The days of Finnish capitalism were numbered, 'the measure of the working people of Finland is full . . . they on the other hand are preparing the collapse of the existing social system as happened in Estonia, Latvia, and Lithuania'.[59] It could easily be deduced from this sort of thing that Soviet policy intended the destruction of Finland's independence, and that the establishment of normal relations with the USSR was an impossible objective. The public must also have got to hear a great deal about, for instance, the behaviour of Zotov, the Soviet ambassador. Certainly official Finland knew more than enough of his aims and methods. He was continuously harassing the Finnish government with his demands that his officials be allowed freedom of movement round the country, or with petty complaints about supposed infringements of the rights of the USSR. It was not only the substance of his demands which irritated, since so many were groundless, but the tone. Zotov invariably 'demanded' what he wanted, his requirements were 'essential minimum conditions'. Paasikivi has remarked that one cannot know whether Zotov's behaviour was caused by excess of zeal or by direct instructions, but in any case 'it showed that the relations of Finland and the Soviet Union were not what they should have been'.[60] Tanner's lawyer, at his trial in 1945, put the case more strongly:[61]

'Minister Zotov did not behave in Finland as the representative of a friendly state, but as a boss. It is understandable that opinion here became embittered, and a basis was formed for some kind of thoughts of revenge.'

In addition to the behaviour of the ambassador, there was a rash of cases of espionage, of spies coming in disguised as refugees from the Baltic states, of embassy officials getting caught in forbidden areas, or trying to contact or recruit agents.

At a higher level, there were several minor disputes which amply illustrated the deplorable state of relations, and rumours of these also penetrated to the public, often no doubt in wildly exaggerated form. In December there was a row about the building of the Kemijärvi railway. Finland had undertaken to construct her section of the line, 'as far as possible', during 1940. It was a difficult job to force a railway through a rocky forested wilderness in a sub-arctic climate, and probably the Finnish authorities were not as enthusiastic in overcoming these difficulties as they might have been in other circumstances. By December it was necessary to report progress to the USSR, and it had to be admitted that the line was unlikely to be open before the summer of 1941. When Zotov was informed of this he took it badly. He suggested that the Finnish government must set a firm date for completion, and if this was not achieved, he warned that it would be a breach of the peace treaty.[62] Soon after Molotov took the matter up with Paasikivi. He expected the railway to be finished in February, and presented a note which declared that Finland had not yet built 'a single kilometre, and thus had not fulfilled the undertaking given in the peace treaty'. Paasikivi suggested to his government that perhaps they could finish the line in the spring of 1941, but that would probably have been impossible. It was in fact not ready until the autumn, when it proved a useful line of supply for the German forces operating against the Murmansk railway.

But the story of the Kemijärvi railway is more than just another illustration of mutual dissatisfaction between Finland and the USSR. It seems to have carried a considerable psychological significance for the Finns. Since the railway made no sense as an economic proposition there was ample scope for wondering what its real purpose was, particularly since the USSR seemed to attach such importance to it. There is good evidence that Ryti, and presumably many other Finns, believed that it was an essential part of a long-cherished Russian design to get direct access to the Atlantic ocean. Such ideas had in fact been discussed in communist circles in the 1920s. Ryti took them as a serious intention of the Soviet government. Mannerheim was haunted by the immediate military implications. The keenness of his apprehensions can be judged by the space which he gives them in his memoirs. He cites various reports collected by Finnish intelligence, of Russian officials connecting the completion of the line with the coming conquest of Finland. One officer was heard to say that 'capitalist Finland will be joined to the Soviet Union this year as soon as the Salla railway is ready'.[63] With such a background, it is easy to see why the Finnish government would put a sinister interpretation on Russia's insistence on a speedy completion of the railway. Yet it is unlikely that the USSR had any plans as precise as the Finnish leaders supposed, and even if they did, Molotov knew by December that Hitler's veto stood in the way of realizing them. Molotov was probably using the Kemijärvi railway as one more stick with which to beat Finland and keep her under pressure.

The game of guessing the intention of the USSR towards their country was being played by Finns at the highest level. Paasikivi was exchanging letters of advice not only with Witting, but with other members of the leading circle on this subject. Paasikivi tended to take a less jaundiced view of Soviet intentions than most of his correspondents. He told Walden in a letter of December 5, that he thought things were easing, and that the worst danger had been during the summer, when, as he had since heard, the USSR had seriously contemplated the annexation of Finland. Paasikivi also exchanged long letters with Tanner, which reflected the movement of thought in Finland. Tanner described how the continual Russian interference and the barrage of scurrilous propaganda were hardening opinion against the USSR. Most people were now convinced that the USSR intended for Finland the fate of the Baltic states. So far the government had generally followed Paasikivi's advice and made concessions, but Tanner felt that they could not do so much longer. People were asking, 'will this help permanently and where will it end?' Tanner continued:[64]

'Already resentful feelings are aroused here, and the more interference there is in purely internal affairs, the more opinion is likely to turn in reaction from it. Before long there could be here the same conflict between the men of concession and the men of resistance as there was forty years back.'

Thus Tanner was afraid that in the end Soviet policy would provoke such a reaction that a policy of concession would have to be abandoned in order to preserve essential national unity. It is likely that Tanner reflected the views of informed, and liberally inclined Finns of that time. At the root of their thinking is the conviction that the USSR intended to annex Finland as she had done the Baltic states, and this conviction was fed by what Tanner called the endless 'pinpricks, which because of their small-ness are felt to intend the maintenance of continuing nervous tension.'

Paasikivi held a point of view that very few of his countrymen shared. He tried to throw doubt on the basic thesis that what had happened to the Baltic states proved what was in store for Finland. 'Finland's position has always been different from the Baltic countries', he wrote, and proceeded to illustrate this by examples from the time of Peter the Great to Stalin. But Paasikivi could not deny that Tanner might be right about the ultimate intentions of the USSR. The Soviet government certainly tried to keep Fin-land weak and isolated. 'It is not impossible, in addition, that the Kremlin, on a suitable occasion perhaps wants to put an end to us, to conquer Fin-land, exploiting our own communists after the fashion of the Baltic states'. So even Paasikivi could not get away altogether from this grim possibility. Even so he poured scorn on the concept of resistance:[65]

'We have lived in a world of illusions, not of reality. We trust in "rights" and by that we mean rights inscribed on paper. We also hold that every sovereign state and nation is equal. Such is not the case . . . there is a great difference between small powers and great powers . . . and history teaches us also that a small power must give way, even endure humiliation before a great power.'

Paasikivi feared that these basic facts of political life were not understood in Finland. As far as the ordinary citizen was concerned he was right. But the Finnish government had been learning fast. Paasikivi did not realize this, because he did not know of the assurances from Germany that were underwriting the government's policy of setting limits to the extent of its concessions. So Paasikivi had to say that concession must go on, even though he could offer no guarantee that even that would save Finland. 'How far we shall get with this policy I cannot say. Possibly we shall get past the worst times with it'. At least he could say that there was no present sign of imminent Soviet attack. Troop movements were normal. *Pravda* and *Izvestia* were silent about Finland, whatever Petroskoi radio might be saying, and 'that is the happiest and surest sign'. It must be said that Paasikivi did not argue that a policy of unending concessions was always right in principle. He was arguing for realism. Unless there was the assurance of counter support from other powers, any policy other than concession 'would lead us in all probability to catastrophe'. If support was available, then Paasikivi certainly believed that improper demands should be resisted. But to this he added one major proviso. Finland must never forget that Russia would always be her neighbour, would always be a great power, and that Finland must always seek for some permanent way of living in peace with her. It was this vital point, rather than the realities of power politics, that the government in Helsinki increasingly forgot.

Debate on foreign policy at a lower level was still being discouraged officially. The government, backed by the press, took the view that 'the direction of foreign policy should remain singly and solely in the hands of the government'.[66] Thus even when the Eduskunta got one of its rare opportunities to debate foreign affairs, on November 8, the main party leaders deliberately declined to take it. The occasion was the presentation of the official report on the activity of the government for the year 1939. This included the report of the foreign ministry. But only the extremists, Wiik on the Left, and the IKL leader Kares on the Right, broke the self-imposed restraint of the members by making controversial remarks on the subject. Even Kares recognized that they could not speak freely in a public session, he wished they could discuss matters in secret. The majority shared the view of Hackzell, the Kokoomus spokesman, that although there were many things they would like to see discussed, it was impossible in current circumstances.[67] But Molotov's visit to Berlin could not fail to stir up a wave of rumour and speculation. The official line was that people should believe the communiqué issued after the meeting which claimed that the two sides were in agreement on all points of substance.[68] In other words the public was warned not to indulge in speculation about a possible breach between Germany and the USSR which might work to Finland's advantage. Svento in particular worked hard to persuade his readers not to indulge in 'building houses of cards'.[69] Germany and the USSR had too strong a sense of the advantages of continued co-operation and would not allow minor differences to affect this. He said that it was well known there had been such differences over the Balkans and 'in the north of Europe', that is Finland, but these fell within the limits of tolerance between the two powers. Svento admitted that developments in the Balkans might put a severe strain on this tolerance, but this was not something on which Finland ought to build any hopes for herself.[70]

But of course no amount of official or press exhortation would stop people discussing their nation's future at so critical a time. The debate increasingly focused on the question of whether Finland ought to cleave to the path of strict neutrality, or whether she should openly throw in her lot with Germany and the New Order in Europe. The government's public line was always for strict neutrality. This is the theme of the two addresses to the nation by Ryti on his inauguration and at New Year. Finland was absolutely neutral. She desired to improve relations with the USSR on the basis of 'respect for each other's rights'. At the same time she wanted 'further to strengthen and deepen friendly relations with Germany, to which there are historic, economic, and cultural ties'.[71] It was therefore admitted that even a neutral Finland had a rather special relation with Germany, although this was not supposed to have a political significance. Thus Finland was neutral, but slightly less neutral to Germany than she was to the USSR. Among the public, the Social Democrats were the keenest exponents of strict neutrality. Svento in particular attacked the idea that Finland must choose her side.[72] This was being stimulated by speeches and press comment in Germany and Italy that the time had come for the neutrals to take sides. Svento said Finland was a genuine neutral, 'there is not and there cannot be any compulsion to make a choice.' The socialist press generally stressed that Finnish workers and peasants would have nothing to do with policies which departed from neutrality.

But outside the socialist ranks, the feeling that Finland should link her fate to Germany was growing. It was fed by the assumption of the non-socialist press that the New Order was an accomplished fact. Typical of this is an editorial in *Uusi Suomi* on November 25, commenting on the adhesion of some neutrals to the Tripartite pact.[73] This was part of the work which Germany and Italy were engaged on in mapping out the new order for Europe. Thanks to their preparatory work, when peace came the transfer from wartime conditions would go smoothly. In December, pro-German circles founded a new weekly periodical for the discussion of foreign affairs. It claimed to be politically neutral, but the board contained such convinced friends of Germany as Koskenniemi and P. H. Norrmen. Its basic assumptions were made clear in the first issue. This declared that:[74]

'The whole political system which followed from the dictated peace of Versailles has broken down, and other states have taken the position of leaders in place of the western powers, and under their leadership a new Europe is rising. Ties of friendship link us to these states strengthened by the influence of centuries of cultural, economic and political influences.'

The aim of the more advanced leaders of this move towards Germany wanted nothing less than the formal adherence of Finland to the Tripartite pact. It has been seen that this view was held at the highest level by Kivimäki and Witting, who told the German ambassador that 'he would gladly see Sweden and Finland join the Tripartite pact. But he added the request not to take this remark any further.'[75] Witting probably made this addition because he knew the idea had been considered by the government and rejected. Others were probably less sure exactly what they expected Germany to do, except that they wanted to be saved from the USSR. This was what Kivimäki referred to when he paid his New Year call on Weizsäcker and said that the public in Finland was now less anxious about the threat from the USSR, because it felt sure that in any future conflict, Finland would not be alone.[76] Thus it is likely that although there were many Finns who had genuine enthusiasm for the idea of a European New Order, and wanted Finland to play a constructive role in it, the pro-Germanism of the majority was a very Fennocentric thing. As long as Germany would protect them against the USSR, the rest of Europe could look after itself.

But for whatever reason Finnish public opinion was moving towards Germany. It is clear that the socialist campaign for strict neutrality had a defensive tone about it. It was the other side that was on the move. Nor was there any dynamic counter movement to this pro-German trend. The radical Left was not quite dead, but it was a spent force. In November, the government had felt strong enough to put an end to SNS. It applied to the High Court for an order delaring it an illegal organization. After a series of secret hearings, the court gave judgement on December 23. It said that the activities of SNS had been prejudicial to the national interest, and that they had in fact 'made difficult and endangered the maintenance of friendly relations between Finland and the USSR'.[77] The SNS put out a final manifesto of protest, which declared that its suppression was 'a new demonstration of hostility against our great neighbour, the Soviet Union'. It would not recognize the decrees made against it by a government that did not represent the real people of Finland. Thus the SNS threatened to continue its work underground, but gradually it expired. In the new year it did manage to raise some 20,000 signatures for an address calling for the release of its arrested leaders, but thereafter gave little sign of life. Its surviving cells turned to the subversion of reservists in face of the approaching renewal of war, but with very slight success. The remaining radical leaders acknowledged that they were beaten. On January 5, 1941, Wiik and his friends held a meeting in Tampere to discuss whether there was any prospect of starting a new organization to campaign for better relations with the USSR. They came to the conclusion that such an attempt was hopeless and that for the time being there was nothing further they could do.[78]

When Ryti was elected president, it became necessary to reform the government, in particular a new prime minister was needed. It was assumed at first that this would be a matter of days. No major alteration of men or measures was contemplated, the government would still be a broad coalition.[79] Further, it seems to have been agreed during the discussions of the presidency, that the new prime minister should be an

Agrarian.[80] It was soon announced that one of the Agrarian leaders, Pekkanen, had been asked to form a government. Unfortunately Pekkanen, who had been a provincial prefect, had had a series of clashes with Social Democratic organizations in his province, and the Social Democrats vetoed him, though they pretended that this was just a matter of personalities and they would accept some other Agrarian.[81] But the Agrarian party took offence and declined to nominate any other candidate.[82] It now seemed logical that the Social Democrats put forward a candidate. But this was impossible. They could not nominate anyone but Tanner, and Tanner refused to come forward on the grounds that it would outrage the USSR. Indeed there had been widespread fears that the USSR might interfere in the formation of the government, and Tanner told Paasikivi that if this did happen, the exasperated politicians would be in a mood to defy Russia.[83] He also revealed that many politicians were reluctant to assume high office under such difficult and unrewarding circumstances.

Then there arose a further complication. The Agrarians and Social Democrats had put down an interpellation in the Eduskunta criticizing the slow progress of the resettlement of the Karelians. The Swedish People's party took this to be an attack on the Swedish-speaking minority, which in part it was, for reasons that will be explained later. There was an acrimonious debate which lasted 12 hours on January 2, which left tempers frayed, and the Swedish Peoples party threatening not to join the government.[84] However, it began to be felt that the long delay in forming a government was a scandalous mockery of yksimielisyys, and the difficulties were overcome on January 4. A non-party prime minister was found in Rangell, and the Swedish People's party was given some kind of promise that its special interests would be taken into consideration.[85] The new government announced that it meant to follow the policies of its predecessor, but feeling was that it represented a shift to the Right. The new prime minister, Rangell, was described by *Uusi Suomi* as 'politically a somewhat unknown person'.[86] He was in fact a banker after the Ryti pattern and some thought that he was simply a Ryti substitute, a man of straw directed by Ryti. It is certain that Rangell never had the power or influence that Ryti had possessed as prime minister, but then Rangell had an active president to work with. Rangell was described as a non-party man, but he had been an early supporter of the Nouseva Suomi movement, and was definitely a man of the Right. The most striking feature of the new government was the inclusion of a minister from the fascist IKL. The socialists, who had wanted to continue a broad coalition, swallowed this in the sacred name of unity, even if the coalition was now a little broader than they had bargained for. The IKL seems to have given an undertaking to cease its attacks on the democratic system in general, and on the socialists in particular, whom they had tended to brand as unpatriotic. The inclusion of IKL meant that the government could expect the support of the whole of the Eduskunta, except the Wiik group. Further it made a gesture to Germany and the New Order in Europe, which seems to have been appreciated. The German press gave a warm welcome to the new government.

Subsequently, Rangell's government came in for quite a lot of criticism. It was charged with being weak in its contacts with parliamentary and democratic life. Rangell had never sat in the Eduskunta, and there was not now a single parliamentarian in the central core of the government. A later critic remarked:[87]

'It has been said that Rangell was anti-parliamentary, but there is no foundation for this allegation. His government could never get the right relation to the Eduskunta's way of working, but not because he deliberately wanted to push the Eduskunta aside.'

He went on to suggest that lack of experience of parliamentary politics among the leading men in this government produced the difficulties which sometimes arose between the government and the Eduskunta, in spite of virtually unanimous support which the government could always call on when needed. It has also been said that this government was in fact more pro-German than its predecessor. As the same critic has remarked, 'nobody could expect a rapprochement with the Soviet Union from their labours'.[88] It is true that the Rangell government seems to have accepted from the beginning that co-operation with Germany was the basis of their foreign policy. It is significant that when, soon after its formation, the Swedish government sent to ask if the Finnish government wished to continue with talks about a union plan, they were told that while the Finnish government remained interested, they saw no point in discussing it in present circumstances.[89] They had come round to Witting's original view that the union plan was useless. As Witting had remarked to Blücher on December 30, the union plan was a dream based on Sweden's memories of past greatness and not a practical proposition.[90]

But much of this criticism seems misplaced. It is a mistake to attach much significance to the change of government in January 1941. Of course the addition of the IKL had a certain symbolic importance, but it made no fundamental difference. The critics tend to overlook the fact that for essential purposes the new government was the same as the old one. The central directing core still consisted of Ryti, Walden, and Witting, with Mannerheim always in the background. The addition of Rangell to this central core made little difference. They were neither more nor less parliamentary than they had been before, and the continuity of policy was quite unbroken. This is especially true of foreign policy. Rangell's government did draw closer to Germany than its predecessor, but it did so under inexorable pressures from outside, rather than any innate disposition to be pro-German. The pro-German tendencies in the inner core of the government were much more a matter of political calculation than the corresponding tendencies among the politicians and the public. So, in January 1941, the Finnish government recognized that the union plan was dead. Some members, led by Witting, felt no regrets at this. But Mannerheim and Walden, and probably Ryti, knew that Finland's brightest hope of escaping unhurt from the perils by which she was surrounded had died with it.

CHAPTER 10

The Petsamo nickel crisis and its aftermath

On January 14, 1941, Vishinski called Paasikivi to the Kremlin and opened the last major Russian effort to put pressure on Finland.[1] Vishinski demanded to know how much longer the USSR was expected to wait for a settlement of the nickel question, since 'our patience is at an end'. Paasikivi had very little to tell. The Finnish government had sent an emissary to London for talks with the British government on the issue and was waiting for his return. Vishinski demanded to know what had been the point of the December discussion in Moscow, if, as now appeared, the Finnish government was still making the whole thing hang on British consent. It just proved that the Finnish government was acting in bad faith. But such procrastination could not continue. Paasikivi reported Vishinski as saying that 'they will find other means of settling the matter'.[2] The Finnish government, ignoring Paasikivi's advice to make some concession, sat tight. On January 21, Paasikivi got another summons, and the same charges were levelled. He had nothing to add. His government was still waiting to hear from London, after which they would be ready to re-open discussions on a mixed company. At this Vishinski exploded in anger. He would not listen any longer to this sort of double talk, the Finnish government must decide by the following day whether they were ready to resume talks about a mixed company. Paasikivi pointed out that this was literally impossible. Vishinski then said that the USSR must have an answer on the 23rd. Paasikivi told his government they must yield to the demand.[3]

As soon as the Soviet pressure had been renewed, the Finnish government had turned to Germany for advice. The German position was unchanged. Hitler had explained it to Mussolini at their meeting on January 18–20. He said that even though the USSR was ready to guarantee Germany 60% of the output, Germany did not trust her, and hoped that Finland would prevent her getting control of the mines. In the last resort Germany would assist Finland, if the crisis led to a Soviet aggression against her. Hitler stressed to Mussolini the economic importance of the nickel because he could not reveal his real primary interest in the Petsamo area. But Hitler understood that the interest of the USSR in the area was also political and military.[4] Indeed Molotov actually said this a few days later to the German ambassador when he told him that the interest of the USSR in Petsamo was political, 'an English concession was completely out of place in the Petsamo region.'[5] However, Hitler still could not afford to be involved in a premature conflict with the USSR over the nickel dispute, so Finland had to be told that she must avoid bringing matters to the point of war, and continue her delaying action. To this end, Ribbentrop sent instructions to Blücher on four successive days between January 26 and 30.

Ribbentrop thought that by exploiting British objections, and asking the USSR to overcome them, there might be further room for procrastination. Finland must stand firm on its demand to remain in control of the mixed company. He promised to have his ambassador in Moscow remind Molotov that Germany insisted on firm guarantees for her 60% of the output, but would not go any further than this. The Finnish government was grateful for this small assistance, and assured the Germans that they would keep control of the mixed company. But it asked very pertinently what was to happen if the USSR accepted the German requirement.[6] To this there was no satisfactory answer, and all the appeals of Witting to Blücher and Kivimäki to the foreign office failed to shift the German position. So the Finnish government was left with the impression that Germany would not make a Russian seizure of the Petsamo area a *casus belli*. Hitler deliberately deceived them about this, in order to restrain Finland from any inopportune defiance of the USSR.

On the other hand, the Finnish leaders did understand that Germany would protect them from a general Russian attack, as opposed to a limited operation against Petsamo. Even so, the renewed Soviet pressure put them under a terrible strain, which can be measured by the fact that for the only recorded time, Mannerheim lost his nerve. There were good reasons for this. In addition to the ultimatum over the nickel question, the Soviet government had suddenly stopped its exports to Finland, and recalled its ambassador to Moscow. They found an excuse for interrupting exports in the terms of the Russo-Finnish trade agreement. This had been a bilateral arrangement which provided that mutual trade was to be kept in balance. If one side failed to do this, the other was entitled to suspend deliveries until the balance was restored. The bulk of the Soviet exports to Finland were of raw materials, of which food grains were the most important. The Finnish exports to Russia were mostly capital goods, such as ships and barges, which took time to build. Consequently, by January 1941, Russia had delivered goods to Finland worth over $3 million, while

Finnish deliveries to the USSR were worth only $139,000. But Finland claimed that if advance payments on goods under construction were added in, there was in fact a balance, and that this was the reasonable interpretation of the agreement.[7] Even so, the USSR had the excuse she needed for starting economic reprisals against Finland for her delaying tactics on the nickel question. Since Finland was in the middle of a serious food shortage at this time, it was a shrewd blow. Mannerheim might well wonder if economic warfare was to be the prelude to armed attack.

Then, in addition to this, he received intelligence reports from the vital south-east frontier of troop movements on the Russian side. This proved the last straw for the Marshal's nerves. A conference was called on January 23 between Mannerheim, Walden, and Heinrichs on one side, and Ryti and Rangell on the other. Mannerheim wanted to mobilize two divisions on the threatened sector at once, and Heinrichs and Walden backed his demand. Ryti and Rangell firmly refused. Mannerheim was astonished, as well he might be, for it was virtually unknown for his advice to be rejected. He declared, somewhat petulantly, that in that case he could take no responsibility for the consequences. Ryti remarked dryly that he supposed that the responsibility would be his. It must be presumed that Ryti was not impressed by Mannerheim's evidence, which seems to have consisted of no more than visual observations of camp fires and movements across the frontier. Further he must have trusted to German assurances, for an attack across the south-east frontier would be a general invasion, which he had been assured that Germany would not permit. Ryti had his way, and was proved to have been right, for two days later, Walden told him that the observed activity had died away. Walden agreed that it was as well that Ryti had taken the stand he did. Mannerheim was considerably put out. He must have felt humiliated by this very uncharacteristic failure of judgement on his part, and was so upset that he talked of resigning, but was persuaded not to.[8] In fairness to Mannerheim, he was not alone in his apprehensions. There was another burst of rumours in January of an impending blow by the USSR at Finland, perhaps as an answer to any new German move in the Balkans. At least, Halder made a note to this effect in his diary on January 18, though it is not clear what the source of his anxieties had been.[9]

In these circumstances, the Finnish government naturally returned a soft answer to the Soviet ultimatum on the nickel question. They agreed to new meetings of the mixed commission in Moscow on January 29, to consider the formation of a Finnish-Soviet company to handle the concession.[10] Further, the Finnish delegation was armed with new proposals which went a long way towards meeting the Russian demands. They were now prepared to agree, without any equivocation, to dispossess the existing concession holders, and to take the sole responsibility for arranging this. Only, if the British government retaliated by cutting off the traffic to Liinahamari, Finland would expect the USSR to make good the lost supplies. About the structure of the company, Finland now proposed that she should hold 51% of the shares, and appoint the chairman and three of the six directors. At the mines themselves, the manager was to be Finnish, but the USSR might appoint two of the four accountants and two engineers. The Russian counter proposal was that the shares and the directorate should be equally divided between the two countries, but the managing director and one fifth of the staff at the mines was to be Russian. It will be noticed that both sides had made concessions, and that the gap between them had narrowed considerably, but the points which remained were vital ones, and involved the question of who was to control the mines themselves. Since the real aim of the USSR was to establish an effective intelligence centre in the Petsamo area, this was a point on which she could not yield.

The Finnish government took good care that the German government was made aware that the negotiation had reached the critical point. By all available channels they sought to impress the Germans that if the Russians controlled the mines, they would in effect control the whole Petsamo area. Blücher believed this, and urged his government to intervene to prevent it.[11] Halder had made a note about it on January 27, observing that the ambiguous attitude of the German government might have adverse effects.[12] There were many channels by which Finland could make her views known in Germany's ruling circles. One such was Mannerheim's personal envoy, General Talvela, who was frequently in Germany. On a visit in January, Talvela got an invitation to send a Finnish officer to Germany to lecture to the General Staff on the Russo-Finnish war. Mannerheim decided to send Heinrichs, since he had reason to believe that the Germans had some questions they wanted to ask, and Mannerheim wanted to learn what he could of German intentions. He told Heinrichs to talk openly if this would stimulate the Germans to reveal how they were thinking.[13]

The evidence about Heinrichs' visit to Germany on January 30, 1941, is patchy. Halder gave Heinrichs lunch, which was a social occasion, so that probably nothing very significant was said. But in the afternoon, Heinrichs and Halder had quite a long conversation, with Paulus, the chief planner for Barbarossa, in attendance. When he appeared at the Nuremberg trial, Paulus could not remember what had passed on this occasion.[14] Heinrichs too had difficulties with his memory. Some years after he could only remember ten or fifteen minutes of general conversation. It seems likely that he was confusing what happened at the lunch with what happened at the afternoon discussion. Certainly Halder was guilty of an indiscretion over lunch. He recalled how the Germans and the Finns had been brothers in arms in 1918. He suggested that it could happen again, and if it did, hoped Finland would join in an attack on Leningrad. Heinrichs had instructions on this, and replied firmly that he was certain neither Mannerheim nor the Finnish government would ever consent to take part in such an attack.[15] However, during the discussion in the afternoon, which Heinrichs forgot about, it is clear from Halder's notes that there was some uninhibited talk about what Finland might do in a possible Russo-German conflict. Heinrichs outlined to Halder the dispositions and the mobilization plan of the Finnish army. This latter required nine days, and would be quiet, 'but cannot go unnoticed'.[16] So now at last Halder had been able to put the question of which he had made a note in December. There would be eight divisions in line on the south-east frontier, and these would be able to move down either side of Lake Ladoga. Two divisions would be needed to mask the base at Hanko, and no offensive action could be expected there unless Finland received heavy artillery and planes. It seems likely that after the careless remark about attacking Leningrad, Halder was content to get the information he wanted without going any further into the circumstances under which a Russo-German conflict might begin. This subject was only touched on again in Halder's concluding remarks:[17]

'Whether you will take part in a possible war with the Soviet Union, and if so in what circumstances and conditions is a question to be cleared up between the political leadership.—Halder said however that he thought it sensible that the military leadership should prepare against the dangers of such a situation in time and at least in their own heads.'

On a superficial view, the meeting of Halder and Heinrichs on January 30 was of slight significance. Halder had got the information he wanted about the disposition and mobilization plan of the Finnish army, and had been warned that the idea of taking part in an assault on Leningrad did not recommend itself to Finland. Heinrichs had learned almost nothing definite about Germany's intentions. But Mannerheim and Heinrichs were intelligent men, well able to draw the obvious conclusions from what had passed. Halder's conversation must in fact have told them a great deal.

First, there could now be no doubt that the German military leaders were seriously thinking about war with the USSR. Further, if it came to a war, they were expecting that Finland would get involved. But more important than this, the German leaders were thinking of an offensive war. The significance of Halder's interest in the Finnish mobilization was unmistakable. It was meaningless to inquire whether this mobilization could be carried out quietly, unless Germany was thinking in terms of launching a surprise blow at the USSR, since otherwise it would not matter whether the mobilization was obvious. Hence the Finnish military leaders could have been in no doubt about the kind of operation in which they might be called on to participate. It would be, in the eyes of an impartial observer, a war of aggression against the USSR, and even if Finland's role in the first place might be to hold possible Russian spoiling attacks, Germany wanted her to take part in the general assault. The vital information which the Finnish leaders did not have, either then, or until the very last moment, was whether the war would come at all, and if so when and in what circumstances. They were led to believe, with a great deal of success, that Germany was sincerely striving for a peaceful solution of her relations with the USSR, and that war could only come if this effort failed.

In fact, at this very time, German military planning was entering the decisive phase. German headquarters in Norway had been busied with consideration of the execution of Renntier, and the securing of Petsamo. For this, they wanted information about the plans of the Finnish forces in the area.

The German military attaché in Helsinki had approached General Airo on January 7. Airo was willing to talk, since everything he had to say was calculated to worry the Germans, and make them more inclined to help with the defence of Petsamo. He told the attaché that in the event of an attack, Finland would evacuate the Petsamo area, including the airfield and the nickel mines. Demolitions would be carried out, but Airo evaded the question of whether the mines would be destroyed.

Falkenhorst, the commander in Norway, had the further task of planning how to develop Renntier into a thrust into the USSR aimed at cutting off Murmansk.[18] He received detailed instructions for this on January 16, and was to assume the use of four divisions, and the co-operation of the local Finnish forces.[19] It was suggested that once Murmansk was cut off, the Germans might turn south and make for Lake Ladoga. Falkenhorst was also to consider how to build up the necessary supplies at Rovaniemi, and what sort of a command structure should be set up, and what was to be done about the Russian base at Hanko. As a result, on January 27, the Norwegian command produced the first draft for the operation code named 'Silberfuchs'. It was a plan of great scope and imagination, and assumed the full-scale co-operation of the whole Finnish army. Finland was to mobilize quietly and man her defences, including the Åland islands. Then a Finnish striking force of eight or ten divisions would concentrate north of Lake Ladoga and strike down east of the lake to the River Svir. The Germans, having executed Renntier, would assemble a force based on Rovaniemi, and strike up the line of the Kemijärvi railway to cut off Murmansk. They would need the use of Swedish railways to bring in the troops for this, and two Finnish divisions to support it. When Murmansk

14

had been cut off, this force would turn north and south, and roll up the Russian forces on both flanks. It was assumed that Mannerheim would take overall command, but that the northern sector would in effect be a separate command under Falkenhorst.[20] Falkenhorst now wanted permission to contact the Finnish and Swedish authorities before he could carry the planning any further. There are two striking features of this plan. One is the German optimism about the possibility of such operations in the wilderness of north Finland and north Russia. The other is the unquestioning assumption that Finland would take part, not in any limited or defensive capacity, but in launching deep thrusts into Soviet territory. It never occurred to any responsible German that this co-operation was not to be had for the asking.

The details of the Silberfuchs plan were discussed by Halder and Colonel Buschenhagen, chief of staff to Falkenhorst, on February 1.[21] On closer consideration it began to appear that the assembly of four divisions from Norway might be too difficult, so that the scope of the plan was cut down somewhat. A more modest scheme had already been devised by the army general staff and embodied in the detailed elaboration of the original Barbarossa plan issued on January 31, and confirmed in a conference with Hitler on February 3. This is the document known as 'Aufmarschanweisung Barbarossa' and is the executive order which set the Barbarossa scheme in motion.[22]

As far as Finland is concerned, the plan embodies the information which Halder had got from Heinrichs. It assumed that the main Finnish forces would deal with Hanko, and launch a general attack to the south-east on both sides of Lake Ladoga. For this they would need powerful support. In the far north, one and a half divisions of Germans would execute Renntier, and if the Swedish railways became available, another one and a half divisions could be brought in and used for a thrust at the Murmansk railway. It was thus a much more modest scheme than that envisaged by headquarters in Norway. Hitler threw in some typical comments of his own on the plan. He was confident of Sweden co-operating and proposed to give her the Åland islands as her reward, and added that the idea of a Swedish-Finnish union would not fit in with his ideas for a new order in Europe. Hitler stressed that the various associated states would not be informed of their tasks until the very last moment. Now Hitler not only assumed that Sweden and Finland would be willing to play their parts, but that Finland would have no objection to losing the Åland islands to Sweden. On the following day, Hitler discussed the naval aspect of the plan with Admiral Raeder. Again it was assumed that Finland would let her harbours and ships be used for laying a mine barrage across the Gulf of Finland, and her airfields for attacks on the Russian fleet and on the locks of the White Sea canal, so that Russian naval forces could not be withdrawn that way.[23]

Meanwhile, the Petsamo nickel affair continued to perplex all the parties involved. The Finns continued their vain efforts to frighten Germany into intervening. On February 8, Mannerheim himself tackled the German military attaché.[24] He said that if Finland gave way over the question of the managing director, the German supply line to the north of Norway would come under Russian control. Then a new factor emerged to complicate things. Paasikivi, who still believed that his government really wanted to settle the question, tried his hand at mediation. He suggested to the Finnish government that they might consider exchanging the Petsamo region for some territory elsewhere, or even drop the whole idea of a mixed company, and give the concession directly to the USSR.[25] These suggestions were not well received either in Helsinki or Berlin. Hitler revealed subsequently that he had given Finland 'strict advice' not to consider them. On February 12, the Russian chairman of the mixed commission in Moscow announced that he regarded the negotiations as having broken down.

The following day, Vishinski summoned Paasikivi. They agreed that deadlock had been reached, but Vishinski suggested that they have an informal discussion of the outstanding issues. This was carried on in a friendly spirit, and Paasikivi had the impression that Vishinski was genuinely anxious to negotiate a compromise. For once the habitual threats were not used. Vishinski tried to pretend that the whole matter was of economic significance only. He said that 'we have no aggressive intentions as you perhaps suppose'.[26] Yet everything he said only went to show that it was not an economic matter, since Paasikivi and Vishinski too got stuck on the question of the nationality of the managing director, and Vishinski could produce no convincing explanation of why he must be Russian. He resorted to such arguments as that the USSR had 'decided' that he must be in order to maintain equality between Finland and the USSR, and that 'the Soviet Union is a great power and Finland is a small one: the prestige of the Soviet Union demands equality'.[27] Finally, Paasikivi said that he would suggest to his government that they agree to concede equality in shares and in the directorate, and that a fifth of the staff should be Russian, leaving the question of the managing director open. Paasikivi had assumed that one fifth of the staff at the mines would amount to no more than five or six, whereas it transpired it would have been 18 or 20. Even so, as Paasikivi pointed out to his government, Finland could surely render that number fairly harmless. Paasikivi followed his recommendation of this compromise with a warning. He had said to Vishinski at one point that they could hardly go to war over a managing director.

Vishinski had replied, 'there is already a trade war between us.'[28] Paasikivi took this to mean that more forceful measures were still possible. On the other hand Paasikivi felt a genuine anxiety on the Russian side to avoid conflict and reach a negotiated settlement. It was significant that on February 15, the mixed commission was reconvened by the Russians, who proposed that it should agree on the points settled by Paasikivi and Vishinski.[29]

To his consternation, Paasikivi found his suggested compromises completely rejected by his government. They had decided that they would make no compromise with the principle that control of the mixed company must remain with Finland. If this principle was accepted, any details could be discussed in the mixed commission. When Paasikivi told this to Vishinski on February 19, Vishinski exploded in what was obviously baffled rage:[30]

'The Soviet proposals were unconditional, they would not be abandoned . . . there was no reason to continue the mixed committee's work. There was nothing to be done. The matter must develop with all its consequences. The Finnish government's answer was intended to delay matters . . . since he had not been given any clear answer he regarded it as an affront and he protested.'

Paasikivi described this discussion as 'the most unpleasant of all my time in Moscow'. But it was not Vishinski's anger and threats that depressed the ambassador. He had realized that his government had rejected the policy of conciliation that he had always urged, and that he regarded as the only one possible for Finland. Paasikivi still did not know why his government acted so. As he understood things, only a firm guarantee from Germany could justify such behaviour, and he did not believe that Germany could possibly have given one. Paasikivi could not conceive that the German government would be so mad as to quarrel gratuitously with the USSR, and certainly not over an issue like Petsamo nickel. So it seemed to him that, as Tanner had suggested in December, the 'men of resistance' had got the upper hand in the government, and he would not be a party to their follies. Paasikivi sent in his resignation on February 20 to his government:[31]

'Since I see that our opinions about our country's foreign policy are not sufficiently close together, since you do not trust my power to make assessments and my experience of politics and since I do not want even the remotest connection with policies which can lead to catastrophe, I am sending to Witting by the first courier my letter of resignation.'

The government did not at once accept his resignation, but recalled him to Helsinki for consultations. Before he left, Paasikivi had one last interview with Molotov on the nickel question. The tone of this was very significant since Molotov went back on the wild and threatening stand taken by Vishinski. He first said that the USSR had just concluded firm agreements with Germany to assure her of her 60% of the output. Molotov was not telling the truth. The USSR had brought itself to offer to guarantee Germany's 60% to the end of 1947, but this had not been considered satisfactory by Germany.[32] Molotov was trying to show that Finland could not hope to use the position of Germany as an excuse for resistance. He stressed that it had been a generous act by the USSR to return Petsamo to Finland in 1940. 'The Finnish government must remember that we gave it to Finland.'[33] They went over the other points of difference and as always reached deadlock on the question of the managing director. Molotov was no more able than Vishinski to produce convincing reasons for his stand over this. He asserted that 'we can discuss all other points but not the managing directorship.' Yet he ended on an unexpected note. Although Vishinski had treated the Finnish answer of February 19 as breaking off the negotiations, Molotov now went back on this, and said that he regarded them as still open, and would hope that Paasikivi would bring an answer back with him. Molotov ended, 'I beg you, who knows the position and circumstances here, so to influence matters that this business gets settled.' The contrast between the tone of this interview on March 5, and the interviews in January with Vishinski is very striking. Molotov, far from using threats, was almost pleading with Paasikivi to help him resolve the conflict. The explanation is probably fairly simple. The USSR had got itself into an impossible situation. They had taken up an extreme position that could only be made good by the threat of force, supposing that Finland must yield to it. But Finland had decided not to yield, and Hitler's veto prevented the execution of the Soviet threats. If the deadlock was to be broken, the USSR would now have to make concessions, and this was a humiliation that Molotov did not care to face. It is no wonder that he wanted Paasikivi to find some way out of the mess that he had got the USSR into.

It is easier to find a theory that will account for the behaviour of the Soviet government than to determine why the Finnish government, on or about the middle of February, decided that it had reached the limit of concessions to the USSR. For it had made such a decision, as Witting told Blücher shortly after:[34]

'Die Regierung sei aber entschlossen, sich nicht irre machen zu lassen. Die Regierung kenne die Erfahrungen, die Randstaaten mit Nachgiebigkeit gemacht hätten. Sie würde deshalb versuchen, ihren Standpunkt so lange wie möglich aufrecht zu halten.*'

---

* 'The Government had decided not to let itself be led astray. The Government knew of the experiences the border territories had had as a result of their compliance. It would therefore attempt to stick to its point of view as long as it possibly could.'

One must surmise that there were one or two factors which came together
to produce the result. It seems likely that Paasikivi's report of his conversation with Vishinski on February 13, and the concessions which he
recommended, was the decisive event. There is evidence that, as Tanner
had hinted in his December letter, the Finnish government was sick and
tired of Paasikivi telling them that they must make another concession or
the USSR would resort to force. They just could not see where such a process was to end, and Paasikivi himself could not tell them. This feeling
of exasperation with their ambassador was reflected in a remark of Witting
to Blücher:[35]

'Er habe dadurch bei einigen ängstlichen Gemutern, Nervösität her-
vorgerufen. Es sei für die Regierung unangenehm, dass der Gesandte,
der natürlich am besten über russische Verhältnisse unterrichtet sein
müsste, desartig defaitistisch wirke.*'

It seems then that the government had, as Paasikivi complained, been
steadily losing its confidence in the ambassador's powers of judgement, and
his report was the last straw. They felt that if they did not take a stand,
Paasikivi might involve them in concessions which they did not wish to
make, and which Germany was constantly advising them not to make.
This was the second factor in the situation. The Finnish authorities were in
constant touch with their German counterparts over the nickel problem,
and although they could never extract the promise of German intervention
which they wanted, they were consistently told to yield nothing that would
give the USSR effective control of the Petsamo area. They were told that
such a degree of concession was not necessary, and gradually the Finnish
government had come to accept this. If the German government advised
that it was safe to take a stand, then the Finnish government could assume
that it had good grounds for its advice, even if it refused to reveal what
they were. The third factor, which reinforced the second, was that there
were an increasing number of signs for the intelligent observer to read,
which pointed to the conclusion that Germany was vitally concerned
about the Petsamo area from a military point of view, so that she was most
unlikely to tolerate any attempt by the USSR to seize it. On this basis it is
possible to make sense of the decision which the Finnish government had
taken. One of the earliest of the signs referred to was a German inquiry,
early in February, about the possible improvement of certain roads in the
Petsamo area, particularly that leading north-east from Ivalo, where there
was a German base, towards the Russian frontier.[36] The Finnish autho-

* 'In this way he had roused certain anxious individuals to a state of apprehen-
sion. It did not please the Government that their ambassador, who would naturally
be better informed than anyone else about the situation in Russia, should thus
encourage defeatism.'

rities took the hint and began with the necessary works as soon as conditions permitted. At about the same time, the German airforce general von Seydl, who was director of billeting and supplies, visited Helsinki.

It is not known who invited him, but he was received by Mannerheim, Talvela, and Heinrichs, so Mannerheim was probably the ultimate authority for the visit. It may have been regarded as a return for the visit of Heinrichs to Berlin. The German Foreign Office made a complete fool of itself over this visit, since it laid down elaborate security precautions to preserve secrecy, which were so complex that the instructions only reached Blücher after Seydl had finished his talks in Helsinki and gone to look at conditions in the far north for himself. Blücher reported that Seydl had discussed supply and communication problems in the north, but did not touch on military operations. This is confirmed from other sources. Seydl was well satisfied with his visit. He had been received by Mannerheim with unusual warmth, indeed the Marshal had 'showed him such marks of favour as had seldom been shown to anyone'. He had 'gotten what he went after', namely information on supply and communications, and had refrained from touching on politics or operations, except 'very superficially'. Seydl probably also refrained from telling anything very significant either, but the mere fact of his being interested in the Petsamo area would have conveyed a great deal to the Finnish military leaders, even if Seydl did not actually say anything.[37]

Almost immediately after von Seydl, the Finnish leaders got another visitor, who confirmed the conclusions they must already have drawn for themselves. This was Colonel Buschenhagen, the chief of staff to Falkenhorst and the German army in Norway. Buschenhagen arrived in Helsinki on February 18, and had a series of discussions with Heinrichs and other Finnish officers.[38] These dealt with both communications and operational possibilities. Since Buschenhagen was not authorized to reveal Germany's intention, the discussion proceeded on the basis of considering a number of hypothetical military situations that would arise if the Russians moved into northern Finland. In the process Buschenhagen revealed a most important piece of information. He confirmed that the German troops in north Norway would intervene in such a situation, or as Mannerheim puts it, 'would not remain passive'.[39] So the Finnish government had been correct in the assumption that it was safe to take a stand over the nickel question. Buschenhagen was told that the Finnish forces had not intended to defend the Petsamo area, but would resist the attack which they anticipated down the line of the Kemijärvi railway. If Germany was indeed willing to assist them, there would be two Finnish divisions available to protect a concentration of German troops at Rovaniemi, and these would then be able to join in combined operations with the Germans.[40] Buschenhagen claimed, some years later, that he had also described Germany's offensive plans as embodied in Silberfuchs, but Heinrichs, the other party to the talks, denied this.[41] According to him, they went no farther than agreeing that for a successful defence of northern Finland, it would be necessary in the end to cross the frontier and capture the Salla highlands.[42]

The letter which the German military attaché in Helsinki wrote immediately after Buschenhagen's visit suggests that the truth lies between these two versions. Although Buschenhagen was careful to insist that he was talking only of hypothetical situations, he did ask about the prospects for offensive operations in the Petsamo area and along the line of the Kemijärvi railway, and further south in the direction of Kem, where the Finnish representatives regarded an offensive as 'possible and desirable'. But Heinrichs was careful to stress that in this case, Finnish participation might not go further than providing a covering force for the German concentration since the Finnish troops would be needed for operations on the main fronts further south.[43] Buschenhagen went on to explore other hypothetical situations, in order to draw the Finns out. The possibility of a general German attack on the USSR was discussed, though Buschenhagen was careful to stress that his listeners must not jump to any conclusions from what he was saying. He asked the Finnish officers what their objectives might be if they ever got involved in such a war. He was told that Finland would certainly want to re-occupy the areas ceded under the Treaty of Moscow, and might, if conditions seemed to favour it, consider an operation to capture the whole of eastern Karelia, the area bounded by Lakes Onega and Ladoga to the east and south, and by the White Sea on the north.[44] Buschenhagen was told that if this were achieved, Finnish interests 'would be completely exhausted. Sympathy or enthusiasm for broader war aims cannot be found among the Finnish people.'

After these conversations in Helsinki, Buschenhagen left on a tour of northern Finland. He himself gave the impression that he had been shown everything by enthusiastic Finnish hosts. The Finnish officers concerned gave a very different version. Colonel Ahonen, who went with him from Ivalo to Liinahamari and back, said they did nothing but inspect the port facilities at Liinahamari. They passed some Finnish field works on the road, but did not stop to look at them.[45] General Tapola accompanied Buschenhagen on the whole of this journey. He said that they never went near the Russian frontier except to look at the Salla highlands, in which Buschenhagen could legitimately take an interest in view of what had been said in Helsinki. Tapola reported that the German was constantly trying to draw him out, but that he had evaded all delicate questions about Finland's military planning. Tapola said that he bore in mind Russo-German co-operation, which was still officially in full force, and thought 'Buschen-hagen's journey somewhat regrettable, that is of a sort which could be-come, taking the existing situation into account, a spy trip damaging to us.'[46]

As a result of the Buschenhagen visit, the Germans learned a lot about the state of communications in northern Finland, and about the problems of co-operating with the Finnish forces there in defence of the area. They were also given interesting information on the offensive possibilities in the north, though with the provision that it was unlikely that any Finnish troops would be available to take part in them. Otherwise, Buschenhagen had learned little beyond the general military objectives which the Finnish command had in mind in the event of an offensive war becoming possible. It seems best to believe the Finnish witnesses who were unanimous that these offensive possibilities were discussed in the most vague and general terms. On the Finnish side, although Heinrichs maintained that he still doubted the reliability of Buschenhagen's statements that German troops would help to defend northern Finland in the event of an attack, it is probable that the Finnish authorities felt fairly confident about this after the visit, and that this confidence is reflected in the government's attitude to the Petsamo nickel question.[47]

It is interesting to note the conceptions held by the Finnish military leaders of the nature of a possible war between Germany and the USSR. They clearly expected such a war to reduce Russia to the rank of second-class power, and they hoped to profit by this. It must be stressed that if the Finnish command had been thinking only in terms of recovering the areas lost in 1940, this was an objective consistent with a moderate adjustment of the power relationship between Germany and Russia, still leaving the USSR as a major power. But when they thought in terms of the occupation of large areas of undisputably Russian territory, they were also thinking of the outcome of a war between Germany and the USSR as being the total destruction of the latter as a European power. In this connection, Hein-richs let fall some very interesting remarks at a dinner given for Buschen-hagen.[48] Heinrichs pointed out that the USSR herself might make an offer to Finland, perhaps to return all or part of the lost territories. If such an offer were made, in return for a Finnish cession of Petsamo, or a guarantee of Finnish neutrality in a Russo-German war, Heinrichs warned that 'Ministers of the Left' might be inclined to accept it. It is to be pre-sumed that Heinrichs was trying to frighten his German listeners with this bogeyman, for which at that stage there was no foundation in fact at all, hoping that it would help to stimulate Germany into supporting Finland in less ambiguous fashion. But it is not unreasonable to suppose that General Heinrichs, enthused at the prospects which Buschenhagen's careful hints had suggested to him, would have been genuinely regretful if Finland were to lose the opportunities which a German attack on the USSR would offer her.

One further important question arises out of the Buschenhagen visit, and that is how far, as a result of the visit, the Finnish military leadership regarded a German attack on the USSR as probable. They had no direct information from the German side since Hitler was fanatically insistent that none should be given. But already, in February 1941, the skilled observer could detect signs of the German military build-up in the east, and the Swedish government in particular seems to have possessed quite reliable sources of information about German policy, and generally passed on any items of interest to Finland. The Finnish command could be certain, as a result of what Buschenhagen had said, and as Halder had revealed in January, that an offensive war was being contemplated, and that if it was executed, Germany was expecting Finland to take part in it. They had got as far as considering what their own military objectives might be in such a war. But they never lost sight of the possibility that it might not take place at all. Germany and the USSR might once more come to terms. For this reason the Finns were extremely wary in their dealings with Buschenhagen. Tapola's caution, if his memory of the visit is reliable, reflected in extreme form the massive reservation in the minds of the military leaders as they contemplated, with evident satisfaction, the pointers towards Russo-German conflict. There was just one thing they never seem to have considered at all. That was the possibility that if the war did come, the USSR might win it.

When Buschenhagen returned from Finland, the military planning of the Norwegian command was still at a very indecisive stage. There were too many imponderable factors in the situation. One of the most irksome was the uncertain attitude of Sweden. In February and early March, various soundings had been made in Stockholm about the willingness of Sweden to grant transit facilities for Germany troops to pass from Norway to Finland. The Swedish authorities wanted to know in what circumstances this might be necessary. If the movements were to help Finland to repel a Russian attack, Sweden would permit transits, otherwise not.[49] Since Germany obviously could not reveal the circumstances in which the facilities would be needed, it was concluded that for planning purposes, the use of Swedish communications could not be assumed. Another important factor was Hitler's personal obsession with the danger of a British landing in Norway. He was very reluctant to permit troops to be taken from the garrison there for the execution of Silberfuchs. This difficulty was suddenly accentuated by a British raid on the Lofoten islands, in which the British carried off German shipping and prisoners. This had a profound effect on Hitler, as Buschenhagen discovered when he presented himself to the Führer on March 8.

Buschenhagen reported that because of the poor road network in the Petsamo area, compared with the much better facilities available to a Russian defending force, any direct attack on Murmansk across the Petsamo area was impossible. At this word, Hitler flew into a rage. He would have no talk of impossibilities, and went on to attack the command in Norway for having permitted the Lofoten raid to succeed. There could be no question of the depth of Hitler's feelings on the matter. Subsequently, on March 12, Hitler issued an order for extensive additions to the defences of Norway, and ruled that it would no longer be possible to weaken these by withdrawing troops for the Barbarossa operation. So the planning of the Norwegian command had to be heavily revised, and Falkenhorst flew back to Germany for a series of conferences. In the course of these Hitler laid down a series of priorities for Falkenhorst's command. First they must defend Norway against the British. Secondly they must be ready at all times to execute Renntier and secure the nickel mines. Hitler put great stress on the importance of the nickel, and revealed that he had followed the current negotiations in Moscow closely. He knew that these had now 'come to a dead end', and said that Germany had urgently vetoed Paasikivi's idea of ceding the Petsamo area to the USSR in exchange for something else. This put Silberfuchs third in order of priority. Hitler now accepted that Swedish railways were not available, and also Buschenhagen's advice that a direct thrust at Murmansk across Petsamo was impractical. Even so, Murmansk must be eliminated, and Hitler now wanted an attack from Rovaniemi, up the Kemijärvi railway, by a strong motorized force.[50]

The plans were further discussed between Hitler, Halder, and Brauchitsch on March 17.[51] It was now decided to use two divisions for Renntier, and when they had executed the plan, they were to push on as far as they could towards Murmansk. But the main attack would be the southern one, launched by the SS Panzer brigade, a German infantry division and a Finnish division. It was still uncertain how these German troops would be got to Rovaniemi, and Hitler stressed that 'as far as actual fighting troops are concerned we can depend only on German forces'. Finland could only be relied on to eliminate Hanko, and tie down Russian forces on her southeastern front.[52] In fact Hitler had a high opinion of the fighting qualities of the Finnish troops, but doubted if they had recovered fully from their recent defeat.[53] Hitler added that the disposal of the occupied areas in the northern USSR presented 'no difficulty', since they would be handed over to Finland. Since it was no longer assumed that Sweden would co-operate, there was no more talk of giving her the Åland islands. The final plans were embodied in an OKW order to Falkenhorst on April 7.[54] It had now been decided how the troops were to be assembled at Rovaniemi. The SS Panzer brigade was to march down the Arctic Highway from Kirkenes to Rovaniemi. The staff, and the infantry division were to go by sea to Finland and move up to meet it. Since the movement would have to be carried out about a week before the opening of Barbarossa, it would be disguised as an exchange of troops for the relief of the garrison at Kirkenes. If, in the end, Sweden did grant the use of her railways, a further German division would be brought in from Norway, and would be available for further operations. In this way, the German planning for operations conducted from Finland reached its mature form. It is obvious that nothing that had been said to Buschenhagen had caused the Germans any doubts that Finland would play her allotted part when the time came. Yet one can believe those Finnish participants, from Mannerheim downwards, who assert that they always made it quite clear to the various German emissaries, that Finland would only fight if she were first attacked by the USSR. The Germans rightly attached no importance to this pious saving clause, since it meant nothing, in the mouths of men like Mannerheim and Heinrichs. In the first place they thought it highly probable that the USSR would attack Finland at some point, independently of anything Germany might do. But even if a German attack on the USSR were launched before this could happen, they were certain that as soon as Germany opened her attack on the main fronts in Europe, the USSR would launch a spoiling attack into Finland, to forestall German action there. All Finnish military planning testified to the firmness with which this belief was held. So the condition which the Finnish leaders set for their participation was, in their own minds, an unreal one, and of no practical effect. And Buschenhagen had learned enough to know that once the attack had been repelled, Finland did not intend to stand strictly on the defensive.

In Finland itself, the momentous decisions being taken in Germany had no obvious or direct repercussions. To a great extent the Finns appeared to be entirely wrapped up in their own domestic problems, which were pressing enough. The ordinary citizen was having a hard winter. He was not only short of food, but he knew there was some doubt whether he might not face much more serious hunger before the next harvest came in. The government knew, though it concealed the fact from the ordinary citizen, that when Russia cut off grain deliveries in January, it had made it very doubtful whether the bread ration could be maintained through the early summer. This was a threat for the future. The most obvious immediate problem was meat. There were persistent reports that in the cities, people were failing to get their ration even after prolonged queueing.[55] This was causing some bitterness, particularly among those who believed

Map to illustrate the proposed German-Finnish operations in northern Finland.

Legend

- ═══ The Arctic Highway
- ┼┼┼┼ Railway
- xxxxx Operational boundary
- ⬤ German unit
- ◯ Finnish unit
- ⤑ German approach move
- ▷ German offensive
- ⟶ Finnish approach move
- ▷ Finnish offensive

Units involved:

1 German Mountain Corps
2 SS Panzer brigade
3 German 169 Division
4 German XXXVI Army Corps
5 Finnish Petsamo battalion
6 Finnish Fifth Army Corps

Map labels

Arctic Ocean

NORWAY

Kirkenes

Petsamo Area

Murmansk

Ivalo

Sodankylä

SWEDEN

Kandalahksa

Sallatunturi

Kemijärvi

Rovaniemi

White Sea

Oulu

Gulf of Bothnia

Vienan Kemi

Sorokka

FINLAND

USSR

that the farmers were living in plenty, and making fortunes by illicit sales of food on the black market. The government stressed that the great task of the coming spring and summer would be to safeguard the nation's food. Townspeople were urged to prepare to go out into the country and help raise crops, and to make the most of their allotments. The press ran a prolonged campaign along these lines as the spring approached. There was also a major scheme sponsored by the ex-servicemen's organization for running summer work camps to win new farmland from the wilderness.[56]

The government was particularly sensitive about the food situation because it rapidly became a central feature of Soviet propaganda attacks. These suggested, naturally, that the rich lived in luxury while the poor starved, and that the food was going to feed the German troops, or was being stored for the future use of foreign armies. They never forgot to suggest also that if Finland had a government which would pursue policies of friendship towards the USSR, the shortages would be remedied at once by the Soviet Union. The Finnish authorities were particularly irritated at the way in which reports of hardship in Finland were picked up and magnified by the communist press in Sweden, and then quoted on Petroskoi radio as though it were an impartial foreign comment. The government got so irritated by these attacks that it actually allowed the Finnish press to comment on them. *Uusi Suomi*, in an editorial on February 23, said that the tone of Petroskoi radio was so incompatible with any prospect of building up better relations with the USSR, 'that one wants to refuse to believe that it is put out with the knowledge of the government concerned'. A few days later, the paper refuted some of the allegations directly. It was not true that rationing and shortages had 'inflamed the working people of Finland', or that 'only the destruction of the bourgeoisie could relieve the food problem'.[57] By April, when public confidence was growing, it was even suggested that the government might make an official protest about the endless barrage of abuse and misrepresentation.

There was also a certain amount of labour unrest which the communists were quick to exploit. The tradition of bad labour relations from the period before 1939, and seasonal unemployment made both employers and workers touchy. The government was always quick to intervene and pacify whenever trouble became overt, for it realized the dangers inherent in any renewal of industrial strife. Inflation too was a problem.[58] In the general absence of consumer goods, or even of the essentials of life, there was not much to spend money on, except the black market. The government became increasingly anxious to siphon off excess purchasing power and divert it into investment for reconstruction. For this purpose, the government launched a Fmk.1,000 million reconstruction loan on February 18. At first the response was a little hesitant, but the press made much of the patriotic duty of the citizen to invest in the future, and help fight inflation, and it was fully subscribed by March 16.[59] This loan is a rather significant declaration of confidence in the government, and in the future of his country, by the ordinary citizen, despite all the discouraging conditions of his daily life.

The main strains and stresses of life were reflected in an outburst of party bickering. The politicians showed themselves less phlegmatic than the ordinary citizen and gave clear signs that their nerves were suffering. There was considerable skirmishing between the Social Democrats and the IKL. The leaders of the Social Democratic party were bound to be embarrassed by their new allies in the government. The IKL leader Annala made things worse by telling his followers that he had agreed to work with the socialists only because they had abandoned their old programme. Since this was exactly the criticism that the Wiik group were making from the opposite wing, the socialists were extremely sensitive about it. An editorial appeared in *Suomen Sosiaalidemokraatti* declaring that the party was still internationalist, marxist, and class conscious.[60] The socialists felt bound to assert themselves, and stressed that defence expenditure must be balanced by social service expenditure, and campaigned strongly for rent controls and price controls. This in turn produced angry counterblasts from the parties of the Right.

The Eduskunta opened a new session on February 2, and it soon became apparent that the revived spirit of partisan politics was becoming a threat to yksimielisyys. Ryti had opened the session in a mood of restrained confidence. Their work was bound to be dominated by problems caused by the war, and in particular national defence must have first priority, but he looked forward to making a start with building for the future and with the works of peace. The political commentators expected a quiet session in which the spirit of unity would be manifested.[61] It was true that in face of the resurgence of fascist and authoritarian opinions, even conservative papers felt bound to defend the reasonable exercise of party functions. *Uusi Suomi* stressed that unity was not inconsistent with the existence of parties, whose work could be one of enlightenment. Other papers thought party politics not merely useful, but essential for the maintenance of democratic life. They condemned the idea of maintaining a 'dead silence'.[62] But the narrow limits which the cult of unity was felt to impose on party activity were reflected in the pained comment in *Uusi Suomi* when the Eduskunta failed to elect its Speaker unanimously. Those who appeared to believe that 'politics is intrigue' were castigated. This was followed by a comment of unusual naïvety, even for the Finnish press of that time. 'Politics, Finnish domestic and foreign politics, consists of course of the open and straightforward playing of cards. That is our conviction . . .'[63]

In a society where a serious national political commentator could publish such a view of politics, and apparently be taken seriously, the subsequent conduct of the Eduskunta was bound to seem irresponsible in the extreme.

Trouble started with the first major item in the government's programme, a measure conferring on it very extensive powers of control over the economy, the so-called 'valtalaki'—enabling law. The government already had most of the powers it conferred, but only under emergency regulations. It now wished to base its powers on regular legislation. The Social Democrats were strongly in favour of the valtalaki. It fitted their ideas about the need for economic planning. The only reservations which they had were on the provisions giving the government power to prohibit strikes.[64] The other parties were dubious about the valtalaki for precisely the same reasons which made the socialists support it. They saw it as a device for the introduction of creeping socialism. The Agrarians were particularly sensitive because they feared that the law could be used to fix low farm prices and requisition food. This fear was actually picked up by Soviet propaganda, which told the farmers that they were threatened by collectivization, and it had the effrontery to suggest that the communists would always take a lead in defending farmers from such a danger.[65] Only the Swedish People's party seems to have taken up the obvious line of attack that the valtalaki was a threat to political liberty. It attacked the law because it would deprive the Eduskunta of its legitimate constitutional right to control legislation. The extent of these fears can be measured by the slow progress of the valtalaki. It had been introduced by the government in December, but by March 18 it had only got out of the constitutional committee by one vote, and still had a long way to go before it finally passed. Already, the press was making indignant noises, attacking the shameful party manœuvring which they held responsible for this.[66] The opposition probably realized that they would have to pass the law, but were expressing their resentment and their impotence by aiming mulish kicks at the government. For instance the Agrarians led the other bourgeois parties in rejecting a government project to establish state fuel reserves, in the name of defending a private enterprise economy.[67] The political commentator of *Helsingin Sanomat* was genuinely shocked at their behaviour and wondered what had got into the members. *Uusi Suomi* solemnly warned them that they would get no thanks from the voters for this shameless reversion to the political habits of pre-war days.[68]

Probably the main reason why the politicians in the Eduskunta were behaving in this way was to be found in another government measure that was published, after long discussion in the cabinet, early in March. This concerned amendments to the law on the resettlement of refugees. The controversial amendment was the one which would have extended until

September 1, 1941, the time during which a landowner whose land was designated for resettlement, might purchase other land elsewhere, and offer it in place of his own.[69] Such land was technically called 'vastikemaa' —substitute land—and the subsequent political trouble centred round the so-called vastikemaa amendment. This amendment was put forward by the government at the demand of the Swedish People's party, and had been their price for agreeing to enter the government in January. In fact the Swedish language minority had been running a constant agitation on the point ever since the original resettlement proposals had been passed. In order to understand the force behind this agitation, it is necessary to explain briefly the position of the Swedish language minority in Finland.

In 1940, nearly ten per cent of the population of Finland spoke Swedish as their mother tongue. The Swedish-speaking population fell into three groups. There were the farmers and fishermen who inhabited much of the west and south coastal plain of Finland, and the islands of the archipelago which skirted this coast. These people, descendants of Swedish migrants in medieval times, were a self-contained group whose numbers were steadily shrinking as the young people left for the cities. They were not politically active, nor inclined to agitate about the future of Swedish culture. Secondly there had been a predominant Swedish language population in most of the coastal towns, including Helsinki. But except in certain small and economically stagnant places, these towns were being infiltrated by a stream of Finnish-speaking migrants. By 1940, the Finnish speakers were a majority in every major urban centre, or if not, were a substantial minority, which gained ground with every year that passed. Further it was an observed social phenomenon that if a Swedish-speaking family moved into town, its children would become bi-lingual, and its grandchildren Finnish-speaking. The pressure of the majority culture proved irresistible. This steady undermining of the Swedish-speaking minority by natural processes would probably have been accepted as natural, and proceeded painlessly to its inevitable end, if there had not existed a third element of Swedish speakers, numerically the least significant, but politically of great importance.

These were the heirs of what had been the Swedish-speaking ruling class of Finland. Until the mid-nineteenth century, the whole ruling class in Finland, the major property owners, the trading community, the professions and the civil service, and all educated persons had been Swedish-speaking. This situation had changed rapidly after the 1860s when the Russians deliberately began to encourage the official use of Finnish, and gave free rein to the Finnish language enthusiasts, who had previously been restrained. The process of making Finnish the language of the ruling group and of society generally had gone far by 1918, but the Swedish-speaking minority was still possessed of enough political and economic power to insist that entrenched rights for Swedish language and culture be written into the constitution. These top people had been slowly edged out of politics, but were still powerful in industry and commerce in 1940. For the defence of the rights of the minority culture, the Swedish People's party had evolved, and existed solely for this purpose, winning most of the Eduskunta seats in the Swedish-speaking areas. The fishermen and farmers of the coastal region were willing to follow the lead of the politicians and intelligentsia who ran the party. They in turn were aware that slowly the whole basis of their special position was being eroded by natural forces, and were the more sensitive to anything which seemed calculated to speed up the process. This was exactly what the resettlement law threatened to do. If large numbers of Finnish-speaking Karelians were settled in the coastal strip, many parishes which had been officially bi-lingual, with a Swedish majority, would become Finnish majority areas. Many others which had been wholly Swedish-speaking would have a large Finnish minority introduced in their midst. The danger was made worse by a kind of historical nemesis. Because they were the heirs of the old ruling class, Swedish speakers formed a disproportionate part of the owners of large farms in the more fertile parts of the country. Hence they would be most severely affected by the compulsory purchase provisions of the resettle-ment law. The only way in which these people could avert the conse-quences of resettlement was to make extensive use of the vastikemaa pro-cedure, buying off the threat to the last surviving strongholds of Swedish language culture in Finland.

The attitude of the majority press, and of the major political parties, had been unsympathetic to the Swedish minority fears. It was suspected that they were trying to contract out of the sacrifices which the rest of the com-munity was making.[70] The government had had the utmost difficulty in framing its proposal. The Agrarians were most strongly opposed, since they held that the amendment would slow down the rate of resettlement. The Social Democrats were less vehement, but disinclined to support the amendment because it seemed to favour big landowners. The Agrarian ministers had threatened to resign on the issue, but Ryti had virtually forced them to remain in the government. The Swedish People's party had made it clear it would go into opposition if the measure were not passed, and in the interests of unity, they were allowed to have their way. The result was that the government's proposal was in fact opposed by a majority of the members of the cabinet, and because of this the govern-ment could not put pressure on the Eduskunta or make it a matter of con-fidence.[71] It announced that it would abide by the decision of the Edus-kunta on the matter. The result was to poison the whole political atmosphere. The Swedish People's party was afraid that the other parties would go back on the agreement made at their entry into the government. They expressed this fear by their part in opposing the valtalaki and other measures. The Agrarian party intended to fight the vastikemaa amendment in the Eduskunta, and were confident of defeating it unless the socialists, in the interests of unity, felt obliged to support it. There were signs that this might happen. It has been pointed out that the refugee vote mattered a great deal to the Agrarians, but comparatively little to the Social Democrats. They could afford to be statesmanlike and offer to pocket their opposition to concessions for big landowners, and condemn the current political row as a vulgar brawl among the bourgeois parties for the Karelian vote.[72] They pointed out how shameful it was for the Agrarians and the Swedish People's party to join together in delaying the valtalaki out of their common but opposite resentments against the government.[73] The more radical Agrarians, led by Niukkanen, were prepared to bring down the government rather than let the vastikemaa amendment pass, and it became increasingly clear that on this issue they had most of their party behind them. They lashed out at the Social Democrats, accusing them of betraying the alliance of the two parties, and Hannula published the accusation in his paper.[74] At this point, all responsible opinion began to take alarm at such a resurgence of old-style political controversy. Tanner published a soothing letter, assuring the Agrarians that his party was as keen as ever on co-operation with them, and the press urged the politicians to hurry and settle their differences.[75] As *Helsingin Sanomat* told them, such quarrels were 'not constructive. And at the present time we Finns must be constructive only'. The politicians were told bluntly that they were letting the people down, and that they had more important work to do.

This pressure began to have its effect. This was made clear when on April 1 the valtalaki at last reached the floor of the Eduskunta after months in committee. Rangell introduced it himself, pointing out that the government was often embarrassed by the need to resort to emergency regulations, and that while the government was a national coalition there was no reason to fear any abuse of the law. The Social Democrat minister Fagerholm stressed how the law would facilitate such measures as rent control, and advised socialist critics not to stand out against it because of the powers to prohibit strikes. It became apparent from the following debate that the opposition to the law had collapsed. Only the Swedish People's party persisted in its opposition. The conservative groups did not conceal their preference for retaining the emergency regulations, nor did the Agrarians hide their anxiety about its use against farmers, while many socialists stood out for the right to strike, but it was clear that none of these groups was now prepared to reject the bill.[76] The Agrarians tried to save face by

proposing that it should expire at the end of 1941, but they got little support on this. Rangell had made it clear that the government regarded the
valtalaki as a question of confidence, and it finally passed, unamended, on
April 29, by 147 votes to 33.[77]

It is likely that the press was correct when it suggested that the ordinary
citizen was much less interested in disputes over the valtalaki or the vastikemaa amendment than were the professional politicians in the Eduskunta. Their attention was focused on the unfolding drama of the European war, and in so far as they were interested in domestic politics, they
were more concerned with whether Finland should adapt her policies to
suit the German New Order in Europe. But the great question was
whether Germany would attack the USSR in the spring or summer and
whether Finland should then take her opportunity of reversing the Treaty
of Moscow. The extent of the speculation can best be judged by the extent
of the condemnation of it in the press. Early in March, the speculators at
last got some solid fact to feed on. German troops moved into Bulgaria,
and the USSR issued a formal protest. Svento, who had devoted so much
energy to proving that a Russo-German conflict was unlikely, was taken
aback by this, but still thought that the two powers would come to terms
rather than fight. The official policy was still one of absolute discretion.
Helsingin Sanomat warned its readers not to jump to conclusions because
of the protest, but in fact it was obvious that conclusions were indeed being
jumped to on a large scale.[78] The socialist press in particular became
alarmed at the increasing advocacy of a 'policy of adventure', which was
the public euphemism for a policy of joining in a German-Soviet conflict.[79]

Another sign of the vigour of this kind of thinking was the lively activity
of Right-wing extremists. There was a rash of new political periodicals, all
of the Right, which openly indulged in the most tactless speculation. This
had been commented on adversely already in January, when it was noted
that 52 had appeared in the second half of 1940, of a kind which 'seek to
fish in troubled waters', and which tended to advocate a 'new order'
which they were generally reluctant to define too closely, but which was
clearly authoritarian and violently nationalist.[80] The more old-fashioned
nationalists, as represented by the AKS, tended to deprecate these new
trends as much as the socialist press. For instance, the AKS periodical,
Suomen Heimo, while agreeing that there could be no return to the pre-
1939 political system, insisted that leadership must remain where it was,
with the properly constituted government, and deprecated those who
advocated patent political remedies imported from abroad.[81] The government found this effervescence embarrassing too. It stood firmly in public
for a policy of strict neutrality, and the building up of proper relations with
the USSR. Ryti's speech to the Eduskunta on February 2 had emphasized

this unchanging resolve by the government. He added the warning that although the government would never waver from a position of neutrality, and a will for peace, this did not always suffice in the present state of the world. Hence the need for strong defences. This theme was echoed in an editorial in *Uusi Suomi* on March 13, on the anniversary of the peace. 'The Finnish people feels deeply the blessings of peace. But it also knows that peace is not procured free of charge in the present world.'[82] Thus there were enough hints for the initiated reader that the mere will to live in peace with the USSR might not be enough, and even that Finnish neutrality might have a slight bias in favour of Germany.

This was made almost explicit in a report by the government to the foreign affairs committee of the Eduskunta in March. This contained a phrase about neutrality that was later to be quoted widely:[83]

'Finland has in some circumstances had to take into account that neutrality, as understood in its old classical form . . . has everywhere had to be set aside.'

The report cited the transit agreement with Germany, and the agreement with Britain allowing her inspectors to operate in the Petsamo area as examples of this. But it was also clear to the observant reader, that in so far as Finland did lean away from classical neutrality, it was towards Germany that she inclined. Public official comment rarely failed to mention that Finland had a special relation with Germany, though it rarely defined with any precision what the relation was. Usually, as in the report mentioned, it used such a phrase as 'Finland and its people have an inheritance of friendly relations with Germany going back for centuries'. Thus it was stressed that the special relation was the most natural thing in the world and of no special immediate significance. The subject was still much too delicate for open speaking. This is apparent in the treatment of a speech by Mussolini. He had referred to Finland as a country 'directly or indirectly within Germany's sphere of influence'. *Helsingin Sanomat*, by quoting a German newspaper, managed to reveal that this phrase had been cut out of the versions of the speech released in Finland.[84] This remained a favourite gambit for mentioning the unmentionable. A more daring use of it in the same paper occurred in March, when by quoting a Swedish newspaper, it not only revealed that there had been a crisis in relations with the USSR the previous summer, something never officially admitted, but said that subsequent relaxation of tension had been directly linked with the granting of transit facilities to Germany.[85]

Even so, the press felt it irksome at being debarred from open participation in the great debate. *Uusi Suomi* complained that proper discussion was impossible when 'at the moment it is not even possible to name everything by its right name . . . Discussion is therefore more or less a battle in darkness.'[86] Still, despite these handicaps, in however veiled a fashion, the press reflected the simple fact that Finland had special ties with Germany, and even that there might be great events ahead and that Finland might be involved in them, as *Uusi Suomi* warned its readers on March 28.[87] The public of course was much less inhibited in its discussions. Paasikivi noted, when he returned to Helsinki in the middle of March, that a Russo-German war was the common topic of conversation, and that most people expected it. In fact the buzz of discussion reached such a pitch by the end of March that Ryti himself intervened to try and calm it down. He invited Svinhufvud to call on him for a discussion of the government's foreign policy and urged him to calm down the enthusiasm of pro-German circles. There was no certainty that Germany would attack the USSR, so that Finland must 'rely on ourselves, do everything possible to strengthen our defensive capacities'. The only safe policy was to give priority to developing relations with Sweden, then to cultivate Germany, but at the same time to avoid conflict with the USSR and try to find some way of living with her. Rash talk among the public was endangering these objectives.[88]

One reason why Ryti felt it necessary to try to restrain the enthusiasms of the pro-German groups was that they had already involved the government in an acutely embarrassing situation by their excessive zeal. The group responsible was dominated by conservative nationalists of the kind who supported Nouseva Suomi, the most prominent of whom were P. H. Norrmen and E. Riekki. They were men with influential friends in Germany, and Mannerheim characterized them as 'activists who had too much time and energy'.[89] They had been in contact with Himmler and the leaders of the German SS, the special private army of the Nazi party. As a part of the building of the New Order, the SS had been recruiting men from all 'nordic' countries who would serve the cause of European National Socialism. Such men had to be racially approved, be prepared to accept the ideology of Nazism, and swear an oath of allegiance to Hitler. Norrmen and his friends had given the SS authorities the idea that there were hundreds of young Finns eager to enlist, and the SS were preparing to send a doctor to Helsinki to conduct medical examinations. There is no doubt that on the Finnish side, most of the promoters had in mind the precedent of the First World War, when young Finns had enlisted in the Imperial German Army in order to fight the Russians, and had formed the 27th Jäger battalion in the Imperial Army. They tended to close their eyes to the fact that because of the ideological factors, joining the SS was rather a different proposition.

At the beginning of March, the SS authorities informed the German foreign office of their plan, and they felt that the matter must be taken up with the Finnish government.[90] Blücher was asked to find out what the position was in Finland, and Kivimäki, who was going home on leave, asked to take up the matter officially. Witting at once reacted favourably, even enthusiastically, and remarked to Blücher that in this way perhaps 'Finland can march into membership of the Tripartite pact'.[91] Witting perceived at once that this scheme would constitute a kind of pledge of future close co-operation between Finland and Germany. The others consulted, Ryti, Mannerheim, and Walden, were clearly less enthusiastic, but basically shared Witting's view that the move would create a new obligation on Germany to stand by Finland, and not sell her out in a possible deal with the USSR. But all the Finnish leaders expressed a preference for enlisting the Finns in the German regular army rather than the SS, and stipulated that if they must join the SS it should be as a separate, purely Finnish unit, and not in units recruited from occupied countries like Holland or Norway. These men, who were decent and civilized men, were never happy about the SS or being associated with it. They knew that in dealing with such an organization they were touching pitch. Hence they were very ready to agree that the actual organization be left to Norrmen, Riekki, and a small private committee, so the hands of the government would not be soiled.

Even so, the ruling circle continued to exhibit all the signs of a bad conscience over the SS battalion. At first nobody wanted to take the responsibility of financing it, until Walden at last consented to the use of defence ministry funds.[92] They tried to get further special conditions for the recruits, such as a pledge that they would not be used to fight the western powers, or that they should not take an oath to Hitler, but significantly, rather than see the scheme founder, they withdrew these proposals.[93] Mannerheim felt so badly about it that when he came to write his memoirs after the event, he supposed that he had opposed the scheme altogether. But contemporary evidence proves quite clearly that he had not. Finally, they were so ashamed that they did not dare to tell their own people of what they had done. Riekki's committee was enjoined to work with the utmost secrecy, and nobody outside a very small circle was informed of what had been done. However, the secret could not be kept. When Riekki's committee got down to work, they discovered that the supposed flood of eager volunteers did not exist. So they had to begin a very discreet recruiting campaign during April, and news of this inevitably leaked out. As soon as it did so, the Social Democratic party and the Agrarian party made a joint protest to the prime minister about the ideological implications of what the government had done. Rangell replied that he too was unhappy about this, and hoped that recruiting would soon cease.[94] However it did not prove difficult to enlist 750 men to serve in the exclusively

Finnish SS battalion that was set up. There were plenty of young Finns, eager for adventure and foreign travel, impressed by Germany's military successes, and easily persuaded that they were continuing the glorious traditions established by their fathers in the 27th Jäger battalion. Most of them probably neither knew nor cared much about the ideology of National Socialism. But the leaders of the Finnish people cannot be absolved from their responsibility. They knew what they were doing, as their attempts to evade responsibility clearly indicated. They were indeed wandering rather far from the classical concept of neutrality. It is understandable that Ryti should have sought to cool down the activists. The government did not want to get caught up in any more episodes of this nature.

The Finnish leaders defended their conduct over the SS battalion on the grounds that in March 1941, the ultimate intentions of Germany were so uncertain, that they could not neglect any opportunity, however dubious, of creating further links with her, or do anything that could conceivably offend her. For they remained convinced that the USSR was bent on their destruction. This became apparent in a series of high-level discussions on foreign policy which took place when both Kivimäki and Paasikivi returned to Helsinki in March.[95] Paasikivi tried to urge on the government the view that Germany could never be so mad as to attack the USSR while Britain was still undefeated. He tried to persuade them that the USSR was much stronger than they supposed. He discussed the current rumours that Germany was determined to get control of the wheat of the Ukraine and the oil of the Caucasus, and said that this was a task beyond Germany's strength.[96] But Paasikivi found nobody to believe him in Helsinki. Ryti was convinced that the USSR had an active plan to gain access to the Atlantic through Scandinavia, and that she had no long-term intention of respecting the Treaty of Moscow.[97] Paasikivi tried to persuade the government to consider further concession on the nickel question, as he was convinced that the USSR would use force in the end if she were denied.[98] This the government declined to do, as they were relying on their assurances from Germany.

At the same time they were constantly seeking to get these assurances in some more concrete form. Kivimäki was able to tell them that the German foreign office no longer denied that relations with the USSR had worsened, and that there might be developments of interest to Finland in the near future.[99] As soon as the ambassador got back to Berlin he sought some amplification of these hints. He asked Weizsäcker whether a Russo-German war was likely, and he was told emphatically that it was not.[100] Then Kivimäki raised the nickel question, ought his government to continue its stand against Soviet pressures? On this the German response was much more specific than before. First Blücher told the Finnish government that even if the nickel negotiations broke down completely, Finland had nothing to fear.[101] And on April 2, Kivimäki was told by Weizsäcker that the Finnish government need have no further anxiety over the nickel question. The USSR was well aware that Germany would not tolerate an outbreak of war in Scandinavia, and the approach of the campaigning season was enough in itself to ensure that the USSR would not risk any breach with Germany.[102] Ryti too received some kind of assurance at this point from Germany that Finland could stand firm, and that matters would be cleared up within the next month or two.

So, by the end of March 1941, Finnish policy entered a new phase. For perhaps the first time since the end of the war, the Finnish government had a degree of security. They knew that for the time being they did not need to fear an attack from the USSR, or that if it did come, Germany would help them to repel it, because she had reasons of her own for wishing to prevent any further Soviet encroachments on Finland. The government could now focus its attention on the remaining open question. They knew that within two months the relations of Germany and the USSR were to be clarified. They knew that Germany contemplated a solution by force, but they believed that a solution by diplomacy was also possible. Their problem was to shape a policy that would meet both eventualities. One thing was clear. They could not alter their commitment to Germany, for they regarded this as the sole possible basis of their future security. They were so obsessed by the menace of the USSR that they never paused to consider the cost of this commitment. This was made apparent when, at the beginning of April, the governments of Great Britain and the USA made official inquiries about the pro-German trends that were now so obvious in Finland. They wanted to know if Finland was going to depart from her declared policy of neutrality. Witting's answer to the two ambassadors showed that by this stage he attached little importance to these two powers. He said in effect that Finland was a small and peaceful country, and would not change her policy voluntarily, but added that if the two powers wanted to keep her that way, they should stop obstructing the traffic to Liinahamari.

It seems as though the war, followed by twelve months of unending unpleasantness and menace from the USSR, had produced in the minds of the Finnish leaders a kind of fatalism, that probably reflected a considerable degree of mental and nervous exhaustion. They had been living with the threat of destruction for too long. It is probable that with one part of their minds they did genuinely wish to stay neutral, and live within the framework of the Treaty of Moscow, rather than be dragged into a fresh war. This was what they always said. But at the same time they could see fairly clearly by the beginning of April the direction in which events were drifting. They had convinced themselves that the USSR would never let them live in peace, and as Paasikivi had found, no arguments would shift them from this belief. On the other hand they could perceive the possibility of Germany smashing the USSR, or drastically curtailing her power, thus delivering them from their nightmare predicament. The prospect was irresistibly attractive.

Witting expressed their attitude to Blücher when he said, 'Finland, as a small country, cannot in the future frame a policy of her own choice, but must adapt herself to circumstances.'[103] He went on to make it clear that as far as he was concerned, only Germany could offer Finland the protection that she needed. Witting admitted that there were still some of his countrymen who hankered after closer ties with Sweden, but he had no sympathy for their ideas. And if the time came to make a public choice, he 'would like to lead his country into the Tripartite pact.'[104] It cannot be asserted that the whole of the ruling group went as far as the foreign minister, and he probably exaggerated his enthusiasm for Blücher's benefit, but they all felt that intelligent adaptation to forces which they could not control was the only policy open to them. As General Heinrichs remarked, 'the current carried the boat along . . .',[105] and nobody in power in Finland believed any longer in the possibility of rowing against it. It was Finland's misfortune that when, in April 1941, she was offered a last opportunity of changing course, her leaders could no longer bring themselves to clutch at it with sufficient energy. They no longer believed that any independent action of their own could alter fundamentally their country's inevitable destiny.

CHAPTER 11

Lost opportunities

I n April 1941, the international situation in eastern Europe was altered by a major shift in the policy of the USSR. This is usually associated with a personal initiative by Stalin himself, of which the outward sign was his assumption of the premiership of the USSR. Until April, the USSR, while seeking to avoid conflict with Germany, and consequent involvement in the European war, had set certain limits to the concessions she was prepared to make in order to preserve the goodwill of Germany. The government of the USSR had made it clear that it expected Germany to honour the agreements made in August 1939, and had entered a firm protest when she failed to do so. The most obvious manifestations of this attitude by the USSR had been the formal protest at the entry of German troops into Bulgaria, and the treaty of friendship with Yugoslavia which had been concluded, amid great publicity, on the eve of the German invasion of that country.

It is assumed that the way in which these demonstrations had been ignored by Germany, and the failure of the German government to take up the discussion of political issues where Molotov had left them in November, added to the obvious signs of German military build-up in the east, had convinced Stalin that he must change his policy. He seems to have concluded that at least Germany would not shrink from war with the USSR even though Britain was still undefeated in the west, and may have perceived that Hitler positively wanted an excuse to launch an attack. Since Stalin seems to have been desperate to postpone a conflict with Germany, he began to do everything possible to deprive Germany of any excuse for action, even when this involved considerable humiliation for the USSR. One part of the new policy was to stop the Soviet harassment of the small border countries which enjoyed German patronage.[1]

For Finland, the change was announced by a change of ambassador. Zotov had been recalled to Moscow early in the year, and on April 5 it was announced that he was not returning.[2] Since Zotov, in Finnish eyes, represented all that they most resented in the policies of the USSR, his

elimination from the scene was a necessary prelude to a change of policy. The
new Soviet ambassador, Orlov, was a very different kind of man. Personally
he made a good impression on all types of Finn, even those who expected
nothing good from the USSR. Ryti met him on April 23, and was obviously
impressed by Orlov's manner, for he noted in his diary that Orlov seemed
much more civilized than Zotov.³ Other Finnish officials who dealt with
him confirmed this impression.⁴ The significance of Orlov's coming was
no secret anywhere. He made it clear that it was his mission to improve
relations, and he was ready to tell this to anyone he could get to listen to
him. Orlov spoke several times with Witting and Paasikivi and always his
theme was the same, 'there is still one thing, the most important of all, the
general improvement of relations between Finland and the Soviet Union.
This problem must be resolved'.⁵ The public too was aware of his mission.
Orlov went out of his way to talk with politicians and to seek to impress
them that the USSR was offering to make a fresh start in her relations
with Finland. The socialists in particular welcomed his coming, *Suomen
Sosiaalidemokraatti* greeted the new ambassador with an editorial which
strongly emphasized that the time had come for a major effort to build
friendly relations.

When Orlov discussed current problems with Paasikivi he agreed that
the Petsamo nickel question was the only one outstanding. The USSR was
waiting for a new move from Finland on this, but Orlov warned Paasikivi
that his government would certainly stand firm on their minimum demands. Witting was encouraged by Orlov's manner, and by his consciousness of the new strength of Finland's position, to talk quite frankly with
Orlov. Witting went over the whole sad story of Finnish-Soviet relations
in the previous year and pointed out what a disastrous psychological effect
this had had. The Finnish government was disinclined to make concessions
on the nickel question because 'we do not know what the Soviet Union's
next demand will be after the nickel question.' Witting revealed that the
Finnish government would make the nickel question a test case for deter-
mining whether there was any substance in the new professions of goodwill. If the USSR would accept the new Finnish proposals, that would
have a very favourable effect.

The new Finnish note on the nickel question was formally handed over
to Vishinski on May 10. It contained alternative suggestions. If the USSR
would now abandon its demand for the concession, and be content with an
agreement to share the output of the mines with Germany, this would
pave the way for a major improvement in relations with Finland. But if the
USSR insisted in its demand to set up a mixed company, then Finland
must insist in turn that the control of the company must be in Finnish
hands and in particular, the management and personnel at the mines must

be Finnish. They would be willing to continue negotiations on this basis by the mixed commission, but in Helsinki, not in Moscow.[6] Thus the reply was made as from a position of strength. The USSR was told either to make concessions or drop the matter. Better relations with Finland would have to be purchased by deeds, not words alone. If the USSR wanted to continue with its previous line of policy, it must realize that the time when Finland had been prepared to make concessions had passed. Vishinski's response to this was mild. As Orlov had forecast, the nickel affair had gone too far for the USSR to make major concessions, great power prestige was involved. Vishinski said that his government could not proceed on the basis proposed by Finland, and that the whole question seemed to be no further forward than it had been three months earlier. But that was all he said.[7] There was no anger and no threats. Since the USSR does not seem to have raised the nickel question again, she must have accepted that Finland now had enough backing from Germany to make further progress impossible. In such circumstances the USSR preferred to defer the whole matter. Finland's first effort to cash in on Orlov's professions of goodwill had failed, her price was too high.

Soon there were other signs that Orlov had come too late. He had hinted very clearly that the government of the USSR regretted Paasikivi's resignation as ambassador, and would have taken his continuance in office as a sign of Finland's desire to improve relations.[8] There was substance in this view. It will be recalled that Witting had told Blücher that Paasikivi had become a liability to his government because he was too ready to urge concessions to the USSR. Subsequently Witting made a similar remark to the American ambassador.[9] The Soviet government knew this, as was revealed when Paasikivi had a farewell interview with Stalin. The Soviet dictator's opening words were, 'they are not pleased with you in Helsinki'.[10] Indeed, the point was not missed in Finland. Svento wrote:[11]

'Wide circles in Finland have gradually got to feel that Paasikivi's being in Moscow was a kind of guarantee that no deterioration would occur in our relations with the Soviet Union . . . it does not have a reassuring effect . . . we are deeply convinced that he would never have refused to serve his country for a little longer . . . if only the conditions for his activity had been different from what, for many reasons, they have clearly been in recent times.'

For the Finnish press of 1941, this was brutally frank speaking. It was also true. The confirmation of Paasikivi's resignation meant the rejection by the Finnish government of the policy which he had advised. That policy would have demanded a positive response to Orlov's advances. Paasikivi had fought hard while in Helsinki for his point of view. He had tried to impress on the government that they could not run away from the facts of geography. They would always have a powerful USSR for a neighbour and must learn to live with her. Their ultimate survival depended on this. Germany could never destroy the Soviet Union by military action, nor would the USSR disintegrate under attack. Paasikivi prophesied correctly that Stalin would, in the event of such an attack, be able to call forth the latent power of Russian patriotism. By using the vast spaces at his disposal, and backed by the power of Britain and the USA, Stalin would defeat Germany in the end. On the other hand, Orlov's coming offered a most favourable opportunity for trying to reconstruct relations with the USSR on a sound basis. Orlov's approaches were backed by a change in the tone of Soviet propaganda. The stream of threats and abuse had ceased, and Petroskoi radio was now stressing that the time had come to improve relations with Finland. But the Finnish leaders were psychologically blind and deaf to Paasikivi's urgings. They dismissed the new Russian policy as insincere, as Blücher noted, 'manch finnischen Politiker sahen darin blose Taktik'.*[12] Paasikivi has recorded how he failed to shake Ryti's belief. He was 'convinced that Soviet Russia would never give up its attempt to conquer Finland . . . Finland's only salvation was that Germany should smash the Soviet Union'.[13] Given this fundamental outlook, there was no prospect of Orlov's advances being taken up, though the Finnish government was prepared to try and extract tactical advantages out of them, as it had done in the nickel affair.

The most important of Orlov's initiatives concerned the question of Finland's relations with Sweden. Orlov persistently hinted that if Finland wanted to reconsider the idea of an alliance with Sweden, the USSR would no longer oppose it.[14] Several Finnish politicians were told this by the ambassador.[15] Sir Stafford Cripps told Paasikivi the same thing when the latter returned to Moscow. Such a turn round in the policy of the USSR was quite natural in the circumstances. They had at last realized that such an alliance was the only thing that might prevent Finland from throwing in her lot entirely with Germany. The Finnish leaders inevitably saw the move as a trap. The USSR would try to encourage them in a move which would, as they knew, be offensive to Germany, and then having undermined Finland's only existing security, would no doubt revert to their old tactics. So that the possibility of alliance with Sweden, which had been the most cherished objective of Finnish policy in December, was now, when it might have been realized, rejected out of hand. The Finnish government, and large sections of the Finnish public, no longer thought that they shared a common foreign policy with Sweden. As they saw it, the paths of the two nations had diverged.

* 'many Finnish politicians saw it as mere tactics.'

The Swedish government had formed a fair idea of just what the divergence was, and was concerned, if it were still possible, to dissuade Finland from entering any Russo-German war as the ally or associate of Germany. It seems to have recognized that Finland could hardly prevent Germany making use of her territory in such a war, and would not regard this as inconsistent with a general policy of neutrality. Even if Finland used the opportunity presented by such a war to repossess the areas ceded in 1940, Sweden was still willing to maintain close co-operation with her. But if Finland openly participated as an ally in an aggressive war against the USSR, close co-operation between Finland and Sweden would no longer be possible. But the aim of the Swedish government remained that of persuading Finland to adopt the same kind of neutrality as Sweden herself.[16] The apprehensions of the Swedish government spread into the columns of the Swedish press. *Svenska Dagbladet* published an editorial in April on the position of Finland which concluded with this passage:[17]

'As long as the direction of policy follows a Scandinavian pattern and unconditional neutrality is pursued, our fates are the same and oblige Sweden to strengthen continuously its inescapable ties with the brotherland to the east.'

The implication of the article was clear. If Finland did not pursue a genuinely neutral policy, Sweden would regard her as betraying her Scandinavian traditions, and might refuse to be associated with her. The Finnish press was outraged by the implied criticism. The lead was taken by *Helsingin Sanomat*, usually a paper of moderate and liberal views. In an editorial on April 26, the paper declared that Finland conducted her own foreign policy, that she had problems peculiar to herself, which demanded policies different from those of Sweden, and that in any case Sweden had given Finnish foreign policy little or no help since the war ended.[18] *Svenska Dagbladet* had started a first-class row between the press of the two countries. At once a lively debate sprang up about Finland's neutrality.[19] Soon the British press joined in. As a result the Finnish readers were suddenly treated to a debate on their front pages for which there was no precedent since the war. Mainly by quoting the foreign press, Finnish papers mentioned many hitherto unmentionable things. The presence of German troops in Finland, the German military build-up in the north, even the exchange of visits between the Finnish and German general staffs were openly talked of. Even worse, the Swedish paper *Dagens Nyheter* drew attention to the activity of Right-wing groups in Finland and the 'very powerful foreign propaganda' which they spread in the country, and said that it was common talk, particularly in the officer corps, that there would be a 'war of revenge'. Such phenomena made close co-operation between Finland and Sweden very difficult. *Svenska Dagbladet* pointed

out that the attitude of the public in Finland and Sweden to the German
troops in transit had been opposite in the two countries.[20] The theme of the
Finnish replies was always that Sweden ought to recognize Finland's
peculiar problems, and the special policies they called forth. *Uusi Suomi*
declared:

'The basic reason for the mistake which the Swedish press is making is
that in Sweden they are not able, or they do not want to see the demands
which arise from the nature of our position. It would be a mistake to
measure values with the same measure in Sweden as in Finland.'

A few days later the same paper pointed out that history, geography, and
politics all produced different attitudes in the two countries, but the most
powerful factor of all was Finland's experiences in the late war. Some of
the Right-wing comment denied that Sweden had any claim to enjoy a
closer relationship with Finland than Germany had. The periodical
Suomen Tie wrote:[21]

'If centuries-old political, cultural, and economic traditions form the
basis of the common effort of the Scandinavian countries, then the state of
the relationship between Finland and Germany is just the same . . .
Europe is being shaped into new patterns of life and it is certain that Finland does not wish, and cannot be kept aside from this new, broad, unfolding, common effort of the nations.'

Naturally, responsible opinion in both countries was horrified at this
massive release of cats from bags, and rushed in to stifle it. There were of
course German troops in Finland, and the two general staffs had exchanged 'courtesy visits', but no normal person could see anything sinister
in this. Swedish papers began to say that of course nobody had really
wanted to cast any doubt on Finland's neutrality and told one another they
ought not to publish things that would embarrass Finland. *Svenska Dagbladet* tried to soothe ruffled feelings in Finland. It said that in face of 'un-
relenting Russian pressure' it had been quite natural that Finland should
turn to her old friends, that is, Germany. *Helsingin Sanomat*, shaken by
what it had started, sternly reproved extremist publications in Finland
that had given rise to many of the Swedish misconceptions about Finnish
policies. Yet in the end, *Svenska Dagbladet* made a last thrust. It asked why
there had been so much excitement in Finland over its original article.
Could it be that there were, after all, some doubts about Finland's neutrality?[22] The significant feature of these exchanges is that in the Finnish
press, apart from the socialist papers, it was accepted that Finnish neutrality was different from Swedish neutrality because Finland had a special
relationship with Germany. This was accepted as a fact, and regarded as
entirely natural. It is a reasonable assumption that by this stage Finnish
public opinion, again with the exception of the socialists, shared the out-

look of the press. This gives some substance to the claims of the Finnish government that its own policy, which rested on a similar assumption, had the support of majority opinion in the country.

It quickly became apparent that the Swedish press had been reflecting the anxieties of the Swedish government. For within a few days of the controversy subsiding, it was announced that Günther, the Swedish foreign minister, would visit Helsinki for talks with the Finnish government. His aim was to discover the truth about Finnish policy, and if necessary try to persuade the Finnish government not to depart from a strictly neutral line. The German foreign office was aware of Günther's purpose, and was alarmed that he might have some success. Ribbentrop sent urgent instruction to Blücher about how he was to handle the Finnish government. They were asked to be evasive in answering questions about the relationship of Finland and Germany. If there was any chance of persuading Sweden to enter the Tripartite pact, then she would be welcome and Finland could join with her. Otherwise Finland should maintain an unattached position, and not enter into any special ties with Sweden.[23] It seems clear that the German government took seriously the possibility that Günther might revive some plan of a Swedish-Finnish alliance, and that Finland might find it attractive. It was still conceivable that the Finnish leaders might think that the safety of strict neutrality was preferable to the risks involved in close association with Germany, despite the alluring prospects of gain which the latter course might open up.

But Ribbentrop went further, with a move designed to take all urgency out of the situation, and suggest to Finland that she had no need to take any hasty decisions at that stage, while at the same time giving Sweden the impression that no crisis was imminent. A German official, von Weissauer, was sent to Helsinki with instructions to tell Witting, as from the highest source, that there was no likelihood of a German-Soviet conflict before the spring of 1942, and that Germany hoped that conflict would be avoided altogether. Blücher was not sure that Witting believed it, but there is good evidence to suggest that he did. He was certainly impressed by von Weissauer, and told Pakaslahti, head of the Finnish foreign office, that his information had come from a source 'directly connected with Germany's higher leadership'. Wasastjerna, the ambassador in Stockhom, who was a close personal friend of Witting, was quite certain that Witting believed that the war was put off.[24]

Thus when Günther came to Helsinki and asked outright whether Finland was thinking in terms of a war of revenge, Witting told him that he had just heard on high authority that a German-Soviet war was unlikely, so that the question did not arise. But he added, according to Blücher, that 'die finnische Regierung denke völkish und nicht territorial und wolle

16

keine Revanche'.* If there was a war, Witting said that Finland would
certainly grant Germany any special facilities she asked for, in spite of
neutrality. Witting criticized the Swedish concept of neutrality as outmoded. Finland at least could not expect to be neutral in the old sense in
any German-Soviet conflict. On the other hand, Finland could expect
some changes to her advantage in any settlement between Germany and
the USSR whether brought about by war or by diplomacy. Witting told
Blücher that Günther had expressed understanding of the Finnish
position.[25] It is not clear whether Günther even mentioned the subject of
an alliance between Finland and Sweden. If he did, Witting showed no
interest, but Günther could have concluded from what Witting said that
the necessary basis for such an alliance, the acceptance of strict neutrality
by Finland, did not exist.

It can be seen from Witting's position during the Günther visit, that the
Finnish leaders saw the situation in May 1941 as rather promising.
Their existing position enjoyed the protection of Germany against en-
croachment by the USSR. This protection was much more powerful than
any which an alliance with Sweden could have conferred. For the future,
if they remained co-operative with Germany, they could expect to profit
out of any settlement that Germany might make with the USSR. If it
came to a war, that would be temporarily unpleasant, but in the end Germany would smash the USSR. Finland could expect to pick up a few of the
pieces, and live happy and secure thereafter. There was the theoretical
possibility that Germany might lose the war, but most Finns thought this
unworthy of consideration. Germany had just given a terrifying exhibition
of her power during the campaign in the Balkans. Nobody doubted that
she would do the same to the USSR if the occasion arose. It is probably
true that if the prospects for real neutrality had been brighter, Finland
would have chosen it, for a small nation does not lightly contemplate a
major war. But the Finnish leaders knew that Germany would use their
territory in the event of war, and that they could not have prevented this if
they had wished to. In such circumstances Russia was almost certain to
retaliate by attacking Finland. Why therefore throw away the security and
possible advantages which co-operation with Germany offered, in order to
pursue a neutrality that could probably not be maintained in any case? It
must have been some such line of reasoning which made the Finnish
leadership uninterested in alliance with Sweden or in seeking a long-term
improvement of relations with the USSR.

However, since the crisis between the USSR and Germany seemed
likely to be postponed until 1942, the Finnish government was quite ready

* The Finnish government thinks in terms of people not of territory, and wants
no revenge.

to try to exploit the more conciliatory mood reflected by Orlov for short-term gains. They were particularly anxious to secure the resumption of grain deliveries from the USSR. The grain position in Finland was becoming critical. On May 12, Kivimäki had tried to enlist German assistance in presenting a request to the USSR to send grain to Finland. The German government declined. Instead, the Finnish government chose to use an oddly indirect approach to the USSR. Wasastjerna approached Günther and the American ambassador in Stockholm, and asked them to suggest to Madame Kollontai that Soviet policy was driving Finland into the arms of Germany. Only positive concessions, as for instance over the nickel question or the revival of trade, could begin to reverse this trend. Madame Kollontai proved unreceptive.[26] The Soviet government must have thought the approaches insincere, and seen no reason to waste its grain in buying very problematical Finnish goodwill. It is difficult not to agree with their attitude. If Finland had really wanted to do business with the USSR then the obvious way was to approach Orlov, or use the occasion of Paasikivi's return to Moscow. There was so little enthusiasm behind this Finnish initiative, that it may have been primarily intended to impress Sweden and the USA with the belief that Finland was genuinely seeking to hang on to her neutrality, and give her an alibi for the pro-German line that she was actually following.

Paasikivi set out for Moscow on May 9. The Finnish proposal on the nickel question had already been sent, and Paasikivi carried no serious instructions. The three weeks which he spent in Moscow were almost entirely taken up with formal diplomatic leave taking. In an interview with Witting before he left, Paasikivi had been given to understand that the attitude of Finland to the USSR was unchanged, and was one of neutrality 'just like Sweden'. Finland had no thought of revenge and wanted 'to remain on the basis of the peace of Moscow'.[27] So Paasikivi took nothing constructive with him, just a bland assurance that everything was all right. The only interest in Paasikivi's last weeks in Moscow lies in the tokens of esteem which he personally received from the Soviet leaders. Of these the most remarkable was the privilege of an interview with Stalin, something rarely granted to foreign diplomats. There was little Paasikivi could say, except to repeat what Witting had told him of Finland's unaltered wish to remain neutral. Paasikivi said that he would continue to use his influence as a private person to improve relations with the USSR, to which Stalin replied, 'you can never be a private person'. They discussed the dispute over the interpretation of the trade agreement, and Finland's desperate shortage of grain. Stalin then said, 'I will do you personally a favour. I will give you 20,000 tons'. In this way Paasikivi personally achieved what his government had failed to do. It was no empty gesture, for the grain was actually delivered to Finland before the outbreak of war.[28] The incident certainly showed that the Soviet leaders had a high opinion of Paasikivi, and believed that he might yet be of use to them. But it was also surely meant to be a hint that there was still time for Finland to reconsider her attitude to the Soviet Union, and that genuine goodwill would bring results. The Finnish government made no response. Paasikivi was not replaced, and no further diplomatic activity occurred. As will be shown, when the crisis came, the Finnish embassy in Moscow had no policy, no instructions, and no leader.

Finnish writers who seek to explain why their government failed to make any effective response to the various gestures made by the USSR frequently appeal to the force of Finnish public opinion, which, they allege, would not have countenanced any line of policy other than the one which was followed. This is not a factor to be ignored. Even Paasikivi, the strongest Finnish proponent of alternative policies, remarked of them that 'the greatest difficulty would have been Finnish public opinion'.[29] To make a realistic assessment of this factor, and to understand the decisive events that were about to happen, it is necessary to look at the working of Finnish government machinery at this point. Finland was a democratic state, and it is undeniable that in the field of domestic policy, the government was extremely sensitive to public opinion, as expressed through the Eduskunta. But in the field of foreign policy the situation was quite different.

One major factor was the degree of autonomy enjoyed by the military authorities. This depended largely on the personal prestige of Mannerheim, as Tanner pointed out,[30] but its effect was to create what Ryti described as a system of dualism, in which the civil and military authorities 'acted unknown to one another', and frequently found themselves confronted by the other 'with an accomplished fact'.[31] This dualism was displayed in its most striking form in the dealings with the German troops in Finland. It is obvious that the numbers and activities of these troops were a vital factor in the making of Finnish foreign policy. But neither the president of the republic nor the Finnish government had any regular or precise information about them. When Ryti was asked about the supervision exercised by the civil authorities over this matter, he had replied that there was none, 'I believed that it was the job of the military authorities'. Similarly Rangell was asked what information came to him as prime minister on the activities of German troops in the country, and he replied, 'I cannot remember any official information ever being sent in'.[32] It is apparent that Ryti and other members of the inner circle of government were kept informed in general terms of the dealings of the military authorities with the Germans, but they remained in ignorance of the details, and exercised no control over policy. To this extent the legal government of the republic was not in full command of the republic's policy.

But in so far as foreign policy was directed by the constitutional authorities, that is by the president and his cabinet, this direction was exercised not by the full cabinet, but by a small inner ring. There were various factors which had produced this situation. For one thing it was well established constitutional practice that individual ministers concentrated on their own departments and did not concern themselves with the activities of their colleagues. The concept of the collective responsibility of the cabinet was imperfectly developed in Finland. In particular, those ministers who were not members of the foreign affairs committee of the cabinet played almost no part in the making of foreign policy. Lehtonen, the minister of justice, thought this entirely natural, 'from force of circumstances foreign policy remained the concern of a small circle'.[33] But Tanner has testified that even the members of the foreign affairs committee did not play much part. 'In the time of Rangell's government . . . the foreign affairs committee was rarely assembled'.[34] Cabinet control was further weakened by the institution of the 'night school', informal evening meetings of the inner circle of the government, which came to make most of the vital decisions. The effect was, as described by Tanner, that 'in the official sessions of the cabinet, fundamental discussions rarely arose, since matters had been settled in private conferences'.[35] It seems clear now that the foreign policy of Finland in this period was in fact being made by an inner ring consisting of Mannerheim, Ryti, Walden, Witting, and Rangell. The minister of the interior, von Born, describing this state of affairs, added that 'the soldiers are now important policy makers, they are strongly oriented towards Germany. But this direction is followed with the understanding of the president.'[36]

This inner group was of all men the least likely to bend to public opinion. They were the non-political element of the government, with no party ties, and no roots in the parliamentary or electoral system. Although they could not insulate themselves from what the nation felt, they were as genuinely independent in framing policy as is practicable. They were men with a high sense of dedication to and responsibility for the fate of their country, they were quite uninterested in courting popularity, they had no need to manœuvre in order to stay in office. They could afford to do what they thought right. These men did on occasion cite public opinion as the justification for their actions, but only because it suited them to do so afterwards.

Even the Eduskunta was quite powerless to exercise any control over their actions. Its foreign affairs committee was fed with information in such a way that it could exercise no influence. Witting made no secret of the fact that he did not tell the committee all that was going on. He stated on one occasion, 'I am not telling you the whole truth. If more than five or six people get to know the truth, it will be all up with us.'[37] In general, the foreign affairs committee was only informed of things long after the event. For instance it was not given any full account of the German transit agreements until May 1941. The Eduskunta was not kept in quite such complete ignorance as this state of affairs might suggest. Tanner has pointed out that there were 'unofficial contacts which were always used when necessary to keep the members of the Eduskunta aware of the course of events'.[38] Thus the Eduskunta, like the general public, had a general idea of the drift of events, but no precise knowledge of what was going on. Most of them seem to have been satisfied that the government's policy, as far as they knew it, was the best possible in the circumstances. But even if they had not been satisfied, there was no effective way of bringing pressure to bear on the policy makers of the inner ring. Members of the foreign affairs committee of the Eduskunta, and members of the cabinet, could and did grumble that they were never consulted about things in advance. But they were in no position to suggest alternatives, either of men or measures, and had to trust their leaders to do the best job they could.

Although the structure of government meant that the public could exercise no direct influence over their leaders in the field of foreign policy, there was nothing to prevent them discussing it, and by May 1941 the discussion was becoming very lively and uninhibited. Both Blücher and Paasikivi noted the great upsurge of public speculation at this time.[39] The press increasingly chafed at the restrictions which stopped it taking part, except in a muted form. They were still forbidden in general to mention awkward truths, and as *Helsingin Sanomat* pointed out, when the public see things happening before their eyes, but find the press is silent about them, their confidence in the printed word gets shaken, and speculation and rumour flourish.[40] The themes of debate were unchanged. The extreme Right was making a great deal of noise. For instance they had imported the idea of anti-semitism. Since the numbers of Jews in Finland could be counted in hundreds, they were far too few to provide ammunition for a genuine anti-semitic movement. The IKL and its allies were deliberately manufacturing one to keep in line with their ideological exemplars in Europe.[41] The extreme Left was virtually silenced. Wiik and his followers had been reduced to impotence, and could very rarely make their voice heard. In April, when the Social Democratic party was holding its area conferences, it was congratulating the leadership on the total defeat of the Left opposition. Speakers pointed out that it would be a healthy development if the Right would deal as effectively with its lunatic fringe.[42]

But the serious debate was between the respectable Right and the socialists. A fair sample of conservative thinking on international affairs was a lecture given by a Swede, Dr. Essen, before a crowded audience in Helsinki. Essen declared that the world consisted of two great power blocs, a continental bloc led by Germany, and a maritime bloc led by Britain and the USA. The USSR did not belong to either and hoped to profit from both. But the USSR had designs for expansion in Scandinavia in order to reach the Atlantic. It followed that Scandinavia must join the continental bloc, since only Germany could counter this threat. The parliamentary system, the old liberal economic order, the old concept of neutrality, had all failed.[43] The future of Scandinavia lay in co-operation with the New Order in Europe. The same themes are found in speech by Reinikka to the Agrarian party. Discussing foreign policy he declared:[44]

'If anyone believes that so small a country as Finland can still in present circumstances be unconditionally neutral, it must be said of him that he is in the grip of old collapsed theories to that extent, that he is unable to grasp the serious realities of life . . . the neutrality question in the form we have thought of throughout the period of independence must be buried, and we must find new signposts and new channels for the development of our country.'

On domestic policies, some typical ideas were presented at a meeting of Nouseva Suomi on May 8.[45] The common theme of speeches was the need for a more authoritarian pattern of government. It was wrong to call the Eduskunta a sovereign body. The Eduskunta should be content with laying down general principles and leave the government to govern. The Eduskunta was not the only means for expressing the national will. Perhaps the direct election of the president should be introduced, or the referendum might be an alternative method. Whatever happened there could be no return to the bad old days of party politics. This is a fair sample of the ideas of the responsible Right in Finland in the spring of 1941. Always the common theme was the rejection of the past, by abandoning a foreign policy based on the old type of neutrality and a domestic policy based on democratic party politics. The future must be built in co-operation with Germany and in harmony with her New Order in Europe.

The socialists battled resolutely against these concepts. Their press declared that small nations had the right to live by their own ideals. No other policy than one based on the strictest neutrality 'was even a possibility'[46] for Finland. They agreed that relations with the USSR were encumbered with such unsolved questions as the future of the nickel concession, but all these could be solved, and there was no cause for anxiety. Finland must of course have good relations with Germany, but 'nobody can imagine that, without a sharp change in circumstances, they can begin to press us away from the path of neutrality on which we wish to remain.'[47] But during April and May, socialist comment was coloured by a growing fear that the government was in fact moving in the direction recommended by the Right. The socialists commented adversely on the cynical tone which was apparent in the press and radio when the misfortunes of the victims of German aggression were discussed. Small countries brave enough to defend their independence should have the open sympathy of every Finn.[48] They asked why the government would not say who was sinking Finnish merchant ships engaged on the traffic to Liinahamari. Everybody knew that it was the Germans, but nobody was allowed to say so.[49]

This open debate demonstrates quite clearly that opinion in Finland was not unanimous about foreign policy in 1941. There is no means of calculating the strength of the opposing views, but the Social Democrats were the largest single party, and represented well over 40% of the electorate. There probably was a majority in favour of pro-German courses, but it could not have been a large one. It was however disproportionately strong in the upper levels of society. The government was probably right when it claimed subsequently that there was majority support for the kind of policy which it was following. But if the Finnish government had wished to slow down, or reverse its current drift into the German camp, and seek refuge in Swedish-type neutrality, it would not have lacked powerful internal support. It will be seen that the socialist attitude remained unshaken up to the very eve of the war.

Foreign affairs, although they dominated, did not quite monopolize the attention of the public. Early in May the question of the vastikemaa amendment produced a minor political crisis. Its future was never bright once it was clear that the government was itself divided over it, and could not make it a matter of confidence. The more it was discussed, the more Agrarian opposition to it hardened. This in part reflected the impatience and dissatisfaction of the Karelians. They were bitterly angered at the slow progress of resettlement. It was now generally acknowledged that most of them would not get on to their own farms before the summer of 1942. Once more they were reduced to cultivating temporary allotments, compulsorily provided by often reluctant hosts. On top of this they saw a threat to their compensation. It was by now apparent that the proceeds of the capital levy, plus the government contribution of 3,000 million marks, would not meet the full claims for compensation. Consequently the government was proposing an amendment under which a quarter of all compensation over 100,000 marks would be withheld. *Uusi Suomi* at once thought that there was no chance of the Eduskunta accepting this. The government was once more revealing its banker's outlook on what was really a humanitarian question. 'The government has not been happy in its proposals about the refugees.'[50] But there was a last straw still to come. At the very end of April, the refugees found themselves being shifted once more, this time to their final places of settlement. The moves were supposed to have been voluntary, but the refugees do not seem to have understood this. For many it was their third major move, and the arrangements proved defective. They often found no billets ready for them on arrival, nor anywhere to store their possessions, while the new host communities were sometimes so unsympathetic that there were cases of the police being called out to enforce billeting orders. The press was severe in its condemnation of the organization of these moves. It was revealed that there were still nearly 70,000 refugees involved, embittered by over a year of idleness and frustrated hopes, deprived of their young people, who had gone away to find work.[51]

In these circumstances it can be imagined that the Agrarian party was in no mood to compromise on the vastikemaa issue. At the party conference in April the leadership came under heavy fire for its alleged softness hitherto. There were strong moves to make conference resolutions absolutely binding on Agrarian members of the Eduskunta. The leaders were left with no choice but to stand firm. The vastikemaa amendment came on to the floor of the Eduskunta on May 2. Rangell did his best to defend it on the grounds of national interest. Food production would be helped by avoiding the break-up of larger and more efficient farms. The fears of the Swedish-speaking minority for its culture should not be lightly brushed aside. But the Eduskunta would not listen.[52] They rejected the amendment, and as it had threatened, the Swedish People's party went into opposition. Their representative in the government, von Born, resigned.[53] This did not cause a serious political crisis. The vacant post was filled almost immediately by Horelli, a member of the Conservative party.

But the episode of the vastikemaa amendment did cause a distinct worsening of the atmosphere of domestic politics. Everyone else blamed the Swedish People's party for selfishly rupturing the unity which the government had represented. They were accused of seeking to revive the bitterness that had existed between the linguistic communities as recently as the mid-1930s. In turn, the Swedish People's party, and its press, became a sulky, if impotent opposition. But there were other signs of unrest. The Social Democrats were unhappy about the appointment of Horelli. They had liked von Born for his liberal ideas, and now complained that the government was overweighted to the Right.[54] This was echoed in other parties. The Progressive party conference in May was told that relations between the government and the Eduskunta were unsatisfactory, and that too many ministers were now strangers to the ways of parliamentary government. Although there were Social Democrats and Agrarians in the government, they were systematically excluded from the exercise of real power. *Uusi Suomi* published an editorial denying these allegations and warning those who made them that the time was not ripe for a return to pre-war party politics. But it seems possible that if the war had not intervened there would have been a growing volume of protest from the professional politicians of the Eduskunta at the way in which the government excluded them from any real share in the making of policy at the highest levels.[55]

While the Finnish people, and the politicians in the Eduskunta were thus preoccupied, the inner circle of the government was being brought to the point of enlightenment and decision. It has been seen that Hitler very strictly forbade any premature revelation of German intentions to his intended allies. The military planners in the Norwegian command had tried in vain to get some alleviation of his orders, so that they could make contact with the Finnish military authorities. Blücher too was worried that the Finnish government was making no preparations for war. There was no shelter programme and no plan for evacuation from Helsinki and no build-up of essential supplies. Blücher felt that his government's efforts to persuade the Finnish government that there was no imminent danger of war were proving too successful.[56] It was in fact very difficult for the Finnish government to know what it should believe. For instance on April 18, Kivimäki reported that relations between Germany and the USSR had suddenly improved, and that the adherence of the latter to the Tripartite pact was again considered possible.[57] On May 9, he was told by the foreign office that important negotiations were in progress between the two governments. He had heard it rumoured that Germany would get some kind of lease of the Ukraine and the Caucasian oilfields. Such reports got into the world press, and were relayed by *Helsingin Sanomat*. They were complete fabrications. On the other hand, the Finnish authorities knew that military preparations were proceeding unchecked. Already in March, the Germans had surveyed and begun to construct a large camp near Rovaniemi, which would be needed for Silberfuchs. The work on this and their other depots had led to an increase in the number of Germans stationed in Finland to over 3,000, in addition to the 900 leave men passing through.[58] Blücher remarked of this activity:[59]

'Diese Dinge liessen sich natürlich nicht verheimlichen und waren Gegenstand lebhafter Diskussion im finnischen Volke. Allgemein wurde mit dem Bevorstehen eines deutsch-russisches Krieges gerechnet.*'

* 'These things were of course no secret, and they were the object of lively discussion among the Finnish people. It was generally reckoned that a Russo-German war was imminent.'

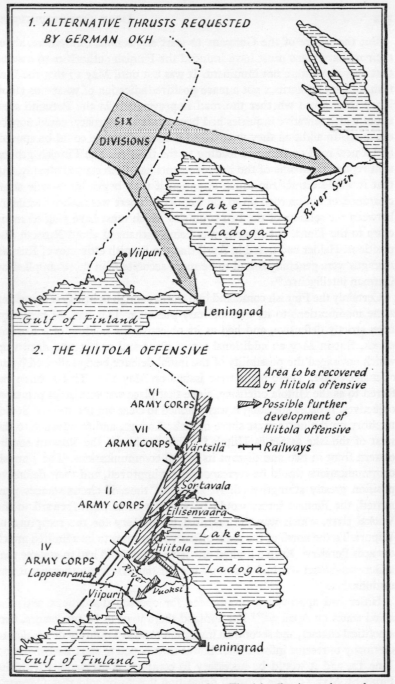

1. Map to illustrate the German proposals for a Finnish offensive to the south-east.
2. Map to illustrate the Finnish plan of May 1941 for an offensive to the south-east (Hiitola offensive).

But the failure of the Germans to start any serious discussions about their military plans must have induced the Finnish authorities to assume that operations were not imminent. It was not until May 17 that the Finnish military authorities got a more positive indication of what was afoot. They were asked whether the road improvements in the Petsamo area, about which tentative inquiries had been made in February, could now be executed. In addition they were asked if snow clearance could be started, and a new road constructed leading to the frontier. The Finnish general staff replied that some of the improvements had been started already, but that it would attract too much attention if they began large-scale snow clearance, or built a road up to the frontier.[60] There were other exchanges between the soldiers of the two countries which must have yielded many clues to the Finns. Intelligence was being exchanged about Russian dispositions. Halder had noted in April that the Finnish estimates of Russian strength were generally found to be more accurate than those supplied by German intelligence.[61]

Certainly the Finnish command had learnt enough to justify it in making some modifications to its own military planning. This had, of necessity, been strictly defensive, and had as its objective the holding of a Russian attack. But in May an additional set of plans and orders was drawn up which envisaged the possibility of the initial defence being followed by an offensive phase. These plans were issued on May 18.[62] This is often referred to as the Hiitola offensive, since that place was one of its principal objectives. Broadly speaking it was planned to clear out the strip of Soviet territory on the north-west shore of Lake Ladoga, and to advance to the west of the lake as far as Hiitola.[63] This would cut the Russian south-eastern front in two and disrupt its lateral communications. The Finnish communications would be correspondingly improved, and their defensive position greatly strengthened. At the same time, if circumstances permitted, the Finnish forces would be well placed to push forward to the Vuoksi river, which was the essential preliminary for the recapture of Viipuri. To the north of the main offensive there was to be a limited attack towards Porajärvi. Even a limited offensive of this kind had to assume that a German-Soviet war had drawn off the Russian reserves, otherwise it was unthinkable.

Hitler had approved a programme for opening discussions with the allied states on April 30.[64] For Finland there were to be two stages, first a political contact, and second an invitation to send a military delegation to Germany to receive information. It was then hoped to start Barbarossa on June 12, and it would be necessary to complete conversations with the Finns by May 15. The Finnish delegation was to be told that Germany was threatened by the current dispositions of the Soviet forces, and that if she could not get a solution by diplomacy, she would launch a preventive war. A general picture of German plans for the northern sector would be given, and the Finns invited to co-operate. The general briefing at Hitler's headquarters would be followed by detailed discussions between the various branches of the services and their Finnish counterparts. Renntier and Silberfuchs would be explained, and the possibility of Finnish action on the south-eastern front discussed. The problems of Hanko and the Åland islands would also have to be settled, while the naval authorities wanted to discuss their plan for closing the Gulf of Finland by a mine barrage. On the issue of this directive, the various departments of the German armed forces began to prepare lists of their requirements for use in the discussions. When the date of Barbarossa was put back to June 22, the date for talks with Finland was changed to May 25. In the course of these preparations it became obvious to the planners of the Norwegian command that the dates of Silberfuchs would have to be later than the main Barbarossa offensive. Buschenhagen reported this to Halder on May 14. Halder's reaction was that the whole offensive in the far north was rendered of dubious value because of this. He noted in his diary, 'the whole undertaking is an expedition, not an operation—it is a shame to waste the men allocated for the purpose'. But Hitler's requirements could not be altered. The final programme for the discussions with Finland was completed by May 22. By that stage all the participants were fretting at the shortness of the time left to them.[65]

The political side of the programme had already been launched. The chosen emissary was a foreign office official, Schnurre, and he was in Helsinki on May 20. Schnurre met Ryti, and gave him an account of recent events, followed by two requests. It is necessary to reconstruct what happened from a variety of brief accounts but the salient features emerge clearly enough. Schnurre's mission was partly one of deception, and the deception worked perfectly. His trump card was the revelation of what Molotov had said about Finland in Berlin. This was coloured up a little for Ryti's consumption. Molotov was said to have demanded a free hand 'to settle accounts with Finland, that is to liquidate Finland'. Hitler was represented as nobly refusing this demand. Hitler's refusal, and subsequent developments in the Balkans had worsened German-Soviet relations, and they had now reached a point of considerable tension. Both sides were making military preparations. The situation would not necessarily lead to war, and certainly Germany would not begin such a war, but it remained a possibility. Russia might launch preventive attacks into Romania or Finland. Ryti said that Finland had no other desire but to live in peace with the USSR and would never launch an offensive war against her, 'although the Moscow peace hurts'. But she would certainly defend herself if

LOST OPPORTUNITIES

attacked. Ryti asked whether Germany would treat an attack by the USSR on Finland as a *casus belli*. Schnurre affirmed that Germany would do so. Then he presented his two requests. First he asked that Finland should send a military delegation to Germany to receive information about Germany's military plans. Second, since Germany was hoping to settle her differences with the USSR by diplomacy, he asked the Finnish government to submit any points that it would wish Germany to raise with the Soviet Union on its behalf.[66]

Most of what Schnurre told Ryti was false. The account of Molotov's visit to Berlin was not far from the truth, but the rest of his story about the negotiations supposedly in progress, and Hitler's desire to avoid a military solution was a complete fabrication, and the request to submit points to be raised in the supposed negotiation a complete deception. But whoever devised the programme for Schnurre had confirmed Ryti's own conviction that the USSR intended Finland's destruction, so that any policy of reconciliation with the USSR was hopeless. Then he had portrayed Hitler as jeopardizing his valuable relationship with the USSR in order to protect Finland, and had assured Ryti that this protection would be continued. Finally he had held out the hope of a negotiated settlement from which Finland might profit. In these circumstances it is no wonder that Ryti proved extremely receptive. Before Ryti gave his answer, he called in the inner circle, Mannerheim, Walden, Rangell, and Witting, and put Schnurre's proposals to them. They were unanimous that Schnurre's proposals should be accepted.[67] On May 22, Schnurre telegraphed to Berlin, 'negotiations here successfully concluded.[68]

The next step lay with the Finnish military authorities, and Schnurre was told to deal with Mannerheim. Since Schnurre indicated that the highest German military leaders would receive the Finnish delegation, Heinrichs was appointed to lead it. Heinrichs received strict orders. He was to acquire all the information that he could, but must give no binding commitments, and make it perfectly clear to the Germans that he had no authority to do so. Mannerheim stressed to him, 'let the Germans talk and explain. You remain as far as possible the receiving party.'[69] But it is clear from the composition of the delegation that Mannerheim had learned, either from Schnurre or from another source, that joint operations between Finland and Germany would be discussed, and which technical experts the Germans wanted to talk to. For the delegation also included the chief of the operations division, the director of the mobilization plan, the chief of the supply section, and a representative of the navy. This delegation was received at the OKW headquarters at Salzburg on May 25.

While they were away, the inner circle got to work on Schnurre's second request. For this, Kivimäki was summoned from Berlin to take part. The

proposals were finally agreed on May 30, after long and careful consideration. It is not certain what the exact form of these proposals was, but they
seem in effect to have contained a minimum and a maximum programme.
The least that Finland wanted was a firm guarantee of her integrity, and
certain minor concessions from the USSR. Curiously there seems to have
been no mention of the Petsamo nickel dispute, perhaps it was assumed
that Germany herself would deal with this. But they did ask for deliveries
of food and raw materials from the USSR, and the settlement in Finland's
favour of another minor dispute over the use of the Vallinkoski rapids,
which lay right on the frontier, for generating electric power. The maximum programme was in effect a demand for a return to the 1939 frontier,
and the overthrow of the Treaty of Moscow. This is a much more serious
demand, and shows that the Finnish leaders thought it possible that the
USSR, in order to make her peace with Germany, would be willing to
surrender important assets. It seems that Mannerheim had a restraining
influence here. He insisted that Finland should offer to modify the 1939
frontier in the interests of the security of Leningrad, against territorial
compensation in eastern Karelia. He also insisted that this compensation
must not be such as to threaten the Murmansk railway, or the White Sea
canal. If the USSR would not consider these adjustments, Finland would
accept a simple return to the 1939 frontier.[70]

These proposals were of no practical significance, since Germany had no
intention of using them. But they do throw light on the thinking of the
inner circle of the Finnish government on the eve of the war. They obviously rated German power, and Soviet fear of it, very highly indeed.
Their maximum programme assumes such a degree of abject terror among
the leaders of the USSR that they would surrender without a fight the
dearly bought gains of the Treaty of Moscow. The minimum programme
was more realistic, but even that supposed that the USSR was prepared
to buy Hitler's goodwill at a high price. The proposals also show an un-
hesitating acceptance of Germany's patronage and protection, and an
implied tie-up of Finland's future with that of Germany. The proposals
are in themselves inconsistent with strict neutrality between Germany and
the USSR. The Finnish leaders showed no awareness of the trick which
Schnurre had played on them. They readily swallowed the story of the
supposed negotiations. It must be said that they were in good company,
for the rest of the world also believed that such negotiations were in progress. Very few conceived it possible that Hitler would be so demented
as to assault the USSR without putting any demands at all. This German
deception was kept up until a very late stage. On June 10, Kivimäki reported to Ryti that there had been 'a very favourable response' to the
Finnish requests.[71] As will be seen, other events made the prolongation of

the farce after that date impossible. But the deception served its purpose. It disguised from the Finnish government the true nature of Germany's intentions, and put a more civilized veneer on her conduct. More important, it put the Finnish leaders in a position where they would be specially anxious not to forfeit Germany's goodwill, and thus render them more amenable to Germany's requirements.

The military delegation was welcomed to Salzburg by Keitel, who conveyed Hitler's greetings, and his regrets that in the late war, the situation had not permitted Germany to help Finland as she would have wished. Major developments were to be expected in the near future, and since Germany believed in preparing in advance for all eventualities, she had wanted to confer with Finland. After this formal beginning General Jodl gave a lengthy discourse on the situation. He asserted that the Russian military build-up in the west was such that an intolerable situation had been created for Germany. It must be resolved by diplomacy if possible, but by military action if diplomacy failed. In any event, Finland was bound to be affected. If it came to war, the war would be a 'crusade' against bolshevism, in which several powers would participate, and Finland might wish to be one of them. At the conclusion, Russia would be dismantled as a great power. The decision would come early in the summer.[72] Thus Jodl did not go much further than Schnurre, except that he revealed that the war, if it came, would be an offensive war initiated by Germany.

Jodl then explained how Germany's current plans affected Finland. He said that it was not Germany's habit to expect others to do her fighting for her, and she realized that Finland was still weakened by her losses in the late war. Finland was entirely free to choose what part she would play. Germany would in any case thrust through the Baltic states to Leningrad, at the same time destroying the Soviet Baltic fleet by closing the Gulf of Finland, and blocking the White Sea canal by air attack. In the far north there would be operations to destroy Murmansk under the command of Falkenhorst. Jodl then explained Renntier, and its continuation into a thrust at Murmansk direct. He hoped that Finland would lend the services of the battalion which she kept in the Petsamo area, and would make certain preparations there, and grant the use of Petsamo airfield to the Germans. Then Jodl described Silberfuchs, but included the fiction that in the event of a peaceful solution, the German forces approaching Rovaniemi from the north and the south would pass each other, and the move would be a simple exchange of troops in northern Norway. Germany hoped that Finland would attach the two divisions of her Fifth Army Corps to cover Silberfuchs, at least up to the point where the Germans captured the Salla highlands and crossed the 1939 frontier. For this purpose it was hoped that Finland could mobilize these two divisions early. Jodl revealed that the forces for Silberfuchs had already begun to move, and that they would assemble at Rovaniemi around June 10–16. Finally, Jodl said that on the main Finnish front to the south-east, Germany asked no more than that Finland should mobilize, and tie down as many Russian troops as possible until the Germans had captured Leningrad.[73]

Heinrichs, who was the only Finnish representative who spoke at Salzburg, had made only two interventions during Jodl's exposition. First he said that it would be possible to detach the battalion in the Petsamo area for service with the Germans. Heinrichs says that he knew Mannerheim was prepared to do this. Second, he said that Finland would like to have the troops of Fifth Army Corps available for her own operations on the main front. When Jodl had finished, Heinrichs was invited to make general comments on what he had heard. Heinrichs was faithful to his instructions. He said that he had no powers to enter into any agreements, either political or military, and that everything which he said was subject to this reservation. However he added that the presence of the Finnish delegation could be taken to indicate Finland's attitude to the idea of co-operation with Germany.

Then Heinrichs came to his detailed remarks. He was surprised that Germany asked for the use of the Fifth Army Corps, since he had assumed that Germany would take sole responsibility for the sector north of Kuhmo. This was an interesting remark. He did not say on what grounds he made this assumption, but it must have been on the strength of discussions with Buschenhagen in February, or some later contacts not recorded, concerning German intention if the Russians attacked Finland. In any case it suggests that such contacts had been a great deal more concrete in their content than Mannerheim and Heinrichs remembered when they came to write about them years later. Heinrichs went on to say that Finland had hoped that Germany would take care of the Åland islands, and eliminate the base at Hanko. The latter was in any case more of a nuisance to Germany than to Finland. Jodl replied that Finland was not being asked to take the offensive on her main front, so that she could spare the forces necessary for Åland and Hanko.

However, Heinrichs had another idea for the Åland islands. He suggested that Germany might herself occupy some of the islands. This would keep the Russians out and give Finland an excuse for mobilization. Otherwise, Finland could spare no more than two regiments for the islands. Jodl was not taken by Heinrichs' suggestion, Germany did not wish to take so overt an action before Finnish mobilization had even started. The problem of air defence was discussed. Heinrichs doubted whether Finland could allow German aircraft to use Helsinki airport, and noted that in spite of Finland's request to purchase aircraft from Germany, none had

been forthcoming. Finally they discussed Finland's mobilization. Heinrichs stressed how important it was to be able to complete it in time, but
Jodl refused to be drawn into naming any firm date by which it might
become necessary. There the discussion ended, with no firm decisions
taken, except that it was agreed that Germany would send an officer to
Helsinki on June 2 to receive the answers of Finland's political and military
leaders to the German proposals.[74] The Salzburg discussions were well
summarized by the German commentator Greiner:[75]

'Dabei waren jedoch keine festen Vereinbarung getroffen, sondern nur
die operativen Möglichkeiten in unverbindlicher Form erörtet und die
Finnen von der deutschen Absicht offiziell in Kenntnis gesetzt
werden . . .'*

Another German writer, who was closely associated with the talks, von
Lossberg, said long after the event that when the Finnish delegation was
asked if it would take part in an attack on the USSR, the answer was that it
would.[76] This is probably a mistake on Lossberg's part. The weight of the
surviving record is against it, and it is most improbable that Heinrichs
would have departed so far from his orders. There is one other point in the
Salzburg conversations which is in dispute. The German record makes
Heinrichs say that on the south-eastern front, 'being the centre of Finnish
interests, the Finnish forces will not limit themselves to waiting, but will
attack as far as is possible'.[77] Heinrichs has always maintained that he has
no recollection of saying this. One can only point out that if he did say it,
it was no more than the truth. As has been seen, the Finnish army did have
plans for an offensive if the circumstances permitted and orders for this
had already been issued. So Heinrichs could easily have said something to
this effect, although the offensive to which he would have been referring
was not the one which was actually delivered when the time came.

On May 26, the Finnish delegation went to Berlin, and entered on a
series of conferences with the various branches of the German armed
forces. The central place was held by the talks between Heinrichs and
Halder on the operational possibilities. Halder had a transcript of the Salzburg discussion, so that he knew beforehand that Heinrichs would enter
into no commitments. Halder was quite content to explore the possibilities
on a theoretical basis. Falkenhorst's operations in the far north did not
concern Halder, since he was not responsible for them, and as has been
seen rather disapproved of them. What Halder wanted to explore was the
prospects for Finnish forces on the south-eastern front co-operating with
the German drive on Leningrad. Unlike Jodl, who had repeated that he

* 'No definite agreement was reached, however, but there was merely an incon-
clusive discussion about operational possibilities, and the Finns were officially informed of German intentions.'

expected no more than a holding operation on this front, Halder wanted
the Finns to make as powerful an offensive thrust as they could, to coincide
with the German approach to the city. He asked if the Finnish army could
be grouped so that it could strike either east or west of Lake Ladoga as
circumstances might require. Heinrichs revealed that there would be six
divisions available for an offensive, But he doubted if they could be
arranged as Halder wished. Halder thought that it ought to be possible to
assemble more than six divisions for an offensive, but Heinrichs said that if
Finland was to look after Hanko and the Åland islands, and give two divisions for Silberfuchs, that was the most she could do. Of Halder's alternatives, Finland would probably prefer the thrust east of the lake, though
they could carry it only a limited way into Soviet territory.

The two men then turned to the problem of the Finnish mobilization.
Halder estimated that the Finnish army would not be required to launch its
main offensive until about 14 days after the opening of a German attack.
So that except for the Fifth Army Corps, there was no need to mobilize
the rest of the Finnish army until after hostilities had started. Heinrichs
pointed out that for a number of reasons, general mobilization could not
be carried out until the concentration for Silberfuchs was complete, that is
on June 16. Finland would prefer to postpone her mobilization in order to
leave the men time for spring ploughing and sowing. Once more, no decisions had been made. Heinrichs and Halder had together explored the
various factors in the situation. The Finnish delegation left Germany on
May 28th.[78] As he was leaving, Heinrichs asked the German officer who
was looking after him, Bürchner, why Halder appeared to expect more of
the Finnish army on the south-eastern front than Jodl did. It was explained that Jodl's was a minimum programme, and Halder's was a maximum, there was no reason to think that Jodl would have any objection to
the Finnish army taking the offensive.[79] This seems a reasonable explanation of what was otherwise an odd discrepancy. It has to be remembered
that Halder was directly responsible for the attack on Leningrad, and further that he believed that the plan for Barbarossa was in any case too ambitious for the forces available. So he was naturally more concerned to get
an active contribution from the Finns. Further if Heinrichs had said something about Finland not sitting on the defensive, that may have prompted
Halder's questions.

The scattered evidence on the visit of the Finnish delegation is at least
quite agreed that Heinrichs had obeyed his orders and given no firm undertakings, with the solitary exception that he had virtually promised the
co-operation of the Finnish battalion in Petsamo for Renntier. The Germans understood this. Buschenhagen, who had been ordered to go to
Helsinki and get the Finnish answers, noted that the delegation had been

'friendly', but that all the military questions were still unresolved.[80] But it would be a mistake to suppose that the German planners were no further forward as a result of the visit. Nothing that Heinrichs had said had indicated any reluctance in principle to engage in co-operation with the Germans. At the least it was obvious that Finland would put no obstacles in the way of executing Renntier and Silberfuchs. The open question was how much more the Finnish armed forces might do, supposing that the USSR refrained from attacking Finland, and left them with a choice. The Germans could be excused for assuming that at least Finland would not be pedantically neutral. A good measure of the optimism of the Germans, and the value of the information they received, is the fact that after the visit of the Finnish delegation, they were able to draw up a timetable for operations in Finland, including operations by the Finnish forces, which in the event proved to be entirely accurate.

Heinrichs presented a report to the inner circle of the Finnish government as soon as he returned to Helsinki. He had concluded from what he had heard that war was 'possible even very probable'. But he could not know it was certain. Jodl had been at pains to give the impression that it was not, and Hitler himself issued an order on May 28, that this deception of the Finns was to be strictly maintained. Heinrichs also reported that the Germans thought a war might be started by Russian attacks on Finland, or Romania, but that in certain circumstances, the Germans would initiate the war themselves. Heinrichs was further able to report that such a war would be of the nature of a 'crusade' against bolshevism, and that its objective was the destruction of Russia as a great power.[81] Heinrichs' report left the Finnish leaders a difficult problem to ponder. There might be no war, and for this reason they did not want to make any commitment that would compromise them with the USSR and the western powers in such a case. On the other hand a war was certainly possible, and they had to decide whether they should try to preserve some kind of neutral, or non-belligerent status, or whether they should agree to take part with Germany, and if so, on what terms. And all the time they had to remember the threat of a Russian preventive strike, and the need to keep Germany's benevolent interest in them. They had three days to think about these things before Buschenhagen came for his answer.

CHAPTER 12

The decision

By the beginning of June 1941, all Finland was openly discussing the chances of a German attack on the USSR. Svento issued a stern warning against speculation on May 30, pointing out that the USSR could hardly fail to notice it, and that it might be considered to be evidence of wishful thinking in Finland.[1] The public knew from the quotations in their newspapers of foreign press items, that this speculation was world wide. Only the two protagonists, Germany and the USSR, preserved their silence. The military preparations in Germany were by now on too large a scale to escape notice. Ambassador Kivimäki sent in a long report on May 26, describing the disruption of rail services in Germany because of the troop movements to the east, and even how German rolling stock was being converted to the Russian broad gauge. The Finnish foreign office assumed that war was probable from the end of May.[2] The inner circle of the government knew from what Heinrichs had told them that this probability was very strong indeed, so much so that Ryti felt it necessary, on May 30, to prepare the cabinet for what might be coming.[3]

Ryti told the ministers that there was growing tension between Germany and the USSR, and that one by-product of this might be an increase in the volume of German transits through Finland. There was an obvious danger that either side might try to secure strategic advantages at Finland's expense. Ryti mentioned Petsamo, the Åland islands, the Salla area, and Hanko as potentially threatened. He said that Mannerheim might be compelled to take military precautions to meet these dangers within the next few weeks. Ryti said that he had told them this so that they would not be taken by surprise if things developed so far. Ryti's statement to his cabinet is open to criticism in that although everything he said was true, it was not the whole truth, even so far as Ryti then knew it. Ryti knew for certain that German transits would increase, and that in the event of war Germany would occupy Petsamo and strike through Salla. Perhaps Ryti wanted to break the cabinet in gently to what was coming. Further there was the danger that some awkward spirit among the ministers might suggest that

261

something ought to be done, or at least some protest made since Germany had declared her intention, in certain circumstances, of committing gross violations of Finland's neutrality.

On June 2, the German delegation arrived in Helsinki. It was led by two colonels, Buschenhagen and Kinzel, and accompanied by specialist advisers. Its mission was to get Finland's consent to participate in an attack on the USSR and to work out the practical details. But the fiction was to be preserved that a diplomatic solution was still possible, and war might be avoided. It is not easy to reconstruct the chronology of the conferences that went on between June 2 and June 6. The evidence about them on the German side consists of reports drawn up after they were concluded, while the evidence from the Finnish side is vague, and even downright confusing about the sequence of events. The broad pattern of the conferences was that Buschenhagen and Heinrichs conducted the main discussions, with Kinzel occasionally present.[4] Mannerheim took no direct part in the discussion, but was constantly consulted by Heinrichs. Walden was probably kept fairly fully informed of what was happening, and passed on such information as he thought fit to the members of the inner circle. Ryti for instance probably did not know the details of the military plans, but he had a good general idea of what was happening.

It seems likely that the proceedings began logically with Buschenhagen trying to find out if Finland would join in Germany's attack. First he tried an indirect approach. Heinrichs was asked what return Finland would expect as the price of taking part in a war between Germany and the USSR. A positive reply would imply a readiness for such participation. Heinrichs reported to Mannerheim, who dodged the issue, and authorized Heinrichs to reply that if Finland got drawn into such a conflict against her will, she expected no reward from Germany. He added that if Finland became the victim of an aggression by the USSR in advance of such a conflict, she hoped that Germany would come to her assistance.[5] This evasion forced Buschenhagen to put the question directly. He asked whether Finland was prepared to participate in a German attack on the USSR, on the lines indicated to Heinrichs during his visit to Germany. This was the vital decision, and the inner circle was called into conference to decide on the answer. The meeting almost certainly took place on June 2, and Mannerheim, Heinrichs, Ryti, Walden, and Witting were present. There seems to be no record of Rangell participating, if so he was the one member of the inner circle to be excluded.[6]

However, it turned out that the decision had already been made by Mannerheim. The proceedings began with Heinrichs explaining to the ministers that the Marshal had decided to put the Petsamo battalion, and the Fifth Army Corps, under German command. According to Heinrichs, the ministers made no comment at all, though this was the vital decision which made all that followed a mere search for a suitable diplomatic formula in which to clothe this decision.[7] This presented problems because it is quite clear that Mannerheim had determined to avoid giving hostages to the Germans by any unequivocal agreement to participate, at least so long as the Germans declined to give an unequivocal assurance that the attack would actually take place. The ministers fully shared Mannerheim's resolution to keep open some kind of escape route until the situation was clarified. Heinrichs read to the meeting the formula which Mannerheim and himself had devised for a reply. They proposed to say:[8]

'The attitude of the Finnish commander in chief to the ideas discussed in Salzburg and Berlin, depends on the decision of Finland's political leadership.'

Then they would say that subject to this condition, Mannerheim was prepared to comment on what the Germans had revealed, and that he welcomed the opportunity of this exchange of views. In other words, Mannerheim would agree that Heinrichs should work out the details of Finnish participation with Buschenhagen's mission, but on the understanding that formal political consent would be needed for the execution of the plans. In the end, the meeting decided that a formula devised by Witting would meet the situation better. Witting proposed that the following reply be given in writing:[9]

'On the assumption that the political side of the question is cleared up by discussion between the competent authorities, the proposed measures can be executed.'

To this there would be a verbal addition, to the effect that Mannerheim was not only interested in the technical military aspects of what had been revealed, but also in the political idea underlying the whole concept—that is the destruction of the USSR as a great power—and that this concept 'aroused joy in Finnish soldiers' hearts' and was recognized as of great historical significance. The answer did not specify who 'the competent authorities' were, but deliberately left it open for the military authorities to arrange everything without involving the government in a formal political decision. Further, the verbal addition left no doubt that Finland welcomed the German plans and wished for their success. It becomes apparent from what followed that what Witting meant by the 'political side of the question' was that matters must be so arranged that Finland should not appear to take the initiative in attacking the USSR.

It would be unnecessary to comment further on this answer, if it were not that Finnish writers have persisted in describing it as negative. The answer, which had the unanimous endorsement of the inner circle, was fogged by a certain obscurity but it was not, by any interpretation of the language used, a negative reply to Buschenhagen's question. Buschenhagen had asked whether Finland would take part in an attack on the USSR along the lines suggested at Salzburg and Berlin. Witting's reply was that Finland would do so, and that she approved of the concept underlying the plan, but that certain political aspects would have to be cleared up. It turned out that the only one of these which mattered was that Finland should not appear as an aggressor state, but that, in the favourite Finnish phrase, she should be 'drawn in' to the conflict after it had started. There was no attempt to set any other relevant political condition for Finland's participation. There is no doubt what the German delegation thought that the Finnish answer meant. They believed that Finland's participation in their plans could be taken for granted. If Witting's answer to Buschenhagen's question was really meant to be a subtle negative it proved rather too subtle, since the Germans were so stupid that they failed to grasp his meaning. Buschenhagen himself informed OKW on June 4 that 'Finland is now ready for full co-operation within the framework of the conversations of Salzburg and Berlin.'[10] That was how he understood Finland's 'negative' reply. All that the Finnish leaders had wanted to do was to leave an escape route open. In politics, and above all in war, everything is so uncertain, and it would have been folly for Finland to make a compromising and unconditional commitment in answer to what was supposed to be a hypothetical question.

The Finnish answer was given to Buschenhagen on June 3. To make quite sure that Germany should not misunderstand the purport of the Finnish reply, Heinrichs had been authorized by Mannerheim to make a further verbal addition. He was to say that 'for the first and probably for the last time in Finland's thousand-year history, the great moment has come in which the Finnish people can free itself for all time from the pressure of the hereditary enemy.'[11] It may be, as Heinrichs claims, that Mannerheim described this as 'polite nonsense', but there can be no doubt about the impression it was intended to leave on its German audience. The two sides then got down to business, the main points had been cleared up by June 4, and the talks were wound up two days later. The following were the main points of agreement.

It was agreed that the Finnish troops in the north, that is the Petsamo battalion, and the Fifth Army Corps, should serve under Falkenhorst's command and could be used to prosecute the German operations based on northern Finland. The operational boundary between Falkenhorst's command, and the rest of the Finnish forces was to be a line from Oulu to Sorokka. Buschenhagen had suggested that the Finnish forces in Fifth Army Corps need not go beyond the line of the 1939 frontier, but Mannerheim said that no such limitation was necessary. If the war was one for the total destruction of the USSR, such considerations were irrelevant.[12] Germany was to be responsible for the supply of the troops under her command in respect of everything except ammunition. The discussion on this point took so little time that there is reason to believe that the outlines of the agreement had already been worked out in Berlin. This impression is heightened by the testimony of General Siilasvuo, the commander of Fifth Army Corps. He received a sudden summons to Helsinki on June 2, and in the following days had the plans for his command explained to him. He was not asked to comment on them, and noticed that there seemed nothing to discuss since 'taking everything into account, the matter seemed to have been settled already'.[13] Siilasvuo did not get detailed operational orders at this stage, since these were to come from the Germans, nor was he told when hostilities would commence.

On the south-eastern front, Buschenhagen found that the Finnish command had been thinking over what had been said in Berlin, and were prepared to meet German requirements. Heinrichs said that the troops could be grouped so as to attack either east or west of Lake Ladoga in a strength of six divisions, provided they had five days' notice of the direction the Germans wanted. Buschenhagen tried to press for a stronger attacking force, and Heinrichs tried to use this as a lever to get the Germans to take over responsibility for the Åland islands and Hanko. But the Germans had no force to spare for this, and Heinrichs in consequence stuck to the figure of six divisions for the Finnish attack. He also warned Buschenhagen not to expect too much of the Finnish troops, and said that at the most, they would not go beyond the River Svir.[14] Heinrichs produced excellent military reasons for this, but there are good grounds for believing that Mannerheim was not interested in going further. He must already have had an idea of his war aims, and as these developed it became clear that the Svir was the limit of his ambitions in that direction. Agreement was also reached on a number of smaller points, including the use of Finnish airfields. Contrary to what Heinrichs had suggested in Berlin, Mannerheim was willing to let the Germans use Helsinki and Kemijärvi airfields, but subject to the condition that operational flights could not be begun without Finnish permission. Mannerheim was not going to risk having Russian reprisals brought on his head before he was ready.

The most complex and delicate problem to be discussed was that of Finnish mobilization. Certain fixed factors were operative here. The forces for Silberfuchs would start moving through Finland on June 8. They would be assembling at Rovaniemi from June 12 onwards. Germany wanted Finnish forces to cover the assembly against the danger of a Russian spoiling attack, but general mobilization could not be carried out while the forces for Silberfuchs were clogging the lines of communication. Further, the German side could not reveal the date for the attack to begin, but did not want Finland to mobilize prematurely and draw attention to what was happening. For this same reason, that general mobilization could not be concealed, and would compromise Finland in the eyes of the outside world, Mannerheim was unwilling to order general mobilization until he was sure that war was coming. Otherwise, if Germany and the USSR did arrive at a negotiated settlement, Finland could be caught in a very awkward situation. In addition, because of the danger of a Russian spoiling attack, it would be necessary while mobilizing to evacuate the frontier regions of civilians. Since these contained important industrial plant that Finland was anxious to keep in production, this constituted a further reason for mobilizing as late as possible. So what Mannerheim wanted was to have as late a mobilization as possible, and to learn the date of the German attack as early as possible. Since Buschenhagen could not satisfy him on the latter point, no final agreement could be reached on a date. But the possibilities were discussed. Heinrichs favoured leaving general mobilization until after the commencement of hostilities on the main fronts in Europe. It was agreed that the earliest possible date for Finland to start mobilizing would be June 16, and that if this date was chosen, the main attack on the south-eastern front could begin any time after June 28. However a plan was drawn up for the first stages of mobilization. On June 10, the units on the frontier, and certain naval and specialist units would be brought up to war strength. These would have to provide the covering force while the Germans were assembling at Rovaniemi. Then on June 15, the troops who were to come under German command would begin general mobilization, which would be completed by June 25. The German operations there could begin at any time after that date. The forces which were to cover Hanko and occupy the Åland islands would begin mobilizing on June 10, and be ready on June 20.[15]

By concluding these plans, all aspects of German-Finnish joint operations were provided for, except the date of general mobilization of the bulk of the Finnish army, and the direction of the main attack on the south-eastern front. The talks then moved on to what Witting's reply to Buschenhagen had called 'the political side of the question'. Here Heinrichs made clear to Buschenhagen what this phrase was meant to cover. First of all, since a peaceful outcome of the crisis was still supposed to be possible, Heinrichs emphasized Finland's hopes as contained in the response to Schnurre's request.[16] But if it was to be war, Heinrichs stressed that Finland could not take an initiative in attacking. He mentioned domestic opinion as a factor, and in particular the strength of the socialists. Hence the Finnish army could not be used to begin hostilities against the USSR, nor could Finland allow the initial attacks to be launched from her territory. He hoped that the war would open elsewhere, and then the Russians could be provoked into giving Finland the excuse for coming in. Heinrichs also mentioned that Mannerheim was unhappy about the SS battalion, and hinted that he would like to get the men back again. He went on to warn Germany against any notion of setting up a Quisling type government in Finland. Any move in this direction would make further co-operation between Finland and Germany impossible. It is not known why Mannerheim should have gone out of his way to make this point. The Germans had never even thought about it. Presumably Mannerheim feared that the effervescence of the pro-German groups in Finland, and the recruiting of the SS battalion, might have given Germany false ideas about the political possibilities in Finland. This is one more piece of the formidable body of evidence that although Mannerheim had resolved to co-operate with Germany if she did attack the USSR, he was equally resolved to preserve his own, and his country's independence, and not to allow Finland to be used as a mere pawn in Germany's game.

The German delegation left Helsinki on June 6, and the reports of Buschenhagen and Kinzel showed that they were well satisfied with what they had achieved. They believed that Finland had agreed to everything necessary, and that she would co-operate with enthusiasm in the German attack. Halder summarized the German impression when he wrote in his diary, 'the Finnish High Command has squared its plans with ours and seems to be going at it with every ounce of energy.'[17] As the Germans saw the situation, the political conditions explained by Heinrichs need cause no difficulty. The point about attempting to set up a puppet government was irrelevant to any German intention at that time. The one point of consequence, the insistence of Finland that she must not appear to take the initiative, involved no problem for the Germans. In the first place their plans provided that operations from Finnish territory, apart from mine-laying by the navy, would not begin until several days after the opening of the main attack. During those first days, there would be German troops on Finnish territory obviously prepared for offensive operations, the Russian base at Hanko would be blockaded by Finnish troops and the Åland islands occupied, there would be German aircraft on Finnish airfields, and the Finnish army would be in process of full mobilization. It seemed obvious, and proved to be the case, that the Russian command would not just sit still and watch these preparations once the main attack had been launched. They were bound to make some kind of preventive move, either by attacks from the air, or by a quick offensive on land. Such attacks would give Finland the *casus belli* she needed. She would be 'drawn into' the war in a way that would meet fully the requirements set by Heinrichs.

Mannerheim has explained that fundamentally he saw the situation in the same light. He realized that he could not prevent the German forces moving into northern Finland, and using it as a base to launch attacks on the Soviet Union. Nor could he prevent the Russian reprisals that were bound to follow. As Heinrichs says:[18]

'The Marshal was certain that, if the tension between Germany and Russia developed into war, the Russians would at once attack our country —in any event from the air, but probably by land and sea as well.'

The Marshal wrote in his memoirs that 'our possibilities of remaining outside the expected conflict were from a practical point of view non-existent'.[19] Mannerheim therefore maintained that the plans which were agreed with Buschenhagen represented an intelligent adaptation by the Finnish leadership to a situation over which it had no control.

The execution of the agreed programme followed without delay, on June 7, Buschenhagen officially confirmed the mobilization timetable that had been laid down, and the following day the German 169 Division began to arrive at Finnish ports for transit to Rovaniemi.[20] The next stage was to be the beginning of Finland's partial mobilization on June 10. Before this could take place, the inner circle realized that the cabinet and the political leaders would have to be told something more, since they could not fail to notice what was happening. The ground was broken by Ryti who made a further report to the cabinet on June 9.[21] Ryti said that there would be extensive German troop movements in northern Finland, but that these were part of a scheme to relieve the German garrison in northern Norway. Ryti concealed what he knew of the intention of the Germans, if war came, to attack to the east, and also Mannerheim's decision to put the Finnish troops in the north under German command. Then he said that Russo-German tension was continuing, and that there was an enormous military build-up on both sides of the frontier. Negotiations between the two powers were in progress, but he believed that Germany was asking a bigger price than Stalin would feel able to pay, even though Stalin was obviously anxious to be conciliatory. It was therefore highly likely that 'a conflict would come to the boil, perhaps before midsummer'. In these circumstances, Mannerheim had decided that in the interests of national security some reservists should be recalled, and this would be done immediately.

Ryti then made a very interesting analysis of the current situation in Europe. If the war came it would probably open on a front from the Baltic to the Black Sea, and only 'spread northwards later'. Ryti then went on to consider what the attitude of Finland ought to be to this conflict, and presented his view of the fundamental aims and policies of the USSR. He thought that her policy towards Finland was sufficiently clear from her behaviour over the previous twelve months, which was recounted in some

THE DECISION

269

detail to the cabinet. The world policy of the USSR was obviously one of remaining neutral while the other powers exhausted themselves in mutual conflict. When this process had gone far enough, the USSR would begin to spread revolution and chaos, and work towards its true aim, 'the world domination of Russia and bolshevism'. This led Ryti up to his conclusion which was that a war between Germany and the USSR 'could be of advantage to the whole world'. Ryti continued:

'Germany is the only power which can now defeat Russia, or at least weaken her considerably, nor would it be any harm for the world if Germany too were weakened in the game. But the greatest possible weakening of Russia is the condition of our salvation. If Russia wins the war, our position will be difficult, perhaps hopeless. If Russia directs matters in the world as victor, nobody can support or help us. But Russia is already enormously strong. If she should be left in peace a further year, while the other powers fight among themselves, neither Germany nor anyone else will any longer be able to defeat her. This being the case, cruel though it may perhaps sound, we must almost hope that war will break out between Germany and Russia, hoping of course, that we ourselves can remain outside it.'

There is an element of deceit in this address by Ryti to his cabinet. By concealing what he knew about the plans drawn up with Buschenhagen, and Ryti certainly knew the broad outline of these, he also concealed that the hope expressed in his final phrase was an unreal one. If Finland did what Mannerheim had just agreed with the Germans that she would do, there was absolutely no chance that Finland could remain outside the coming conflict. But for obvious security reasons it was impossible to tell the cabinet about such plans, and equally impossible for political reasons, since Finland was officially supposed to be following policies of neutrality, even if these departed from the old-fashioned significance of that term. Only the socialist ministers showed any wish to challenge Ryti's analysis. The more radical of them, Pekkala, was against the recall of reservists, 'the nation does not want war when it has not even got bread,' he declared. Fagerholm supported him in thinking that there was as yet no justification for mobilization. Ryti was unmoved by their argument, he said that the nation would expect the government to take reasonable precautions, and every other minister agreed with him. Since the socialists made no move to press their doubts to the point of resignation, Ryti was entitled to assume that he had the whole cabinet behind him. It must be said that Ryti and the majority of the ministers were obviously right. Given the international situation, and the presence of large numbers of German troops on Finnish soil, the precautions which Mannerheim proposed to take were entirely reasonable. This does not alter the fact that the cabinet was misled into approving the Marshal's measures by the deliberate suppression of relevant information known to Ryti and the inner circle. Pekkala's remark suggests that he at least may have sensed the deception that was being practised on them.

On the following two days, the leaders of the various party groups in the Eduskunta were given a similar report on the situation by Rangell, and the editors of the principal papers were also informed. The Social Democrats discussed the position on June 12, and decided to support the government's action. But they added the strict condition that if war came, Finland must do no more than defend herself, and 'in no circumstances attack across the national frontier'.[22] This suggests that there were others besides Pekkala who suspected the real direction of the thinking of the nation's leaders. The other parties seemed to have accepted the government's policy without comment. The Swedish government had been informed of the increased German transits, and the intention to recall reservists on June 9. They were not favourably impressed, since as they told the Finnish ambassador, they knew about them already, and thought that if co-operation between Sweden and Finland was to be maintained, Finland ought to give better notice of what she was doing.[23] The obvious displeasure of the Swedish government could be ignored, but it was a more delicate matter to inform Britain and the USA.

The suspicions of the British government had already been thoroughly aroused, and it was usually well aware of what happened in Finland. Already on June 5, the British ambassador in Helsinki had called on Ryti and asked about Heinrich's visit to Germany. Ryti, according to his own notes, had been obliged to tell lies, saying that as far as he knew Heinrichs had not been to Germany, and if some other officers had been there, it was only to discuss technical aspects of the transit agreement.[24] The British government was not deceived. Witting discussed his problem with Blücher on June 10. He said he would take the line that Finland was unable to oppose German activity in the north, but that she would not enter a war unless attacked.[25] The principal Finnish embassies abroad were sent a telegram on June 11 instructing them how to announce the arrival of the Germans and the partial mobilization.[26] By the time the ambassador in London had called on the British foreign office on June 13, the British government, which had known of the situation as soon as it happened, had already decided on its counter measures.

It was on or around the period June 11–12, that the Finnish leadership finally became certain that Germany had no intention of seeking a diplomatic solution with the USSR. Confusing reports continued to come in. On June 12, the embassy in Budapest reported that opinion there discounted the possibility of war, and that both the German and Soviet ambassadors had been positive that it was out of the question.[27] But on the same day, Kivimäki was sent instructions to find out from the German foreign office if there really were any negotiations in progress between Germany and the USSR. The terms of the instruction indicate that the government in Helsinki was convinced that there were not. This impression is reinforced by a report sent to Berlin by Blücher on June 11, after a long conversation with Witting.[28] This said that political circles in Finland were increasingly certain that war with Russia was coming, but that the ordinary people were not well informed about the situation. The government's precautionary measures were being executed according to plan. The inner circle of the government and the military authorities, and the two leading Social Democrats, Tanner and Hakkila, 'are looking the situation straight in the eyes'. But Witting had stressed that it was important that to the Finnish nation, the enemy should be made to appear to be the aggressor.

The military preparations were certainly rolling forward as planned. The German Mountain Corps, which was to execute Renntier, was told to be ready by June 22, the first possible date for occupying Petsamo. The attack on Murmansk would open nine days after the occupation. The Finnish troops in Petsamo would come under German orders from the date of the occupation, and preparatory talks could be begun immediately about the necessary advance measures. The German command in Norway was drawing up the operational orders for the Finnish Fifth Army Corps, and the headquarters for the German 36th Army Corps, which was the designation of the troops who were to execute Silberfuchs, would begin to function at Rovaniemi on June 15.[29] In Berlin, Halder had briefed the liaison staff who were to be attached to Mannerheim's headquarters. He assured General Erfurth, who was to lead the delegation, that the Finnish army would go over to the offensive as soon as the Germans gave them the wink.[30] Erfurth arrived in Helsinki on June 13, and began work at once, though at Mannerheim's request, the German officers did not appear in uniform for the time being. On the Finnish side, the recall of the reservists proceeded smoothly. The men involved were mostly specialists, such as the anti-aircraft troops in north Finland, the men of the Petsamo battalion, and the men in the third battalions of the thirteen active peace-time brigades.[31] Further all leave was stopped, and all staffs put on regular duty. On June 12, the Fifth Army Corps was ordered to take up defensive positions to cover Rovaniemi and the German concentrations, and to dig in as quickly as possible. The Cavalry brigade, the élite mobile unit, was ordered to be brought up to war strength and the discharge of time-expired conscripts stopped. It was now possible to put the various units of the army on to 'alternative 2', which meant no danger of surprise attack, and order them to take up battle stations.

Mannerheim was apparently seriously worried about the dangers of a Russian spoiling attack being the answer to his partial mobilization. During Buschenhagen's visit, the Finnish side had strongly favoured leaving general mobilization as late as possible for political and economic reasons. By June 10, Mannerheim had changed his mind, and sent Heinrichs to the German military attaché to announce that he would begin general mobilization on the earliest possible date, June 16.[32] This would mean that he would be able to take the offensive on June 28, but he still insisted on at least five days' notice of the direction in which the Germans wanted the attack launched.

On June 13, Witting carried the process of enlightening the politicians a stage further. He reported to the foreign affairs committee of the Eduskunta. Witting followed the same general line as Ryti in speaking to the cabinet. He said that war was 'at the door', and that was the reason for the partial mobilization. Witting revealed Molotov's demand in Berlin to liquidate Finland, and how Hitler had stopped the USSR by his veto. He gave an account of the affair of the SS battalion, and said that the government had felt obliged to consent to its formation as a gesture which would show where Finland stood. Witting recognized that the government's policy had already compromised Finland in the eyes of Britain and America, but expressed the view that Finland had had no choice. He had no illusions about German policy, 'Germany is behaving now the same way as England [in 1940] wanting and trying to make use of us'. Witting did not believe that neutrality was now a possible policy for Finland.[33]

Witting's statement differed from Ryti's four days earlier, in that he did not conceal that Finland had almost no chance of staying out of the war when it came. This disturbed some members of the committee. Voionmaa pointed out that Finland had joined her fate to Germany, but that the government had made no attempt to consult the Eduskunta. He complained that 'we are told things only after they have happened.' Salmenoja took the same line, 'there has been a decision of war and peace, although not even the foreign affairs committee has had the chance to speak its mind on the question.' Hannula was one of the few non-socialists to support these protests. He declared:[34]

'The truth is that a foreign power has occupied Finland. The picture which the foreign minister gave by talking of two divisions does not correspond with the truth. . . . The government will achieve nothing without the Eduskunta, and without the Finnish people.'

The significant feature of these criticisms is that they were not directed at what the government had done, which the committee seemed to accept as inevitable, but at the fact that it had not consulted the Eduskunta first. Most members of the committee did not even complain of this, their attitude was that of Linkomies, 'there is no other policy but that which the government is following.' According to Blücher, only the radical socialist Aatos Wirtanen criticized the policy of the government for departing from strict neutrality.[35] Thus the Finnish leaders could claim with some justice that, although they had not felt able to consult with the Eduskunta in advance, they had been correct in assuming that the bulk of the nation would approve of what they had done, and recognize that they had had no choice. But once more the reservation has to be entered that Witting had not told the committee the whole truth, the war he pictured was a defensive war against a Russian aggression, so that the committee was not in a position to make a proper assessment of government policy.

The next major problem for Mannerheim and the inner circle was to decide the date of general mobilization. On June 13, the Soviet news agency Tass put out a statement which denied that there were any grounds for rumours of conflict or tensions between Germany and the USSR. It is now known that this was a last desperate attempt by the government of the USSR to elicit from Hitler some statement of his intentions. But the Finnish leaders did not know this, and it becomes apparent that Mannerheim at least suspected that there might be truth in it, and that in fact the USSR and Germany were negotiating a settlement of their problems. So he began to reconsider the decision of a few days earlier to start mobilization on June 16. In consequence, June 14 became a crucial day in the consideration of the mobilization question. There was at least one conference of the inner circle, at which Mannerheim explained the military considerations which necessitated this move, and the political leaders gave their consent. There was of course never any doubt that Ryti, Walden, and Witting, who shared all Mannerheim's basic conceptions, would approve of mobilization. There may, however, have been some discussion of the date. There is evidence that Ryti argued strongly for a late date, preferably after the opening of hostilities between Germany and the USSR, and that Witting supported him, mainly on political grounds.[36]

Mannerheim himself was now undecided. Buschenhagen, who was again in Helsinki, went to see the Marshal on the 14th and took Erfurth along with him. Mannerheim made it clear that he was now unwilling to order mobilization unless the Germans would give him an unequivocal assurance that there would be a war.[37] He revealed how the Tass statement had impressed him by discussing seriously the guarantees that Finland would expect if Germany did after all make a peaceful settlement with the USSR. Erfurth could give no such assurances, but he promised to send to Germany and ask for them. A telegram was sent immediately to OKW reporting Mannerheim's doubts, and asking for authority to set them at rest. Otherwise, Mannerheim would undoubtedly refuse to mobilize. The same

18

evening, Erfurth saw Heinrichs, who urged him to get an answer by the following day. He also said that Mannerheim wanted to send a liaison officer to OKH to keep in closer touch with military developments. It is likely that during these conferences on the 14th, Erfurth revealed that the critical period was likely to be June 20–22, and that a final decision would be made within that period.

Erfurth's telegram had been considered by Hitler himself, who dictated the form of the answer to be given. The exact form which it took is not quite certain, since the exchange was confused by the irrepressible reluctance of all concerned to call a spade a spade. The Finnish request had been to know whether they were to reckon on a military solution or a diplomatic solution of the tensions between Germany and the USSR. According to some sources it was Erfurth who brought the reply that 'the demands and conditions raised by Finland concerning the measures to be taken are to be regarded as fulfilled'.[38] But Jodl subsequently told the German foreign office that Hitler had said the reply was to be that the first alternative, a military solution, could be counted on with certainty.[39] Whatever version finally reached Mannerheim, and perhaps they both did, his doubts should have been set at rest. So Erfurth considered, and he was surprised when, on the evening of June 15, Heinrichs informed him that Mannerheim wanted to put back the date of mobilization by five days, and not begin until June 21. This would mean that operations on the southeastern front could not begin before July 3, that is after the commencement of the German attacks in the north. Heinrichs urged this on political grounds, and indicated that Ryti was pressing for it, insisting strongly that Falkenhorst should start operations before the main Finnish army took its 'first step'. In this way it would be much easier to carry the Eduskunta and the general public along with the government's policy. One cannot know whether Mannerheim continued to hesitate because of urgings from Ryti, or whether he was still not satisfied with the German assurances. But the decision was in fact delayed until June 16, and the order for general mobilization did not go out until June 17.

These hesitations had had no effect on the programme agreed with Buschenhagen for the north of Finland. On June 15, as arranged, Fifth Army Corps began to mobilize, and received orders to submit to the command of Falkenhorst's headquarters at Rovaniemi.[40] The number of Siilasvuo's command was now altered to Third Army Corps. The orders to Siilasvuo were quite straightforward. While the mobilization took place, his military task was to repel 'possible military operations from the east into Finnish territory'.[41] When the mobilization was complete on June 26, the Army Corps would take its operational orders from Falkenhorst. These were in fact issued to it on June 16. Siilasvuo's two divisions were to make deep thrusts into Soviet territory on the right flank of the German attack up the line of the Kemijärvi railway to the junction with the Murmansk railway at Kandalahksa. Only the date of commencing operations was left open. It would be superfluous to comment further on this transaction, which merely fulfilled the agreement arrived at with Buschenhagen at the beginning of the Helsinki talks, if it were not that various Finnish commentators have tried to make out that the orders to the Fifth Army Corps did not mean what they obviously say.

It is true, that when a supposedly neutral state puts a part of its army under the operational command of a foreign power, knowing that that power contemplates launching a war of aggression against a neighbouring state, some explanation is called for. The obvious explanation is that the neutral state has no real intention of remaining neutral if the war should break out. But this, the common sense explanation, and the only one that really squares with the known facts, is a luxury that most Finnish commentators have denied themselves. Mannerheim himself is less than truthful in suggesting that his motive in issuing the orders was to prevent the supply and communications difficulties caused by the simultaneous presence of two different armies in the same area.[42] Such difficulties would undoubtedly have arisen but they were not the reason for issuing this order. The reason was that Mannerheim had agreed with Buschenhagen that if the war came, the troops of Fifth Army Corps could be used by the Germans for their Silberfuchs operations. Mannerheim and others have stressed that the order could have been cancelled at any time, and that Siilasvuo knew that if he got operational orders, he must first refer them to Mannerheim. This is undoubtedly true. But to argue, as General Tapola did afterwards, that this meant the order involved no obligation to participate in a German attack is to make a technical point of no practical significance.[43] Siilasvuo got his operational orders on June 16, and presumably, as instructed, referred them to Mannerheim. Since Siilasvuo's command then proceeded to make all necessary preparations to execute the orders, it can be presumed that Mannerheim said nothing which indicated that they were not to be carried out. The order to Fifth Army Corps on June 15 meant exactly what it implied. That if there was a war between Germany and the USSR the agreements for Finnish participation in Silberfuchs, which Heinrichs had concluded with Buschenhagen some ten days earlier, would be honoured. In theory, Mannerheim could still have cancelled his consent to the proposed operations. In fact, nobody on either the Finnish or the German side considered for a moment the possibility that he would.

By this stage it had become very difficult for Finland to maintain even the semblance of neutrality as between Germany and the USSR. The suspicions of the British government had been confirmed when, on June 12, they were asked to withdraw their inspectors from the Petsamo area. The reasons why Mannerheim insisted on this are obvious. The counter move of the British government was inevitable, and it announced the cancellation of all permits for the traffic to Liinahamari.[44] Two days later the Finnish ambassador in London reported to his government that Finland was regarded there as under German occupation. Britain continued to hope that Finland might at least maintain some kind of non-belligerent status, but without much conviction. The British ambassador called on Witting on June 19 to deliver a warning to Finland not to risk backing the losing side. He is said to have told Witting that by 1943 he would see an English fleet sailing into the Baltic with flags flying. It is conceivable that even in 1941 there were still British ambassadors who considered it appropriate to talk to the foreign ministers of small powers in the language of gunboat diplomacy. Witting is said to have answered dryly, that if Finland used force to oppose the German troops on her territory, there would be very few Finns alive in 1943 to witness this splendid sight. Witting denied that Finland had ceased to be neutral, but admitted that she would do nothing to prevent Germany making use of her territory. The ambassador noted that they were 'sitting in different camps'.[45]

In Sweden the last illusions were quickly vanishing. On June 14, Finland broke with a Scandinavian custom of long standing and ended freedom of travel between Sweden and Finland for the nationals of both countries. In future passports and visas would be required. The Swedish press commented adversely on this. *Dagens Nyheter* talked of a major change in Finnish policy, and it was generally recognized that Finland had diverged from the line of policy pursued by Sweden. It was openly said that in a war between Germany and the USSR, Finland was likely to take part on the German side. The Finnish press quoted these opinions extensively, as it did the current speculation in the British press.[46] Some papers, like those of the socialists and *Helsingin Sanomat*, still protested that the Swedish papers were mistaken, and that Finland was still as neutral as Sweden. *Helsingin Sanomat*, while recognizing that the position of the two countries could not be the same at all points, thought that Sweden, as a good neighbour, should show more understanding of the difficult position in which Finland found herself.[47] But *Uusi Suomi* saw no reason to deny what was becoming all too obvious. It agreed that if there were a war between Germany and the USSR, Finland could not be unaffected. Germany was a power 'with which we have formed ever closer and firmer relations'. But the public was still urged to shun speculation, to keep calm, and trust the government to act wisely.[48]

However, when the order for general mobilization was issued on June 17, the point had been reached at which the public must be told something. For general mobilization touched every family in the land, and its significance was known to all. Ryti had a series of conferences with the politicians on June 18 and 19.[49] There is no certainty what he said, but he seems to have admitted that if war came between Germany and the USSR, Finland would almost certainly come under Russian attack, and that was the reason for mobilization. Some alleged later that Ryti had said that if Russia did not attack Finland within a few days of the opening of such a war, Finland would herself take the initiative. But it seems improbable that even if Ryti thought this, which he might well have done, he would have been so incautious as to say it in public. But there is plenty of evidence that in fact people were not deceived, and that they expected Finland to take the offensive if the situation permitted. It was widely realized that in some way Finland was committed to participation with Germany if war should come.

The socialists showed that they realized what was happening by the vigour of their reaction. At a meeting of party leaders on June 17, Tanner had told the other parties that the social democrats would not support an offensive war. Hakkila had told Paasikivi on the previous day that the socialists still believed that Finland should stay out of a war between Germany and the USSR.[50] The socialist press attacked those who advocated 'a policy of adventure', and called on the government to issue a declaration of neutrality. On June 19, all the socialist organizations, including the trade unions, held an emergency conference. They resolved to send deputations to present their views to the president and the prime minister, and to issue a manifesto to the nation. While they were prepared to support the government's measures to date, because they seemed to be justified by the tense international situation, they insisted that there was no cause for Finland to depart from a policy of strict neutrality, and that the working class would not support such a departure.[51]

This was more than a routine claim to speak for the workers. There was genuine confusion and dismay among ordinary people, who could not understand why they should be called up when there was no war. The writer Paavolainen, who was himself a reservist, has described such reactions. He saw a unit on June 20 which was in a state of near mutiny because the ordinary soldier could not see why he was there. To him the approaching war was 'the gentry's war', and he was showing his opinion by an 'open and cynical lack of enthusiasm'.[52] On the other hand there was plenty of evidence of a contrary opinion in the country. Paasikivi noted how wide was the belief that Germany would beat the USSR in a short time, and how this gave rise to public optimism about Finland's opportunities. Still, the opposition to an offensive war was sufficiently strong and well organized to make it understandable why Ryti was so anxious that Finland should not appear to take the initiative against the USSR. If serious internal discontent was to be avoided, the USSR must somehow be made to seem the aggressor.

The military authorities recognized the validity of the fears of the politicians to the extent that they were quite ready to press their point of view on the Germans. But nothing was allowed to prevent the smooth driving forward of their war plans. On June 16, certain frontier zones were evacuated and mined. The following day operational orders for the occupation of the Åland islands were distributed to the forces concerned.[53] On June 18, the main forces on the south-eastern front got their operational orders. These were in two parts covering a defensive phase, and an offensive phase. The offensive plans were those drawn up in May for the Hiitola offensive.[54] It has been pointed out that the Hiitola offensive would in the first place greatly improve the Finnish defensive position, and at the same time open the way for a speedy reconquest of the ceded areas. The plans were not entirely inconsistent with what Heinrichs and Buschenhagen had agreed, but they were not in accord with the spirit of that agreement, which was that the Finnish forces should hold themselves ready to strike either east or west of Lake Ladoga, in accordance with German wishes. Further Heinrichs had more than once suggested that the Finnish command preferred an offensive east of Ladoga, whereas these orders were for an offensive predominantly west of the lake.

There is a minor mystery here, the secret of which may well have died with Mannerheim himself. He had a great reputation for impenetrability. The easiest explanation is that since Mannerheim had not been told which direction of attack the Germans preferred, he had simply issued the operational orders drawn up in May, before Heinrichs had been to Salzburg, with the intention of changing them if necessary after the German command had declared its preference. This has the merit that it is what actually happened in the event. It may be that Mannerheim felt that if the war was to get the necessary political support from the nation, he must make the reconquest of the ceded areas his first offensive aim. Mannerheim said as much to Erfurth when they were discussing this problem after the outbreak of hostilities. Or it may be that Mannerheim, as he consistently showed in the months to come, was determined to keep control of the operations of the Finnish armies, and not to become the puppet of the German command. Or finally, Mannerheim may just have wanted to wait and see what happened, and seen no point in changing the army's operational orders until he could see how the situation was developing. At this stage the Marshal was still much preoccupied with the danger of a

Russian spoiling attack. On June 17 he asked the government to begin the evacuation of the frontier areas, particularly of the women and children. Mannerheim urged that 'the gain of a single day is significant.'[55] It seems that the government did not agree with him, since the orders were not issued until June 20. Probably this is evidence of Ryti's preoccupation with keeping up appearances, and not alarming domestic and foreign opinion more than was needed. In the following days over 60,000 people were moved, testimony to the seriousness with which the belief in a Russian attack was held.[56]

On June 19, the Finnish command learned the date of the German attack. It is not on record how this happened. It may have come from Rovaniemi, since the German troops there had begun to move towards the frontier on June 17, and had been told that they need no longer conceal their intentions from the Finns.[57] Finland also received a German warning on June 17 to stop any further sailings of ships to Russian ports. The evidence that the Finnish command knew the date is to be found in the orders issued on June 19. The Åland force was told to execute the occupation of the islands on the morning of June 22. The navy was ordered to lay its minefields in territorial waters during the night of June 21–22. The army was told that it must be ready for battle, and prepared against air attack on the morning of June 22.[58] At the same time, with the assurance that the German offensive would open within three days, it was possible to make some modifications to the mobilization plan, so as to facilitate an early offensive.

It has been mentioned that the basic scheme of mobilization was intended to meet a Russian offensive, and that it placed heavy emphasis on the defence of the vital coastal sector, which offered the shortest and easiest route into the interior. By June 19, Mannerheim, knowing that the Germans were going to thrust at Leningrad, and that this must tie up the forces of the Leningrad garrison, decided that the danger of a massive Russian offensive had diminished. So he ordered the transfer of one division from the coastal sector, and added it to the Finnish Second Army Corps which would be the spearhead of the Hiitola offensive. The First Division, which was part of the commander in chief's reserve, was to assemble at Lahti, also behind Second Army Corps, and the Nineteenth Division, also from the reserve, was ordered to Pieksämäki, from where it could easily move either behind Second Army Corps, or in support of the more northerly Seventh Army Corps. These changes show that Mannerheim was now losing his fear of serious Russian spoiling attacks by land, though the danger of air attack was taken seriously still, and that his opinion in favour of the Hiitola offensive was hardening. This was obvious to Erfurth, who discussed the Finnish dispositions with Heinrichs on June

19, and expressed concern that the build-up of a force that could strike
north and east of Ladoga was being neglected.

Erfurth got no satisfaction, he was told that Mannerheim was not yet
ready to begin the moves which Erfurth suggested. In fact, Mannerheim
had a well-developed technique for dealing with the Germans. He was a
master of evasion by silence, always ready to listen to what they had to say,
and thus find out what was on their minds, but extremely chary of committing himself in return. So on this occasion he listened to Erfurth's
comments, but went on with his own plans, and reserved his answer. He
meant to go to war alongside Germany, but he would do it in his own way,
and for the objectives which he preferred. There was other evidence on
June 19 that Finnish-German co-operation was imperfect. It had long been
part of the German plan to send the 163rd Division from Norway to Finland, provided Sweden would grant the use of her railways. It was thought
that the Division might tackle Hanko. But since it was not certain that it
could come at all, Swedish consent being doubtful, the Germans had not
bothered to discuss with the Finnish command the role of this force.

Then on June 19, General Engelbrecht, the commander of 163rd Division, presented himself to Heinrichs, and announced that he was going to
deal with Hanko. Heinrichs was surprised, especially as he had more than
once suggested to the Germans that they should take responsibility for
Hanko, and always been told that they had no troops available. It was decided that since the Finnish disposition to cover Hanko had now been
made, some other task should be found for Engelbrecht's troops if they
did eventually arrive.[59] At the same time Schnurre had arrived in Stockholm and among his other duties was expected to get the Swedish government to consent to the transit of Engelbrecht's troops. Blücher had been
instructed to ask Ryti if Finland would send a delegation to Stockholm to
support Schnurre's request. Ryti agreed to send the delegation, but it
busied itself asking Sweden for economic assistance, and when Schnurre
asked for its backing with the Swedish government, he was told that the
mission had no instructions on this, and would have to refer to Helsinki.
It is likely that Ryti knew nothing of the plans of 163rd Division, and regarded the German request as likely to compromise Finland prematurely
in the eyes of the Swedish government. So Schnurre remained unsup-
ported for the time being, and made little headway with the Swedish
government.

The German military authorities seem to have had a clearer appreciation of the Finnish position than the German foreign office. They respected
the insistence of Mannerheim and Heinrichs that Finland must not appear
to be the aggressor. On June 20, German airforce units were reminded
that they must not make operational flights from Finnish airfields until the

Finnish authorities gave their permission. At the same time the German naval units were reminded that they could not commence their mine-laying operations before the outbreak of hostilities. That same day, the Germans had been reminded that Mannerheim needed careful handling. His personal liaison officer, General Öquist, arrived at OKH, and had a talk with Halder.[60] He said that it was most important to delay the start of the Finnish main attack as long as possible and that Finland would need seven rather than five days' notice of the date. He also said that Manner-heim would like to get Siilasvuo's troops back under his own command at the earliest possible date. But the most surprising of Öquist's points was his insistence to Halder that the main Finnish attack should be made to the east of Lake Ladoga, rather than the west. This is at first sight inconsistent with the way in which Mannerheim was currently resisting Erfurth's efforts to persuade him to alter his dispositions so as to facilitate a thrust on the east of the lake. The explanation is probably simple. It was one of Mannerheim's obsessions that Finnish troops must not take part in a direct attack on Leningrad. There were both military and political reasons for this. It is almost certain that what Öquist said to Halder was just this, and that Halder reasonably concluded that the Finnish command would prefer to strike east of Ladoga. But the Hiitola offensive was not even remotely aimed at Leningrad, and so was quite consistent with what Öquist was telling Halder. It is to be noted that Öquist took Finland's participation in the attack on the USSR absolutely for granted. He was only anxious to stress that the Finnish main attack be delayed sufficiently for the situation to develop to the point where Russia must react in some way which would give Finland her *casus belli*.

Thus matters stood on June 21. Outwardly Finland's position was obscure, but the men who were directing events had no doubts. Hitler wrote to Mussolini explaining his decision to attack the USSR. He said, 'I assume, that is I am convinced, that Finland and likewise Romania will forthwith take part in this conflict'.[61] At midday, Erfurth came to Hein-richs and told him that the official order to begin the attack had come.[62] Erfurth noted that Heinrichs seemed surprised, and wondered if this was because to the end the Finns had doubted if the attack would actually be launched. It is hard to believe that Heinrichs was really surprised. No doubt he was deeply moved, as anyone might be at receiving such news. He took Erfurth's hand and said, 'A historic moment. May everything go well.' There was no nonsense about neutrality in Heinrichs' feelings. Only in the USSR did the government cling to its belief that Hitler could not attack them because they had given him no cause. Orlov came to Witting on the same day, and solemnly assured him that a war between the USSR and Germany was most improbable. Witting must have got a certain grim satisfaction out of hearing this. The same evening, the German naval attaché in Helsinki called on Heinrichs. He had just got the text of Hitler's speech, to be broadcast the following morning, and it contained the following passage:[63]

'In alliance with their Finnish comrades, the victors of Narvik stand on the shore of the Arctic Ocean. German divisions, led by the conqueror of Norway, along with Finnish liberation fighters under their Marshal, protect Finland's territory.'

The naval attaché, misreading this, thought it untrue and compromising to Finland, since it suggested a stronger degree of association than actually existed. Heinrichs went to Mannerheim's house, and Walden was summoned, to consider the text. They decided to take no action.

Finnish commentators, led by Mannerheim, have tried to suggest that Hitler was deliberately misrepresenting Finland's position in order to drag her into the war. The Marshal writes that Hitler meant 'to face Finland with an accomplished fact',[64] and provoke Russian counter-measures. They then go on to explain that in the circumstances they could hardly make any protest. In fact, there was nothing to protest about. For once Hitler was being almost pedantically truthful. One may cavil at the phrase 'im Bünde' as being too strong to describe the relationship between the two countries. When the Finnish censorship passed the speech, it took the liberty of translating this 'side by side', which is certainly no more accurate as a description of the arrangements which existed between Siilasvuo's troops and the Germans. Mannerheim and Walden must have perceived as they read the text that there was nothing to complain of. It said that these troops were 'protecting' Finland. Since neither the Finnish nor the German troops intended to take the offensive for some days, this was a very fair way of putting it. As will be seen, even the government of the USSR was uncertain what interpretation to put on this passage. They did not assume that it meant that Finland was committed to war. It is probable that a much more important passage in the speech was that in which Hitler described Molotov's visit to Berlin. He represented Molotov as demanding the right to liquidate Finland. Rumours to this effect had long been in circulation, and the politicians had heard the story from Ryti and Witting, but ordinary people had only heard rumours, and now these were confirmed by an eye-witness account. To judge by the Finnish press comment, this revelation made a deep impression, and must have done much to help make the government's policy acceptable.

When the German attack on the Soviet Union was opened in the early hours of June 22, the Finnish armed forces were still in the middle of their mobilization. This fact dominated the course of events. Mobilization would be completed on June 28, and the longer that the formal outbreak of hostilities could be postponed, the better it would be. This was the factor which dictated the way in which Finland's military leaders made their methodical preparations to enter the war. At 2.30 a.m. on the 22nd, the German Mountain Corps entered the Petsamo area and occupied it without incident, the Finnish troops there coming under its command according to plan.[65] Later in the day the Finnish command was informed of the date of the opening of the northern offensives. The direct thrust at Murmansk would begin on June 29.[66] Silberfuchs would begin on July 1. The operations could not be started simultaneously, since the same air-force units had to cover both. This suited Finnish planning very well, since their mobilization would be completed before operations from Finnish soil had begun. Hence they proved to be unreceptive when the German command at Rovaniemi proposed action which would have upset this situation. Erfurth came to Heinrichs on June 22, and said that the Germans would like to send patrols into the Salla area, since they thought it was unoccupied, and it might be possible to seize the important heights without a struggle. Heinrichs refused this request. He said that such premature activity might bring on Russian reprisals which would upset the smooth working of the Finnish mobilization.[67] Before making this decision, Mannerheim had consulted Ryti, who fully approved of it. An attack by the Germans from Finnish territory at that stage would have made nonsense of the government's efforts to represent Finland's position as still unsettled.

The only incidents involving the USSR had occurred on the naval front. The occupation of the Åland islands had been carried through without a hitch, and was completed by 9.30 a.m. There was no Russian reaction. The centre of tension was at Hanko, and in the neighbouring waters. Here Russian aircraft had attacked Finnish shipping, and the Russian batteries had opened fire at 6.50 a.m. The Finnish batteries were authorized to return this fire. The navy was anxious to drop the mask and start full-scale operations; particularly, they wanted to begin laying mines outside territorial waters. But their request was refused by headquarters for 'political reasons'.[68] Otherwise, the outbreak of war enabled the Finnish command to set the date by which the units concerned in the Hiitola offensive should be ready to move, June 28. Further preparations for the opening of this offensive were made in the course of the day, when the First Jäger Brigade, one of the *élite* units of the army, was ordered to move to Varkaus, behind the front of Second Army Corps, and orders went out to remove some fortress artillery for use in the offensive. The final move on the 22nd was an order to stop the Russian transits to Hanko on some suitable pretext.[69]

This was followed by a further move against Hanko in the early hours of

June 23. The Hanko–Helsinki, and the Helsinki–Tallinn cables were cut, breaking direct telegraph communication between Hanko and the USSR. Otherwise, June 23 was an uneventful day. There were scattered flights over the frontier by Russian aircraft, and the Hanko area continued restless. This was understandable, since the garrison had not only had its communications cut, but it was heavily bombed by German aircraft coming from East Prussia. Finnish naval headquarters reported vigorous 'enemy' preparations in the area all day. The interesting developments all took place inside Mannerheim's headquarters. One was an order which in itself reveals clearly the ultimate intentions of the Finnish command. An order was sent out to form a special battalion of refugees, then serving in the Finnish army, who were natives of Soviet eastern Karelia or of Ingria, the hinterland of Leningrad where the original rural population was of Finnish-speaking stock. This special battalion was to be assembled at Kajaani on July 7.[70] This order makes no sense at all unless Mannerheim had already decided, on June 23, to carry an offensive over the 1939 frontier into areas which, although largely inhabited by peoples of Finnish race, had never been politically part of Finland.

Preparations for the Hiitola offensive also went forward. Orders to the heavy artillery to proceed to the front allotted four batteries to Second Army Corps, and two to its northern neighbour, Seventh Army Corps. At the same time, General Talvela was appointed to command Second Army Corps. He at once submitted a strong recommendation to follow up the Hiitola offensive with an advance to the Vuoksi, preparatory to the recovery of Viipuri. The distribution of the artillery, and the fact that Talvela was one of Mannerheim's most trusted commanders, were signs that the Marshal was still bent on giving priority to the Hiitola offensive. Erfurth had again come to Heinrichs during the 23rd with a request to start patrolling over the frontier, and was again refused. But by the evening of that day, Mannerheim was satisfied that his plans were so far developed, that he could risk inviting Russian reprisals. One sign of this was the order for headquarters to move from Helsinki to its war station at Mikkeli. This was issued at 9 a.m. on June 24, and the move was to be completed by June 26. The other sign was that when Erfurth came back to Heinrichs on the evening of June 23, he was told that the Germans could begin land and air reconnaissance after midnight on June 24. At the same time, the navy was at last authorized to lay its offensive minefields.[71]

It has been necessary to establish that the offensive plans and preparations of the Finnish armed forces were well advanced by the end of June 23, so well advanced that Mannerheim saw no further point in concealing them after midnight on the 24th. This is because the Russian reaction, which formed the formal *casus belli*, did not occur until the morning of

THE DECISION

285

June 25. During that morning, there was a series of heavy Russian air attacks on places in southern Finland. There is no doubt that they constituted a serious effort to disrupt Finnish communications and delay war preparations. There is equally no doubt that both in scale and weight, these attacks were an act of aggression under international law, and a fully adequate *casus belli*. These attacks were the crowning folly of the Finnish policy of the USSR. Either the Soviet government had decided that there was nothing further to be gained by treating Finland as a non-belligerent, or else the local Russian commanders, having sat still for three days and watched the obvious preparations being made for an offensive, lost their nerve and lashed out. If the Russians had restrained themselves until June 29, when the first major attack would have come from Finnish territory, they would have lost nothing militarily, and created the most horrible embarrassments for the Finnish leaders on both the internal and the international political fronts.

These air attacks created no serious military problems for Finland. The military preparations proceeded without interruption, only the artillery was authorized to shoot up any promising targets that might offer.[72] Then on June 25, the Germans at last declared their preference for Finnish offensive action on the south-eastern front. Erfurth came to Mannerheim and asked him to launch his attack east of Lake Ladoga. To his evident surprise, Mannerheim proved difficult. There was a long discussion 'before the great wall map', in which Mannerheim explained the advantages of the Hiitola offensive. Erfurth pointed out that this did not at all fit in with German plans, and tried to frighten Mannerheim off by saying that the Hiitola attack would run into 'a wasps' nest'. At least he urged Mannerheim to launch a simultaneous attack to the east of the lake. Mannerheim ended the discussion with the words, 'we will think about it'.[73] Mannerheim's political arguments were undoubtedly sound. The Finnish people would expect priority to be given to the recapture of the ceded territories. But since it is known that Mannerheim also intended to strike into eastern Karelia, it can be assumed that he was not certain that the time was yet ripe for this. Mannerheim did not want to advance east of Ladoga and towards the River Svir until he could be sure that the northern wing of the German thrust at Leningrad had advanced far enough to undermine Russian resistance, and offer the prospect of a link up between Finnish and German forces on the Svir. It may also be that in part his long argument with Erfurth was a demonstration of his independence. It was meant to show the Germans that he was not to be commanded at their convenience. Probably all these factors fed Mannerheim's hesitations.

Mannerheim did in fact consider it. On June 26 he got a memorandum from his operations section on an attack east of Ladoga, and on the following day orders were sent to the First, Fifth, and Nineteenth divisions to be prepared to move north at short notice. During this time Mannerheim was moving in his headquarters train along the rear of the front towards Mikkeli. It was probably on the evening of June 27, when the train was standing at Varkaus, that Mannerheim decided on a compromise. The Germans were informed that he would launch his first attack in a strength of six divisions north and east of Lake Ladoga. What he failed to add was that when this attack had reached roughly the line of the 1939 frontier, he would break it off and execute his Hiitola offensive. The necessary orders went out on June 28. The three divisions were ordered to move north, and General Talvela was transferred from command of Second Army Corps to the Sixth Army Corps, which would play the decisive part in the new attack. On June 29, the whole northern force was formed into the 'Karelian Army', and the command given to Heinrichs.[74] The same day Halder noted in his diary that 'Finland presents a new plan of attack conforming to our wishes'.[75] It only remained to set the date, and this was finally established as July 10. The planning cycle that had been set in motion when Heinrichs came to Salzburg on May 25 was completed. It had, after some vicissitudes, worked out very much in accordance with the Germans' original intentions.

Prior consideration has been given to developments in the military sphere in the period after June 22 because those were the decisive events which determined all else. It has been shown that Mannerheim was not blind to the political implications of what he was doing, but he executed his plans, and thereby determined the fate of his country, with only the scantiest reference to the political authorities. If there is an air of unreality surrounding the activities of the government after June 22, it arises because the government was not controlling events. It was comforming to decisions made elsewhere, and the reactions which these decisions had produced. The government was no longer making policy after June 22, it was improvising some kind of decent political covering for the activities of the military authorities.

The Finnish foreign office, although it had reckoned with the probability of war since the beginning of June, had made scant preparations to meet the situation. The key embassies in Moscow, London, and Stockholm had no instructions. The ambassador in London read with astonishment the reports in the British press that his country had joined in the German attack. He sent an urgent telegram to Helsinki to ask what he was to say to the British government.[76] In Moscow, the chargé d'affaires, Hynninen, seems to have done nothing. In Stockholm, the embassy was approached by Schnurre, and asked to support him in his negotiations with the Swedish government, but the embassy had no authority to do this. In

Helsinki, the foreign office issued a statement, which said that Finland was not 'at present' involved in the war, and that the German troops movements could be considered as falling under the terms of the transit agreement.[77] This statement was all the comment that the Finnish government had to make. The latter part was obviously untrue, and the whole was far short of the declaration of neutrality which would normally be issued in such circumstances. At most it was an expression of provisional non-belligerency. The American ambassador called at the foreign office to inquire about the position, and he was given an answer to the same effect, that Finland would remain outside the war 'as long as possible.'

But the key event of the day in the diplomatic field was a call by Orlov on Witting. This produced a conversation lasting an hour and a half. First the two men tried to exchange protests, Witting against the bombing of Finnish ships, Orlov against alleged air attacks on the USSR from Finnish territory. Orlov declined to receive the protest but did undertake to make inquiries. Orlov then raised the question of Hitler's speech. He pointed out that the presence of German troops on Finnish soil seemed inconsistent with neutrality. This put Witting in a difficulty. He did not want to repudiate Hitler in any way, since Hitler had only spoken the truth about Finland, and he feared that any attempt to put a gloss on Hitler's words would be exploited by Soviet propaganda. So Witting stressed that Hitler spoke only of defending Finnish territory. He then added that the government would be making a statement of its position to the Eduskunta on June 25.[78] It seems clear that Orlov was inviting Witting to declare his non-belligerency at least. For later in the day, Orlov gave an interview in Helsinki to the correspondent of United Press in which he said that the USSR was willing to regard Finland as neutral, so long as her territory was not used for attacks on the USSR.[79] Since there is only the official Finnish account of this interview, one cannot be sure that Orlov said the same to Witting, but it is reasonable to assume that he did. The significant point seems to be that Witting avoided giving an answer, he told Orlov that the USSR must wait until the Eduskunta had met. By then, the mobilization would be fairly safe from serious interruption. The final event of the 22nd was a meeting of the foreign affairs committee of the cabinet, with Ryti presiding. Rangell made a statement on the position to the effect that Finland was not yet involved in the war.[80] He gave some account of the numbers of German troops and then told the committee what he, and Ryti, certainly knew to be a lie. The committee was told that it remained to be seen what the German troops in the north would do. In fact Rangell and all the inner circle knew exactly what they were going to do, and may well have known by that time when they were going to do it.

On June 23, there were reactions from the side of the USSR. One ugly

one was in the field of propaganda. A statement appeared in both *Pravda*
and on the radio, which declared that the Finnish fascists had once more
joined the enemies of the USSR and should bear in mind that a nation of
200 millions might, in its wrath, wipe them from the face of the earth. It is
not clear whether it was the Finnish fascists, or the whole Finnish people
that was thus threatened.[81] The authorities in the USSR quickly perceived that this statement, which was probably meant mainly for domestic
consumption, might have a bad effect abroad. It got withdrawn from later
editions of *Pravda*, and attempts were afterwards made to deny that any
such statement had been issued. At the official level, Molotov called Hynninen to the Kremlin. Molotov complained of various incidents, such as
the firing on Hanko, and demanded to know what the position of Finland
was. He said that the USSR had no demands to make of Finland, but he
must warn her of the serious consequences if she joined the enemies of the
USSR. Hynninen had nothing to say. Indeed, since he had received
nothing from Helsinki since the 21st, he expressed doubt whether the
cable was working. Molotov assured him that it was, and concluded, 'I
will wait for your answer.'[82] It seems clear that Molotov, like Orlov, was
inviting Finland to declare her neutrality.

The Finnish foreign office did circulate the principal embassies abroad
on the 23rd, but told them no more than had been contained in the official
statement of the previous day, that Finland was not at present involved in
the conflict. Hitler's statement was correct if rightly interpreted. The
German troops in Finland could 'at least for the moment be considered as
falling within the terms of the transit agreement'.[83] When Grippenberg
reported this to the British government, it was received with satisfaction,
but he got a warning against joining in the war.[84] Orlov was again called to
Witting on June 23, but only to be informed of the occupation of the Åland
islands, and the request of the Soviet consul there to be taken to Helsinki.[85]
So far, the activities of the Finnish government had resulted in the creation
of a fog of ambiguity around their position. This was done deliberately, as
the German ambassador in Helsinki was well aware. He sent a despatch on
developments to Berlin on June 23. First he reported the receipt by Ryti
of a letter from Hitler. The text of this has been lost, but it seems to have
contained three points. Hitler welcomed the fact that Finland and Germany stood side by side in the conflict with the USSR. He declared that
Germany would never leave Finland in the lurch, and he personally confirmed what had been agreed upon between the military authorities.
Blücher reported that this letter had been received in Finland 'with satisfaction'. He went on to explain the real significance of the various public
statements made by the Finnish government. 'The Finnish army needs
six more days for its strategic concentration. The Foreign Minister has to

consider this and intends to temporize until then.' Blücher urged the foreign office to back up the deception, and refrain for the moment from talking of Finland as an ally.[86]

The same day, the Finnish press got its first opportunity to comment on the war. First it featured the official government statement to the nation. This was a warning that Finland was 'directly in the danger zone', and must be watchful. The public was urged to stay calm and do its duty while awaiting developments. Most space was given to Hitler's speech, and it was the theme of the editorial comment. The revelations about the Molotov visit got more attention than any other point. The socialist press, led by *Suomen Sosiaalidemokraatti*, said that there had been revelations of things hitherto unknown. The ground was being prepared for the socialist leadership to change its stand on neutrality. The paper did not in fact mention neutrality, and its only reference to Germany was to stress that Finland must preserve its national independence. *Helsingin Sanomat*, commenting on Hitler's speech, said that Finland must feel grateful to Hitler for the protection that he had given her. *Uusi Suomi*, which carried quotations from the German press in which Finland was referred to as an ally, called Germany's action a historical turning point, and hoped that it would profoundly affect the future of Finland.[87]

June 24 was a quiet day on the political and diplomatic front. The British government, on the strength of the information given by Grippenberg, informed the House of Commons that Finland appeared to be neutral.[88] It was the policy of the British government to try to keep her so. Schnurre, in Stockholm, sent an exasperated telegram to Berlin, in which he poured out his complaints that he was making no progress with the Swedish government, and that the Finnish embassy was not supporting his request, on the ground that Finland was still neutral. In fact the failure of Schnurre to make headway was due to an intense division of opinion in the Swedish cabinet. Halder already knew on June 24 that Sweden would give the necessary permission, but he probably got information from Swedish military sources. At 9 p.m. Hynninen's telegram arrived from Moscow, reporting his conversation with Molotov. For a reason that is still unexplained, it had been nearly 24 hours on the way. That spared the Finnish government the trouble of thinking up an answer, since the air-raids on the 25th intervened before it had been considered.

The great preoccupation of the government on the 24th was the wording of the statement that must be given to the Eduskunta when it met on the next day. If Mannerheim were to be believed, it would be thought that this statement was to have been a declaration of Finland's neutrality.[89] It has frequently been referred to as though it were, but not often quoted. The text shows quite plainly that it was nothing of the sort. Presumably, when

19

Mannerheim came to write his memoirs, he could not remember what the government had proposed to say. The statement began with a justification of the call up, saying that events had shown that the government had acted just in time. It announced to the Eduskunta that the president had decided to issue a formal mobilization order. The order issued on June 17 had been for 'general training exercises'. The statement continued that the task of the armed forces was 'to safeguard the land of our fathers'. They did not specify whether this phrase was supposed to mean the Finland of the Moscow peace or whether it bore some wider significance. Then the statement, which was clearly being drafted in its final form during the air-raid on Helsinki on the morning of the 25th, continued:[90]

'Since our country is within the area of military operations, the danger of war is apparent. Soviet forces have several times violated our territorial integrity. This morning we had to use anti-aircraft guns to drive off Russian machines on a bombing mission over Helsinki. We are compelled to protest to the government of the USSR about these incidents. At any moment the offences may be renewed on such a scale, that we are forced to defend ourselves with all our forces. . . . The immediate future may be rich in events, and may bring great burdens, and with them great decisions.'

This draft is rather remarkable for what it does not say. It was supposed to be a situation report on the strength of which the Eduskunta could decide whether the government had acted rightly, and could judge what its future intentions were. Yet it said no word about Germany from beginning to end, nothing about Hitler's speech, nothing about the German troops in the north. The word neutrality, or any reference to the concept of neutrality is entirely absent from the statement. It is, on the face of it, a warning to the Eduskunta to expect to be at war with the USSR in the very near future, and an indication that Russian aerial activity was to be made the *casus belli*.

This was the situation on the morning of June 25. That morning's papers nearly all ran leading articles on the ideological implications of Hitler's attack on the USSR. Bolshevism was a menace to western culture and civilization, this was the starting point. *Helsingin Sanomat* declared 'that all civilized nations recognized this fact.' Finland among them. Sweden was reproved for failing to appreciate the true nature of the war, and allowing herself to be abused still by the bolshevik conspiracy. *Uusi Suomi* also addressed Sweden, and reproached her for lack of understanding. Finland had special knowledge of the evils of bolshevism. The paper continued, 'the great moment for accounting has come, and nobody, who feels responsible for the future of his nation and of western culture, can be indifferent to it'. The provincial paper, *Savon Sanomat*, addressing a less-sophisticated audience, had expressed itself more bluntly. Hitler's attack on the USSR was 'a holy war for the freedom of humanity'. The sentence speaks volumes for the editor's conception of the nature of Hitler's Germany. He went on to express the hope that the war would bring Finland 'some kind of compensation for what we have lost'. The Finnish government may have been technically non-belligerent on the morning of June 25, but the press had already gone into battle.[91] The Finnish papers could have provided the answers to a set of questions which the German foreign office put to ambassador Kivimäki on the morning of June 25.[92] He was asked to find out what was Finland's attitude to bolshevism, what was its exact relationship with the USSR at that date, and what were the offences which the USSR had committed against Finnish neutrality. The nature of these queries showed clearly that they were meant to elicit material for use in German propaganda about Finland. The German foreign office knew from Blücher's report of June 23 what the real situation was.

As soon as the air-raid on Helsinki was over, Blücher hurried to see Witting, and said there was no longer any need of concealment. Finland could tell the whole world that she had become the victim of aggression. The Finnish government needed no urging. As the reports came in, and it was apparent that the Soviet attacks had been widespread and heavy, the cabinet met to consider whether they should now alter their statement to the Eduskunta. It was agreed unanimously that the Eduskunta should be told that Finland had become the victim of a renewed Soviet aggression and that this would be repelled with all her strength.[93] In the haste of revision they left out all mention of a presidential order for mobilization, the one positive measure included in the original draft, and this was never given. They also omitted to ask the Eduskunta for a formal declaration of war. The following day, *Suomen Sosiaalidemokraatti* had to tell its readers that the situation 'may be interpreted as war, although no official declaration of war has been given'.[94] It never was.

When the Eduskunta gathered, late in the afternoon of June 25, it became apparent that the *casus belli* had been well chosen. Everyone present could remember that the previous war had started in just this way, with a series of Russian air-raids. It was assumed that the parallel was an exact one, and that the country had once more become the victim of a Russian aggression. The Eduskunta met in secret session and Rangell read the government's statement. He asked for a formal vote of confidence. One after another the leaders of the party groups rose and indicated their assent. Even Wiik and his followers were prepared to support the government. They accepted that the *casus belli* was genuine. There were few discordant notes. The spokesman of the Swedish Peoples' party, after noting that as usual the Eduskunta had been faced with an accomplished fact, wondered whether they had yet been told everything. The government had said nothing of any commitments they might have entered into. The IKL representative criticized the obvious omissions in the government statement. Finland had joined Germany in a fight to destroy bolshevism. Why not say so? Why not put the cards on the table? Finland must move her eastern frontier to the White Sea. Such blunt speaking seemed almost obscene to an audience that was more accustomed to the kind of verbal cotton-wool through which the Finnish leaders generally preferred to conceal from others, and perhaps from themselves, what they were really doing. Tanner expressed the sense of outrage caused when he called out, 'the speaker is profaning the whole occasion.' Another representative observed, 'it is not necessary to say everything that you think.' Wiik was one of the last to speak. He accepted that war had begun, but pointed out that the danger of this had long been apparent, and he asked what the government had done to avoid it. Finland had let herself be used a pawn in the game of great-power politics. Nobody bothered to answer him, and the Eduskunta gave its vote of confidence without dissent, and adjourned.[95] The government's task was completed. It remained for the soldiers to do theirs.

The answer to Wiik's query about what the government had done to avoid a conflict is that it had done virtually nothing. The sequence of events after June 22 gives an impression that the Finnish government was gripped by passivity and a desire to procrastinate. It had not issued a clear declaration of its position either to its own people, or to foreign powers. Instead it had put out obviously evasive statements, which said no more than that it was not at the moment belligerent. The government had failed to communicate its intentions to the government of the USSR, either through Orlov, or through its own embassy in Moscow, or through any other channel, although this was obviously the most essential of first steps if conflict was to be avoided. Instead, Witting had deliberately evaded the questions which Orlov had put to him. Such dilatory and casual behaviour, in a situation of gravity and urgency, would have amounted to criminal negligence, if the government had really wanted, or been able, to preserve Finland's neutrality. In fact, the intention was absent, and the power of decision lay elsewhere. The government's attitude to the preservation of the country's neutrality calls to mind the famous lines of Hilaire Belloc:

> *Thou shalt not kill, but needs't not strive*
> *Officiously to keep alive.*

Professor Korhonen has written, 'it is quite impossible to put forward more than uncertain conjectures about the course of events, if the Soviet Union had not made its air attacks on Finland on June 25.'[96] This seems unnecessarily pessimistic, and exaggerates the importance of these attacks.

It has been shown that the activities of the military authorities were quite unaffected by them. The only mark which the attacks left on their planning was the order to the army to shoot over the frontier if suitable targets offered. If there had been no air attacks on June 25, the course of events would have been substantially unaltered. The Germans would have started their northern operations on June 29, with Finnish troops in support, and on July 10, the main Finnish army would have opened its offensive. Before that date, the government would have had to find some other plausible *casus belli*, but who can doubt that some useable incident would have occurred.

It seems clear in retrospect that Mannerheim, and the members of the inner circle who shared in, and helped to implement his decisions, made an appalling mistake in June 1941. It has cost their country over 50,000 lives, vast material damages, and the permanent restriction of its political independence. In fact the bills are still coming in. These men, who usually exercised their stewardship of the nation's affairs with skill and shrewdness, were finally guilty of one terrible error of judgement. Finnish commentators have almost universally evaded discussion of how this happened. They offer determinist explanations, which assert that really no choice was ever made. But in reality, the destiny of nations, even of small nations, is determined by the choices of men, not by impersonal historical forces.

It is not difficult to understand the mistake. Mannerheim, Ryti, Walden, Witting, all believed that Germany would be able to destroy the USSR. Even after events had proved him disastrously wrong, Ryti affirmed that he had believed in German victory. Mannerheim too admitted that he and his military advisers, in June 1941, believed that Germany had 'very great possibilities of winning a war against the Soviet Union'. They were in good company in their error. Most expert opinion in 1941 refused to believe that a system of government so generally hated and despised could have built a society strong enough to resist the attacks of Hitler's Germany. Nor must it be forgotten how nearly they were proved right. If Hitler had destroyed the Soviet Union, history would have acclaimed the foresight of the Finnish leaders. The judgement of Mannerheim and the other members of the inner circle was certainly affected by their innate dislike of the communist ideology, and their vivid experience of the crude brutalities of Soviet foreign policy. Paasikivi was the only Finn holding a high position who did not let such feelings warp his judgement. The Finnish leaders had good grounds for the belief that, in June 1941, they were faced with a great historical opportunity to create a better future for their country.

Ryti expressed this belief in the address which he delivered to the Finnish people on the evening of June 25.[97] He told them that the time had come to destroy the centuries-old threat from the east. 'And this time, we have perhaps better possibilities of succeeding than ever before.' A few days later, Mannerheim called his soldiers to follow him in a final 'holy war against the enemies of our society'. He assured them that 'a new day dawns for Finland'. These were men of sufficient character and courage to be willing to grasp the opportunity when they saw it. Lesser men would have been afraid. If there is a moral to this story, it is perhaps that a small nation can pay too highly for entrusting its affairs to men of boldness and vision. Such men will seize the great historical opportunities when they are offered, but such opportunities usually involve a risk of equal magnitude. The cost of a mistake may be more than a small nation ought to be called upon to bear.

NOTES

The following abbreviations are used for the principal Finnish language newspapers:

HS — *Helsingin Sanomat* (*Helsinki News*)
SS — *Suomen Sosiaalidemokraatti* (*The Finnish Social Democrat*)
US — *Uusi Suomi* (*New Finland*)

Chapter 1

1. The term 'hereditary enemy'—perivihollinen—was commonly used in this period in referring to Russia. The historical significance of this is discussed below.
2. The term 'unity' or 'unanimity'—yksimielisyys—had a special meaning for the Finns in this period, which is discussed below.
3. Finnish accounts of the war of 1939–40 usually assume that there was no internal opposition to the war in Finland. This is almost true, there were cases of notable communists who broke with the party and rallied to the national defence, but there was also a hard-core of Leftwing opposition, whose leaders were kept in preventive custody during the war.
4. Colonel Veltjens, a German arms

dealer friendly to Finland, did send a consignment of AA-guns to Finland at the beginning of the war. The Swedish press picked up the story and published it. The consequence was that the German government, to conciliate the USSR, stopped any further shipments.
5. J. K. Paasikivi, *Toimintani Moskovassa ja Suomessa, 1939–41*, 2 vols. (Porvoo, 1959), I, 198. Hereafter cited as Paasikivi.
6. Ibid., I, 178.
7. Ibid., I, 186, 196.
8. Ibid., I, 189.
9. Erik Heinrichs, *Mannerheim Suomen kohtaloissa*, 2 vols. (Helsinki, 1959), II, 161. Hereinafter cited as Heinrichs.
10. *The Times*, 13.3.40, 14.3.40: *358 House of Commons Debates*,1833–43.

Chapter 2

1. SS, 14.3.40.
2. V. Tanner, *The Winter War* (Stamford, 1957), 252.
3. Ibid., 246.
4. G. Mannerheim, *Muistelmat*, trans. Lauri Hakulinen, 2 vols. (Helsinki, 1952), II, 218. Hereafter cited as Mannerheim.
5. Ibid., II, 218–221.
6. HS, 13.3.40.
7. Ibid., 17.3.40.
8. O. Paavolainen, *Synkkä yksinpuhelu* (Porvoo, 1946), 374.
9. K. Vilkuna, *Maan puolesta: Urho Kekkosen puheita ja kirjoituksia, 1938–55* (Helsinki, 1955), 313.

10. V.Tanner, *Itsenäisen Suomen arkea; valikoima puheita* (Helsinki, 1956), 289fl.
11. C. O. Frietsch, *Suomen kohtalonvuodet* (Helsinki, 1945), 249. Hereafter cited as Frietsch.
12. HS, 13.3.40.
13. US, 22.3.40.
14. SS, 14.3.40.
15. SS, 6.4.40.
16. Heinrichs, II, 184.
17. Paasikivi, I, 95.
18. W. von Blücher, *Gesandter zwischen Diktatur und Demokratie* (Wiesbaden, 1951), 189–190. Hereafter cited as Blücher: *Documents on*

296 NOTES

German Foreign Policy, Series D, 12
vols. (London 1956–62), IX, 32.
Hereafter cited as DGFP.
19. US, 22.3.40.
20. SS, 14.3.40.
21. SS, 16.3.40.
22. Paasikivi, II, 7.
23. Loc. cit.
24. Tanner, Itsenäisen Suomen arkea, 269.fll.
25. Ibid., 247fll.
26. Ibid., 154fll.
27. SS, 15.3.40.
28. SS, 28.3.40.
29. SS, 15.3.40.
30. SS, 17.3.40.
31. US, 15.3.40.
32. Paasikivi, II, 43. The Times, 15.3.40.
33. HS, 16.3.40.
34. Paasikivi, II, 43.
35. Ibid., II, 1. The Times, 21.3.40.

36. Paasikivi, II, 45–46.
37. Ibid., II, 47.
38. Loc. cit.
39. HS, 22.3.40.
40. The Times, 30.3.40.
41. Paasikivi, II, 47.
42. Mannerheim, II, 276.
43. US, 22.3.40, 12.4.40.
44. E.W. Juva, Rudolf Walden, 1878–1946 (Porvoo 1957), 416.
45. US, 17.3.40.
46. SS, 18.3.40.
47. SS, 19.3.40.
48. Sotasyyllisyysoikeudenkäynnin pöytäkirjat, 4 vols. (unpublished), I, 119. Hereafter cited as SSOK(P).
49. Sotasyyllisyysoikeudenkäynnin asiakirjat, 4 vols. (unpublished), I, Österholm's testimony. Hereafter cited as SSOK(A).
50. Ibid., IV, 479.

Chapter 3

1. Paasikivi, II, 120.
2. Y. Kilpeläinen, Suomi Neuvostoliiton radiossa (Helsinki, 1942), 70. Hereafter cited as Kilpeläinen.
3. E. Hiitonen, Vääryyttä oikeuden valekaavussa (Hyvinkää, 1953), 410.
4. Paasikivi, II, 121.
5. SS, 6.7.40.
6. SS, 11.7.40.
7. HS, 9.7.40; US, 10.7.40.
8. HS, 8.10.40.
9. SS, 14.10.40.
10. US, 26.10.40.
11. US, 18.5.40, 8.6.40, 15.6.40.
12. US, 8.6.40.
13. SS, 27.6.40.
14. HS, 12.8.40; US, 4.8.40, 23.8.40.
15. US, 12.4.40.
16. US, 20.3.40, 13.4.40.
17. US, 14.6.40.
18. US, 20.6.40.

19. US, 5.5.40.
20. US, 7.4.40.
21. US, 21.4.40.
22. US, 28.4.40, 14.5.40.
23. HS, 30.4.40.
24. US, 7.6.40, 14.7.40, 29.8.40.
25. US, 1.5.40.
26. HS, 25.5.40.
27. HS, 23.6.40.
28. US, 25.4.40, 8.5.40.
29. HS, 21.6.40.
30. US, 1.5.40, 3.5.40, 4.5.40.
31. HS, 25.5.40; US, 4.6.40, 5.6.40, 6.6.40.
32. HS, 21.6.40; US, 5.6.40, 6.6.40, 11.6.40, 21.6.40.
33. HS, 30.6.40.
34. US, 2.7.40.
35. SS, 11.7.40.
36. HS, 7.7.40; US, 10.7.40.
37. HS, 27.7.40, 28.7.40; US, 30.7.40.

Chapter 4

1. L. Puntila, book review, Historiallinen Aikakauskirja (1958), 63.
2. Juva, Walden, 485–486.
3. Ibid., 489.
4. Heinrichs II, 208.
5. Ibid., II, 209.
6. Juva, 491.

7. Mannerheim, II, 286–287.
8. Heinrichs, II, 206.
9. Ibid., 205.
10. Mannerheim, II, 286.
11. Heinrichs, II, 192.
12. Ibid., II, 193.
13. Mannhereim, II, 287.

14. Juva, 492.
15. SS, 11.4.40, 13.4.40, 14.4.40, 16.6.40; US, 15.4.40, 25.4.40.
16. Heinrichs, II, 204.
17. Mannerheim, II, 286.
18. M. J. Terä, 'Ratkaisun vuodet ja

Veltjens', *Uusi Suomi* (19, 20, 22 December 1957).
19. Mannerheim, II, 286.
20. See above 18.
21. See above 18.
22. Mannerheim, II, 300.

Chapter 5

1. Paasikivi, II, 10. *The Times*, 30.3.40.
2. Paasikivi, II, 12.
3. Ibid., II, 12.
4. Heinrichs, II, 199.
5. Kilpeläinen, 78.
6. *Nazi-Soviet Relations 1939–1941: documents from the archives of the German foreign office*, ed. R. J. Sonntag and J. S. Beddie (Washington, 1948), 138.
7. Heinrichs, II, 201. *The Times*, 8.4.40.
8. Paasikivi, II, 26.
9. Ibid., II, 27.
10. Ibid., II, 29; Wolf H. Halsti, *Kesäsota*, 1941 (Helsinki, 1956), 21.
11. Paasikivi, II, 22.
12. Ibid., II, 32.
13. SS, 23.5.40.
14. Paasikivi, II, 38.
15. Ibid., II, 37: *DGFP*, IX, 402.
16. Paasikivi, II, 39.
17. Ibid., II, 39.
18. *Suomen Sinivalkoinen kirja II* (Helsinki, 1941), 20.
19. Tanner, *Winter War*, 246.
20. Paasikivi, II, 41.
21. Ibid., II, 41.

22. HS, 6.4.40.
23. SS, 6.4.40.
24. SS, 12.4.40.
25. Blücher, 194.
26. Ibid., 193.
27. HS, 11.5.40.
28. SS, 8.5.40, 19.5.40.
29. Paasikivi, I, 214.
30. *Nazi-Soviet Relations*, 137; Frietsch, 308.
31. Mannerheim, II, 278–279.
32. Frietsch, 309.
33. HS, 26.4.40, 27.4.40.
34. Paasikivi, II, 4.
35. Ibid., II, 5.
36. Heinrichs, II, 199.
37. HS, 20.5.40.
38. SS, 21.5.40, 25.5.40, 26.5.40.
39. HS, 12.4.40; SS, 27.4.40.
40. SS, 16.5.40.
41. HS, 31.5.40; SS, 31.5.40.
42. SS, 5.6.40, 9.6.40.
43. HS, 8.6.40; SS, 8.6.40.
44. Hiitonen, 409.
45. Ibid., 411.
46. HS, 26.5.40.
47. SS, 31.5.40, 2.6.40.
48. US, 20.3.40, 7.4.40.

Chapter 6

1. Paasikivi, II, 61.
2. HS, 21.6.40; SS, 15.6.40; US, 15.6.40.
3. Halsti, 25.
4. SS, 21.6.40; US, 21.6.40.
5. Frietsch, 301.
6. Paasikivi, II, 63.
7. Many details about the activities of SNS have been taken from Mika Waltari, *Neuvostovakoilun varjossa* (Helsinki, 1943), particularly chapters 4, 5, and 6. Although this work is not now usually included in the list of the collected works of this distinguished author, and although

its tone is blatantly propagandist, there is no reason to doubt the authenticity of the incidents described.
8. Paasikivi, II, 121.
9. Ibid., II, 140.
10. *DGFP*, X, 237.
11. Hiitonen, 414.
12. Paasikivi, II, 141.
13. Ibid., II, 93.
14. Ibid., II, 121.
15. HS, 27.6.40.
16. SSOK(P), IV, 142: *DGFP*, IX, 402.
17. Ibid., IX, 597.
18. Ibid., IV, 143.

19. Paasikivi, II, 94–95.
20. Ibid., II, 141.
21. Frietsch, 318.
22. HS, 5.7.40; SS, 4.7.40, 5.7.40.
23. Hiitonen, 445.
24. Ibid., 416; Paasikivi, II, 64.
25. Blücher, 194: *DGFP*, X, 121.
26. E. F. Ziemke, *The German northern theatre of operations, 1940–1945* (U.S. Department of the Army pamphlet, 1960), 114.
27. The Halder Diaries (unpublished), IV, 111. The version used was the English translation, prepared in co-operation with Halder himself, and mimeographed.
28. Paasikivi, II, 141: *DGFP*, X, 185.
29. Ibid., II, 111.
30. Ibid., II, 113.
31. Ibid., II, 177.
32. Ibid., II, 114.
33. Loc. cit.
34. US, 10.7.40.
35. SS, 13.7.40.
36. US, 27.7.40.
37. US, 4.8.40.
38. HS, 11.7.40; SS, 14.7.40, 15.7.40.
39. SS, 16.7.40.
40. SS, 15.6.40.
41. HS, 15.7.40; SS, 17.7.40, 27.7.40; US, 30.6.40.
42. US, 26.7.40.
43. HS, 14.7.40.
44. Paasikivi, II, 65.
45. Kilpeläinen, 80. *The Times*, 3.8.40.
46. Paasikivi, II, 71.
47. Blücher, 195.
48. G. L. Weinberg, *Germany and the Soviet Union, 1939–1941* (Leiden, 1954), 109.
49. Arvi Korhonen, *Barbarossa-suunitelma ja Suomi, Jatkosodan synty* (Porvoo, 1961), 61. Hereafter cited as Korhonen.
50. *The Times*, 20.7.40.
51. Paasikivi, II, 73.
52. Ibid., II, 74.
53. Halder Diaries, IV, 111.

54. Korhonen, 85.
55. Paasikivi, II, 72.
56. Korhonen, 47–48: *DGFP*, X, 331.
57. Paasikivi, 11, 178.
58. Ibid., II, 96.
59. Ibid., II, 66–67.
60. Hiitonen, 417; HS, 27.7.40; SS, 27.7.40.
61. Hiitonen, 417.
62. HS, 27.7.40, 31.7.40.
63. *The Times*, 3.8.40; 8.8.40.
64. SS, 1.8.40; US, 2.8.40, 3.8.40, 7.8.40, 9.8.40, 10.8.40, 13.8.40.
65. Paasikivi, II, 65.
66. HS, 2.8.40, 13.8.40.
67. Mannerheim, II, 288; Korhonen, 53.
68. Kilpeläinen, 80, 81.
69. *The Times*, 2.8.40.
70. Paasikivi, II, 70.
71. HS, 3.8.40, 9.8.40; SS, 7.8.40.
72. Paasikivi, II, 69–70, 72.
73. Blücher, 197: *DGFP*, X, 405.
74. Korhonen, 51, 52.
75. Paasikivi, II, 72.
76. Ibid., II, 114.
77. SS, 4.8.40; US, 5.8.40.
78. SS, 7.8.40.
79. US, 10.8.40.
80. US, 12.8.40.
81. Paasikivi, II, 74.
82. *The Times*, 5.8.40, 14.8.40: *364 House of Commons Debates*, 182.
83. Korhonen, 49.
84. Halder Diaries, IV, 157: *DGFP*, X, 460.
85. Paasikivi, II, 74.
86. HS, 16.8.40; SS, 16.8.40.
87. SS, 12.8.40.
88. Paasikivi, II, 76.
89. Ibid., II, 76–77.
90. *DGFP*, X, 478.
91. Blücher, 198.
92. *Sinivalkoinen kirja II*, 82.
93. Paasikivi, II, 77; SS, 19.8.40.
94. Paasikivi, II, 78–80.
95. Ibid., II, 81.
96. Ibid., II, 82.

Chapter 7

1. *DGFP*, X, 108, 185, 237, 368, 428.
2. Halder Diaries, IV, 157; Korhonen, 49; M. V. Terä, *Tienhaarassa*, (Helsinki, 1962), 21.
3. Korhonen, 80.
4. H. Greiner, *Die oberste Wehrmachtführung, 1939–1943* (Wiesbaden, 1951), 297; *International Military*

Tribunal, Documents in Evidence XXXIV, 688; Halder Diaries, IV, 165; Weinberg, 127.
5. Korhonen, 82; M. J. Terä, 'Ratkaisun vuodet ja Veltjens', *Uusi Suomi* (20.12.57) and *Tienhaarassa*, 29–30.
6. Halder Diaries, IV, 168.
7. Ibid., IV, 165.
8. Korhonen, 86.
9. Korhonen, 91; Terä, op. cit., *Uusi Suomi* (22.12.57) and *Tienhaarassa*, 37–39.
10. Heinrichs, II, 225.
11. M. V. Terä, *Tienhaarassa*, 44; Korhonen, 90.
12. M. V. Terä, *Tienhaarassa*, 43–46; Korhonen, 99.
13. Ibid., 85.
14. Halder Diaries, IV, 179; Korhonen, 100.
15. Loc. cit.
16. Halder Diaries, IV, 179; Korhonen, 101.
17. SSOK(P), I, 37–38.
18. Juva, 505; Korhonen, 110.
19. Paasikivi, II, 115–116.
20. Ibid., 116.

21. Frietsch, 311.
22. Korhonen, 95.
23. Halsti, 31.
24. Blücher, 201.
25. Halder Diaries, IV, 193.
26. International Military Tribunal, XXXIV, 691.
27. Nazi-Soviet Relations, 188: DGFP, XI, 92.
28. Korhonen, 117.
29. Ibid., 114.
30. Ibid., 110, 113; SSOK(P), I, 371.
31. DGFP, XI, 148.
32. Korhonen, 115.
33. A. Seidl, *Die Beziehungen zwischen Deutschland und der Sowjetunion, 1939–1941. Dokumente des Auswärtiges Amtes* (Tübingen, 1949), 223.
34. SSOK(P), 11, 435, 438, 439.
35. DGFP, XI, 148.
36. Korhonen, 116.
37. DGFP, XI, 160.
38. Korhonen, 116; SSOK(P), I, 91.
39. SSOK(P), II, 519; Frietsch, 326–327.
40. SSOK(P), II, 456.

Chapter 8

1. Many of the details about the plan for a Swedish-Finnish Union are taken from two articles by Per Gudmund Andreen, 'Svensk-finska unionsplaner 1940–1941' and 'Unionsplanens förlisning', *Svenska Dagbladet* (8 and 9 August 1961).
2. Paasikivi, II, 98.
3. DGFP, XI, 35, 41.
4. Ibid., II, 142.
5. Ibid., II, 142.
6. Frietsch, 260.
7. Ibid., 261.
8. US, 12.10.40.
9. Blücher, 200; US, 7.9.40, 8.9.40; SS, 11.9.40.
10. Korhonen, 102: DGFP, XI, 105.
11. Paasikivi, II, 142.
12. Sinivalkoinen kirja II, 82.
13. Paasikivi, II, 143.
14. Ibid., II, 144.
15. Halder Diaries, IV, 196.
16. DGFP, XI, 34, 44.
17. Kilpeläinen, 85: US, 22.10.40.

18. SS, 9.9.40.
19. HS, 29.9.40.
20. US, 2.11.40.
21. US, 9.11.40.
22. Sinivalkoinen kirja II, 85.
23. Nazi-Soviet Relations, 197.
24. Paasikivi, II, 54.
25. Korhonen, 123.
26. Paasikivi II, 54.
27. Ibid., II, 103.
28. Ibid., II, 105.
29. DGFP, XI, 361.
30. Nazi-Soviet Relations, 201; SSOK(A), IV, 452.
31. Loc. cit.
32. Nazi-Soviet Relations, 203. DGFP, XI, 244.
33. Korhonen, 123.
34. Paasikivi, II, 54.
35. Ibid., II, 145.
36. Korhonen, 107: DGFP, XI, 234.
37. Nazi-Soviet Relations, 205: DGFP, XI, 270, 328.
38. SSOK(A), IV, 452.

39. Blücher, 202.
40. SSOK(P), IV, 272.
41. *DGFP*, XI, 425.
42. *Sotasyyllisoikeudenkäynnin asia-kirjoja* (Helsinki, 1946), 3 vols, III, 29.
43. Korhonen, 127.
44. HS, 27.10.40, 3.11.40; US, 29.10.40, 2.11.40, 8.12.40.
45. HS, 21.10.40; SS, 24.10.40.
46. SS, 11.10.40.
47. SS, 4.10.40, 6.10.40, 9.10.40, 11.10.40, 27.10.40, 12.11.40, 19.11.40; HS, 5.10.40.
48. US, 6.10.40.
49. SS, 9.10.40.
50. HS, 5.11.40.
51. SS, 19.10.40; US, 19.10.40.
52. HS, 26.10.40; US, 26.10.40, 19.10.40.
53. Kilpeläinen, 96, 97.
54. *DGFP*, XI, 397.
55. Ziemke, 117.
56. Paasikivi, II, 132.
57. Ibid., II, 145; *Sinivalkoinen kirja II*, 96.

58. *DGFP*, XI, 452.
59. Paasikivi, II, 133, 146; *Sinivalkoinen kirja* II, 99.
60. Paasikivi, II, 146.
61. Ibid., II, 133; HS, 12.11.40; SS, 13.11.40.
62. Paasikivi, II, 134; US, 8.11.40, 12.11.40, 14.11.40, 15.11.40.
63. US, 14.10.40.
64. Korhonen, 139: *DGFP*, XI, 527.
65. Weinberg, 144.
66. *Nazi-Soviet Relations*, 217.
67. Ibid., 234.
68. Loc. cit.
69. Loc. cit.
70. Loc. cit.
71. Ibid., 247.
72. *International Military Tribunal*, X, 293.
73. *Nazi-Soviet Relations*, 245.
74. Seidl, 191.
75. *Nazi-Soviet Relations*, 258.
76. Blücher, 205.
77. Halder Diaries, V, 26.

Chapter 9

1. *DGFP*, XI, 478.
2. US, 7.11.40.
3. *DGFP*, XI, 925. Ibid., XI, 478.
4. Ibid., XI, 783.
5. Korhonen, 129.
6. Ibid., 130.
7. Paasikivi, II, 146.
8. Ibid., II, 148.
9. Ibid., II, 148.
10. SS, 28.11.40.
11. *DGFP*, XI, 611.
12. Korhonen, 156.
13. Ibid., 157: *DGFP*, XI, 722.
14. Ibid., XI, 813.
15. Korhonen, 159; Ziemke, 117.
16. Paasikivi, II, 149.
17. Ibid., II, 151. *DGFP*, XI, 781.
18. Loc. cit.
19. Ibid., II, 152.
20. Greiner, 325.
21. Halder Diaries, V, 56.
22. Korhonen, 166.
23. Ibid., 171; Halder Diaries, V, 71.
24. *International Military Tribunal*, XXVI, 47fll.
25. Loc. cit.

26. *Sinivalkoinen kirja II*, 110.
27. Loc. cit.
28. Paasikivi, II, 55.
29. SSOK(A), IV, 481.
30. Paasikivi, II, 56–57.
31. A. Rossi, *Deux ans d'alliance Ger-mano-Sovietique* (Paris, 1949), 196–197: *DGFP*, XI, 854.
32. SSOK(P), I, 114; II, 39.
33. Korhonen, 172; Halder Diaries, V, 71.
34. Ziemke, 123: *DGFP*, XI, 917, 959.
35. *International Military Tribunal*, VII, 327.
36. Halder Diaries, V, 71.
37. Korhonen, 158.
38. HS, 30.11.40; SS, 29.11.40.
39. US, 29.11.40, 30.11.40.
40. HS, 4.12.40.
41. *DGFP*, XI, 763.
42. Blücher, 215.
43. Paasikivi, II, 129.
44. SS, 18.12.40; US, 17.12.40.
45. HS, 10.12.40.
46. Korhonen, 172; Heinrichs, II, 217.
47. Blücher, 210–211: *DGFP*, XI, 774.

48. *DGFP*, XI, 799.
49. Ibid., XI, 763, 813.
50. Ibid., XI, 884.
51. Paasikivi, 11, 127.
52. Ibid., II, 128.
53. Ibid., II, 129.
54. *DGFP*, XI, 841.
55. US, 20.12.40.
56. SS, 20.12.40.
57. Heinrichs, II, 218.
58. *The Times*, 21.12.40, 24.12.40.
59. Kilpeläinen, 103.
60. Paasikivi, II, 177.
61. SSOK(P), 467.
62. Paasikivi, II, 174.
63. Mannerheim, II, 300.
64. Paasikivi, II, 179.
65. Ibid., II, 179–187.
66. HS, 12.11.40.
67. US, 9.11.40.
68. HS, 12.11.40; SS, 16.11.40.
69. SS, 28.11.40.

70. SS, 16.11.40, 4.12.40.
71. SS, 22.12.40, 3.1.41; HS, 3.1.41.
72. SS, 28.11.40.
73. US, 25.11.40.
74. US, 28.12.40.
75. Blücher, 213.
76. Korhonen, 159: *DGFP*, XI, 995.
77. Paasikivi, II, 83–84.
78. Hiitonen, 447.
79. US, 21.12.40.
80. HS, 28.12.40, 1.1.41.
81. SS, 1.1.41, 27.3.41.
82. HS, 31.12.40, 1.1.41.
83. Paasikivi, II, 179.
84. HS, 3.1.41; SS, 31.12.40, 3.1.41, 4.1.41.
85. HS, 3.1.41, 8.1.41; SS, 7.1.41.
86. US, 5.1.41.
87. Frietsch, 317.
88. Ibid., 271.
89. SSOK(A), IV, 481.
90. Korhonen, 179.

Chapter 10

1. Paasikivi, II, 152.
2. *Sinivalkoinen kirja II*, 126.
3. Paasikivi, II, 253.
4. Greiner, 347; *International Military Tribunal*, XXXIV, 698.
5. Blücher, 216: *DGFP*, XI, 1235.
6. Ibid., XI, 1199, 1206, 1212.
7. Paasikivi, II, 125.
8. *Sotasyyllisoikeudenkäynnin asiakirjoja*, I, 17; SSOK(P), II, 563; SSOK(A), II, 300.
9. Halder Diaries, V, 88.
10. Paasikivi, II, 154.
11. Heinrichs, II, 213.
12. Halder Diaries, V, 96.
13. Korhonen, 219.
14. *International Military Tribunal*, VII, 254.
15. Korhonen, 219; Mannerheim, II, 301.
16. Halder Diaries, V, 101.
17. Korhonen, 220.
18. Korhonen, 199; Ziemke, 124.
19. Korhonen, 200; Halder Diaries, V, 84.
20. Korhonen, 202–203; Ziemke, 124.
21. Halder Diaries, V, 102.
22. Korhonen, 188, 204–205; Greiner, 353–357; *International Military Tribunal*, XXVI, 394; Ziemke, 125.

23. *The Fuehrer Conference on naval affairs* (London, 1947), *1941*, 19.
24. Greiner, 363.
25. Paasikivi, II, 159.
26. Ibid., II, 158.
27. Ibid., II, 159.
28. Ibid., II, 159; *Sinivalkoinen kirja II*, 122.
29. Paasikivi, II, 161.
30. Loc. cit.
31. Ibid., II, 202.
32. *DGFP*, XII, 75, 196.
33. Ibid., II, 163.
34. Blücher, 216.
35. Blücher, 216.
36. Korhonen, 244.
37. Ibid., 225–227: *DGFP*, XII, 122.
38. SSOK(A), IV, 470.
39. Mannerheim, II, 301.
40. Korhonen, 229; Ziemke, 127.
41. *International Military Tribunal*, VII, 309; SSOK(P), 111, 48fll.
42. Ibid., IV, 183fll.
43. *DGFP*, XII, 122.
44. Korhonen, 229; Ziemke, 127: *DGFP*, XII, 122.
45. SSOK(A), IV, 478.
46. Ibid., IV, 473.
47. SSOK(P), IV, 195.
48. *DGFP*, XII, 122.

49. Ibid., XII, 319, 321, 322, 633.
50. Korhonen, 267; Greiner, 363.
51. Ibid., 368; Halder Diaries, VI, 27; Korhonen, 208.
52. Halder Diaries, VI, 27.
53. Ibid., VI, 42.
54. Korhonen, 210.
55. SS, 25.1.41, 27.2.41, 4.4.41; HS, 9.1.41, 26.2.41, 7.3.41, 18.3.41, 1.4.41.
56. HS, 2.4.41, 3.4.41, 6.4.41, 10.4.41.
57. HS, 20.2.41, 4.3.41, 7.3.41, 3.4.41; US, 23.2.41, 5.3.41.
58. HS, 23.3.41; SS, 14.2.41, 21.2.41, 12.3.41.
59. HS, 18.2.41, 2.3.41, 6.3.41, 9.3.41, 16.3.41.
60. SS, 11.2.41, 14.2.41.
61. HS, 4.2.41; SS, 1.2.41, 3.2.41, 4.2.41.
62. HS, 6.2.41; US, 19.2. 41.
63. US, 2.2.41.
64. SS, 1.2.41.
65. Kilpeläinen, 114.
66. HS, 20.3.41; SS, 19.3.41; US, 20.3.41, 21.3.41.
67. HS, 19.3.41, 22.3.41.
68. US, 27.3.41.
69. HS, 9.3.41; US, 9.3.41, 11.3.41.
70. HS, 14.3.41; SS, 14.3.41; US, 16.2.41, 17.2.41, 1.3.41.
71. US, 14.3.41.
72. SS, 16.3.41.
73. HS, 29.3.41; SS, 21.3.41; US, 14.3.41, 25.3.41.
74. HS, 27.3.41.
75. SS, 27.3.41.
76. HS, 1.4.41, 2.4.41; SS, 2.4.41, 3.4.41; US, 2.4.41.
77. HS, 23.4.41, 30.4.41; SS, 30.4.41; US, 30.4.41.
78. HS, 6.3.41.
79. SS, 25.2.41, 27.2.41.
80. SS, 22.1.41; US, 27.1.41, 28.1.41.
81. HS, 14.2.41.
82. SS, 3.2.41.
83. HS, 6.3.41.
84. HS, 4.3.41.
85. HS, 10.3.41.
86. US, 30.4.41.
87. US, 28.3.41.
88. SSOK(A), II, 159.
89. Mannerheim, II, 302.
90. Korhonen, 232; Ziemke, 119.
91. Korhonen, 233.
92. SSOK(A), I, Testimony of A. Pakaslahti; Juva, 508.
93. Korhonen, 234.
94. SSOK(P), II, 341.
95. Paasikivi, II, 203.
96. Ibid., II, 208.
97. Ibid., II, 209.
98. Korhonen, 222.
99. SSOK(P), IV, 143.
100. Loc. cit.
101. Korhonen, 223.
102. Loc.cit.
103. Blücher, 218.
104. DGFP, XII, 433.
105. Heinrichs, II, 247.

Chapter 11

1. Weinberg, 160.
2. SS, 6.4.41.
3. SSOK(P), I, 501.
4. Paasikivi, II, 213.
5. Ibid., II, 214.
6. Ibid., II, 163–164; Sinivalkoinen kirja II, 124.
7. Ibid., 125.
8. Paasikivi, II, 211.
9. A. J. Schwartz, America and the Russo-Finnish War (Washington, 1960), 53.
10. Paasikivi, 11, 217.
11. SS, 28.5.41.
12. Blücher, 219.
13. Paasikivi, II, 208, 209.
14. Ibid., II, 213.
15. Ibid., II, 216; Frietsch, 258.
16. Korhonen, 238.
17. HS, 22.4.41.
18. HS, 26.4.41.
19. The Times, 1.5.41, 13.5.41; 371 House of Commons Debates, 829.
20. HS, 26.4.41, 27.4.41, 28.4.41; SS, 29.4.41, 30.4.41; US, 27.4.41, 30.4.41.
21. US, 11.5.41.
22. HS, 30.4.41.
23. Korhonen, 240; SSOK(P), I, 373; Ibid., II, 584; DGFP, XII, 678, 684, 702, 717.
24. Korhonen, 244; SSOK(P), I, 373; Ibid., II, 584; SSOK(A), II, 302.
25. Blücher, 220; Korhonen, 241.

26. Ibid., 245; SSOK(P), II, 43.
27. Paasikivi, II, 209.
28. Ibid., II, 217.
29. Ibid., II, 219.
30. *Sotasyyllisoikeudenkäynnin asia-kirjoja*, III, 5.
31. SSOK(P), I, 134.
32. Ibid., II, 515.
33. Ibid., III, 71.
34. *Sotasyyllisoikeudenkäynnin asia-kirjoja*, III, 6.
35. Ibid., III, 5; L. Puntila, book review, *Historiallinen aikakauskirja* (1960), 469.
36. Frietsch, 326.
37. Ibid., 318.
38. *Sotasyyllisoikeudenkäynnin asia-kirjoja*, III, 6.
39. Paasikivi, II, 203; Korhonen, 244.
40. HS, 21.5.41.
41. SS, 19.4.41, 22.4.41, 16.5.41, 1.6.41.
42. SS, 19.4.41.
43. HS, 19.4.41.
44. SS, 3.5.41.
45. HS, 9.5.41.
46. SS, 18.4.41.
47. SS, 11.5.41.
48. SS, 19.4.41, 18.4.41, 23.5.41.
49. SS, 24.5.41.
50. HS, 1.5.41.
51. US, 29.4.41, 4.5.41, 11.5.41.
52. SS, 3.5.41.
53. HS, 9.5.41; SS, 10.5.41.
54. SS, 11.5.41, 25.5.41.
55. US, 25.5.41.
56. Korhonen, 211–212; Ibid., 243; Ziemke, 129.
57. SSOK(P), IV, 143.
58. Korhonen, 243.
59. Ibid., 244; Blücher, 221.
60. Korhonen, 244.
61. Halder Diaries, VI, 49.
62. The Finnish military archives for this period are still closed to researchers. But the author had the privilege of interviews with officials of the Historical Section of the Fin-

nish General Staff, who are familiar with these documents. They answered a number of the author's questions and discussed points involved. Much of the information about the Hiitola offensive, and other aspects of Finnish military activity, is based on the notes taken by the author during these interviews. The officials concerned are in no way responsible for these notes or the views based on them, but the author is greatly indebted to them for their patient assistance.
63. Heinrichs, II, 265–266.
64. Korhonen, 247; Halder Diaries, VI, 91.
65. *Fuehrer Conference on naval affairs, 1941,* 57.
66. *Sotasyyllisoikeudenkäynnin asia-kirjoja*, I, 9; SSOK(P), I, 91.
67. Ibid., I, 91; *Sotasyyllisoikeudenkirjoja*, I, 9; Mannerheim, II, 303; Korhonen, 255.
68. Ibid., 255.
69. Mannerheim, II, 304; Heinrichs, II, 231.
70. SSOK(P), I, 506; Mannerheim, II, 308; Heinrichs, II, 236; Korhonen, 256.
71. Ibid., 257.
72. Ibid., 261–262; Heinrichs, 232.
73. Korhonen, 263-264; SSOK(P), IV, 190; SSOK(A), IV, 472, 473, 475: DGFP, XII, 879.
74. SSOK(P), IV, 90; Korhonen, 268.
75. Greiner, 387.
76. B. von Lossberg, *Im Wehrmacht-führungsstab* (Hamburg, 1950), 114.
77. DGFP, XII, 879.
78. Korhonen, 270–272; Halder Diaries, VI, 133; Ziemke, 132.
79. Korhonen, 273; SSOK(A), IV, 475.
80. Korhonen, 274.
81. Ibid., 275–276; SSOK(P), II, 534; SSOK(A), IV, 475.

Chapter 12

1. SS, 30.5.41.
2. SSOK(P), IV, 143.
3. *Sotasyyllisoikeudenkäynnin asia-kirjoja*, I, 9–10; SSOK(P), I, 94.
4. Korhonen, 280.
5. Ibid., 280; Heinrichs, II, 237.
6. Korhonen, 281; Heinrichs, II, 237; SSOK(P), IV, 183fll.
7. SSOK(P), IV, 195.
8. Korhonen, 282.
9. Ibid., 283; Heinrichs, II, 238.
10. DGFP, XII, 963.

304 NOTES

11. Ibid., 240; Ziemke, 264.
12. Korhonen, 287; Heinrichs, II, 241.
13. SSOK(P), II, 574; Ibid., III, 315; SSOK(A), II, 301.
14. Korhonen, 289.
15. Ibid., 291; Halder Diaries, VI, 145.
16. Korhonen, 285; Ziemke, 134.
17. Halder Diaries, VI, 145.
18. Heinrichs, II, 240.
19. Mannerheim, II, 18.
20. Korhonen, 294.
21. SSOK(P), I, 96fll.
22. SSOK(P), I, 98; Ibid., II, 341.
23. Korhonen, 306; SSOK(P), I, 377.
24. SSOK(P), I, 380, 96.
25. Blücher, 223.
26. SSOK(P), I, 372.
27. Ibid., II, 49.
28. C. L. Lundin, *Suomi toisessa maailmansodassa* (Jyväskylä, 1960), 204.
29. Korhonen, 309.
30. Ibid., 310.
31. SSOK(A), I, Päämajan sotapäiväkirja (HQ War Diary).
32. Korhonen, 312; Halder Diaries, VI, 148.
33. Frietsch, 362: *DGFP*, XII, 1023.
34. Ibid., 363.
35. Blücher, 224.
36. Ziemke, 134.
37. Korhonen, 313.
38. Ibid., 314; Ziemke, 134.
39. Korhonen, 315: *DGFP*, XII, 1039.
40. SSOK(P), II, 106fll; Päämajan sotapäiväkirja.
41. SSOK(P), III, 321–324.
42. Mannerheim, II, 312.
43. SSOK(A), IV, 476.
44. Päämajan sotapäiväkirja.
45. Blücher, 226.
46. *The Times*, 17.6.41; 18.6.41.
47. HS, 17.6.41, 19.6.41; SS, 14.6.41, 18.6.41, 19.6.41.
48. US, 18.6.41.
49. Frietsch, 368.
50. Paasikivi, II, 220; Frietsch, 366.
51. SS, 18.6.41, 19.6.41; SSOK(P), II, 342; Frietsch, 367.
52. Paavolainen, 108–109.
53. Päämajan sotapäiväkirja.
54. Loc. cit.
55. SSOK(A), II, 186.
56. Mannerheim, II, 311; SSOK(A), II, 188.
57. *International Military Tribunal*, XXXIV, 217fll.

58. Päämajan sotapäiväkirja.
59. Korhonen, 329; SSOK(P), IV, 183fll.
60. Korhonen, 318; Halder Diaries, VI, 157.
61. *Nazi-Soviet Relations*, 349.
62. Heinrichs, II, 245; Korhonen, 321.
63. Heinrichs, II, 246.
64. Mannerheim, II, 313.
65. G. L. Dietl and D. K. Herrmann, *General Dietl* (Munich, 1951), 220.
66. Ziemke, 139.
67. Korhonen, 327.
68. Päämajan sotapäiväkirja.
69. Ibid.
70. Ibid.
71. Ibid.; Korhonen, 328.
72. Päämajan sotapäiväkirja.
73. Heinrichs, II, 266.
74. Ibid., II, 267.
75. Halder Diaries, VI, 185.
76. G. A. Grippenberg, *Lontoo—Vatikaani—Tukholma; suomalaisen diplomaatin muistelmia* (Porvoo, 1960), 184.
77. SSOK(P), IV, 360.
78. *Sinivalkoinen kirja II*, 129: *DGFP*, XII, 1083.
79. Halsti, 64; Lundin, 219.
80. SSOK(P), I, 385.
81. Kilpeläinen, 123.
82. Mannerheim, II, 314; *Sotasyllisoikeudenkäynnin asiakirjoja*, I, 11; SSOK(P), IV, 37.
83. J. H. Wuorinen ed., *Finland and World War II, 1939–1944* (New York, 1948), 106.
84. Grippenberg, 184. *The Times*, 25.6.41.
85. *Sinivalkoinen kirja II*, 129.
86. SSOK(P), I, 44; Lundin, 218: *DGFP*, XII, 1083.
87. HS, 23.6.41; SS, 23.6.41; US, 23.6.41.
88. Korhonen, 327; Grippenberg, 187: *372 House of Commons Debates*, 976.
89. Mannerheim, II, 315.
90. SSOK(P), III, 310.
91. HS, 25.6.41; US, 25.6.41.
92. Korhonen, 337.
93. SSOK(P), IV, 536.
94. SS, 26.6.41.
95. Lundin, 224–225.
96. Korhonen, 336.
97. US, 26.6.41.

SELECT BIBLIOGRAPHY

1. *Unpublished sources:*
Sotasyyllisyysoikeudenkäynnin pöytäkirjat, 4 vols. (Transcripts of the War Guilt trial held in Helsinki, 1945–1946).
Sotasyllisyysoikeudenkäynnin asiakirjat, 4 vols. (Documents given in evidence at the War Guilt trial).
These records may be consulted with the permission of the Oikeusministeriö (Ministry of Justice).
The Halder Diaries, 7 vols. An English translation of these diaries, prepared in co-operation with the author, exists in mimeographed form, but has not been published. The copy used was that in the Imperial War Museum, London.
W. Kohlhammer Verlag, by whose kind permission the quotations from the diaries appear, are publishing the diaries under the title: *Generaloberst Halder, Kriegstagebuch.*

2. *Published sources:*
House of Commons Debates, 358, 364, 371, 372.
The Fuehrer Conferences on naval affairs (London, 1947).
The proceedings of the International Military Tribunal, vols. VII, X, XXVI, XXXIV.
Nazi-Soviet Relations 1939–1941: documents from the archives of the German foreign office, ed. R. J. Sonntag and J. S. Beddie (Washington, 1948).
Die Beziehungen zwischen Deutschland und der Sowjetunion 1939–1941: Dokumente des Auswärtiges Amtes (Tübingen, 1949), ed. A. Seidl.
Sotasyyllisoikeudenkäynnin asiakirjoja (Helsinki, 1946), 3 vols. (Documents of the War Guilt trial.) This consists of very brief excerpts from the proceedings published unofficially.
Suomen sinivalkoinen kirja II (Helsinki, 1941). (The Blue-White Book of Finland, II). An official collection of documents on Finnish-Russian relations, published by the Finnish foreign office.
Documents on German Foreign Policy, Series D, 12 vols. (London, 1956–62).

3. *Newspapers:*
The Times (London)
Helsingin Sanomat. (*Helsinki News*)
Suomen Sosiaalidemokraatti. (*The Finnish Social Democrat*)
Uusi Suomi. (*New Finland*)
These are preserved on microfilm in the library of Helsinki University.

4. *Secondary works:*
W. von Blücher, *Gesandter zwischen Diktatur und Demokratie* (Wiesbaden, 1951).
G-L and K. Dietl, *General Dietl* (Munich, 1952).
W. Erfurth, *Der Finnische Krieg, 1941–1944* (Wiesbaden, 1950).
W. Erfurth, *Murmannin radan ongelma* (Helsinki, 1952). (The problem of the Murmansk railway)
C. O. Frietsch, *Suomen kohtalonvuodet* (Helsinki, 1945). (Finland's fateful years)
G. Gafenco, *Preliminaires de la Guerre de l'est* (Fribourg, 1944).
H. Greiner, *Die oberste Wehrmachtsführung, 1939–1943* (Hamburg, 1951).
G. A. Grippenberg, *Lontoo—Vatikaani—Tukholma: suomalaisen diplomaatin muistelmia* (Porvoo, 1960), tr. L. Karen. (A Finnish diplomat's memoirs)
Wolf H. Halsti, *Kesäsota 1941* (Helsinki, 1956). (The summer campaign, 1941)

Erik Heinrichs, *Mannerheim Suomen kohtaloissa* (Helsinki, 1959), tr. V. Suomi, 2 vols. (Principal biography of Mannerheim)
E. Hiitonen, *Vääryyttä oikeuden valekaavussa* (Hyvinkää, 1953).
H. Hölter, *Armee in der Arktis* (Bad Neuheim, 1953).
C. Hull, *The Memoirs of Cordell Hull*, 2 vols., (New York, 1948).
E. W. Juva, *Rudolf Walden* (Porvoo, 1957).
F. Kersten, *The Kersten memoirs*, 1940–1945 (London, 1956).
K. Killinen, *Demokratia ja totaalinen sota. Tutkimus poliittis-sotilaallisen sodan-johdon teoriasta, järjestelystä, ja toiminnasta* (Porvoo, 1956). (Study of the relation-ships of political and military leadership in war)
Y. Kilpeläinen (Jahvetti), *Suomi Neuvostoliiton radiossa* (Helsinki, 1942). (Finland on the Soviet radio)
Arvi Korhonen, *Barbarossa suunitelma ja Suomi*, Jatkosodan synty (Porvoo, 1961). (The Barbarossa plan and Finland)
Arvi Korhonen, *Viisi sodan vuotta* (Porvoo, 1958). (Five years of war)
B. von Lossberg, *Im Wehrmachtsführungsstab* (Hamburg, 1950).
C. L. Lundin, *Suomi toisessa maailmansodassa* (Jyväskylä, 1960), tr. J. Aaltonen. (Revised and translated version of the author's *Finland in the Second World War*)
G. Mannerheim, *Muistelmat*, tr. L. Hakulinen, 2 vols. (Helsinki, 1952). (Manner-heim's memoirs)
J. K. Paasikivi, *Toimintani Moskovassa ja Suomessa 1939–1941*, 2 vols. (Porvoo, 1959.) (Paasikivi's memoirs)
O. Paavolainen, *Synkkä yksinpuhelu* (Porvoo, 1946).
L. A. Puntila, *Risto Rytin valtiomiehentyö* (Helsinki, 1956). (Brief memoir of Ryti.)
A. Rossi, *Deux ans d'alliance Germano-Sovietique* (Paris, 1949).
Y. Ruutu, *Suomen politiikka, 1939–1944* (Helsinki, 1945).
P. Schmidt, *Statist auf diplomatisches Bühne, 1923–1945* (Bonn, 1949).
A. J. Schwartz, *America and the Russo-Finnish war* (Washington, 1960).
H. Shearman, *Finland, the adventures of a small power* (London, 1950).
V. Tanner, *Itsenäisen Suomen arkea* (Helsinki, 1956). (Selected speeches)
V. Tanner, *The Winter War* (Stamford, 1957).
M. V. Terä, *Tienhaarassa. Syksyn 1940 tapahtumat Barbarossa-suunitelman taustaa vasten* (Helsinki, 1962). (At the crossroads. The events of the autumn of 1940.)
M. J. Terä, 'Ratkaisun vuodet ja Veltjens', *Uusi Suomi* (19, 20 and 22 December 1957).
K. Vilkuna, *Maan puolesta; Urho Kekkosen puheita ja kirjoituksia, 1938–1955* (Helsinki 1955).
K. Vilkuna, *Urho Kekkonen* (Jyväskylä, 1949).
M. Waltari, *Neuvostovakoilun varjossa* (Helsinki, 1943). (In the shadow of Soviet espionage)
L. G. Weinberg, *Germany and the Soviet Union 1939–1941* (Leiden, 1954).
E. von Weizsäcker, *Erinnerungen* (Münich, 1950).
J. H. Wuorinen ed., *Finland and World War II, 1939–1944* (New York, 1948).
E. F. Ziemke, *The German northern theatre of operations 1940–1945* (Washington, 1960).

Index

Index